The Newer Therapies: A Sourcebook

The Newer Therapies: A Sourcebook

Edited by

Lawrence Edwin Abt, Ph.D.
Irving R. Stuart, Ph.D.

 VAN NOSTRAND REINHOLD COMPANY
NEW YORK CINCINNATI TORONTO LONDON MELBOURNE

Copyright © 1982 by Van Nostrand Reinhold Company Inc.

Library of Congress Catalog Card Number: 81-21847
ISBN: 0-442-27942-6

Manufactured in the United States of America

Published by Van Nostrand Reinhold Company Inc.
135 West 50th Street, New York, N.Y. 10020

Van Nostrand Reinhold Publishing
1410 Birchmount Road
Scarborough, Ontario MIP 2E7, Canada

Van Nostrand Reinhold Australia Pty. Ltd.
17 Queen Street
Mitcham, Victoria 3132, Australia

Van Nostrand Reinhold Company Limited
Molly Millars Lane
Wokingham, Berkshire, England

15 14 13 12 11 10 9 8 7 6 5 4 3 2 1

Library of Congress Cataloging in Publication Data
Main entry under title:

The newer therapies.

    Includes index.
    1. Psychotherapy.   I. Abt, Lawrence Edwin,
1915–   II. Stuart, Irving R.
RC480.N46   616.89'14   81-21847
ISBN 0-442-27942-6   AACR2

Preface

About five years ago, the National Institute of Mental Health conceived of the idea of a multi-institutional clinical study that would compare two forms of psychotherapy with drugs in the treatment of depression. During 1980, a three-year, $3.4 million study actually got underway, and is the first of its scope attempted for the study of psychotherapy.

Among the many problems the investigators initially faced was that of what types of psychotherapy, useful in treating depression, could be most profitably studied in a scientific manner. A survey of the American psychotherapy scene revealed that perhaps as many as 150 or more kinds of psychotherapy are actually being practiced at present and that many of them claim success with depressed persons. The picture is both exciting and confusing, with all sorts of claims advanced by those who prefer one therapeutic approach to others.

Two psychotherapeutic approaches were finally chosen by the National Institute of Mental Health for scientific evaluation in the treatment of depression, frequently regarded as "the common cold" of the mental health field — the cognitive behavioral therapy Aaron Beck and his associates at the University of Pennsylvania developed in trying to prove the classical psychoanalytic theory of depression, and interpersonal psychotherapy, which was developed by Gerald Klerman of the Massachusetts General Hospital in Boston, as well as a group at Yale University.

As this book suggests, many other psychotherapies were candidates for investigation. The range of possibilities for such choices is large, and the editors do not know the grounds for the two choices finally made. But the implications of such a wide-ranging and scientific study are significant.

Both the government and insurance carriers in recent years have become increasingly concerned about whether to reimburse for psychotherapy, and, if so, whether all forms of psychotherapy merit equal treatment. This issue, which has important political as well as financial dimensions, may be in part determined by the outcome of the present investigation.

The Newer Therapies: A Sourcebook, since it cannot possibly consider the whole range of theory and practice of psychotherapy in the United States, seeks to look at a representative sample through the eyes of some of the leading practitioners of the various approaches. Although it cannot be encyclopedic in its coverage, the editors believe that it is catholic in its consideration of many different approaches.

Part I — The Cognitive Therapies — raises the question of whether there is a common core in psychotherapy and then proceeds to look closely at some current and representative approaches to cognitive therapy.

Part II — Therapy with Children — offers a view of new and interesting therapeutic work with children.

Part III — Group Approaches — focuses on different group experiences with psychotherapy as well as family therapy.

Part IV — Adjuvant Therapies — offers a picture of the ever-widening multidimensional approaches to intervention with different sorts of patients and different kinds of problems.

We believe that this book offers the perceptive reader the means to appreciate views of psychotherapy that may be different from those with which he/she is most familiar, and that at the same time it provides those who are newer to the field of psychotherapy with a statement of what's going on in psychotherapy at the present time.

We wish to thank the 23 contributors to this volume who have worked with us to present a statement of where American psychotherapy stands today.

L. E. A. and I. R. S.

Contents

The Newer Therapies: A Sourcebook

Part I
The Cognitive Therapies

Part I consists of eight chapters, the first one of which, by William B. Stiles, searches for a core that is common to all psychotherapy, of whatever sort, and whether cognitive or not. But it appears clear from the way he writes that he has principally in mind those approaches that are usually called cognitive.

It has, of course, long been suspected by some perceptive therapists that some kind of common core runs through various approaches to handling the problems in living with which they deal. How otherwise can one understand why the therapist, as a therapist, is more important, in relation to the outcome of therapy, than the particular theoretical view that he or she espouses?

Samuel Berkowitz's contribution on behavior therapy, setting forth the different sources of this widely practiced approach, is helpful in disclosing not only what is going on among therapists of this persuasion but also in demonstrating the newer directions, and newer applications, now coming to the fore.

David D. Burns, in his chapter on hope and hopelessness, clearly shows the influence of Aaron Beck and others at the University of Pennsylvania in their concern with more fully understanding the psychodynamics of depression as well as fashioning technical procedures adequate to handling it in its many (both overt and covert) forms. This chapter makes us aware of the involvement of Burns himself in the process still under development in Philadelphia, and, as such, in our view, it is a significant addition to the literature.

Patricia Carrington's thoughtful and sensitive statement of the uses and advantages of techniques of meditation as new, enhancing dimensions of therapeutic practice is especially welcome for clinicians whose knowledge of the applications of meditation is perhaps less complete than it might be. In Carrington's view, meditation provides a focalizing of therapy that might not otherwise be possible.

Rebecca Propst offers the reader a discussion of personal belief systems, either "scientific" or "supernatural," in her chapter. She discloses the influence of

Jerome Frank, who urged psychotherapists to entertain belief and value systems different from their own in working with their clients. Her point is that there may well be considerable therapeutic efficacy in the use of supernatural and transcendent belief systems, and she suggests a model for their conceptualization even in the absence of a significant body of empirical evidence for their support.

Chapter 6, by Joseph Rychlak, presents learning theory, in its therapeutic applications, as a type of logical phenomenology. Introducing the concept of telosponsivity, Rychlak offers it as a counter-poise to responsivity as the more traditional learning theories formulate it. The author favors a form of dialectical interpretation that may be new to most readers, who will find it grounded in a form of teleological structuring that is illustrated in some of Rychlak's work with children.

Transpersonal psychotherapy is examined by Frances Vaughan and Seymour Boorstein in a three-fold manner — by means of its context, its content, and its beliefs. This chapter sets forth the centrality of consciousness and self-awareness in the shaping of experience against a full appreciation and integration of the complete range of other elements — emotional, physical, spiritual — that collectively, through their interactions, are the essense of a sense of well being.

The final chapter in Part I is by John and Helen Watkins, who, together and singly, have practiced for some years what they call "ego-state" therapy. Their view of personality and its conflicts rests, in part, on the notion that various ego-states function together as a kind of "family of self" within a single individual, and that members of this "family" are often in a state of conflict. The conflict the authors encounter within their unique frame of reference is susceptible to resolution through various techniques of family and group therapy. Central to their presentation, as the reader will note, is the concept of dissonance, which, when cognitively recognized or experienced, serves as the focus for the development of symptoms.

Part I offers a picture of cognitive therapies that stand at the "cutting edge" of therapeutic thinking.

The question of what links together various theoretical views of the nature of psychotherapy has long been largely unanswered. Now, under pressure from the federal government and third-party insurance sources for payment of therapy fees, steps are underway to seek an answer.

The author of the following chapter deals with two related hypotheses: (1) that different psychotherapies aim to promote qualitatively different kinds of psychological health and (2) that the "common core" of the therapies is to be found not in any of their technical similarity but rather in the revelation of clients of their own growing knowledge or insightful experience.

Taken together, the two hypotheses and the support for them that is mustered suggest that it is essential to pay attention to the actual process of therapist-client interaction and not merely to the labels or theoretical claims given by advocates of one therapeutic point of view or technique.

1

Psychotherapeutic Process:
Is There a Common Core?*

William B. Stiles, Ph.D.

Coverage in the popular and scientific press[15, 26, 40] suggests that the major question about psychotherapy over the next few years will be its efficacy. Perhaps the central public debate in the United States will concern third-party payments, including national health insurance, for psychotherapeutic services.

How can process research contribute to this debate?

Questions of efficacy seem to suggest outcome studies rather than process studies. Legislators and underwriters are likely to ask *whether* some therapy works rather than *how* it works.

But their question assumes that psychotherapy is homogeneous, as if it were a drug manufactured to specified high standards of purity and uniformity. In fact, as anyone who studies or practices psychotherapy knows, there is great variation in what happens from session to session, even in therapy by the same therapist.[16, 31, 44] Asking "Is psychotherapy effective in general?" makes as little sense as asking, "Are pills effective in general?"

A crucial question, which seems obvious enough in the case of a pill, is "What is in it?" That is, what are the ingredients? Which of those ingredients are active?

---

*This chapter is based on a symposium presentation at the Convention of the American Psychological Association, Montreal, P.Q., Canada, September 1980.

Which are flavors and fillers? This, of course, is where measurement of process is essential.

Below, I will review some evidence that psychotherapy process is systematically different, depending on the therapist's theoretical orientation. There *are* different ingredients in different psychotherapies — although whether various ingredients are active ones or fillers is not so easy to determine.

Process research's long-standing problem has been its failure to be cumulative, which I believe can be traced to a lack of consensus on what the basic elements of process are. For 30 or 40 years — ever since the advent of audio tape recording — process researchers have been struggling to identify the units of therapeutic interaction and to name them and classify them. Donald Kiesler, in his 1973 review of systems of process analysis,[22] put it this way:

> Psychotherapy process research has to rank near the forefront of disciplines characterized as chaotic, prolific, unconnected, and disjointed, with researchers unaware of much of the work that has preceded and the individual investigator tending to start anew completely ignorant of closely related previous work. (p. xvii)

I don't believe this chaotic state of affairs can be solved by fiat or by compromise. Investigators invent new systems of classification because they judge that existing systems are inadequate, or at least because previous systems have so failed to capture the scientific community's favor that they are never heard of. Consensus on what the basic ingredients are must come by evolution and natural selection. That is, investigators must continue to invent and modify coding systems until the result reflects the complexity and richness of psychotherapeutic process in a way that is generally convincing.

However, since Kiesler's book first appeared, there has been some progress. Investigators seem to be reading one another's work and communicating with one another, and some convergence in the categories they use can be seen. Not that we have agreed — almost every psychotherapy process researcher uses a different coding system. But the categories are starting to sound more alike across systems, so results of studies can be compared.

TECHNICAL DIVERSITY WITHOUT DIFFERENTIAL EFFECTIVENESS

The demonstration that therapists' verbal behavior in psychotherapy varies systematically depending on their theoretical orientation has now been replicated by several different investigators.[4, 14, 34, 43, 49] Although the coding systems differ in detail, they are similar enough so that Table 1-1 can be constructed. The table abstracts the results of four different studies — three published recently (one by Brunink and Schroeder,[4] one by Hill, Thames, and Rardin,[14] and one

TABLE 1-1. Percentages of Responses in Selected Coding Categories by Therapists Differing in Theoretical Orientation.

THERAPIST ORIENTATION	CODING CATEGORIES				
	Interpretation (Confrontation)	Advisement (Direct Guidance)	Question (Exploratory Operations)	Reflection (Restatement, Clarification)	Acknowledgment (Facilitation, Encouragers)
Client-centered					
Hill *et al.*	9	0	3	18	53
Stiles	1	1	3	45	46
Strupp	4	1	10	76	5
Gestalt					
Brunink and Schroeder	7	42	23	15	10
Hill *et al.*	18	19	16	6	8
Stiles	26	37	20	4	5
Psychoanalytic					
Brunink and Schroeder	9	14	20	15	30
Stiles	49	3	12	10	18
Strupp	10	6	36	14	16
Behaviorist					
Brunink and Schroeder	5	27	17	12	35
Rational-Emotive					
Hill *et al.*	13	21	9	7	14

Sources: Brunink, S. A. and Schroeder, H. E. *Journal of Consulting and Clinical Psychology* 47:767–774 (1979); Hill, C. E., Thames, T. B., and Rardin, D. K. *Journal of Counseling Psychology* 26:198–203 (1979); Stiles, W. B. *Psychiatry* 42:49–62 (1979); Strupp, H. H. *Journal of Consulting Psychology* 19:1–7 (1955).

of my own[43]) and one that is over 25 years old (the published report of Hans Strupp's doctoral dissertation[49] — and it should be noted that Strupp's was not the first such demonstration; William Snyder had made one a decade earlier[39]).

I have used my categories — which I call *verbal response modes* (VRMs) — to head the columns, but I think others can recognize their own categories. My VRM system[43] derives from the work of Gerald Goodman at UCLA.[12]

Considering the differences in coding systems and research design, I believe these results are remarkably congruent with one another.

1. Client-centered therapists use almost entirely Reflections and Acknowledgments — "mm-hm" and "yeah" — and avoid other responses.
2. Gestalt therapists use very few Reflections and Acknowledgments. They do use lots of Advisements (Goodman's word for commands, suggestions, permission, and advice — guiding information).
3. Psychoanalytic therapists generally avoid Advisements (which would be treatment by suggestion).
4. Rational-emotive therapists and behavior therapists use many Advisements; these can be called directive therapies.

To repeat, the conclusion is that there are different ingredients in different therapies. Furthermore, we have the technology to specify what those ingredients are. Theories of therapy have real, measurable consequences for process.

This conclusion may seem obvious to practitioners, but, in a peculiar example of dissociation, there has been a persistent piece of lore that all therapies are fundamentally alike and all therapists converge on a common core of techniques. This is not so. Furthermore, there has been published evidence that this is not so for over a quarter of a century.

On the other hand, as research on process becomes less disjointed, we see how disjointed psychotherapy really is. Every school is systematically doing something different from every other school.

The clear demonstration of process differences contrasts with the general failure to find clear differences in the rate of successful outcomes among different types of therapy.[2,24] Virtually all therapies that have been studied show modestly positive effects overall, as compared with controls.[1,2,24,30,38] It appears that "everybody has won and all must have prizes" (Luborsky *et al.*[24] quoting the dodo bird in Lewis Carroll's *Alice in Wonderland*).

Partly for this reason, many of us would like to believe that there is a common core to different therapies, despite the process differences. It is not hard to see where this resistance comes from: If every school does something different and none is demonstrably better than any other, then perhaps it doesn't matter what you do! This seems devastating for professional psychotherapy, since it suggests that you don't have to be a professional: Whatever technique you happen to use, you end up with about the same results.

In this chapter I would like to suggest two possible ways out — that is, two researchable hypotheses that acknowledge that different therapists may do clearly different things to similar mixes of clients, with similar rates of success, and that nevertheless respect the subtlety, skill, and experience of professional therapists. I believe that in the coming years the profession of psychotherapy will be compelled to defend some such hypothesis as a condition of its continued claim on public resources.

DIFFERENT THERAPIES MAY ACCOMPLISH DIFFERENT ENDS

My first hypothesis is that *different therapies may produce different kinds of healthy people.*

By calling the people we treat "mentally ill," we invoke an analogy with physical illness that may be misleading. Physical illness is usually construed as a deviation from normal, and physical treatment is tailored to the direction of the deviation. It brings the person back to normal — which is more or less the same for everybody — by killing invading organisms, giving supplements for deficiencies, and otherwise restoring homeostatic balance.

However, applying this medical analogy to psychotherapy may be seriously misleading. Unlike physical disease, in which the object is to return the patient to normal, psychotherapy promotes individuality — actualization of the self, freedom from aversive control, release from a compulsion — and thus permits an *increase* in individual variation. Most models of personality describe a healthy individual as having a wide range of options.[13] Freedom from psychopathology opens up many paths rather than converging on a single pattern of good adjustment.

We all recognize that the old, popular stereotype of a "well-adjusted" person is false — a picture of rigid conformity rather than of psychological health. A better picture includes creativity, spontaneity, and, in some ways, unpredictability. My suggestion is that different therapies may open up systematically different ranges of options for their clients. There may be many different paths away from maladjustment.

I do not mean to suggest that all clients of a particular therapist emerge from the same mold. Presumably, all successful clients become less rigid, less constricted, and less like one another. Nevertheless, perhaps it does make a difference which therapy you choose; you may become a different person as a result of each.

Even the most superficial look around shows that there are many different varieties of psychological health. There may, therefore, be reasons to choose one therapy over another beyond effectiveness at overcoming psychopathology.

The existence of many paths does not eliminate the need for a guide, nor does it imply that just any path leads away from psychological disorder. Each new path that is discovered is probably best traveled with someone who knows that path, its hazards, and its requirements.

This view fits the observation that therapists tend to stick with what they do well, across the whole range of their clients. And it supports the common clinical injunction that each new therapist must carefully develop his or her own way of being effective.

CLIENT VERBAL BEHAVIOR AS A COMMON CORE

My second hypothesis — which is not entirely inconsistent with the first — is that *there is a common core to the psychotherapy process, but it is in the client's behavior rather than in the therapist's.* This is the hypothesis that I have been researching recently. It was suggested by the finding that, at least in terms of the coding system I've been using, clients behave very similarly regardless of their therapists' theoretical orientations.[46] Even though therapists systematically use different modes, the client profile of modes remains essentially the same.

The client profile shown in Table 1-2 (based on ten sessions representing varied types of therapy) consists primarily of Disclosures and Edifications, as defined by the verbal response mode (VRM) system.[43] According to this system, each utterance is coded twice, once for its grammatical form and once for its communicative intent. Disclosure (D) form is first person ("I"), and Disclosure intent is to reveal subjective information — thoughts, feelings, perceptions, intentions. Edification (E) form is third person ("he," "she," "it," or a noun), and Edification intent is to convey objective information — observable from the outside.

More technically, both Disclosure and Edification intents concern the speaker's knowledge or experience, but Disclosure intent uses the speaker's internal frame

TABLE 1-2. Verbal Response Mode Use by Clients in Psychotherapy.

MODE*	MEAN PERCENTAGE OF UTTERANCES
D(D)	37.9
E(D)	22.3
E(E)	10.7
D(E)	4.7
K(C)	4.2
K(K)	3.4
K(D)	3.0
Other	13.8
Total	100.0

*Mode abbreviations: Disclosure (D), Edification (E), Acknowledgment (K), Confirmation (C). Form is written first, intent second (in parentheses).
Source: Stiles, W. B. and Sultan, F. E. *Journal of Consulting and Clinical Psychology* 47:611–613 (1979).

of reference, whereas Edification intent uses an external frame of reference.[43] Thus, utterances whose truth can be determined only through access to the speaker's private experience are coded Disclosure intent, whereas utterances whose truth can *in principle* be assessed by an external observer are coded Edification intent.

In the VRM abbreviation system, form is written first and intent second (in parentheses). Thus, "I am delighted to be here" is D(D) — a pure Disclosure — whereas "It is delightful to be here" is a *mixed mode*, E(D) — a third person statement that reveals subjective experience. "My house is eight blocks from here" is E(E) — a pure Edification — whereas "I walked eight blocks from my house this morning" is D(E) — a first person statement that conveys objective information. About 75 percent of client utterances were in one of these four modes (Table 1-2). Some further examples are:

I'm very frightened. D(D)
I understand what you're saying. D(D)
I think she should apologize. D(D)
It's very annoying. E(D)
He made me feel better. E(D)
My favorite color is blue. E(D)
She said she was wrong. E(E)
The tablecloth was blue. E(E)
He hit me first. E(E)
I bought a blue tablecloth. D(E)
I failed my history exam. D(E)
I'm a second-generation Italian. D(E)

In addition, about 10 percent of client utterances were Acknowledgment (K) in *form* — brief, contentless forms such as "mm-hm," "yeah," "no," "well," or "hello." Their intent must be inferred from context. K(K) conveys simple receipt of communication; K(D) conveys subjective information, as in "yes" or "no" answers to closed questions; K(C) conveys agreement or disagreement, as when a client says "yeah!" to confirm an accurate reflection of interpretation.

This client profile is very different from any therapist profile, and stays about the same despite wide variations in the content of what clients say as well as across different schools of therapy. Perhaps this profile is the common core.

The main process variation from one client's session to another is within this profile — in the relative proportions of Disclosures and Edifications. This suggested that simple hypothesis that perhaps some part of this profile is a common active ingredient of psychotherapy.

The most obvious candidate is client Disclosure. Pure Disclosures — D(D) — involve voicing personal responsibility for one's own internal experience, as opposed to talking about external events or someone else's experience. Also, Disclosure is a very large part of the profile — D (D) and E (D) account for an average of about 60 percent of client utterances[46]. Clients must be doing this for some reason.

To give a more formal formulation of this hypothesis, according to client-centered theory,[35, 36] psychotherapy involves an alteration of the client's "self" through recognizing, facing, and reevaluating its inconsistencies. Because the client is the only person who can fully know his or her own field of experience, the best vantage point for facilitating change is from the client's internal frame of reference.

A frame of reference can be described as the constellation of associated experiences, perceptions, ideas, feelings, memories, and so forth from which a particular experience gains its meaning. An experience may be expressed either in an external, objective frame or in an internal, subjective frame of reference. That is, a client can give objective descriptions of events or reveal the events' personal meanings, feelings, and values.

The self, according to Rogers,[35] is a differentiated portion of the organism's perceptual fields; hence, it consists of experiences — "an organized, fluid, but consistent conceptual pattern of characteristics and relations of the I or the me together with the values attached to these concepts." (p. 498) Thus, at least in part, the self *is* the client's internal frame of reference. When a person reveals the personal meaning of an experience, that meaning consists of the experience's relation to the self. Talk that uses the client's internal frame of reference (i.e., VRM Disclosures) should thus be therapeutic because it brings distorted or mis-valued experiences and inconsistent feelings to awareness, where they can be reevaluated, reconciled with the self, and accepted. Talk that uses an external frame of reference (i.e., VRM Edifications) may be a waste of time; it fails to expose the relation of events to the self.

The first thing we did in examining this hypothesis was to compare client verbal response mode use with expert ratings of good therapy process, using the Experiencing (EXP) scale.[45] The EXP scale was developed some years ago by Gendlin, Tomlinson, Kiesler, Klein, and others in the client-centered group to measure the degree to which clients face and explore their own inner experience in a segment of dialogue.[9, 10, 11, 21, 23, 51] In our study,[45] transcripts of 90 interview segments (two to eight minutes long) that had been previously rated by expert EXP raters were coded according to the VRM system. The percentages of each client mode were then correlated with the EXP ratings. The results, shown in Table 1-3, were encouraging. The strongest correlate of EXP was pure Disclosure. These correlations — positive with Disclosure, negative with Edification — imply that our idea of good process is similar to the client-centered group's idea of good process. So the notion has some convergent validity.

TABLE 1-3. Correlation of Verbal Response Mode Percentages with Experiencing Scale Ratings in 90 Interview Segments.

MODE*	r
D(D)	0.58***
E(D)	0.31**
D(E)	-0.29**
E(E)	-0.48***
K(C)	0.07

*Mode abbreviations: Disclousure (D), Edification (E), Acknowledgment (K), Confirmation (C). Form is written first, intent second (in parentheses).
**$p < 0.01$.
***$p < 0.0001$.
Source: Stiles, W. B., McDaniel, S. H., and McGaughey, K. *Journal of Consulting and Clinical Psychology* 47:795–797 (1979).

As Kiesler[21] has noted, the concept of EXP is very similar to other theoretical ideas of good process, such as the psychoanalytic concepts of insight, absence of resistances, and working through.[3, 41]   All imply that good process requires clients' revealing or exploring their own inner life. VRM Disclosures can be considered as a way of specifying and measuring this conception in terms of individual utterances, and hence, perhaps, as a common active ingredient of psychotherapy. There is also a large theoretical and empirical literature on self-disclosure,[7, 48] with many suggestions that disclosing is therapeutic (Sidney Jourard's work[18, 19] is an illustration). Most of this literature defines disclosure in terms of intimacy of content, which is different from the VRM definition, but there is probably a good deal of overlap.

In view of strong theoretical reasons why client self-disclosure, experiencing, or self-exploration should be therapeutic, available evidence on the relation of such measures to psychotherapy outcome is surprisingly mixed and inconclusive.[10, 21, 23, 29, 33, 37, 47]   The mixed results may reflect the formidable methodological problems involved in studying the relation of process to outcome.

The only study so far comparing VRM Disclosures to outcome failed to show the expected positive relationship,[28, 29] but it illustrates some of the methodological problems. This study, which was Susan McDaniel's dissertation research, involved VRM coding of tape-recorded therapy sessions gathered as part of the Vanderbilt Psychotherapy Project.[50]   Subjects were 31 male college students who had *t* scores of 60 or above on the MMPI scales of Depression, Psychasthenia, and Social Introversion, and who indicated they would like some counseling. They were offered up to 25 sessions, free of charge, on a twice-a-week basis, and they eventually averaged about 17 sessions each. At intake, at termination, and at one-year follow-up, they were assessed with a substantial battery of tests and rating scales intended to measure level of distress or adjustment at each point in time and change from point to point.   In McDaniel's study,[28, 29] all client utterances in the second, middle, and next-to-last sessions were coded according to the verbal response modes system — in all, this included 93 sessions and nearly 50,000 client utterances.

The results showed that the percentage of Disclosures was higher for clients with greater psychological distress and disorder.   This finding is consistent with previous reports relating excessive self-disclosure to depression and maladjustment.[5, 6, 27, 42]   However, there was no evidence that amount of Disclosure was correlated with amount of change in therapy.

Nevertheless, I am not ready to abandon the hypothesis that high levels of client Disclosures are therapeutic.   For several reasons, this study may not have adequately tested the hypothesis.   First, the level of client Disclosures may have been below that necessary for therapeutic effects.   After reviewing data relating the seven-point EXP scale to outcome, Gendlin and his associates[10] concluded that unless the process is at level four or above, no real therapy takes place.   On the average, D(D) and E(D) accounted for only a little over 40 percent of the Vanderbilt clients' utterances, which corresponds to about level two or three on the Experiencing scale,[45] as compared with an average of 60 percent D(D) and E(D) in our earlier work,[46] which corresponds to about level five on the Experiencing scale.   The possibility that little real therapy occurred would be consistent with the very modest mean differences found between the treatment and waiting-list control groups in the Vanderbilt study.[50]

Second, if different clients change differently in psychotherapy, as my earlier hypothesis, stated above, suggests, then it may be inappropriate to measure all clients' improvement on the same scales, as was done in the Vanderbilt study.[50] Perhaps a much more individualized approach to outcome measurement is necessary.[25]

Finally, the sample of process used to characterize each client's level of Disclosure may have been insufficient.   The coded sessions included about 17 percent of the total time the clients spent in therapy, which is higher than in most process-outcome comparisons, but which probably included the good hours for some clients and missed many others, haphazardly.   Outcome was assessed at the end of a long, probably very heterogeneous, series of sessions.   Comparing some *sample* of process to eventual outcome makes little sense if the underlying assumption — that process is consistent throughout a client's therapy — is false.[20] In the Vanderbilt data, clients' use of particular modes in different sessions — for example, the percentage of E(E) in the second session versus the middle session — correlated only about 0.4 on the average.[29]   Thus, there was some consistency, but it accounted for only 15 to 20 percent of the variance in mode use.   This low consistency of VRM-coded process corroborates results of a variety of studies that rated whole sessions.[16, 31, 44]   The process in which therapist and client participate is not stable from session to session.

On the other hand, it does not seem feasible to code every utterance in a whole course of therapy for comparison with outcome measures taken months or years later.

An alternative approach is to measure the *impact* of each session. If psychotherapy has a long-term effect, then some residue must remain after each session, even though any obvious external improvement or life changes may require incubation or cumulation of small effects. It might be useful to develop measures and concepts to understand the impact of particular sessions, as a bridge between process and long-term outcome. Several researchers have taken preliminary steps in this direction.[8, 17, 32, 44]

In any case, the difficulties in demonstrating that a particular part of the client VRM profile (i.e., Disclosure) is the active ingredient should not be permitted to obscure the striking commonality of client verbal behavior across gross differences in therapists' techniques and theoretical approaches.[29, 45, 46]

CONCLUSION

I have suggested two hypotheses that seek to reconcile the technical diversity of the psychotherapies with their lack of demonstrated differential effectiveness. Each of these hypotheses has implications for how new therapies, such as those described in the other chapters of this volume, should be regarded.

The first — and more radical — hypothesis is that different psychotherapies promote qualitatively different kinds of psychological health. This hypothesis requires abandoning any preconception of normality as conformity to a norm, in favor of a pluralistic view of healthy personhood. There may be no common core to the psychotherapies because each is aimed at accomplishing something different. An implication is that new therapies must be evaluated as to *what* they seek to do — what sort of change they seek to produce — as well as how well they do it.

The second hypothesis is that the common process core of the various psychotherapies lies in the clients' revealing their own knowledge or experience through Disclosures and Edifications, rather than in any technical similarity in the behavior of therapists. In contrast to the first hypothesis, this one suggests a common metric on which new therapies can be compared — how well they facilitate the core client process. On the other hand, there may be many ways to facilitate clients' self-exploration, and different clients may be more responsive to different techniques. Perhaps what is crucial are the therapist's skill, experience, and attitude rather than his or her theoretical orientation or technical preferences.

The two hypotheses are not necessarily incompatible with each other. It may be that clients' revealing their own experience is a necessary precondition for any therapy, but that the nature and direction of personal growth and change depend on how the revealed experience is dealt with by the therapist, following the philosophy and technical procedures of his or her school.

Both hypotheses suggest that in evaluating a new therapy, it is essential to pay attention to the actual process of the interaction – not merely to the labels or theoretical claims given by proponents. Any rational choices about which therapy to prescribe must rest on knowledge of its ingredients – its technical procedures and mechanisms of action.

REFERENCES

1. Bergin, A. E. The evaluation of therapeutic outcomes. *In:* Bergin, A. E. and Garfield, S. L. (Eds.). *Handbook of Psychotherapy and Behavior Change.* New York: Wiley (1971).
2. Bergin, A. E. and Lambert, M. J. The evaluation of therapeutic outcomes. *In:* Garfield, S. L. and Bergin, A. E. (Eds.). *Handbook of Psychotherapy and Behavior Change: An Empirical Analysis* (2nd Ed.). New York: Wiley (1978).
3. Bordin, E. S. Free association: An experimental analogue of one psychoanalytic situation. *In:* Gottschalk, L. A. and Auerbach, A. H. (Eds.). *Methods of Research in Psychotherapy.* New York: Appleton-Century-Crofts (1966).
4. Brunink, S. A. and Schroeder, H. E. Verbal therapeutic behavior of expert psychoanalytically oriented, gestalt, and behavior therapists. *Journal of Consulting and Clinical Psychology* 47:567–574 (1979).
5. Coyne, J. C. Depression and the response of others. *Journal of Abnormal Psychology* 85:186–193 (1976).
6. Coyne, J. C. Toward an interactional description of depression. *Psychiatry* 39:28–40 (1976).
7. Cozby, P. C. Self-disclosure: A literature review. *Psychological Bulletin* 79:73–91 (1973).
8. Elliott, R. How clients perceive helper behaviors. *Journal of Counseling Psychology* 26:285–294 (1979).
9. Gendlin, E. T. *Experiencing and The Creation of Meaning.* New York: The Free Press of Glencoe (1962).
10. Gendlin, E. T., Beebe, J., III, Cassens, J., Klein, M., and Oberlander, M. Focusing ability in psychotherapy, personality, and creativity. *In:* Shlein, J. M. (Ed.). *Research in Psychotherapy* III. Washington, DC: American Psychological Association (1968).
11. Gendlin, E. T. and Tomlinson, T. M. The process conceptualization and its measurement. *In:* Rogers, C. R., Gendlin, E. T., Kiesler, D. J., and Traux, C. B. (Eds.). *The Therapeutic Relationship and its Impact: A Study of Psychotherapy with Schizophrenics.* Madison, WI: University of Wisconsin Press (1967).
12. Goodman, G. and Dooley, D. A framework for help-intended communication. *Psychotherapy: Theory, Research, and Practice* 13:106–117 (1976).
13. Hall, C. S. and Lindzey, G. *Theories of Personality* (3rd Ed.). New York: Wiley (1978).
14. Hill, C. E., Thames, T. B., and Rardin, D. K. Comparison of Rogers, Perls, and Ellis on the Hill Counselor Verbal Response Category System. *Journal of Counseling Psychology* 26:198–203 (1979).
15. Hilts, P. J. Federal government seeks to analyze role of psychotherapy. *The Cincinnati Enquirer,* H-6 (September 28, 1980).
16. Howard, K. I., Orlinsky, D. E., and Perilstein, J. Contributions of therapists to patients' experiences in psychotherapy: A components of variance model for analyzing process data. *Journal of Consulting and Clinical Psychology* 44:520–526 (1976).

17. Hoyt, M. F. Therapist and patient actions in "good" psychotherapy sessions. *Archives of General Psychiatry* **37**:159-161 (1980).
18. Jourard, S. M. *Disclosing Man to Himself.* New York: Van Nostrand Reinhold (1968).
19. Jourard, S. M. *The Transparent Self* (Rev. Ed.). New York: Van Nostrand Reinhold (1971).
20. Kiesler, D. J. Experimental designs in psychotherapy research. *In:* Bergin, A. E. and Garfield, S. L. (Eds.). *Handbook of Psychotherapy and Behavior Change: An Empirical Analysis.* New York: Wiley (1971).
21. Kiesler, D. J. Patient experiencing and successful outcome in individual psychotherapy of schizophrenics and psychoneurotics. *Journal of Consulting and Clinical Psychology* **37**:370-385 (1971).
22. Kiesler, D. J. *The Process of Psychotherapy: Empirical Foundations and Systems of Analysis.* Chicago: Aldine (1973).
23. Klein, M. H., Mathieu, P. L., Gendlin, E. T., and Kiesler, D. J. *The Experiencing Scale: A Research and Training Manual* I. Madison, WI: Wisconsin Psychiatric Institute (1969).
24. Luborsky, L., Singer, B., and Luborsky, L. Comparative studies of psychotherapies: Is it true that "everyone has won and all must have prizes"? *Archives of General Psychiatry* **32**:995-1008 (1975).
25. Malan, D. H. The outcome problem in psychotherapy research. *Archives of General Psychiatry* **29**:719-729 (1973).
26. Marshall, E. Psychotherapy works, but for whom? *Science* **207**:506-508 (1980).
27. Mayo, P. R. Self-disclosure and neurosis. *British Journal of Social and Clinical Psychology* **7**:140-148 (1968).
28. McDaniel, S. H. Clients' verbal response mode use and its relationship to measures of psychopathology and change in brief psychotherapy (doctoral dissertation, University of North Carolina at Chapel Hill, 1979). *Dissertation Abstracts International* **41**:359B (1980) (University Microfilms No. 8013966).
29. McDaniel, S. H., Stiles, W. B., and McGaughey, K. J. Correlations of male college students' verbal response mode use in psychotherapy with measures of psychological disturbance and psychotherapy outcome. *Journal of Consulting and Clinical Psychology*, in press.
30. Meltzoff, J. and Kornreich, M. *Research in Psychotherapy.* New York: Ahterton Press (1970).
31. Mintz, J., Luborsky, L., and Auerbach, A. H. Dimensions of psychotherapy: A factor analytic study of ratings of psychotherapy sessions. *Journal of Consulting and Clinical Psychology* **36**:106-120 (1971).
32. Orlinsky, D. E. and Howard, K. I. The therapist's experience of psychotherapy. *In:* Gurman, A. S. and Razin, A. M. (Eds.). *Effective Psychotherapy: A Handbook of Research.* Oxford: Pergamon Press (1977).
33. Orlinsky, D. E. and Howard, K. I. The relation of process to outcome in psychotherapy. *In:* Garfield, S. L. and Bergin, A. E. (Eds.). *Handbook of Psychotherapy and Behavior Change: An Empirical Analysis* (2nd Ed.). New York: Wiley (1978).
34. Pope, B. Research on therapeutic style. *In:* Gurman, A. S. and Razin, A. M. (Eds.). *Effective Psychotherapy: A Handbook of Research.* Oxford: Pergamon Press (1977).
35. Rogers, C. R. *Client-Centered Therapy.* Boston: Houghton-Mifflin (1951).
36. Rogers, C. R. A theory of therapy, personality, and interpersonal relationships, as developed in the client-centered framework. *In:* Koch, S. (Ed.). *Psychology: A Study of a Science* 3. New York: McGraw-Hill (1959).
37. Sloane, R. B., Staples, F. R., Cristol, A. H., Yorkston, N. J., and Whipple, K. *Psychotherapy versus Behavior Therapy.* Cambridge, MA: Harvard University Press (1975).

38. Smith, M. L. and Glass, G. V. Meta-analysis of psychotherapy outcome studies. *American Psychologist* **132**:752–760 (1977).
39. Snyder, W. U. An investigation of the nature of non-directive psychotherapy. *Journal of General Psychology* **33**:193–223 (1945).
40. Sobel, D. Freud's fragmented legacy. *The New York Times Magazine,* 28–31; 102–208 (October 26, 1980).
41. Speisman, J. C. Depth of interpretation and verbal resistance in psychotherapy. *Journal of Consulting Psychology* **23**:93–99 (1959).
42. Stanley, G. and Bownes, A. F. Self-disclosure and neuroticism. *Psychological Reports* **18**:350 (1966).
43. Stiles, W. B. Verbal response modes and psychotherapeutic technique. *Psychiatry* **42**:49–62 (1979).
44. Stiles, W. B. Measurement of the impact of psychotherapy sessions. *Journal of Consulting and Clinical Psychology* **48**:176–185 (1980).
45. Stiles, W. B., McDaniel, S. H., and McGaughey, K. Verbal response mode correlates of experiencing. *Journal of Consulting and Clinical Psychology* **47**:795–797 (1979).
46. Stiles, W. B. and Sultan, F. E. Verbal response mode use by clients in psychotherapy. *Journal of Consulting and Clinical Psychology* **47**:611–613 (1979).
47. Strassberg, D. S., Anchor, K. N., Gabel, H., and Cohen, B. Self-disclosure in individual psychotherapy. *Psychotherapy: Theory, Research, and Practice* **15**:153–157 (1978).
48. Strassberg, D., Roback, H., D'Antonio, M., and Gabel, H. Self-disclosure: A critical and selective review of the clinical literature. *Comprehensive Psychiatry* **18**:31–39 (1977).
49. Strupp, H. H. An objective comparison of Rogerian and psychoanalytic techniques. *Journal of Consulting Psychology* **19**:1–7 (1955).
50. Strupp, H. H. and Hadley, S. W. Specific versus nonspecific factors in psychotherapy: A controlled study of outcome. *Archives of General Psychiatry* **36**:1125–1136 (1979).
51. Tomlinson, T. M. and Hart, J. T. A validation study of the process scale. *Journal of Consulting Psychology* **26**:74–78 (1962).

In the chapter that follows behavior modification is examined not as a set of techniques but rather as a comprehensive theoretical orientation and a group of practices essentially grounded in operant conditioning principles and procedures. The author indicates in what ways treatment strategies that aim to bring about changes in behavior are based upon the identification and control of environmental factors and processes.

In examining on-going research and thinking, the author considers the relationship between the older behavior modification theory and practice and newer, more comprehensive views that place additional emphasis on more specifically cognitive factors. Within such a frame of reference, behavior modification principles and procedures are projected onto a larger and larger vista as they find application in a wide variety of fields not originally contemplated.

2

Behavior Therapy

Samuel Berkowitz, Ph.D.

Behavior modification originally emerged as a departure from the traditionally held psychodynamic therapeutic view and the techniques practiced in the mental health fields, primarily clinical psychology and psychiatry, in the 1940's and 1950's. The basic characteristic of the many diverse behavior modification techniques used today is adherance to an experimental, empirical, and objective approach toward developing principles and procedures used in clinical practice.

Behavior modification is more than a set of techniques. It is a comprehensive orientation and practice that treats behavior problems and is based primarily on operant conditioning principles and procedures. Operant conditioning provides a rather unique way of conceptualizing and developing treatment strategies to bring about changes in behavior. The goal of operant conditioning is to identify and control factors in the environment that result in the modification of behavior.

This chapter will provide the reader with a brief history of the experimental and clinical origins of behavior modification, and then discuss specific techniques used in the field, with a focus on current and recent applications. The material discussed should be considered a short introduction to a field whose literature is both extensive and diverse.

HISTORY

Unlike the more traditional treatment approaches, behavior modification has drawn extensively from experimental laboratory findings and the research methods of psychology. The works of both Ivan Pavlov, the Russian physiologist, and the American psychologist-educator Edward Thorndike, laid the original groundwork by developing principles, concepts, and procedures to study both human and animal behavior. Later work in the early part of the present century by John B. Watson, followed in the 1920's and 1930's by Edwin Guthrie and Clark L. Hull, demonstrated how basic scientific research can lead to the development of techniques that can be applied to the resolution of behavioral problems.

More recently, the experimental work and writings of B. F. Skinner in the area of operant conditioning have had a tremendous effect on treatment programs in clinical psychology, psychiatry, nursing, education, social work, and rehabilitation. In the early 1950's, Skinner's influence led to the development of systematic applications of basic laboratory findings to clinical problems.

During this period, several other seminal, but independent, attempts were being explored and delineated by Joseph Wolpe, a South African psychiatrist, Arnold A. Lazarus, a South African clinical psychologist, and Hans J. Eysenck, an English experimental psychologist. These parallel efforts converged and today encompass a wide spectrum of multifaceted philosophies, treatment procedures, and theoretical assumptions. The basic characteristic of all these approaches is the experimental analysis and evaluation of treatment techniques.

DEFINITION

When we understand behavior modification's experimental and empirical origins, it is then clear why Kazdin[4] has defined behavior modification as "the application of basic research and theory from experimental psychology to influence behavior for purposes of resolving personal and social problems and enhancing human functioning."

Some writers differentiate between the terms *behavior modification* and *behavior therapy*. Most, however, use the terms interchangeably owing to a lack of clear, widely adopted, or meaningful distinctions between the two.

BASIC ASSUMPTIONS

Virtually all behavior modification techniqes rest on the assumption that behavior, whether it be labeled as abnormal or socially appropriate, is a function of its relationship to the environment. The principles of learning apply to all behaviors, and it is assumed that unacceptable behaviors can be unlearned and replaced by more adaptive behaviors.

Research findings from the experimental-learning laboratory provide the objective basis for the techniques used in behavior modification, which are to be replicated, evaluated, and validated in clinical practice. Consistent with this empirical, experimental approach, the focus is on overt behavior as the subject matter rather than on behavior that is conceptualized and treated as a symptom of an underlying problem. Therapy focuses on changing behavior directly, not through changes in intervening or hypothesized states, such as inner mental or psychic processes.

Behavior modification is characterized by a reliance on rigorous treatment-assessment procedures. Within its historical and experimental origins, techniques are systematically subjected to empirical scrutiny through intrasubject-replication designs. This experimental analysis seeks to determine the effectiveness of the technique in bringing about behavior change, rather than through the more traditional approaches of group comparisons, pre- and post-testing, and statistical analysis. The emphasis is on systematic assessment, refinement, and reevaluation of treatment procedures. All clinical problems are operationally specified and objectively quantified.

BASIC PROCEDURES

Those who use behavior modification procedures seek to answer these four questions:

1. What is the target behavior to be changed? Which observable behavior is to be strengthened, maintained, or weakened?
2. Which empirical events in the environment — antecedents and consequences — are currently maintaining the behavior?
3. What environmental changes, or systematic interventions, can be introduced to modify — establish or eliminate — the behavior?
4. How can the behavior, once established, be maintained and/or generalized to new situations over a period of time?

The initial step in designing a behavioral program is the pinpointing or specification of the target behavior to be changed. The behavior is operationally defined — that is, described in concrete, observable, measurable terms. Next, environmental conditions in which the behavior occurs are delineated. Since the focus of the treatment apporach is to change behavior in relation to the situation or stimulus conditions of the environment, such specifications need to be identified at the outset.

A recording or measurement technique (e.g., frequency or duration) is next selected to obtain a baseline meaure of the target behavior prior to the introduction of any treatment/intervention procedure. The behavior and its antecedent stimulus conditions and consequences (reinforcing and aversive) are also recorded. The baseline measure provides an initial measure of the level, frequency, or extent of the problem behavior and provides information regarding environmental factors and consequences that may be influencing or maintaining the behavior. It is these environmental factors that are to be systematically changed during the treatment phase to bring about a concomitant change in the target behavior.

This initial analysis of problem specification and baseline measurement is the first step taken in all the specific behavioral techniques to be discussed below. This first step is important for making decisions about treatment strategies, even before goals are established.

By stating the problem in behavioral, observable terms, one can select specific treatment techniques to alter the target behavior. By specifying the environmental factors, the behavior therapist can evaluate and change them to modify the behavior.

This initial analysis, or diagnostic stage, like the subsequent intervention and assessment phases, rests on direct, objective observation and measurement of behavior for making treatment decisions. Explicit specification at the outset facilitates observation, recording, and assessment throughout the modification program. This point cannot be overemphasized.

SPECIFIC TECHNIQUES

Several of the major behavior modification techniques will be discussed. The purpose of this section is to briefly describe the actual steps in the application of the technique subsequent to the baseline phase and to provide a discussion of applications and outcomes. Space restrictions do not allow for a thorough, more comprehensive analysis than is presented.

Operant Conditioning

Although behavior modification encompasses a wide variety of behavioral techniques and conceptual views, it is this one sub-area, operant conditioning, that has stimulated more work than any other field of research and clinical application. This approach to studying learning has been developed by B. F. Skinner over the past 50 years and is based on the use of reinforcers and punishers to modify behavior. Skinner's work stems from the early work of Thorndike.

Significant contributions have been made in the application of operant procedures to the modification of such diverse population groups as retardates, autistic children, chronic schizophrenics, and adult neurotics. These techniques have been used by mental health professionals, as well as paraprofessionals (e.g., parents, teachers, psychiatric aids), and in a wide variety of situations.

A brief chart follows, outlining the basic sequence of steps in conducting an operant program.

Conducting an Operant Conditioning, Behavior Modification Program

1. *Define the target behavior to be modified. Describe the target behavior; what is the patient now doing that is to be changed?*
   A. On-task behavior: The desirable behavior, to be increased.
   B. Off-task behavior: The undesirable behavior, to be decreased.

2. *Select the recording technique.*
   A. How will the target behavior be counted and measured? (e.g., frequency, duration, sampling, interval, products).
   B. Construct a recording sheet to count the behavior.

3. *Baseline behavior:*
   A. Count the target behavior under the present conditions without making any other changes.
   B. Count the antecedents to and consequences of the target behavior, without making any other changes.
   C. Construct a cumulative graph to record observations.

4. *Terminal goal:* Establish goals for the target behavior; identify the acceptable level (frequency) of the behavior and the conditions under which it will occur; at the end of the treatment program, at what level would behavior have to be to consider the program a success?

5. *Establish assessment procedures.* (This step is optional and not usually done in clinical practice. It is performed in behavior analysis studies to determine functional relationships between treatment and behavioral variables.)
   A. Reversal design (ABAB).
   B. Multiple-baseline design.

6. *Intervention:*
   A. *Design program:*
      (1) On-task behavior: Reward (e.g., praise, tokens, consumables, attention, privileges, points).
      (2) Off-task behavior: Punish (e.g., ignore, response cost, time out, aversive stimuli, overcorrection).
   B. *Implementation:*
      (1) *Antecedents:*
         a. Give clear signals ("rules").
         b. Clearly specify the desired behavior that is to be followed by reward. The desired behavior should be one that the individual can readily engage in (at or below baseline).
      (2) *Consequences:*
         a. Catch them being good! Follow desired behavior with reinforcement. Catch them *on-task!*

   b. Praise improvement. Although progress is slight, reward be-
      havior moving in desired direction (toward terminal behavior).
      Individual must be successful.
   c. Ignore off-task behavior if possible (extinction). If not, use a
      punishment procedure (e.g., response cost, time out, overcor-
      rection).
(3) *Shaping, modeling, and fading procedures.*
(4) *Intermittent reinforcement.*
(5) *Behavioral contracting.*
7. *Continue to count, evaluate, and revise.*

Following the baseline measures discussed in the previous section, one makes
decisions concerning the modification of the target behavior. Selection and designing (6A in above chart) operant conditioning techniques to increase the socially acceptable or on-task behavior(s) and/or to decrease the inappropriate,
maladaptive, off-task behavior(s) are a further step. Reinforcement procedures
(positive or negative) increase the frequency of the acceptable behavior, and
punishment (positive or negative) or an extinction procedure weakens or eliminates the unacceptable off-task behavior (6B).

Positive reinforcement increases behavior by making a stimulus event or consequence immediately contingent upon the occurrence of the desired on-task behavior. This is called "positive" reinforcement becasue the consequence is *added*
following the on-task behavior and not because the consequence is "good" or
desired. Negative reinforcement also increases behavior, but here the increase is
due to the removal, avoidance, or *subtraction* of a stimulus event following the
occurrence of the off-task behavior. Negative reinforcement is often confused
with punishment procedures. The former increases behavior; punishment decreases behavior.

Punishment following an undesired behavior can take the form of presenting
or adding an aversive stimulus, such as a sharp reprimand, a "dirty look," or a
shock, following the behavior. "Adding" something following the behavior is
positive punishment. Negative punishment is the removal (subtraction) of a
reinforcer or privilege following the occurrence of the behavior. A fine, a penal-
ty, and being sent to one's room are examples of negative punishment. The other
procedure to reduce behavior is extinction. Here the unwanted (off-task) behavior is not attended to and is completely ignored, while the on-task behavior is
followed by reinforcement.

Typically, reinforcement and punishment procedures are scheduled together
in a behavior modification program to simultaneously strengthen on-task behavior
through reinforcement, while at the same time weakening incompatible off-task
behavior through punishment or extinction. For example, a teenager may earn
additional TV viewing time by returning home before a specified curfew time,
and lose TV viewing time by coming home after the curfew time. In this case,

positive reinforcement increases the on-task behavior, while at the same time negative punishment (taking away the TV privilege) is applied to decrease the off-task behavior.

These contingencies can be clearly spelled out in a behavioral contract. Here the behaviors and the consequences are written out. Both parties (parent and child, therapist and patient, teacher and student) first negotiate the contract, then sign it, and review and perhaps revise it weekly or periodically. The written contract specifies the behaviors that each party is to engage in and what the consequences for each will be (reinforcers and punishers).

Another important procedure is shaping. Shaping is used to establish new behaviors, not currently in the repertoire, and to strengthen those that are initially infrequent and unstable. Here the initial behavior is reinforced, and then successive approximations of the behavior are systematically reinforced until the behavior more closely resembles and finally reaches the terminal behavior or goal.

Operant techniques were originally applied in such areas as individual therapy, school problems, and mental retardation and institutional behavior management programs. Today many new areas of assessment, research, and modification are being studied in a broadening concept of applied behavior techniques. Recent successful applications have gone well beyond the original clinical/mental health areas. Several areas of recent interest are traditional medical problems, biofeedback, problems in business and industry, employment, energy conservation, penal reform, pollution control, racial integration, and the use of mass transit. Areas of application are both rapidly expanding and continuously changing.

Systematic Desensitization

Systematic desensitization, formally developed by Joseph Wolpe[11] in the early 1950's, is one of the most widely used and experimentally researched techniques in behavior modification. It is used primarily in eliminating maladaptive behaviors that are anxiety- or fear-based. Desensitation procedures typically include three basic components:

1. Relaxation training.
2. A hierarchy of anxiety-provoking stimulus, raking from least to most anxiety-provoking.
3. Systematic replacement of the anxiety response with an incompatible relaxation response to each of the situations, by pairing relaxation with imagery of each hierarchy item.

Besides imaginary presentations of the anxiety-eliciting stimuli, desensitization can also take place *in vivo*. Here the client learns to engage in incompatible relaxation responses in the presence of the actual anxiety-provoking situation.

"In-life" seems to be more effective than exposure to imaginary or verbal stimuli.

Systematic desensitization has also been successful in alleviating maladaptive behaviors in other areas where fear and anxiety interfere with appropriate and effective functioning, such as assertive responses, sexual responses, social situations, depression, illness, and death.

Wolpe's original three treatment components have recently been demonstrated not to be necessary in bringing about effective desensitization. Although his explanation or conceptualization for desensitization's success has been brought into doubt and several alternative explanations have been offered, the empirical evidence as to the techniques's effectiveness is not questioned. Operant reinterpretations explain desensitization through such mechanisms as counterconditioning, shaping, and fading.

Cognitive Behavior Modification Techniques

At the opposite end of the scale from operant conditiong are the cognitively-oriented techniques, which deal with covert, private, or internal events. Seemingly inconsistent with a behavioral approach, these techniques grew out of a disenchantment with operant explanations that ignore mediating events and covert variables such as perceptions, interpretations, feelings, meanings, and thoughts. Cognitive research focuses on the role that these private events play in controlling behavior.

Many behaviorists, including Pavlov, Watson, Guthrie, Hull, and Tolman, have long acknowledged the influence of cognition on behavior. Each dealt conceptually or experimentally with private events in his own way.

The goal of the therapy is to change cognitions, internal dialogues, interpretations, beliefs, and perceptions in order to modify behavior. The goal is always to change overt behavior, and the cognitively-based techniques use private events to achieve this goal. Wolpe's use of imagery is an example of this. Obviously, difficulties in methodology and verification exist, although many, including Skinner, make the assumption that private, covert events follow the same laws of behavior as do overt events.

There are several techniques, all not necessarily developed within behavior modification research, that fall under the heading of behavior modification, and these are described below.

Rational-Emotive Therapy (RET). RET considers the alteration of cognitions as the essential ingredient to effect behavior change. (Because of space limitations, RET is the only cognitively-oriented technique discussed and is used as a general model of other cognitive approaches.)

RET was set forth by Albert Ellis over 25 years ago. Ellis' basic assumption is that faulty thought patterns or irrational beliefs are the basis of psychological disorders, emotional and behavioral. Ellis discusses behavior and treatment in terms of a chain of events, labeled A-B-C-D-E. The focus of therapy is to examine the client's implicit assumptions and irrational beliefs (B) about him/herself and his/her world, which are prompted by the external activating events (A) that precede them. These beliefs, which in turn result in emotions and responses (C), are to be changed during the course of therapy. The activating event (A) occurs first, and is perceived, evaluated, and interpreted through the irrational belief system (iB), resulting in inappropriate, self-defeating emotional and behavioral consequences (C). Ther therapist encourages the client to engage in disputing and debating (D) the faulty beliefs (iB), and the effect (E) of disputing replaces the irrational beliefs (iB) with more desireable, rational beliefs and cognitions (rB), which in turn result in more appropriate emotions and desirable responses (E). The scheme, then, is:

$$A \rightarrow B \rightarrow C \rightarrow D \rightarrow E$$
$$\text{(Activating Event)} \rightarrow \text{(Belief)} \rightarrow \text{(Consequence)} \rightarrow \text{(Dispute)} \rightarrow \text{(Effect)}$$

For example, a teenager's parents have refused to loan their daughter their car (A) although they had previously promised they would do so. The teenager says to herself (B) that "it is awful and unfair for them to go back on their word. They should do what they say. They don't love me! They always do this to me. They never think of me!" The undesirable emotional consequences (eC) are that she feels angry and depressed; the behavioral consequences (bC) are screaming at her parents, sulking, and locking herself in her room.

Disputing (D) the irrational beliefs (iB) would take the form of directly and systematically questioning and confronting the evidence for each of the beliefs. Why is it "awful" for them to act the way they did? Why is it "unfair"? Why "should" they do what they say? What evidence is there that her parents don't love her? Is it so that they "never" think of her?

Actively disputing (D) and demonstrating the lack of evidence for each of these exaggerated, globalized, irrational beliefs may lead to the effect (E) of her seeing her situation as inconvenient, annoying, or frustrating, to be sure, but not as "awful," or questioning their love, etc. Behaviorally, she may now attempt to persuade her parents to change, rather than yelling and slamming doors. She may even attempt to borrow an uncle's car, rather than locking herself in her room. The self-defeating intensity of her anger may also subside.

The therapist's goal is to alter the client's beliefs or automatic self-statements. The therapist directly attacks the irrational beliefs (iB) that lead to maladaptive emotional (eC) and behavioral (bC) consequences. This process demonstrates to the client that the irrational cognitions do not need to be maintained, and as a result the client learns how to function better and more logically in life situations. RET also assigns "homework" in the form of practicing the disputes (D) discussed in therapy, and writing down specific A-B-C-D sequences as they occur in various situations. The homework is then discussed in the therapy session.

Recent applications of RET have been made to speech anxiety, sexual anxiety, group therapy, parenting, assertiveness training, social and interpersonal encounters, etc. Also, recent empirical investigations, rather than the earlier reliance on case studies, have begun to support the efficacy of the technique.

Self-Instructional Training. Another cognitive behavior modification technique is self-instructional training, developed in the last decade by Meichenbaum.[6] Here the client is taught to present instructions or statements to himself. These act as discriminative stimuli for directing and guiding a person's behavior. Meichenbaum's work has been effectively applied to schizophrenic patients, deliquents, and impulsive children, among others.

Problem-Solving. Problem-solving, another cognitive behavioral approach, has recently been formalized as a technique used in therapeutic relationships. Problem-solving enables individuals to develop a pattern of behavior to deal with various problems. The client is taught first to define problems in concrete terms, then to identify possible alternative solutions or behaviors of problems, to evaluate the solutions, and finally to implement the solution that seems to be the best course of action to take. The client is trained to succeed at each step of the process and to apply the strategy to increasingly more complex problems.

Covert Conditioning. Covert conditioning, developed by Joseph R. Cautela in the late 1960's, is another prominent technique used in cognitive behavior modification therapy. In covert conditioning, reinforcement and punishment consequences are imagined, as are the behavioral events themselves. These consequences are presumed to operate on the imagined events in the same manner as do overt consequences in operant conditioning, and then to generalize to overt behavior.

In the use of one of Cautela's techniques, "covert sensitization" (as opposed to desensitization), the goal is to eliminate or reduce a specific behavior with imagery of an aversive event. The imaginary scenes are developed by the therapist to focus on the specific behavior to be modified. For example, an obese client may imagine himself or herself as starting to eat a rich dessert. This is followed by an imagined aversive consequence, which may be for the person to imagine vomiting convulsively and profusely. Together with this imagined punishing consequence for the off-task behavior, alternative reinforcing imagery for on-task behaviors may include imagining oneself being praised for refusing a dessert, or accepting a diet drink rather than a thick milkshake, followed by a scene of lying on the beach and having a slim waistline.

Cautela has developed specific techniques for many operant procedures, such as covert extinction and covert negative reinforcement. Because of its rather recent origins, serious conceptual, clinical, and outcome questions remain to be resolved concerning covert conditioning, although the techniques have been implemented in a wide range of behavioral intervention programs — such as phobias, homosexuality, drinking, overating, smoking, and social anxieties.

Flooding. This technique has the same goal as desensitization, the treatment of fear and anxiety. In contrast, though, the flooding procedure immediately exposes the client to the intense fear-evoking stimulus, rather than the gradual hierarchical fashion used in desensitization. The rationale is to repeatedly expose the client to the feared stimulus at its extreme strength so that the stimulus will weaken and eventually lose its capacity to evoke anxiety.

This procedure is based on the Pavlovian extinction procedure, which suggests that anxiety and avoidance responses are conditioned to specific stimuli; namely, to the anxiety-provoking conditioned stimulus (CS). Flooding has been extended to clinical cases, and is historically founded on extensive animal research, which suggests that forced inescapable, prolonged exposure to a fear-eliciting stimulus will eliminate the anxiety and the avoidance response.

In clinical practice, the client imagines an extremely frightening scene for extended periods. The exposure time to the scene is continued until the stress dissipates. As in desensitization, *in vivo* exposure has been found to be more effective than imaginary stimuli exposure.

Implosive Therapy. Implosive therapy, or implosion, is a variation of flooding in that psychodynamic components are added to the behavioral procedures. The client is also asked to imagine symbolically provocative scenes developed by the therapist from his/her knowledge of psychoanalytic principles. In implosive therapy, the imagined scenes are heightened to obtain the highest impact from the anxiety-eliciting stimuli. These two components differentiate this technique from flooding.

Flooding and implosion have been successful in reducing a wide varity of anxiety and fear responses, such as fear of animals and insects, test-taking anxiety, obsessions, and social anxieties. Like desensitization, the imaginary components in these techniques also qualify them as cognitive procedures.

Many differences still exist between the clinical application of flooding and animal analogues. These unresovlved theoretical and procedural questions await empirical clarification. Obviously, the question of maximizing a client's anxiety during treatment sessions raises many ethical considerations, especially when effective alternatives (such as desensitization) are readily available.

Other Techniques. The following techniques are used in their own right, and can also be used in conjuction with a wide variety of other techniques, especially the major ones discussed above. Some of these are: (1) self-control (or self-management) techniques; (2) aversion therapy, in which, for example, an aversive stimulus (e.g., a shock or a loud noise) is paired with alcohol to reduce alcohol consumption, or in which shock is made contingent upon drinking; (3) observation learning, in which imitation and modeling procedures are utilized to alter behavior; (4) behavioral rehearsal and role-playing; (5) negative practice or stimulus satiation; (6) thought-stopping; and other empirically-derived techniques.

FUTURE DIRECTIONS

Behavior modification's history exemplifies the blend of experimental evaluation with clinical issues into an empirical body of diverse techniques. Present day behavior modification is characterized more by an advocation of a scientific approach to clinical and treatment questions rather than the adherence to any one theoretical orientation.

As discussed above, behavior modification's influence has already gone well beyond its original clinical/mental health focus. Behavioral techniques will continue to expand the work that has recently begun in attacking such diverse areas as behavioral medicine, town planning, obesity, environmental problems, creativity, personalized education instruction (PSI) — developed by Fred Keller, unemployment, sex therapy, racial attitudes and biases, marriage and family therapy, production in industry, and energy conservation.

The deprofessionalization of treatment and a focus on preventive measures (rather than crisis orientation) are obvious in the current extensive training of paraprofessionals.   Closely related is the emphasis on self-control procedures, enabling individuals to transform their own lives and to be more responsible for their own experiences.

The significant growth and influence of cognitive behavioral techniques have further broadened the domain of behavior modification. Even this "traditional" area, the study and treatment of private events, demonstrates the commitment to, and the effectiveness of, methodological rigor and empirical validation.

The last issue to be successfully brought to the consciousness of individuals in our society will probably be the issue of control. Skinner has dealt with social control and the issue of freedom in the design of a more just and effective society in *Walden Two* and *Beyond Freedom and Dignity*.

In any society, managing and influencing individuals to behave in certain cooperative ways for the benefit of all in the society are crucial. Laws, religion, education, families, and government itself develop appropriate and acceptable customs and codes, intending to guide and direct ways of behaving. By applying experimental findings and insights based on them to the design of harmonious, reinforcing living environments, we can possibly achieve more satisfaction, aliveness, and spontaneity in our lives.

REFERENCES

1. Bandura, A. *Principles of Behavior Modification.* New York: Holt, Rinehart and Winston (1969).
2. Ellis, A. and Harper, R. A. *A New Guide to Rational Living.* North Hollywood, CA: Wilshire Books (1975).
3. Goldfried, M. R. and Davison, G. C. *Clincial Behavior Therapy.* New York: Holt (1976).
4. Kazdin, A. E. *History of Behavior Modification: Experimental Foundations of Contemporary Research.* Baltimore: University Park Press (1978).
5. Mahoney, M. J. *Cognition and Behavior Modification.* Cambridge, MA: Ballinger (1974).
6. Meichenbaum, D. *Cognitive-Behavior Modification: An Integrative Approach.* New York: Plenum (1977).
7. O'Leary, K. D. and Wilson, G. T. *Behavior Therapy: Application and Outcome.* Englewood Cliffs, N.J.: Prentice-Hall (1975).
8. Skinner, B. F. *Science and Human Behavior.* New York: Macmillan (1953).
9. Stampfl, T. G. and Levis, D. J. Essentials of implosive therapy: A learning theory-based psychodynamic behavioral therapy. *Journal of Abnormal and Social Psychology* 72:496–503 (1967).
10. Whaley, D. L. and Malott, R. W. *Elementary Principles of Behavior.* New York: Prentice-Hall (1971).
11. Wolpe, J. *The Practice of Behavior Therapy.* New York: Pergamon (1969).

Hopelessness is common in depressed patients and is closely related to the presence of suicidal thoughts and urges. For these reasons, the therapist must be prepared to intervene actively and forcefully to counter the patient's hopelessness.

Cognitive therapy has been shown to be efficacious in the treatment of depression. This therapeutic approach is founded on Aaron Beck's theory that negative feelings and moods (including depression, anxiety, and hopelessness) are the product of irrational, distorted thoughts. In cognitive therapy, the patient learns to alleviate negative moods by learning to talk back to negative irrational thoughts and to replace them with more realistic, rational ones.

This chapter presents a demonstration of the application of the basic techniques of cognitive therapy to the problem of hopelessness, as well as a number of specialized anti-hopelessness techniques developed by cognitive therapists.

3

Hope and Hopelessness: A Cognitive Approach

David D. Burns, M.D. and Jacqueline Persons, Ph.D.

"I feel hopeless."

"I'm sure you can't help me. I've been to dozens of therapists, and none of them has helped me."

"I've been depressed and anxious all my life and I'll never get better."

"Life is not worth living."

These are typical statements of hopelessness given by depressed patients. The patient believes that he or she will always be depressed, that psychotherapy cannot help, and that the future holds no hope. The patient is certain that no recovery is possible. This attitude is present in 85 percent of moderately to severely depressed patients.[1]

Cognitive therapy has been shown to be efficacious in the treatment of these patients.[8, 13] Because of the importance of the issue of hopelessness in the treatment of depression, cognitive therapists have developed a set of specialized anti-hopelessness interventions, and these are presented here. In addition, the basic cognitive techniques of eliciting and answering the patient's negative "automatic thoughts," and the application of this approach to the issue of hopelessness will be demonstrated.*

---

*Readers wishing to learn more about the practice of cognitive therapy should consult Burns[5] and Beck, Rush, Shaw, and Emery.[4]

It is imperative that the therapist intervene promptly and actively when he hears a statement of hopelessness. The patient's belief that his moods and life situation cannot improve greatly intensifies his suffering. Most things can be endured if the possibility of eventual change exists. The patient's distorted belief that his discomfort will go on forever adds greatly to his burden. In addition, the sense of hopelessness can substantially undermine the patient's motivation to engage productively in therapy because he will feel less willing to devise and carry through a meaningful self-help program. He will reason: "Since I'm hopeless, there's no point in trying. Why frustrate myself and waste the effort?" This thinking can seriously impede progress in therapy, and it functions to a certain extent as a self-fulfilling prophecy because if the patient does little productive work to help himself, his mood is likely to remain unchanged. He may conclude: "See, I was right. I really am stuck, and nothing can change, so there is no point in trying. I'm hopeless." Essentially, the patient fools himself with circular reasoning.

Most important, the patient's belief that he is hopeless will quite often be accompanied by suicidal impulses. This has been demonstrated repeatedly.[7,9,11] The patient who feels trapped in a no-exit situation may have the urge to end his life, seeing this as the only imaginable escape. Fast-acting, effective interventions are all the more important because of the epidemic increase in attempted and successful suicides since the mid-1950's.[12] As patients in therapy overcome their feelings of hopelessness, they experience a significant improvement in mood along with a reduction in suicidal urges.

Because of the close association between feelings of hopelessness and suicidal impulses, the therapist who hears statements of hopelessness must carefully assess the potential for suicide and work actively to prevent it.

ASSESSMENT OF SUICIDE

Some therapists hesitate to raise the issue of suicide for fear that discussing it will push the patient over the brink. Nothing could be further from the truth. In fact, the opposite is more often the case. The ventilation of suicidal urges can at times provide a sense of relief, and rarely, if ever, does it make the patient feel worse. Without an assessment of the situation through careful questioning, the therapist is powerless to assist the patient with this serious matter and may be stunned by an unexpected suicide. This sad result is especially tragic, since if the therapist intervenes actively, he is likely to be able to convince the patient that his hopelessness and his desire to commit suicide are the product of irrational, distorted thinking. Thus, a needless death can be prevented.

The presence of suicidal thoughts and impulses can be elicited with straightforward questioning along these lines. "Do you at times have thoughts that you might be better off dead? . . . . Do you sometimes have active suicidal impulses that are hard to control? . . . . Have you decided about which method you might use? . . . . Do you think you might be willing to call me if a strong suicidal impulse arises?" A good outline for the therapist wishing to assess the strength of the patient's suicidal urges is the Scale for Suicidal Ideation (SSI) developed by Beck and his colleagues.[3] In addition to assessing hopelessness about the future, the 19-item scale includes an assessment of the frequency and duration of suicidal thoughts, the degree to which the patient accepts these thoughts, the presence of deterrents (e.g., religious beliefs or concern for the care of children), the amount of planning and preparation for an attempt, and the presence of the opportunity and the method for a suicide attempt. The existence of past suicide attempts should always be a danger signal to the therapist, since for many people these first attempts seem to be "warm-ups" in which they flirt with suicide but have not yet mastered the particular method they have selected.

INTERVENTION TO PREVENT SUICIDE

The therapist must intervene actively and forcefully to prevent suicide. We believe that the therapist who does not do so, out of respect for a patient's "right" to commit suicide, is misguided. We believe that hopelessness and the wish to commit suicide are always products of distorted thinking. We have never encountered a depressed patient for whom suicide was a rational solution to life's problems.

THE THEORY OF COGNITIVE THERAPY

Cognitive therapy, as developed by Aaron Beck, is based on the theory that negative moods and feelings are the product of distorted, irrational cognitions.[1] The patient develops a negative view of himself, the world, the past, the present, and the future. His mind is flooded with negative cognitions, which are called "automatic thoughts" because they occur involuntarily, without effort, and often without awareness. For example, at a social gathering a patient may automatically be telling himself, "I'm not nearly as interesting or successful as these people." Because the patient is unaware of how unreasonable these negative thoughts frequently are, he takes them at face value and becomes upset. His painful feelings in turn convince him that his self-critical perceptions are valid. He reasons: "I feel so nervous and inferior to these people. This shows how inadequate I really am." He may even begin to isolate himself and to cut himself off from his normal activities and relationships. The ensuing self-created isolation convinces him further of his lack of worth. The role of the cognitive therapist is to break this vicious cycle by teaching the patient to elicit and refute his negative automatic thoughts and to overcome the self-defeating behaviors that perpetuate the depressive syndrome.

TALKING BACK TO THE THOUGHTS THAT LEAD TO HOPELESSNESS

The therapist can teach his patient to monitor and dispute the negative automatic thoughts that maintain the depression and lead to feelings of hopelessness. An important consideration is that if he is to use this method effectively, the therapist must be certain 'not to accept the patient's feelings and statements of hopelessness, which are often presented in a deceptively persuasive manner. The therapist who believes that a given patient *is* hopeless needs to spend some time examining and learning to answer his own negative automatic thoughts about that patient. It can be helpful to consult a colleague for assistance in providing a fresh strategy when the therapy seems temporarily stalemated.

One of the first steps in cognitive therapy involves training the patient to identify his distorted thoughts. He can use negative feelings as a cue to monitor and write down the thoughts he is having at that time. For a detailed description of this process, see Burns[5] or Beck *et al.*[4] For example, a patient in treatment asked one of this chapter's authors: "Do you like me?" The therapist responded: "Yes, I think quite highly of you." The patient immediately broke into angry tears. While this response appears surprising, it was readily understood when the patient explained his negative thought: "I've even fooled my therapist. Even you can't see what a fraud I am." This indicates the depressed patient's profound capacity to screen out positive experiences that are not consistent with his negative self-image.

As a second step, the therapist and patient work together to produce "rational responses" to these illogical negative thoughts. These rational responses are *not* excessively positive statements that present an unrealistically rosy view of the world, but objectively valid statements that contradict the distorted beliefs and perceptions that upset the patient. It is not wise to confront the patient with the illogic in his perceptions. Instead he should be led to this realization on his own through a process of gentle questioning. In the previous example, the therapist continued by asking the patient: "Apparently, if people react negatively to you this means they have seen the 'real you,' whereas a positive reaction means you have fooled them. Does this sound logical to you?" By questioning the patient, using a Socratic style, the therapist was able to lead the patient to an understanding of his illogical tendency to disqualify positive events and to dwell exclusively on his shortcomings. As the patient learned to assess his strengths and shortcomings more objectively, his mood improved.   Elimination of the distortions in the patient's automatic thoughts is nearly always sufficient to produce a reduction in the strength of negative emotions.

It is important that the therapist guide a patient to new, more realistic views, rather than arguing or haranguing the patient, or trying to convince him that he is "wrong."   Similarly, presenting the depressed person with an overly glib, optimistic view of life is liable to alienate him. During a therapy session, one of the authors of this chapter's patients produced the thought: "The fact that I'm divorced means I'm a failure in life." The therapist might be tempted to counter this thought with the argument: "That's quite an irrational statement, because many people who are divorced lead useful, productive lives. You can, too — just think of all your good qualities."

The patient's response to such an intervention is likely to be resentment and frustration. The therapist's quick, positive response will probably cause the patient to conclude that the therapist is not empathetic and does not understand his feelings.

One example of a more effective approach is the following dialogue:

Therapist: I see. Being divorced makes you a failure in life?
Patient: Yes.
Therapist: Let me ask you this: Do you know any other people who are divorced? Are any of your friends divorced?
Patient: Yes, lots of them are divorced!
Therapist: And do you consider these people to be failures in life because of their divorce?
Patient: No — that doesn't make sense.
Therapist: And what about you — does your divorce make you a failure?
Patient: No, I can see that doesn't make sense.

Notice that the therapist's first intervention was to repeat the patient's irrational statement in a questioning manner. As Rogerian therapists are well aware, the therapist's repetition of the patient's statement will cause the patient to view his therapist as empathetic and understanding of his feelings, and this can open the door to a collaborative exploration of the perception.

The Daily Record of Dysfunctional Thoughts form[4,5] can be used to facilitate this process. The patient writes down the distorted negative thoughts that upset him in a variety of situations and learns to substitute more objective cognitions. Figure 3-1 presents an example of the use of this approach in the case of several patients wrestling with hopelessness.

	SITUATION	EMOTION(S)	AUTOMATIC THOUGHT(S)	RATIONAL RESPONSE	OUTCOME
DATE	Describe: 1. Actual event leading to unpleasant emotion, or 2. Stream of thoughts, daydream, or recollection, leading to unpleasant emotion.	1. Specify sad/anxious/angry, etc. 2. Rate degree of emotion, 1–100%.	1. Write automatic thought(s) that preceded emotion(s). 2. Rate belief in automatic thought(s), 0–100%.	1. Write rational response to automatic thought(s). 2. Rate belief in rational response, 0–100%.	1. Re-rate belief in automatic thought(s), 0–100%. 2. Specify and rate subsequent emotions, 0–100.
3/4/81	Feeling suicidal during my therapy session.	Hopeless, 99% Sad, 99% Frustrated, 99%	I will always be depressed, 99%. I've been working on this depression for several years with no success, so it's hopeless, 100%.	I cannot predict what my feelings will be in the future – just because I'm depressed doesn't mean I will always be depressed. Since I haven't always been depressed in the past, there's no convincing way to predict that I'll always be depressed in the future, 90%. I've had some periods of improvement so it can't be true that I've had "no success." Furthermore, many other patients have recovered from a several-year depression, so there's no reason to conclude I'm hopeless. Finally, there are many treatments available, including antidepressants and psychological interventions, and all of these have the potential for being beneficial to me, 85%.	My belief in the "automatic thoughts" was substantially reduced. My feelings of hopelessness and frustration went down by half.

I didn't respond to an anti-depressant – that shows that no drug can help me, 90%.	Failure to respond to one anti-depressant does not mean that I will fail to respond to all of them, 100%.
My father is a skid row alcoholic so I'm destined for the same, 60%.	Many people have had an alcoholic parent who did not themselves become alcoholics, 100%.
I'm a burden to my family and myself so I should kill myself, 50%.	There's no proof that my suicide would ease their burden; indeed, it could make it far worse, 90%.
I have no close family ties – all my relatives hate me because I'm a complete loser, 85%.	That's "mind-reading." I'm not a "complete loser," and there's no real evidence that everyone hates me, 75%.
I'm fed up with trying to get into graduate school – it's hopeless, 60%.	It's a lot of work to apply, but a counselor at the school advised me that my chances for admission are excellent, 95%.

Figure 3-1. Daily record of dysfunctional thoughts.

EXPLANATION: When you experience an unpleasant emotion, note the situation that seemed to stimulate the emotion. (If the emotion occurred while you were thinking, daydreaming, etc., please note this.) Then note the automatic thought associated with the emotion. Record the degree to which you believe this thought: 0% = not at all; 100% = completely. In rating degree of emotion: 1 = a trace; 100 = the most intense possible.

The list of Definitions of Cognitive Distortions developed by Burns,[5] reproduced in Figure 3-2, can guide the therapist and the patient in identifying the forms of twisted thinking that are contained in the various automatic thoughts. Patients who understand the basic rationale of cognitive therapy are usually quite receptive to the idea that many of their thoughts contain cognitive distortions. The therapist can ask his patient to examine the list of thinking errors to determine which are present in a given automatic thought. Patients often accept

- *All-or-Nothing Thinking.* You see things in black-or-white categories. If your performance falls short of perfect, you see yourself as a total failure.
- *Overgeneralization.* You see a single negative event as a never-ending pattern of defeat.
- *Mental Filter.* You pick out a single negative detail and dwell on it exclusively so that your vision of all reality becomes darkened, like the drop of ink that discolors the entire beaker of water.
- *Disqualifying the Positive.* You reject positive experiences by insisting they "don't count" for some reason. In this way you can maintain a negative belief that is contradicted by your everyday experiences.
- *Jumping to Conclusions.* You might make a negative interpretation even though there are no definite facts that convincingly support your conclusion.
  - a. *Mind Reading.* You arbitrarily conclude that someone is reacting negatively to you, and you don't bother to check this out.
  - b. *The Fortune Teller Error.* You anticipate that things will turn out badly, and you feel convinced that your prediction is an already-established fact.
- *Magnification (Catastrophizing) or Minimization.* You exaggerate the importance of things (such as your goof-up or someone else's achievement), or you inappropriately shrink things until they appear tiny (your own desirable qualities or the other fellow's imperfections). This is also called the "binocular trick."
- *Emotional Reasoning.* You assume that your negative emotions necessarily reflect the way things really are: "I feel it, therefore it must be true."
- *Should Statements.* You try to motivate yourself with shoulds and shouldn'ts, as if you had to be whipped and punished before you can be expected to do anything. "Musts" and "oughts" are also offenders. The emotional consequence is guilt. When you direct should statements toward others, you feel anger, frustration, and resentment.
- *Labeling and Mislabeling.* This is an extreme form of overgeneralization. Instead of describing your error, you attach a negative label to yourself: "I'm a *loser.*" When someone else's behavior rubs you the wrong way, you attach a negative label to him: "He's a goddamn louse." Mislabeling involves describing an event with language that is highly colored and emotionally loaded.
- *Personalization.* You see yourself as the cause of some negative external event for which in fact you were not primarily responsible.

Figure 3-2. Definitions of cognitive distortions.*

*Reprinted from *Feeling Good: The New Mood Therapy* by David D. Burns, with permission from the William Morrow Publishing Company.

this task as a challenge and a problem to be solved. When he finds the distortion, the patient has taken the first step toward eliminating it.

Role-playing offers another powerful tool for talking back to distorted cognitions.[2] For example, a 25-year-old married housewife was referred to one of the authors of this chapter because of a 5-year-history of severe intractable depression. She described two serious unsuccessful suicide attempts, numerous episodes of self-mutilation with razor blades, multiple hospitalizations, and continuous closed-ward confinement for the previous three months. She had not responded to several years of intensive analytically-oriented psychotherapy, and the recommendation of the referring psychiatrist was for long-term hospitalization. At the initial evaluation, her ratings on the Beck Depression Inventory indicated a severe depression, and her score on a test designed to measure the degree of hopelessness was quite high. She expressed the belief that her life was not worth living, that her problems were insurmountable, and that her case was hopeless.

The therapist used a modified version of role-playing in which the patient was asked to imagine that two attorneys were arguing her case in court. She, as the prosecutor, would try to convince the therapist that she deserved a sentence of death. The therapist, as the defense attorney, would challenge the validity of the accusations of the prosecution.

Patient (as Prosecutor): For this patient, suicide would be an escape from life.

Therapist (as Defense Attorney): That argument could apply to anyone in the world. By itself, it is not a convincing reason to die.

Patient: The patient's life is so miserable she cannot stand it.

Therapist: The patient has been able to stand it up until now and maybe she can stand it a while longer. She was not always miserable in the past, and there is no proof that she will always be miserable in the future.

Patient: But her life is a burden to her family.

Therapist: Suicide will not solve this problem, since her death by suicide may prove to be a greater burden.

Patient: But she is self-centered and lazy.

Therapist: What percent of the population is lazy?

Patient: Probably 20 percent . . . . No, I'd say only 10 percent.

Therapist: That means 20 million Americans are lazy — and they don't have to die for this, so there is no reason the patient should be singled out for death. Do you think laziness and apathy are symptoms of depression?

Patient: Probably.
Therapist: Well, individuals in our culture are not sentenced to death for symptoms of an illness. Furthermore, the laziness may disappear when depression goes away.

The patient appeared involved in and amused by this repartée. After a series of such "accusations" and "defenses," she agreed that there was no convincing reason that she should have to die and that any reasonable jury would rule in favor of the defense. More important, she began to challenge and answer the negative thoughts herself. This brought some immediate emotional relief, the first she had experienced in many months.

At the end of the first therapy session, she expressed a sudden return of hopelessness and depression because of her automatic thought: "This new therapy may not prove to be as good as it seems." With the therapist's help, she was able to generate the following rational response: "If it isn't, I'll find out in a few weeks, and I'll still have the alternative of long-term hospitalization, so I'll have lost nothing. Furthermore, it seems to have helped a little bit already, so there is no reason to make a pessimistic prediction." Once again, her mood lifted and her sense of hopelessness diminished.

In the following sections, we present a number of specialized anti-hopelessness interventions to assist the therapist in developing strategies to reverse the patient's illogical belief that his suffering can never end.

An Experimental Test of the Hopelessness Hypothesis

One useful antidote to hopelessness involves helping the patient perform an experiment to test his belief that he is irreversibly depressed. Although the patient predicts that he cannot improve, the therapist can ask him to evaluate this in an objective fashion by participating in the therapy program over a reasonable period of time and assessing his degree of improvement objectively, according to criteria that the patient and therapist agree on ahead of time.

To measure improvement, any of the scales developed to measure depression, such as the Beck Depression Inventory, can be used. The patient may prefer to keep his own records of his negative and positive emotions (as will be illustrated later). Behavioral measures can also be used: Change can be measured in terms of time spent in productive or pleasurable activities.

If the patient agrees to this, he has, in effect, agreed to suspend his hopelessness temporarily and to make an active effort to use the therapy to work for improvement in his mood and level of functioning. This commitment to therapy and involvement in the effort to help himself usually leads to an improvement in mood.

As the patient evaluates his progress, it is important that he learn to give himself credit for *mastering* the *processes* that will ultimately lead to recovery. The depressed person's tendency to evaluate his progress in terms of *results* and to measure his success in an all-or-nothing manner may actually impede his recovery. The patient can be instructed to avoid evaluating his progress exclusively in terms of the way he is *feeling,* since his moods may not yet seem within his control. Instead, he can focus on doing potentially productive things that *are* under his control, with the understanding that these efforts will eventually bring about the improvement in mood he desires. He can ask himself the following questions.

	Yes	No	Somewhat
		(check one)	
Am I learning to understand the role of negative thoughts in generating my painful feelings?	☐	☐	☐
Am I learning to identify and talk back to these negative thoughts?	☐	☐	☐
Can I identify the various cognitive distortions that are present in my upsetting thoughts?	☐	☐	☐
Am I participating in a bibliotherapy program (reading self-help books)?	☐	☐	☐
Do I spend time each day doing psychotherapy homework to help myself between therapy sessions?	☐	☐	☐
Am I learning to schedule my time more effectively?	☐	☐	☐
Am I using the Pleasure Predicting Sheet[5] to see how much satisfaction I might experience in response to a variety of activities?	☐	☐	☐
Am I working on improving my interpersonal relations with other people?	☐	☐	☐
Am I practicing assertive skills?	☐	☐	☐
Am I mastering the verbal methods that will allow me to respond to criticism and disapproval without getting unduly upset?	☐	☐	☐
Am I learning to break large problems down to their smallest component parts so I can attack these one step at a time?	☐	☐	☐
Am I learning to identify basic attitudes and assumptions that make me vulnerable to excessive depression, anxiety, or anger?	☐	☐	☐

The patient can be reminded that patients who develop and adhere to a self-help plan along these lines eventually experience an improvement in outlook and a reduction in depression. Since no one can predict precisely when this improvement will occur, the patient can avoid frustration if he will evaluate progress in terms of adhering to a personal growth program rather than insisting on immediate results. His focus can be redirected to giving himself well-deserved credit for the many things he is doing in the spirit of learning to cope more effectively. This itself will serve as an antidote to the sense of hopelessness and helplessness and will help alleviate depression.

Prognosis for Improvement is Good

The patient can gain hope from the knowledge that depression is one of the psychiatric disturbances that has the best outlook for eventual recovery. The therapist can remind the depressed person that a variety of treatment approaches exist, ranging from psychological interventions to antidepressant medications, and that all of these treatments have been demonstrated to be effective in the treatment of depression and anxiety. If one approach is not helpful, another is likely to be.

When the therapist provides this information, it is important to elicit the patient's response. The capacity of depressed persons to disqualify and distort positive input is quite remarkable. A common reaction is a feeling of even greater hopelessness owing to a thought like this: "I know that most other patients have recovered, but I know that *I* am the one who really won't get better." We hear this complaint quite frequently. The patient may insist that he is *the only person* who is different from everyone else in the world who has recovered from a depression, and he may feel convinced that he definitely will not and cannot respond to any known treatment. The tendency of a depressed patient to view himself as an unintelligent loser and at the same time to insist that he can predict with a great degree of certainty the prognosis for his own case of depression is a remarkable paradox.

The therapist can ask: "What makes you so certain you can predict without a shadow of a doubt that you will never improve or recover? What qualifies you as an expert?" The instant retort will usually be: "I know how I've been *feeling. That* makes me an expert. *You've* probably never felt this way, so you aren't in a position to understand how bad it is."

The patient can be reminded that he may be an expert in knowing about the symptoms he experiences but that he is certainly not an expert in predicting his response to a variety of treatment interventions. The patient can be asked: "If you had pneumonia with a high fever, you would certainly know how uncomfortable it *feels,* but would this qualify you to diagnose the infectious agent, prescribe the correct treatment, or predict the outcome of your illness? Of course not! Similarly, no matter how powerful your feelings of depression may be, they do not qualify you as an expert who can predict recovery accurately."

If, in spite of this discussion, the patient still insists he knows he is hopeless, the therapist can avoid a power struggle or an argument in the following way. Point out that neither of you can predict the future with certainty and propose that the patient *maintain* his skepticism but *test it* by actively participating in his treatment program for a number of weeks or months. Progress can be evaluated along the lines suggested in the previous section. It is important to set up specific criteria for "improvement" ahead of time. For example, a modest reduction in the severity of depression on a self-assessment test such as the Beck Depression Inventory can be viewed as evidence for "moderate improvement." Setting up the criteria for improvement ahead of time undercuts the patient's tendency to disqualify his progress by saying, "It doesn't count because I'm not completely happy yet."

Some refractory patients will find it helpful if the therapist arranges an interview with another patient who initially felt convinced he was hopeless and then went on to recover. This can be especially useful for a patient who believes his therapist is overly optimistic about his chances for recovery.

The depressed patient who chooses this option must be warned that he may tend to disqualify arbitrarily whatever he is told by the recovered patients. You can tell the patient he may have negative thoughts like this: "Well, she got better because she's younger (or older, or married, or employed, etc.), so her good outcome doesn't really apply to me." The therapist can rehearse with the patient how he may develop rational responses to such thoughts. For example, the patient may substitute this thought: "The fact that she is younger doesn't prove I cannot also recover, since younger patients frequently have just as tough a time defeating depression as older patients. Since she felt hopeless and went on to recover, maybe I can also."

"I Can't" Versus "I Don't Want To"

Depressed patients often convince themselves they are hopeless by saying, "I can't" when they mean, "I don't feel like it" or "I don't want to." For example, the patient may say, "I just *can't* get out of bed," when in reality he knows he *could* get up if he had to, but he just can't see the point of doing it. The problem with saying, "I can't" instead of, "I choose not to" is that the patient begins to take this language seriously and begins to view himself as inadequate and helpless. Many depressed people find it a surprise to discover that in reality they *can* do many things they've told themselves they can't do.

Similarly, when the patient says, "I can't possibly get better," he may mean, "I don't really want to." This attitude is not usual, since most depressed individuals *do* in fact desperately want to get well. An empathic dialogue with the patient who claims, "I *want* to feel depressed" often reveals a considerable amount of anger and resentment. The patient may feel that he is being coerced or treated unfairly by someone important to him. A 39-year-old unemployed television announcer verbalized that his low level of activity and his "inability" to carry out the basic activities of daily living were an expression of anger toward his wife, whom he viewed as continually nagging him to stop feeling sorry for himself and go out and find a job.

Patients who insist they want to feel depressed often benefit substantially by making one list of the advantages and disadvantages of being depressed and another list of the advantages and disadvantages of being happy. The list in Figure 3-3 was prepared by a young woman who felt suicidal and trapped in an unsatisfactory marriage. She indicated that as long as she was very depressed, she would be more motivated to leave her husband. She feared that if she allowed herself to recover, she would become complacent and lose her desire to separate.

However, when she listed the advantages and disadvantages of continuing to feel depressed and angry, she found the disadvantages were far greater (see Figure 3-3). In contrast, when she listed the advantages and disadvantages of getting better, she found the advantages were greater (see Figure 3-4). Consequently,

ADVANTAGES OF STAYING DEPRESSED AND ANGRY	DISADVANTAGES OF STAYING DEPRESSED AND ANGRY
1. I don't have to appear to be happy.	1. I won't feel fulfilled and satisfied.
2. I can spite people who expect me to be happy all the time.	2. I'll still have all of my problems and won't try to solve them.
3. I can be lazy.	3. I'll probably stay with my husband no matter how I feel.
4. I don't have to be nice to people.	4. I may kill myself and that wouldn't help anything.
5. I can fail.	

Figure 3-3. The patient found that the advantages of remaining depressed outweighed the advantages by a 65/35 ratio.

ADVANTAGES OF GETTING BETTER	DISADVANTAGES OF GETTING BETTER
1. I'll be able to make mistakes without getting so upset or getting defensive.	1. I won't have excuses when I avoid doing the things I know would make me feel better.
2. I'll be able to make decisions and feel good about them.	2. I won't be able to feel sorry for myself a large part of the time.
3. I'll feel more fulfilled and satisfied.	3. I may lose the urge to leave my husband.
4. I won't worry so much.	
5. I won't want to commit suicide.	
6. I can get on with my plans to go to graduate school.	
7. I can learn to be assertive and I can try to improve my marriage.	

Figure 3-4. The patient found that the advantages of getting better outweighed the disadvantages by a 75/25 ratio.

she made a committed effort to her therapy program and experienced substantial improvement in the following weeks.

Jumping to Conclusions

The patient can be taught that one source of his sense of hopelessness is a common cognitive distortion called "jumping to conclusions" (see Figure 3-2). He is jumping to the conclusion that he cannot improve under any conceivable circumstances even though he has no convincing information for making such a prediction. It can be helpful to point out that since he hasn't always felt depressed in the past, there is no valid basis for predicting he will always feel depressed in the future.

Some patients immediately feel better when this is pointed out, whereas some others are not so easily convinced. A young woman who consulted one of the authors for treatment of severe anxiety reasoned: "But I always *have* felt anxious my entire life!" When she was questioned closely about this, however, she admitted her anxiety first developed around the time she attended college and graduate school. Since then it had been present only half the time. She was able to calculate that the actual amount of time during her life she had felt anxious was less than 10 percent. This was not consistent with her notion that she had "always been anxious." Because she had focused exclusively on those moments when she had been upset, she completely overlooked her many reasonably happy and contented periods.

She then went on — as some clever patients will — to counter with a new argument that "proved" she was nevertheless hopeless. She said, "But as you can see, my anxiety has been on the increase in recent years since I went to college. As I project this trend into the future, it becomes blatantly obvious I am getting worse and worse as I get older. The only good times in my life are behind me! This is *proof* that I'm hopeless, so treatment can't possibly help me!"

The therapist simply pointed out that she had once again fooled herself with the same cognitive distortion, jumping to conclusions. She irrationally predicted that her anxiety levels would continue to increase in the future simply because they had increased during her college years. However, the anxiety could conceivably get worse, stay the same, vanish, fluctuate, etc. The patient's insistence that her anxiety would continue forever to get worse was simply not supported by any evidence or logic.

Disqualifying the Positive

Many patients feel hopeless about achieving relief from depression and anxiety because they discount any episodes of improvement as "temporary flukes." A law student having trouble finding a summer job recently told one of the authors: "I couldn't possibly be happy unitl I get my career organized." When questioned about things he'd enjoyed recently, he reported numerous experiences that he'd enjoyed "over 95 percent." When he was asked how he reconciled this with his hypothesis that he *couldn't* feel good until his career plans were secure, he immediately retorted, "Those experiences were just temporary flukes." The evidence showed he *could* enjoy himself by getting productively involved with daily living even though his career plans were unsettled. However, he so firmly believed this wasn't possible that he discredited the evidence by labeling his happy periods as "flukes."

Patients using this type of distorted reasoning need to be reminded that *all* experiences — good or bad — are "temporary" because nothing lasts forever. Even if a good feeling lasts only an hour or a day, it is nevertheless real and valid. Such times of improvement can profitably be studied in order to learn *why* they occurred so that the patient can learn to feel better for longer and longer periods of time. If the therapist allows the depressed person to discount his happy moments as "flukes," he will minimize his capacity to enjoy them.

Depressed, hopeless patients often forget that they have ever experienced any other feelings and have difficulty recalling any pleasant events from the past. There is good experimental evidence to support the notion of "state-dependent recall."[10,14] A depressed businessman told one of the authors: "I've *never* been happy. I've actually felt miserable every day of my life." He estimated his average mood during his lifetime as -90 on a scale from -100 (the worst) to +100 (the best). After he began to improve, he estimated his mood at +80 on this scale, indicating that he felt quite happy. When the therapist suggested it must be quite new and different for him to experience such positive emotions after so many years of never-ending despair, he replied, "Oh no, I've felt good like this most of my life except for the brief spell of depression I had recently!" He had fooled both himself and his therapist by selectively focusing on his suffering and forgetting about everything else.

Emotional Reasoning

Emotional reasoning is one of the most powerful thinking errors that convinces depressed patients of their hopelessness. The patient reasons: "I *feel* hopeless, therefore I must *be* hopeless." It is important that the therapist point out this cognitive distortion and remind the patient that hopelessness is a *symptom* of mood disorders, especially depression. Hopelessness is a *feeling*, not a *fact*. Therefore, it indicates the need for treatment, *not* for giving up. Actually, the patient can be told that his *feeling* of hopelessness is strong evidence that he is *not* hopeless. That is, it is an indication that he has a disorder that is likely to respond to treatment.

The patient can be taught that his feelings are the product of his thoughts. If he *believes* he is hopeless, he will *feel* hopeless. The feeling doesn't mean anything except that he has a certain thought in his mind. If the thought is distorted and unrealistic, the feeling will not reflect truth in an objective manner, regardless of how intense and persuasive the feeling might seem.

An example of this type of thinking error is provided by the person with an elevator phobia who felt very frightened when standing in an elevator. He had the thought, "I *feel* frightened; therefore, this elevator must be dangerous!" Most patients readily see the irrationality of this sort of thinking.

All-or-Nothing Thinking

All-or-nothing thinking is a cognitive distortion that lurks behind many symptoms of depression and anxiety and is a major cause of the sense of hopelessness. Depressed individuals are in the habit of looking at things in extremes — life seems *either* black *or* white; shades of grey do not exist. This thinking error leads to many painful and misleading conclusions. For example, a patient of one of the authors, an unemployed television announcer, had the following exchange with his therapist:

> *Patient:*   I'm feeling even more depressed. No one wants to hire me (he had not been offered the two jobs he had sought), and I can't even clean up my apartment. I feel completely incompetent!
>
> *Therapist:* I see. The fact that you are unemployed and have a messy apartment proves that you are completely incompetent?
>
> *Patient:*   Well . . . I can see that doesn't add up.

A stylistic point is again illustrated here: Leading the patient to the unreasonableness of his thinking through Socratic questioning is far more effective than arguing with his statements. The latter strategy often leads to an oppositional, non-productive interaction that will frustrate the patient and may inttensify the feelings of hopelessness.

To expose the all-or-nothing thinking that lurks behind the sense of hopelessness, the therapist can ask the patient precisely what he means when he insists he cannot get better. He may be maintaining one of three positions:

1. "I can't even feel *slightly* better for a little while."
2. "I might feel slightly less upset at times, but I can't feel *significantly* less upset."
3. "Even if I do feel significantly better at some point, this improvement will only be temporary, and it can't last. Therefore, I can't feel *permanently*

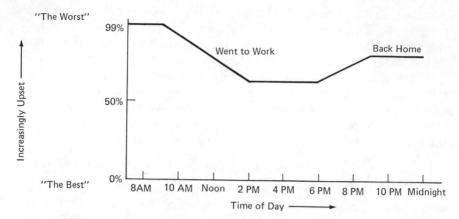

Figure 3-5. This severely depressed patient recorded how badly he felt from the moment he got up to the time he went to bed. His depression was 99 percent the moment he woke up, and improved somewhat as he got out of bed and went to work.

better. This means I will continue to cycle in and out of depression for the rest of my life, so it's useless to think I could ever be cured. Therefore, I am hopeless."

The therapist can examine each of these three views with the patient and show him why each argument is highly unrealistic and self-defeating. The patient who doubts that he cannot ever feel slightly better for even a brief period can be asked to keep a graph of his moods each day between 0 percent (not at all upset) to 99 percent* (the most upset one could feel). As shown in Figure 3-5, this severely depressed individual's blue moods ranged from 99 percent to 65 percent as the day progressed. The graph clearly demonstrated that his moods were not irreversibly stuck at one point. He admitted that his argument that he couldn't even feel *slightly* better was disproven.

Suppose the patient agrees with this argument but responds by saying: "Well, that's *trivial*, doctor. Of course I can feel a *little* better. Maybe I can go from 99 percent bad to 65 percent bad, but I want to feel *good*!"

There are a number of answers to this argument. In the first place, once the patient admits he can feel *slightly* less depressed, he can see that it is highly likely that he has the potential for getting even less depressed than that. For example, the patient can be shown that since becoming more active and productive

---

*The patient can be told that the reason the worst possible feeling is assigned a score of 99 percent instead of 100 percent is because, no matter how miserable he feels, he can always imagine how it might be worse. The therapist can suggest: "Suppose, for example, in addition to feeling severely depressed, that you were in chains, being slowly tortured. Clearly, that would be even worse!"

helped him reduce his level of depression from 99 percent to 65 percent, there is no reason to suspect he couldn't learn to reduce it further on another day to 60 percent, and then perhaps to 50 percent, and so on until his symptoms have been eliminated entirely.

Once the patient realizes that eventually he can and will improve, his only remaining argument in support of the hopelessness hypothesis is that he can't remain happy forever, so sooner or later he will slip back into the depression. The patient argues, "Since I am bound to get depressed again, there's no point in trying to beat the game." Since the cycle of feeling better and then feeling worse again seems inevitable, he concludes that he is, in fact, hopeless.

This argument is quite a subtle one, and like most good deceptions, it does contain a grain of truth. Many depressed patients do experience a relapse, sometimes more than once. However, the patient's conclusion that this means he is hopeless can be challenged. The therapist can point out that none of us can feel happy all the time, and that feelings of sadness, depression, anger, and guilt are an inevitable part of living. Does this mean we are all "hopeless"? Or does it mean, instead, that we are human?

The patient can be asked to look at the graph of his moods, and notice how his moods continually fluctuate. These fluctuations occur in all of us. In everyone's life, there are thousands of times when we are in the process of "feeling worse" (this would be indicated by an upswing on a graph such as Figure 3-5). Point out to the patient that if he thinks that these episodes of "feeling worse" mean that he is hopeless, then remind him: "There are exactly the same number of times in your life when you are 'feeling better.' " (These would be indicated by downswings on a graph like Figure 3-5.) "If 20,000 episodes of 'feeling worse' during your lifetime make you 'hopeless,' then, by the same token, 20,000 episodes of 'feeling better' must mean you are 'non-hopeless.' Apparently you must be both 'hopeless' and 'non-hopeless' at the same time. How can this be?" The patient reaches this nonsensical conclusion because the premise of hopelessness is based on all-or-nothing thinking, and this way of thinking just doesn't fit reality.

Some patients will nevertheless argue that while they are not fixed forever at a certain level of depression, the fact that their moods will forever change means they are hopeless since *this pattern of going up and down* cannot change. The patient can be shown that this argument is invalid since the *pattern* of his moods is itself always changing. Mood patterns change because of the wide range of internal and external factors that affect the way we feel. The fact that this is true for all of us does not make us all "hopeless."

The Mental Filter

Some depressed individuals, especially adolescents, feel that it is *necessary* to feel despair because so many aspects of life are truly negative. They filter out positive experiences and focus on one or more genuinely tragic events. Because they then see all of reality as negative, they resist the notion of hope and discount the possiblity for happiness as a dishonest con. They reason, "My problems are absolutely real. Life is bad, people are no good, and the way I feel is the only *valid* way to feel! The only *genuine* thing to do is to feel terrible about life and kill myself. At least then I'll be *honest* and not a hypocrite."

This, in fact, is similar to Freud's view of depression, as described in his paper, "Mourning and Melancholia."[6] He argued that the depressed patient

> . . . has a keener eye for the truth than others who are not melancholic. When in his exacerbation of self-criticism he describes himself as petty, egoistic, dishonest, lacking in independence, one whose sole aim has been to hide the weaknesses of his own nature, for all we know it may be that he has come very near to self-knowledge; we only wonder why a man must become ill before he can discover truth of this kind.

Depressed patients exhibit a type of cognitive distortion known as the "mental filter," or "selective negative focus." They tend to pick out genuinely negative events and dwell on them at the expense of everything else. Thus, the importance of these events becomes artificially inflated. At the same time, they filter out or fail to notice anything positive.

One patient who was particularly prone to make this type of thinking error was so aware of the frightening things that might happen to her when she went out of her apartment (rape, mugging, shooting, stabbing) that she stayed at home alone most of the time, and could not even read about a crime in the newspaper without her anxiety level shooting up to 100.

Depressed and anxious patients are usually not aware of the arbitrary nature of this mental filtering process. While it is true that many negative and frightening events occur, a more realistic view of life shows that the universe involves a mixture of good, bad, and neutral events. The genuinely negative aspects can usually be coped with if the patient is willing to overcome his tendency to dwell on them at the expense of everything else. As the patient learns to develop a more realistic perspective, the sense of hopelessness diminishes.

Some patients, however, believe these negative views are *necessary*. They are unwilling to give them up because of the mistaken belief that it is to their advantage to hold them. Thus, a young college student treated by one of the authors had an excessive apprehension of her own death that prevented her from falling asleep at night for fear she would not wake up; this had so incapacitated her that she was forced to drop out of college. She reasoned, "I *should* worry about death. It will happen someday, and if I don't focus on it I won't be prepared, and I won't be able to handle it." In reality, her attention to this issue paralyzed her and prevented her from engaging life and thereby gaining the appropriate coping skills. A depressed patient might reason, "I *should* worry about all the evil in the world. After all, it exists!"

One approach to this issue is to ask the patient to list the advantages and disadvantages of feeling depressed or focusing on the frightening, negative aspects of life. This analysis will often convince him that even though there *are* many negative and frightening events in life, it is not realistic or helpful to focus on them disproportionately.

A Definition of Hopelessness

A method that has helped some patients is to instuct the patient to ask himself: "When I claim I am hopeless, what precisely do I mean?" Ask the patient to write down his definition of "hopeless" in a clear, specific way, using simple language. Once he has done this, he can usually see either that his definiton is meaningless or that it does not apply to him. No matter how many ways he tries to define "hopeless," he will be able to attack the definition successfully. This demonstration repeated over and over can usually convince the patient that the concept is irrational.

Here's how it works. An industrialist sought relief for three decades of unrelenting depression and anxiety. In spite of continual treatment by numerous therapists using a wide variety of therapeutic and psychopharmacological approaches, he claimed he had experienced little, if any, significant progress.

After several months of cognitive therapy, he began to experience some periods of improvement in mood and self-esteem that would last up to several weeks. These were typically followed by blue spells lasting from a few days up to several weeks. What made these relapses especially painful was his thought at such times that he was "hopelessly sick" and not getting anywhere. These thoughts were associated with suicidal fantasies and urges.

During one such episode, his therapist asked him to write down his definitions of "hopelessly sick," and then the therapist helped him challenge each definition as follows.

1. *Definition.* "Hopelessly sick" means a non-changing degree of depression and anxiety.
   Rebuttal. Then I am not hopelessly sick because my moods fluctuate substantially. Therefore, they cannot be non-changing.
2. *Definition.* "Hopelessly sick" means that I have constant thoughts of suicide.
   Rebuttal. Since the greatest amount of time I have spent thinking about self-destruction is five minutes per day, and since this occurs only during my most depressed phase, it follows that I don't "constantly" have such

thoughts. Most depressed patients have thoughts of suicide, but these thoughts cannot make them hopeless since depressed people usually recover. As my mood improves, these thoughts tend to disappear.

3. *Definition.* A "hopelessly sick" person is one who will actually commit suicide or make a suicide attempt. Since I plan suicide at times, I am "hopelessly sick."

   Rebuttal. In point of fact, I fantasize about suicide but I'm not planning a suicide attempt. Furthermore, even making a suicide attempt does not prove you are hopelessly sick, it just shows that you *think* you are. Many people who make suicide attempts eventually go on to recover from depression. This shows that their sense of hopelessness was not valid.

4. *Definition.* "Hopelessly sick" means I can't get better. "Getting better" means feeling less depressed on tests that measure depression and happier on tests that measure happiness.

   Rebuttal. It is extremely likely that I will "get better" since this has happened on numerous occasions in the past and since even now I feel slightly less depressed than I did this morning. This shows I can, and will, "get better."

5. *Definition.* "Hopeless" means that your overall condition is such that you are more than 50 percent depressed and anxious more than 70 percent of the time.

   Rebuttal. I have recorded my degree of happiness and depression every day for the past year, and the data show that I have *not* felt more than 50 percent depressed and anxious more than 70 percent of the time. Therefore, I am not "hopeless" according to this definition. Furthermore, *any* such cut-off point for "hopeless" would be ludicrous, because according to this view, a person who was upset 70 percent of the time would be "hopeless," while a person who was upset 69 percent of the time would be "non-hopeless." This is obviously nonsensical.

6. *Definition.* "Hopeless" is a sliding scale then. The *more* depressed I am, the more hopeless I become. Since I have been quite depressed much of the time, it follows that I am "quite hopeless."

   Rebuttal. This amounts to emotional reasoning and is illogical. If I am quite depressed, I will *feel* quite hopeless, but it doesn't follow that I *am* in fact hopeless. Severely depressed people can and do recover.

As he continued to try to define "hopeless," he found he could always produce an effective rebuttal. This helped him see that the hopelessness he felt was not realistic. He then found himself more willing to go to work on what was bothering him, using the cognitive and behavioral techniques he was learning. He consequently experienced a substantial improvement in his mood.

DATE	SITUATION	EMOTION(S)	AUTOMATIC THOUGHT(S)	RATIONAL RESPONSE	OUTCOME
	Describe: 1. Actual event leading to unpleasant emotion, or 2. Stream of thoughts, daydream, or recollection, leading to unpleasant emotion.	1. Specify sad/anxious/angry, etc. 2. Rate degree of emotion, 0–100%.	1. Write automatic thought(s) that preceded emotion(s). 2. Rate belief in automatic thought(s), 0–100%.	1. Write rational response to automatic thought(s). 2. Rate belief in rational response, 0–100%.	1. Re-rate belief in automatic thought(s), 0–100%. 2. Specify and rate subsequent emotions, 0–100%.
	I imagine how I might be thinking and feeling if I experience a relapse of depression.	Frustrated, 90% Hopeless, 99% Sad, 90%	This shows I'm hopeless, 99%. This shows the therapy didn't work, 100%. I'm back at the zero point again — what's the use?, 100%. I feel so bad there's no point in writing down my negative thoughts. My problems are real, so that stupid exercise couldn't help, 90%.	This only shows I'm having a relapse of depression. Since I worked it out before, I can work it out again. Therefore, I can't be "hopeless," 90%. Actually the therapy did work because I felt better. The therapist predicted I might have several relapses. This is not so unusual, 90%. I'm not "back at the zero point" because I have learned many tools for coping with bad moods. I can profit from working my way out of this relapse because it will give me a chance to reapply the techniques that helped me originally. This can give me greater mastery and understanding, 80%. In the past I also felt so bad I was convinced the therapy couldn't help, but it did. If I give it a try I can find out if the methods will help me again, 75%.	The belief in my automatic thought was reduced to about 50%. My feelings of frustration and hopelessness were reduced to about 25%.

EXPLANATION: When you experience an unpleasant emotion, note the situation that seemed to stimulate the emotion. (If the emotion occurred while you were thinking, daydreaming, etc., please note this.) Then note the automatic thought associated with the emotion. Record the degree to which you believe this thought: 0% = not at all; 100% = completely. In rating degree of emotion: 1 = a trace; 100 = the most intense possible.

Figure 3-6. Daily record of dysfunctional thoughts.

Relapse Management

When a chronically depressed patient experiences a substantial and rapid improvement in mood, it is crucial to advise him that just as depression doesn't last forever, feelings of happiness usually don't either. It is important to point out that many patients experience one or more relapses after their initial recovery.

A return of a depressed mood can actually be viewed as positive because it provides some information about the patient's particular vulnerabilities, thinking errors, or coping styles, and provides the opportunity to reapply the coping skills he is learning.

The patient can be instructed to develop a personal blueprint for recovery he can reapply each time he is upset. This self-help plan might include: (1) a list of the types of negative events most likely to trigger emotional upsets for him; (2) a clear understanding of those upsetting thoughts and self-defeating behavior patterns that are most likely to occur during such depressive periods; and (3) a step-by-step description of what he can do to cope more effectively.

It can be especially useful to rehearse talking back to the negative thoughts that may arise during a relapse before they occur. This can help prevent a sudden resurgence of hopelessness and suicidal impulses. The therapist can suggest typical automatic thoughts that arise in patients who relapse and help the patient generate rational responses, using the Daily Record of Dysfunctional Thoughts (See Figure 3-6).

Sometimes creative solutions are called for. One man with 30 years of unsuccessful psychotherapy had a terror of being alone. He learned that when he became upset, he could alleviate his fear by sitting alone in his darkened basement room in the middle of the night until his fear dissipated. This intervention put the lie to his belief that being alone would lead to overwhelming anxiety and insanity and was associated with an improvement in his mood and outlook.

The techniques described in this chapter are part of a systematic treatment program being developed at the Center for Cognitive Therapy at the University of Pennsylvania. This group is engaged in an active training and research program in the further refinement of these methods. The address is: Aaron T. Beck, M.D., Director, The Center for Cognitive Therapy, 133 S. 36th Street, Philadelphia, PA 19104.

REFERENCES

1. Beck, A. T. *Depression: Causes and Treatment.* Philadelphia: University of Pennsylvania Press (1967).
2. Beck, A. T. and Burns, D. Cognitive therapy of depressed suicidal outpatients. *In:* Cole, J. O., Schatzberg, A. F., and Frazier, S. H. (Eds.). *Depression: Biology, Psychodynamics, and Treatment.* New York: Plenum, pp. 199–211 (1977).

3. Beck, A. T., Kovacs, M., and Weissman, A. Assessment of suicidal intention: The scale for suicide ideation. *Journal of Consulting and Clinical Psychology* 47(2):343-352 (1979).

4. Beck, A. T., Rush, A. J., Shaw, B. F., and Emery, G. *Cognitive Therapy of Depression.* New York: Guilford (1979).

5. Burns, D. D. *Feeling Good: The New Mood Therapy.* New York: William Morrow (1980); also New American Library (1981).

6. Freud, S. Mourning and melancholia. *In:* Rieff, P. (Ed.). *General Psychological Theory: Papers on Metapsychology.* New York: Collier (1917/1963), pp. 167-168.

7. Kovacs, M., Beck, A. T., and Weissman, A. Hopelessness: An indicator of suicidal risk. *Suicide* 5(2):98-103 (1975).

8. Kovacs, M., Rush, A. J., Beck, A. T., and Hollon, S. D. Depressed outpatients treated with cognitive therapy or pharmacotherapy. *Archives of General Psychiatry* 38(1):33-41 (1981).

9. Lester, D. and Beck, A. T. Suicidal intent, medical lethality of the suicide attempt, and components of depression. *Journal of Clinical Psychology* 31(1):11-12 (1975).

10. Miller, H. Psychological deficit in depression. *Psychological Bulletin* 82:238-260 (1975).

11. Minkoff, K., Bergman, E., Beck, A. T., and Beck, R. Hopelessness, depression, and attempted suicide. *American Journal of Psychiatry* 130(4):455-459 (1973).

12. Murphy, G. E. and Wetzel, R. D. Suicide risk by birth cohort in the United States, 1949 to 1974. *Archives of General Psychiatry* 37:519-523 (1980).

13. Rush, A. J., Beck, A. T., Kovacs, M., and Hollon, S. Comparative efficacy of cognitive therapy and pharmacotherapy in the treatment of depressed outpatients. *Cognitive Therapy and Research* 1(1):17-37 (1977).

14. Weingarten, H., Miller, H., and Murphy, D. L. Mood-state-dependent retrieval of verbal associations. *Journal of Abnormal Psychology* 86(3):276-284 (1977).

Modern forms of meditation, simplified and divested of esoteric trappings and religious overtones, can possess unique therapeutic properties when used as adjuncts to psychotherapy. In the following chapter, clinically relevant effects of meditation are discussed. These include (1) anxiety reduction; (2) amelioration of stress-related conditions such as bronchial asthma, hypertension, cardiac disorders, insomnia, stuttering, and psychiatric illness; (3) increased alertness; (4) improved ideational fluency and productivity; and (5) greater energy, which can manifest itself as increased ability to "free-associate" in psychotherapy or to reach innovative solutions to emotional problems.

The anti-addictive effects of meditation are also of benefit in psychotherapy. There is often a relationship between the amount of time patients have spent meditating and their ability to reduce abuse of such drugs as marijuana, amphetamines, barbiturates, cigarettes, and alcohol: The longer the patient has been practicing meditation, the more likely he/she is to cut down markedly on intake of these substances.

Other benefits of meditation that appear relevant to therapeutic use are increased "field independence" resulting in a greater ability to withstand social pressures without abandoning one's own opinions and in improved self-assertiveness. Elevation of mood is also noted in many of those who meditate, with chronic low-grade depressions and reactive depressions responding particularly well to meditation. Lowering of hostility and lessened irritability are other effects of meditation that contribute to the therapeutic gains derived from its practice.

Explanations for why meditation achieves these effects include consideration of the effects of internally generated rhythms on mood; "global desensitization" brought about by meditation; and shifts in hemispheric dominance occurring during meditation, which may lead to a balancing of the active and passive-receptive modes of experiencing. It is concluded that meditation does not duplicate the process of psychotherapy, but complements it, with meditation more likely to bring about global changes at a nonverbal *level, while psychotherapy can zero in on the specifics of emotional problems.*

Potential difficulties in the use of meditation are reviewed and recommendations are made for a thorough training program in the practical managment of the meditation process, with an essential part of such a program being adjustment of each trainee's practice to suit his/her individual needs. Several currently available approaches to teaching meditation in clinical settings are discussed.

Lastly, the value of meditation for the psychotherapist is considered. Advantages cited include increased awareness and sensitivity to the clients' primary process thinking; increased responsiveness to nonverbal communications; enhanced empathy; greater ability to sustain the type of evenly suspended attention necessary for therapeutic listening; and greater stamina and alertness over long hours of patient sessions scheduled closely together. It is concluded that meditation can be of significant value in facilitating psychotherapeutic change.

4

Meditation Techniques in Clinical Practice

Patricia Carrington, Ph.D.

Meditation is practiced by directing one's attention to a single unchanging or repetitive stimulus, usually when sitting still in a quiet, isolated environment. While a seemingly simple procedure, this technique has been used by diverse societies throughout recorded history to alter consciousness in a way that has been perceived as deeply beneficial. Traditionally its benefits have been defined as spiritual in nature, with meditation used as an integral part of advanced religious practices. Today, however, new meditation techniques, streamlined for modern use by being greatly simplified in procedure and divested of esoteric and religious overtones, are being used to counteract pressures unique to contemporary society.

These modern meditation techniques appear to serve an all too neglected human need — the need to retreat periodically from the pressures and cares of the external world and turn inward to experience a special kind of mood, which, for want of a better term, we may call the "meditative mood."

This mood is characterized by a drifting state of consciousness that may be accompanied by an unusual openness to experiences ordinarily obscured by the active goal-directed mental set of everyday life. It can thus bring the practioner into harmony with his or her own inner rhythms, and sometimes with the greater rhythms of the universe as well, as the person comes to sense his/her own "aliveness" and interconnectedness with nature.

Meditation is, however, not a strange or unfamiliar state. All of us have experienced the meditative mood at times, perhaps when we were close to nature and were able to sense the tranquility and depth of this experience. This mood may have been evoked when we were watching snow drifting gently to the ground, or when we were attending to embers fading in a fireplace. Or it may have been experienced on a quiet beach as we relaxed and became inwardly silent, listening to the sounds of the gulls overhead and the surf beating on the shore, or as we breathed in a mountaintop's stillness. Moments of tranquility often evoke the "meditative mood" and can approximate the experience brought about by formal meditation techniques.

Even in today's hurried world, some of us are still fortunate enough to experience moments of true inner silence with sufficient frequency so that they have a profound effect on our lives — bringing us back periodically to an inner balance between outer and inner experience, as though a psychological gyroscope were at work. For such people, too much outward focus is automatically followed by a period in which the motor seems to "idle," as it were, so that a balance is regained between inner and outer selves — between experiencing activity and experiencing simply "being." Perhaps such fortunate people do not need *formal* meditation practice to maintain an optimal adjustment to life, although they may freely elect to pursue meditation as a means of personal development.

For the bulk of those living in modern industrialized societies, however, in which the pace of life is determined largely by economic considerations rather than by the rhythms of human life (or those of growing things), there is a dearth of spontaneously occurring quiet inner space into which the individual may retreat for refurbishing. In past centuries, periodic formal prayer probably served such a purpose for large segments of the population, but prayer is sufficiently unfashionable today so that few people can justify interrupting the all-important work day to enter a chapel for quiet contemplation. In the same way, a leisurely stroll to break up work, or simply sitting by a window and listening to the gentle patter of rain as "change of pace," is not possible for most of us during work hours. And even our leisure time is apt to be spent in *increasing* sensory bombardment rather than diminishing it (watching television and listening to music on stereo systems are key aspects of modern life).

Within this context of perpetual stimulation, the average human being moves from task to task with almost no rest and little opportunity to reaffirm his/her own basic existence. It is scarcely surprising, therefore, that the conflicts engendered by an uncertain and stressful environment are all too often left unresolved — since there is no quiet space or time in which to resolve them — and that their effect upon the human organism may accumulate until a variety of psychosomatic problems and other psychopathological manifestations emerge. Although most people will not become actively ill as a result, they will in all likelihood experience a sense of meaninglessness or unease about their lives; in an important sense they will have lost touch with the core of their beings.

It is within the context of hyperactivity so characteristic of the modern world that modern meditative techniques have gained their popularity. The widespread acceptance of such commercially available forms of meditation as, for example, Transcendental Meditation (TM), undoubtedly reflects a hunger on the part of westerners for the meditative mood. Not being supplied this kind of inner refurbishing by other modalities, a significant number of people appear to be turning to formal meditation as a means for attaining it.

Psychotherapists thus find themselves needing to evaluate the impact of meditation on their patients who have taken up this practice, and an increasing number of clinicians see the use of meditation as a promising adjunct to psychotherapy. This seems particularly to be the case where nonverbal conditionings remain unresponsive to more conventional therapeutic interventions.

Contributing to the interest of psychotherapists in the meditative techniques is the fact that these methods are related to biofeedback techniques (which also emphasize a delicately attuned awareness of inner processes) and to relaxation techniques, widely used in behavior modification.

Let us now turn to the question of how psychotherapy and meditation interact.

PERSONALITY CHANGE AND MEDITATION

Meditation appears to affect personality attributes both in an immediate sense and in terms of its ability to alter more permanent traits. The former is not surprising — we might expect a state of deep relaxation to reduce stress and to do so rather quickly — but the latter effect may be somewhat difficult to comprehend. If we consider the practice of meditation in light of its meaning to the practitioner, however, it can be seen that regular use of this technique has an opportunity to exert considerable influence on one's personality.

An individual practicing one of the modern forms of meditation often spends two periods of up to 20 minutes each (i.e., approximately 40 minutes a day) in meditation, plus a few additional minutes coming out of meditation. This brings the total time spent in meditation per day close to that of the typical 50-minute psychotherapeutic session. Since the meditator often spends this time with him/herself *seven days* a week, not for just one or a few hours per week (as in psychotherapy), it is reasonable to suppose that meditation, over time, can become a genuine agent for personality change.

Both clinical and research evidence suggests that some beneficial personality changes do take place in people who meditate regularly. Based on data from my own cases and those reported by colleagues and supervisees using meditation in clinical practice, as well as on data accumulating from research, I have arrived at an overall clinical impression of the usefulness of meditation in effecting personality change, as follows.

Tension Reduction

After commencing meditation, a marked lessening of tension is noted in many meditators, with inappropriate "alarm" responses often dropping out of the behavioral repertoire. The result of this amelioration of the alarm response may be more efficient handling of both large and small tasks and less of a sense of urgency in matters that formerly caused distress.

This increased coping ability often seen in meditators differs, however, in several respects from the effects brought about by psychotropic drugs. Taking certain medicines may restore a patient to feeling "more like himself," but it does not generally promote emotional growth. By contrast, meditators frequently report that meditation leads them to react in ways quite new to them. What is more, the relaxation brought about by drugs may slow a patient down, causing grogginess, while the relaxation resulting from meditation does not bring with it any loss of alertness. On the contrary, meditation seems, if anything, to *sharpen* alertness. Groups of meditators have been shown to have faster reaction times,[1] to have increased refinement of auditory perception,[29] and to perform more rapidly and accurately on perceptual motor tasks[30] than nonmeditating controls. Meditation can, therefore, be profitably used in place of a tranquilizer in a number of cases. For example, Glueck,[15] in a study conducted on a group of psychiatric inpatients, found that dosages of psychotropic drugs could be greatly reduced after patients had been meditating for several weeks, and that in a large number of these cases, sedatives could be reduced or eliminated as well.

Greater Productivity

As noted by Edmund Jacobson,[21] successful relaxation may bring about increased efficiency by eliminating unnecessary expenditures of energy, such as those used in maintaining excessive (counterproductive) muscle tension, or the effort wasted in straining to do something "well." The manner in which anxiety and emotional conflict drain energy has been noted in the literature on psychotherapy, with clinicians frequently reporting an increase in available energy in patients following the resolution of disabling inner conflicts.

Similarly, clinical observation suggests that the practice of meditation in certain patients brings about a striking increase in energy as well as productivity. This beneficial surge of energy after commencing meditation can manifest itself variously as a lessened need for daytime naps, increased physical stamina, increased productivity on the job, increased ideational fluency, the dissolution of writer's or artist's "block," and the release of hitherto unsuspected creative potentials.   With patients undergoing psychotherapy, this release of energy is often reflected in the greater ease with which the patient is able to free-associate in psychotherapy or is able to reach innovative solutions to his or her problems.

Lowered Anxiety

In all controlled research conducted to date where the effects of meditation on anxiety have been measured, results showed anxiety sharply reduced in a majority of subjects after they commenced the practice of meditation, even when the stressors in their lives remained high.   Not surprisingly, therefore, many stress-related illnesses respond to meditation.   Research has shown meditation to have positive effects on bronchial asthma[19] to decrease blood pressure in both pharmocologically treated and untreated hypertensive patients,[26, 6, 27] and to reduce premature ventricular contractions in patients with ischaemic heart diseases.[5] The use of meditation techniques has also been associated with increased rate of autonomic recovery from laboratory-induced stressful events[13, 17] and with reduction in serum cholesterol levels in hypercholesterolemic patients.[12]   It has also proven useful for treating insomnia,[37, 25] stuttering,[24] and psychiatric illness,[16] among other common conditions.

With respect to amelioration of anxiety in the psychotherapeutic setting, clinical observers report that after commencing meditation, patients are frequently better able to tolerate emotionally charged material during their psychotherapy sessions, a distinct advantage for the therapeutic process. There also seems to be less necessity for the therapist to spend time helping the meditating patient cope with his/her common, everyday problems since these seem to be better coped with as a result of the regular practice of meditation, leaving the patient free to concentrate on core problems in the psychotherapeutic process.

Lessening of Self-Blame

A useful by-product of meditation appears to be the increased self-acceptance frequently experienced by meditating patients. This is often evidenced in the therapeutic session as a lessening of unproductive self-criticism. Along with the tendency to be easier on oneself in this fashion, there can also be a concurrent increase in tolerance for the human frailties of others, with a decrease in self-defensiveness. This lessening of self-criticism appears to be a cumulative gain, the result of continued practice of meditation. The final outcome is a more objective outlook on the problems posed in psychotherapy, as well as those that must be faced in everyday life, and often an improvement in interpersonal relationships as well.

Anti-Addictive Effects

A series of studies[3, 31, 32] have shown that, at least in those persons who *continue* meditating for long periods of time (usually for a year or more), there is a marked decrease in the use of nonprescription drugs, such as marijuana, amphetamines, barbiturates, and psychedelic substances such as LSD. In fact, many long-term meditators appear to have discontinued use of such drugs entirely.

Interestingly, similar anti-addictive trends are seen in ordinary cigarette smokers and abusers of alcohol. When Shafii *et al.*[33] measured reduction in cigarette smoking in persons who had practiced meditation for more than two years, he found that 71 percent of these meditators had significantly decreased their use of cigarettes and 57 percent had stopped smoking altogether, while cigarette usage figures for a control group of nonmeditators remained approximately the same over a two-year period.

Apparently there is relationship, in combating addiction, between the amount of time the person has been meditating and the effectiveness of this practice. According to surveys, the attrition rate for the popular forms of meditation runs about 50 percent among adults in a typical community, with about half of those who learn to meditate discontinuing the practice within three years of having learned it, and an even larger number cutting down to once instead of twice a day, or even to only occasional use of the practice. This factor must be taken into account when considering the usefulness of meditation to combat addictions. The optimistic figures reported in the experiment literature clearly relate to those individuals who had the stamina and motivation to continue meditating for an extended period of time, most likely a select group to begin with. However, the fact remains that these particular people, who had been motivated to continue meditation, *did* markedly change their drug intake habits.

Anecdotal reports of lessened interest in excessive usage of common drugs such as marijuana in meditating patients, as well as decreased cigarette smoking and alcohol intake in such patients, suggest that the technique is well worth trying as an adjunct to psychotherapy with a patient suffering from an addictive problem, particularly if that problem is in it's incipient stage.

Mood Elevation

Patients suffering from mild, chronic depression or from reactive depression may experience a distinct elevation in mood after commencing meditation.[11] Such patients may become both more optimistic and more willing to engage fully and energetically in the work of psychotherapy. It has been the experience of a number of clinicians, however, that patients with *acute* depressive reactions do not as a rule, respond well to meditation. Such patients are likely to discontinue practicing meditation even if it is having a markedly elevating effect on their mood.[9]   The tendency of severely depressed patients to drop meditation may be due to the general apathy such patients typically display, or to the complex role depressive symptoms can play in the psychic economy; possibly it reflects a strong unconscious reluctance on the part of certain patients to relinquish a maladaptive pattern.   This reluctance is suggested in cases where meditation has been abandoned by a depressed patient precisely *because* it seemed to be ameliorating the depressive reaction.[8]

Glueck[15] has also noted that certain patients seem unable to accept the pleasurable feelings resulting from meditation and may stop meditating rather than face the guilt engendered.   In such instances, it may be useful to confine meditation to sessions conducted immediately prior to, or during, the patient's psychotherapy, so that any guilt reactions to the pleasure can be immediately worked through.

Increase in Available Affect

Patients who have commenced meditating will frequently report that they are now experiencing stronger feelings of pleasure, sadness, anger, love, or other emotions that had previously been partially suppressed.   This emotional release may occur during a meditation session or apart from it.

Because of the facilitating effects of meditation on the expression of emotions, it may be useful to ask certain patients to meditate immediately prior to their psychotherapeutic sessions.   Similarly, if a session in progress is blocked and the patient is unable to deal genuinely and meaningfully with his or her problem during it, meditating together *with* the patient during the psychotherapy session (usually for about 10 minutes) may be a useful maneuver, bringing patient and therapist into excellent rapport.   I have found this to be invariably helpful, and a number of colleagues have confirmed this observation. Each time a patient and I have meditated together, our communication has been much better afterwards, with the patient relaxed, thoughtful, and in touch with his or her feelings.

With respect to release of feelings during meditation, Glueck[15] has noted that the reduced level of anxiety resulting from meditation seems to facilitate entry into consciousness of "previously repressed anxiety-laden material," and I have observed some dramatic instances of traumatic, repressed memories recovered during a meditative session.   In one instance, repressed memories of having been a battered child first returned to a patient of mine during her meditation session —a breakthrough for her therapy.   This woman had had a psychotic mother who had brutally abused her during childhood, but it was only in the patient's meditative session that memories of this severe childhood stress emerged for the first time.   The memories were then worked on in psychotherapy and were eventually successfully integrated into her conscious life.   The result was a marked change, with a remission of deeply troubling psychosomatic symptoms.[9]

It is important to note, however, that had the above patient experienced this meditation-induced release of memories at a time when she was *not* concurrently undergoing psychotherapy, she almost assuredly would have abandoned the practice of meditation. According to her, the anxiety she experienced over having to face the hitherto unrecognized and potentially threatening emotions that accompanied these memories would have been too painful to bear without the support of a therapist. For such reasons, a combination of psychotherapy and meditation has often been noted as being more effective than either of these interventions used alone.

Increased Sense of Identity

An effect of meditation that is both subtle and important in terms of its effect on the therapeutic process is the increased "psychological differentiation" experienced by many meditating patients. A person possessing a high degree of psychological differentiation is said to experience him/herself in a more articulated, less global fashion; to be "inner-directed" rather than "outer-directed"; to be better able to use his or her own self as reference point when making judgments or decisions; to have a clear sense of his/her separate identity; and to be aware of needs, feelings, and attributes that are recognized as the patient's *own,* distinct from those of others. Internal frames of reference serve as guides for definition of this sense of identity, and such persons have been termed "field-independent." Persons with a less developed sense of separate identity — those who tend to rely on external sources for definition of their attitudes, judgments, sentiments, and views of themselves — have been termed "field-dependent."

It is interesting to find that where meditators have been tested for field-dependence/independence before learning to meditate, and then retested several months later, studies from several different laboratories have shown changes in the direction of greater field-*independence* following several months of meditation. In one study, performed at Princeton University, subjects were even shown to display significantly more field-independence (as measured by the embedded figures test) *following* a 20-minute meditation session than they had shown just before meditating.[20] Such studies suggest that a fundamental change in the person's perception of self may take place as a result of mediation.

Because of the experience of a new sort of identity during meditation, one that is nondemanding and deeply reassuring, meditating patients frequently report that they are now becoming more aware of their own opinions, that they are not so easily influenced by others as they were previously, and that they can now arrive at decisions more quickly and easily. They may also be better able to sense their own needs and thus become more outspoken and self-assertive, thus standing up for their own rights more effectively.

Such changes, however, can pose difficulties for certain patients. If the patient is not prepared to assimilate the independence and self-assertion that meditation can engender, he/she may quit the practice altogether rather than suffer a crisis of self-image. This difficulty is particularly liable to occur if the person has been clinging to a nonassertive role for a long period of time and if such a role has played an important part in his or her psychopathology. Unless the threat, posed by a growing sense of individuation derived from meditation, is successfully dealt with in psychotherapy, the patient may abandon meditation rather than experience the acute conflict engendered.

Other Effects

A withdrawal of projections often accompanies the readmittance into the self-system of previously disowned aspects of the self. Meditators may now view their own formerly compulsive complaints about others with a newfound sense of perspective. Along with these changes, paranoid tendencies may become lessened in some persons after commencement of meditation, with this anti-paranoid effect even experienced by some psychotic patients. For example, when conferring with a research team studying the effects of mediation on psychiatric in-patients at the Institute for Living in Hartford, I spoke with a paranoid schizophrenic patient who had recently learned to meditate, who told me that meditation was making him feel "much less paranoid."

Other effects noted in meditating patients are increased spontaneity, increased self-confidence, greater ability to take risks, decreased obsessive-compulsive behavior, and lessened irritability. The lowering of irritability and of impulsive outbursts of anger may be one of the most appreciated benefits, the meditating patient often becoming less volatile and explosive in his or her interpersonal relationships.[11]

THEORETICAL CONSIDERATIONS

If meditation has effects such as these on a sizable number of people who practice it, we must question why this should be the case. Clearly, meditation "works," when it does, for a number of reasons. Some are as follows.

Effects of Rhythm

In *mantra* meditation, where a lilting sound is continuously repeated, rhythm is a prime component; but rhythm also plays a role in all other forms of meditation, as the inner stillness involved allows the practitioner to become profoundly aware of his or her own bodily rhythms. In the unusual quiet of the meditative state, breathing may be intimately sensed, pulse may be faintly perceived, and sometimes even such subtle bodily sensations as the flow of blood through the veins, generally obscured by the activity of daily life, may be perceived. Certain meditative techniques, such as Zazen meditation, even use bodily rhythms as their object of focus, when the meditator is instructed to concentrate on his/her own natural, uninfluenced breathing.

Rhythm has been universally recognized as a natural tranquilizer, with regularly repeated sounds or rhythmic movements spontaneously used, for example, to quiet agitated infants. Parents the world over may rock a child gently, hum a lullaby, recite a nursery rhyme, repeat affectionate sounds in a lilting fashion, or bounce the baby rhythmically on their laps with an intuitive awareness of the soothing effects of these activities on mood.

If contacting deep biological rhythms in oneself is a prominent component of meditation, then regular meditation might be expected to have a deeply soothing effect. One might, so to speak, gain considerable stabilization from returning periodically to a source of well-being (in meditation) from which one could draw strength in order to deal more effectively with an outer environment whose rhythms are, more often than not, out of phase with one's own.

Global Desensitization

An interesting similarity exists between the situation occurring during a meditation session and that which occurs during the technique of systematic desensitization used in behavior therapy. In the latter process, increasingly greater increments of anxiety (prepared in a graded hierarchy) are systematically "counter-conditioned" by being paired with an induced state of deep relaxation. If the treatment is successful, presentation of the originally disturbing stimulus is supposed to cease producing anxiety.

In meditation, the meditative "focus" (whether this is a *mantra,* breathing, a candle flame, or whatever) becomes a signal for turning inward and experiencing a state of deep relaxation. At the same time, the meditator maintains a permissive attitude with respect to thoughts, images, or sensations experienced during meditation. Neither rejecting nor unduly holding on to these thoughts, the meditator lets these impressions "flow through the mind" while continuing to direct attention to the focal point of the meditation.

This dual process — free-associative thoughts occurring simultaneously with a repetitive stimulus that induces a state of calm — sets up a subjective state in which deep relaxation is paired with a rapid, self-initiated review of an exceedingly wide variety of mental contents and areas of tension, both verbal and non-verbal. As thoughts, images, sensations, and amorphous impressions drift through the mind during meditation, the soothing effect of the meditative focus appears to neutralize the disturbing thoughts. The result is that no matter how unsettling a meditation session may feel to the person, a frequent response of meditators is that they find themselves emerging from meditation with the "charge" taken off their current concerns or problems.

We may then ask whether the modern forms of meditation "work" when they do merely because they are a form of systematic desensitization. Such a reductionist point of view seems to overlook certain important factors. In systematic desensitization, therapist and patient work together to identify specific areas of anxiety and then proceed to deal with a series of single isolated problems in a sequential, highly organized fashion. During meditation, the areas of anxiety to be "desensitized" are selected by the responding organism (the meditating person) in an entirely automatic or unself-conscious manner. The brain of the meditator may be said to act like a computer programmed to run certain material through "demagnetizing" circuits capable of handling large numbers of data at one time. We might conceptualize subsystems within the brain that scan vast memory stores at lightning speed during the meditative state, with the aim of selecting those contents of the mind most urgently in need of being handled and most likely to be currently tolerated without undue anxiety. The decision to surface certain mental contents rather than others for processing would presumably be made by automatically weighing such considerations as the above and arriving at the best possible compromise. For these reasons, meditation seems to operate with considerably wider scope than systematic desensitization, though for exactly this reason it may lack the precision of the latter.

Shift in Hemispheric Dominance

Research suggests that during meditation a greater equalization in workload of the two cerebral hemispheres may occur.[2] Verbal, linear, time-linked thinking (typically processed through the left hemisphere) is minimal during meditation compared to the role it plays in everyday life, while holistic, intuitive, wordless thinking (usually processed through the right hemisphere) is prominent. Some of the effects of meditation may reflect this shift in emphasis.

Many societal or "superego" values are rooted in verbal-conceptual frames of reference. Restrictive moral systems, for example, are for the most part transmitted verbally, and much of role-modeling is dependent upon verbal imitation. The previously noted ameliorative effects of meditation on self-blame may be explained by this basic shift away from the *verbal mode* during meditation. Minimizing verbal-conceptual experience (yet still remaining *awake*) appears to afford the individual temporary relief from his/her own self-blame as well as from excessive self-demands that are formulated as internalized verbalizations. Having obtained a degree of relief from these verbal injunctions *during* the meditative state, when returning to active life, the meditator may now find himself less subject to severe self-criticism and/or guilt reactions. The reduction in the strength of the self-criticism will have generalized from the meditative state to the life of action.

MEDITATION AND PSYCHOTHERAPY

As a therapeutic intervention, meditation differs in several important respects from conventional psychotherapy, which seeks to pinpoint conflicts (often of an unconscious nature) and then attempts to bring into play the conscious integrative functions of the ego. Unlike psychotherapy, meditation does not provide any "conceptual handle" with which to reorganize one's cognitions of self. The rational elements of the psychodynamic psychotherapies and/or cognitive therapies are conspicuously absent in meditation, and the interpersonal elements take a back seat as well. In a fundamental sense, one is alone with oneself during meditation, while simultaneously removed from the verbal-conceptual world.

There is, therefore, a vast flow of ideation available to the meditator during the meditative session which cannot be translated into language, so rapidly does it occur and so diffuse is its quality. Such free flow of inner experience is curtailed in the psychotherapeutic patient, however, because he/she must continually translate experience into language *while it is occurring* – a limitation that while unquestionably useful for some aspects of therapy, may actually hinder certain other aspects of personal growth.

In addition, patients in psychotherapy allow their thoughts to run with a clear purpose in mind – the purpose is to reveal to the therapist and to the patient alike certain concerns now hidden or only partially or hazily identified. By contrast, the meditator allows thoughts to drift through his/her mind with *no goal* whatever. The thoughts need serve no purpose, and there is usually no attempt to contemplate their meaning. Even the most fluent of free-associative processes may thus be said to approximate a type of work in comparison with meditation, which approaches a type of play, two different modes of experiencing.

A final difference stems from the fact that psychotherapy is to a great extent *inter*personal in nature while meditation is strictly *intra*personal. Transference reactions, a part of the normal psychotherapeutic process, may thus restrict therapist-patient communication but not the meditative process. Only gradually, through the progression of psychotherapy, can the influence of punitive self-blame be mitigated, for example, while during meditation, lessening of such self-blame may occur automatically with a particular kind of freedom unavailable at other times because the meditator is alone and answerable to no one on this "inward voyage."

Changes brought about by meditation seem to be more global in nature than those resulting from psychotherapy. Meditation might be said to affect broad field-tension states within the organism, bringing about complex but *nonspecific* adjustments. By the same token, however, it may leave intact *specific* inner conflicts and their psychopathological solutions, even as it fosters positive personality traits on a more general level.

I have seen long-term meditators who, through meditation, have become more emotionally responsive, tranquil, personally insightful, energetic, and sensitive to the world around them. But these same persons still carried burdens of unresolved conflicts concerning sexual adjustments, social relationships, maturity, marriage, or career — conflicts that remained to be handled by conventional psychotherapeutic intervention.

I have also seen individuals who meditated regularly and were benefiting considerably from it, who, after commencing the practice of meditation, entered psychotherapy for the first time to work out some specific personality problems. According to these people, meditation had reduced their anxiety level to a point where they could now contemplate exploring their emotional problems in depth — something they had not previously been prepared to do.

The complementarity of the two processes, meditation and psychotherapy, is as impressive as their differences. I have not known of a single instance in which meditation has been used by a patient as a way of "resisting" psychotherapy, or where it has caused the patient to terminate psychotherapy prematurely. Nor (provided the therapist has a thorough knowledge of and positive attitude toward meditation) have I seen any instance where a patient has felt that psychotherapy has in any fashion interfered with his or her practice of meditation.

PROBLEMS IN THE USE OF MEDITATION

Tension-Release Side Effects

Like all techniques used to effect personality change, meditation has its limitations. One of these is the stress-release component of meditation, which must be thoroughly understood if this technique is to be used effectively. Particularly in the new meditator, physiological and/or psychological symptoms of a temporary nature may appear during or following meditation. These have been described elsewhere.[9] They appear to be caused by the release of deep-seated nonverbal tensions and their occurrence can be therapeutically useful, provided the therapist is schooled in handling them properly. However, too rapid a release of tension during or following meditation can cause difficulties and discouragement in a new meditator and may result in a patient's backing off from meditation or even abandoning the practice altogether. For this reason, careful adjustment of meditation time and other key aspects of the technique must be made if this modality is to be used successfully. Such adjustments usually eliminate any serious problems of tension-release, and for this reason adjusting meditation to suit each practitioner's individual needs is central to the form of recorded teaching of meditation presently widely used in clinical settings, Clinically Standardized Meditation (CSM).[10] With the proper adjustment, meditation becomes a sensitive and versatile tool.

Rapid Behavioral Change

Another problem that can arise with the use of meditation stems from the rapidity with which certain alterations in behavior may occur. Sometimes these changes may be incompatible with the lifestyle or defensive system of the patient. Should positive behavioral change occur before the groundwork for it has been laid (i.e., before the patient's value system has readjusted through therapy), an impasse can occur, which must then be resolved in one of two ways: (1) the pathological value system must be altered to incorporate the new attitude brought about by the meditation; or (2) the practice of meditation must be abandoned. If the meditator facing such an impasse has recourse to psychotherapy to work through the difficulties involved, this usually allows the individual to continue with meditation and make use of it to effect a basic change in lifestyle, but the therapist must be alert to and ready to handle such difficulties.

Some of the ways in which meditation-related behavioral changes may threaten a patient's pathological life style are as follows:

1. Meditation may foster a form of self-assertion that runs into conflict with an already established neurotic "solution" of being overly self-effacing. The tendency toward self-effacement must then be modified before meditation can be accepted into the person's life as a permanent and beneficial practice.
2. Meditation tends to bring about feelings of well-being and optimism, which may threaten the playing out of a depressive role that may have served an important function in the patient's psychic economy.
3. The deeply pleasurable feelings that can accompany or follow a meditation session can cause anxiety. For example, patients with masturbation guilt may unconsciously equate meditation (an experience where one is alone and gives *oneself* pleasure) to masturbation, and thus characterize it as a "forbidden" activity.
4. Meditation can result in an easing of life's pace, which may threaten to alter a fast-paced, high-pressured lifestyle used neurotically as a defense, or in the service of drives for power, achievement, or control. Patients sensing that this may happen may refuse to start meditating in the first place, or, if they start, may quickly discontinue the practice unless the larger problems are attended to.
5. The patient may develop what might be termed "negative transference" reactions to the meditation process itself, or to a meditational object of of focus such as a *mantra*. Some individuals seem to view meditation as if it were an "ideal parent." When they are forced to recognize that the technique actually varies in its effectiveness according to external circumstances, or according to their own moods or their own states of

health, they may then become irrationally angry at the meditation process and sometimes attempt to "punish" the meditation by quitting the practice.[9]

Fortunately, such complications as the above do not occur in *all* meditating patients. Often, meditation assists the course of psychotherapy in such a straightforward fashion that there is little necessity to analyze the patient's reaction to it.

APPROACHES TO TEACHING MEDITATION

Optimal use of meditation in a clinical setting depends in large part upon teaching the patient to manage the technique, a consideration that can easily be overlooked. The therapist must be thoroughly versed in meditation techniques and familiar with some of the routine problems that may arise in their practice.

With respect to the actual method of teaching, meditation can rarely be taught properly by written instructions alone. Correct learning of the technique relies upon communication of a subtle mood and an almost indefinable attitude of ease and permissiveness that is best transferred from one human being to another through nuances of voice and tone. Interestingly, meditation can be taught successfully through tape recordings, provided the latter effectively convey the elusive meditative mood (i.e., they are not "cold" or "mechanical" in nature), and that the teaching system is sufficiently detailed in terms of the information it conveys so that the trainee is instructed in handling the minor problems that may arise before the technique becomes truly workable.

The success of the CSM technique, which teaches meditation through cassette tapes and a programmed instruction text, may be because CSM recordings are "personal" in nature and accompanied by a full instructional system. CSM has been shown to be superior in its therapeutic impact to recorded methods of teaching progressive muscle relaxation,[11] a finding consistent with research showing that progressive muscle relaxation taught by *recordings* is often less effective in bringing about deep relaxation than progressive relaxation taught "live."[7,28] The fact that recorded teaching of meditation can be effective, while recorded teaching of progressive relaxation is less apt to be so, may stem from the fact that effective teaching of muscle relaxation depends upon physical cues and immediate feedback from an observing teacher, who must be present to check the degree of relaxation obtained, while correct meditation practice can be conveyed entirely through tone of voice and verbal instructions, cues that lend themselves easily to a recorded method.

THE MEDITATING PSYCHOTHERAPIST

Data concerning the value of a regular meditation practice for the therapist himself or herself are accumulating, with meditating colleagues reporting on its benefits and research studies confirming its value. Aside from the personal benefits that may derive from the therapist's own practice of meditation (which no doubt contributes to his/her work with patients), the following effects have been noted by my colleagues and myself after we commenced the practice of meditation.

1. An increase in awareness and acceptance of our own spontaneous perceptions of psychodynamics, or of unconscious conflicts, in our patients, and an increase in our ease in communicating these perceptions to our patients. One colleague, for example, reports that during his own meditation sessions, he often visualizes vivid scenes of a symbolic nature, which, on post-meditation analysis, have proven to contain valuable insights into one or another of his patients' psychodynamics.

2. Increased sensitivity to *nonverbal* elements of communication between patient and therapist. This clinical observation has been confirmed by the recent experimental findings of Hattauer,[18] who has shown that psychotherapists who meditate immediately prior to an interview with a client are rated by judges as being more sensitive to nonverbal cues, during the subsequent interview, than are therapists who have not meditated beforehand.

3. Increased "staying power" when patient hours follow one another in succession during a long day. This is consistent with the experimental literature on energy increases following meditation. Many therapists who meditate also report less of a tendency toward drowsiness from their therapeutic work.

4. Greater tolerance of patients' negative therapeutic reactions. If a patient's sudden verbal attack catches the therapist off guard, the therapist who practices meditation may be able to "roll with the punch" more, and as a result be less startled and unsettled. This greater tolerance for aggression in others appears to be part of an increased tolerance to all noxious stimuli (interpersonal or other), which frequently occurs in those who meditate.

5. Greater sensitivity to the difficulties patients may be experiencing in their meditation, because of the therapist's own practice of it.

Because such experiences are commonly reported by therapists, meditation training appears a promising addition to the routine training of psychotherapists. Certain ingredients essential to the practice of psychotherapy cannot, for example, be taught by formal methods, empathy being one. In a preliminary attempt to investigate this problem, Lesh,[23] studied the effects of meditation on the development of empathy in psychological counselor-trainees. The results showed a significant improvement in empathic ability in counselors who regularly practiced meditation during the course of the study, as compared to two control groups of counselor-trainees who did not practice meditation.

Meditation may also foster the kind of "evenly suspended attention" to patients' comments that Freud considered essential to the practice of psychoanalysis and which today is used in many of the derivative psychoanalytic therapies. Freud advised the analyst to "simply listen, and not bother about whether he is keeping anything in mind." Put into a formula: "He must turn his own unconscious like a receptive organ toward the transmitting unconscious of the patient."[14] In this light, a recent study by King[22] is interesting. Her study showed that "focusing" ability, as defined by Eugene Gendlin (a measure of openness and acceptance of the flow of inner experience), can be significantly increased by the regular practice of meditation. Meditation may therefore be considered an exercise designed to strengthen the precise "psychic muscle" necessary to achieve Freud's state of "evenly suspended attention." Experience suggests that it may also help to strengthen the ability for adaptive regression or "regression in the service of the ego," another valuable attribute for the psychotherapist.

THE FUTURE OF MEDITATION IN CLINICAL PRACTICE

The newer forms of meditation can now be taught or supervised by clinicians themselves rather than requiring instruction from a formal meditation organization, and training in supervision of the technique is becoming readily available.[10] We may, therefore, be on the threshold of a new era in the clinical use of meditation. No longer dependent on outside agencies or teachers (such as the TM organization), psychotherapists can now take the clinical management of meditation into their own hands. Accordingly, the use of meditation as an adjunct to psychotherapy is likely to be expanded in the near future.

What is needed at this point is increased research into the use of meditation as an adjunct to psychotherapy, as well as innovative pilot programs using meditation in therapeutic settings and as part of the curriculum of professional training centers. As psychotherapists gain greater familiarity with the technique, there will almost surely be more imaginative, as well as more extensive, use of this valuable modality, and a broadened understanding of the ways in which it can facilitate psychotherapeutic change.

REFERENCES

1. Appelle, S. and Oswald, L. E. Simple reaction time as a function of alertness and prior mental activity. *Perceptual and Motor Skills* 38:1263–1268 (1974).
2. Banquet, J. Spectral analysis of the EEG in meditation. *Electroencephalography and Clinical Neurophysiology* 35:143–151 (1973).
3. Benson, H. and Wallace, R. K. Decreased drug abuse with transcendental meditation: A study of 1,862 subjects. *Congressional Record, 92nd Congress, First Session,* Serial #92–1. Washington, DC: U.S. Government Printing Office (June 1971).
4. Benson, H. and Wallace, R. K. Decreased blood pressure in hypertensive subjects who practice meditation. *Circulation* (Supplement II) 45, 46:516 (1972).

5. Benson, H., Alexander, S., and Feldman, C. L. Decreased premature ventricular contractions through use of the relaxation response in patients with stable ischaemic heart disease. *Lancet* **2**:380 (1975).
6. Benson, H. Systemic hypertension and the relaxation response. *New England Journal of Medicine* **296**:1152–1156 (1977).
7. Borkovec, T. C. and Sides, J. K. Critical procedural variables related to the psysiological effects of progressive relaxation. *Behavior Research and Therapy* **17**:119–125 (1979).
8. Carrington, P. and Ephron, H. S. Meditation as an adjunct to psychotherapy. *In:* Arieti, S. (Ed.). *New Dimensions in Psychiatry: A World View.* New York: Wiley, pp. 262–291 (1975).
9. Carrington, P. *Freedom in Meditation.* New York: Anchor Press/Doubleday (1977); Doubleday Paperback (1978).
10. Carrington, P. *Clinically Standardized Meditation (CSM) Instructor's Kit.* Kendall Park, NJ: Pace Educational Systems (1978).
11. Carrington, P., Collings, G. H., Benson, H., Robinson, H., Wood, L. W., Lehrer, P. M., Woolfolk, R. L., and Cole, J. W. The use of meditation-relaxation techniques for the management of stress in a working population. *Journal of Occupational Medicine* **22**:221–231 (1980).
12. Cooper, M. J. and Aygen, M. M. A relaxation technique in the management of hypercholesterolemia. *Journal of Human Stress* **5**:24–27 (1979).
13. Daniels, D. Personal communication. *Cited in:* Carrington, P. *Freedom in Meditation.* New York: Anchor Press/Doubleday, pp. 60–61 (1977).
14. Freud, S. (1912). Recommendations to physicians practicing psychoanalysis. *In:* Strachey, J. (Ed.). *Standard Edition of the Complete Psychological Works of Sigmund Freud.* London: Hogarth Press, p. 112 (1958).
15. Glueck, B. As quoted in the *Hartford Courant,* p. 6 (May 27, 1973).
16. Glueck, B. C. and Stroebel, C. F. Biofeedback and meditation in the treatment of psychiatric illness. *Comprehensive Psychiatry* **16**:302–321 (1975).
17. Goleman, D. J. and Schwartz, G. E. Meditation as an intervention in stress reactivity. *Journal of Consulting and Clinical Psychology* **44**:456–466 (1976).
18. Hattauer, E. A. Clinically standardized meditation (CSM) and counselor behavior. Doctoral dissertation, Columbia University (1980).
19. Honsberger, R. W. and Wilson, A. F. Transcendental meditation in treating asthma. *Respiratory Therapy: The Journal of Inhalation Technology* **3**:79–80 (1973).
20. James, D. The short-term effects of transcendental meditation on field independence: A pilot study. Unpublished senior thesis, Princeton University (1976).
21. Jacobson, E. *Progressive Relaxation.* Chicago: University of Chicago Press (1929).
22. King, J. W. Meditation and enhancement of focusing ability. Doctoral dissertation, Northwestern University, Evanston, IL (1979).
23. Lesh, T. V. Zen meditation and the development of empathy in counselors. *Journal of Humanistic Psychology* **10**:39–74 (1970).
24. McIntyre, M. E., Silverman, F. H., and Trotler, W. D. Transcendental meditation and stuttering: A preliminary report. *Perceptual and Motor Skills* **39**:294 (1974).
25. Miskiman, D. E. Long-term effects of the transcendental meditation program in the treatment of insomnia. *In:* Orme-Johnson, D. W. and Farrow, J. T. (Eds.). *Scientific Research on the Transcendental Meditation Program* I. Livingston Manor, NY: Maharishi European Research University Press, pp. 331–334 (1978).
26. Patel, C. H. Yoga and bio-feedback in the management of hypertension. *Lancet* **2**:1053–1055 (1973).

27. Patel, C. H. 12 month follow-up of yoga and bio-feedback in the management of hypertension. *Lancet* 1:62–64 (1975).
28. Paul, G. L. and Trimble, R. W. Recorded vs. "live" relaxation training and hypnotic suggestion. Comparitive effectiveness for reducing physiological activity and inhibiting stress response. *Behavior Therapy* 1:285–302 (1970).
29. Pirot, M. The effects of the transcendental meditation technique upon auditory discrimination. *In:* Orme-Johnson, D. W. and Farrow, J. T. (Eds.). *Scientific Research on the Transcendental Meditation Program* I. Livingston Manor, NY: Maharishi European Research University Press, pp. 331–334 (1978).
30. Rimol, A. G. P. The transcendental meditation technique and its effects on sensory-motor performance. *In:* Orme-Johnson, D. W. and Farrow, J. T. (Eds.). *Scientific Research on the Transcendental Meditation Program* I. Livingston Manor, NY: Maharishi European Research University Press, pp. 326–330 (1978).
31. Shafii, M., Lavely, R. A., and Jaffe, R. D. Meditation and marijuana. *American Journal of Psychiatry* 131:60–63 (1974).
32. Shafii, M., Lavely, R. A., and Jaffe, R. Meditation and the prevention of alcohol abuse. *American Journal of Psychiatry* 132:942–945 (1975).
33. Shafii, M., Lavely, R. A., and Jaffe, R. D. Verminderung von zigarettenrauchen also folgc transzendentaler meditation (Decrease of smoking following meditation). *Maharishi European Research University Journal* 24:29 (1976).
34. Wallace, R. K. Physiological effects of transcendental meditation. *Science* 167:1751–1754 (1970).
35. Wallace, R. K., Benson, H., and Wilson, A. F. A wakeful hypometabolic state. *American Journal of Physiology* 221:795–799 (1971).
36. Wallace, R. K. and Benson, H. The physiology of meditation. *Psychosomatic Medicine* 35:341–349 (1973).
37. Woolfolk, R. L., Carr-Kaffashan, K., Lehrer, P. M., *et al.* Meditation training as a treatment for insomnia. *Behavior Therapy* 7:359–365 (1976).

There is some evidence in the literature suggesting the potential coping value of transcendent or supernatural belief systems. It is the contention of this chapter that this coping value can be harnessed if a proper approach is used with the client with such a belief system. The model or approach presented is not meant in any way to imply that this is the only framework by which transcendent values may be made use of in therapy. It suggests, however, that concepts arising from both cognitive psychology and information processing theory and from work in cross-cultural psychology must be taken seriously when a therapist confronts a value system that may be somewhat alien to her/his own system. Taken together, these concepts suggest that all individuals, therapists and clients alike, approach their world through personal belief systems. If the therapist's system is not a transcendent belief system (e.g., humanistic-scientific), he or she must find concepts within his/her own belief system which will allow full acceptance and therapeutic use of the transcendent beliefs of the clients.

5

Cognitive Therapy via Personal Belief Structures

L. Rebecca Propst, Ph.D.

Non-religious therapists often experience a great deal of difficulty in working with religious clients, particularly those clients with a Christian fundamentalist orientation. These difficulties may arise both from the therapists' personal intellectual convictions and from previous negative experiences with such clients. In terms of convictions, therapists suspect that the religious references and allusions in which their religious clientele persist are, at best, irrelevant to the therapeutic task, and thus they interpret persistent attempts by their clientele to discuss such matters as efforts to avoid the really important therapeutic matters, much as if they persisted in discussing a particular hobby in a therapy hour. Some therapists go so far as to regard religious beliefs as not merely irrelevant to the client's emotional problems, but as contributing to their clients' problems. Thus, Ellis[8] asserted that "devout faith in suprahuman entities and powers almost always leads to poor emotional health and to decreased long-range effectiveness." Therapists' difficulties may also arise from previous negative experiences in which they found the religious terminology of the client incomprehensible, or were put on the defensive by a proselytizing client.

The aforementioned difficulties have provided substantial roadblocks for therapists attempting to work with clients with religious or transcendent value systems. The purpose of this chapter is to suggest a potential theoretical framework and set of techniques whereby clients' religious values may be worked with more comfortably in therapy.

Franks'[10] contention in a 1977 article in *American Psychologist*, that all individuals have a cognitive map with which they make sense out of experiences, and that such maps are termed belief systems, may provide us with a theoretical mechanism whereby therapists can work with their clients' belief systems in therapy.   According to Franks, ultimately all belief systems rest on value premises that for the believer are not open to question and that cannot be disproved by appeal to experience — that is, they are articles of faith. This is as true of the scientific-humanistic world view as for the transcendental world view. Familiarity with Franks' contentions should enable therapists to become less absolutist in their own belief systems and more open to the mental health value of other belief systems. Indeed, much work in cognitive psychology also asserts that individuals have prior abstract categories that help them process and make sense out of incoming information.

This chapter will describe a therapeutic rationale and accompanying techniques whereby therapists can more comfortably and easily work with the transcendent belief systems of their clients. A brief discussion of previous work in this area will also be used to support the notion that a transcendent belief system has much coping potential.

The terms *transcendent* or *supernatural* will be used here, rather than the term *religious* because they are more exact terms. The dictionary defines religious as only belief that is strongly held. This could refer to either a transcendent or humanistic scientific belief, and could be used to describe the belief structures of an atheist as well as those of a Jew or a Christian. Using the term *religious* to describe all people's belief systems will make therapists more sensitive to their own religious beliefs. A *transcendent* religious belief system, however, according to Franks, refers to a belief in a reality that is not accessible in the ordinary senses or consciousness.   This is somewhat consistent with the philosopher's notion in that the individual who can transcend his or her surroundings must do so by means of an alternative perspective. A supernatural religious belief system is even more specific and refers to belief in a specific reality or entity (God) that is beyond, above, or outside the natural scheme of cause and effect. Finally, a *humanistic-scientific* religious belief system, according to Franks, refers to belief only in a reality that operates according to the laws of natural cause and effect and that is learned of by making an intellectual analysis of sensory data.

EARLIER WORK

There are many divergent cues to the mental health value of a supernatural or transcendent belief system. Some of the earlier works in this area, for example, really began to hint at the conceptual similarity of the therapeutic relationship and one's relationship with a supernatural being. Thus, one or the other could serve the same purposes in the individual's life. For example, the therapist has been seen as similar to the priests or shamens of the ancient rites, in which the believer or client is asked to submit to an authority so that she or he may be healed.[21,22] Other analysis compared a conversion process to the therapeutic process of gaining insight, and one's relationship to an accepting therapist as being synonymous to a relationship with an accepting God.[20] Still other rational and observational analyses of the supernatural or transcendent experience and the therapeutic experience have given a psychoanalytic interpretation to the former and have seen it as an example of repression, a manisfestation of the individual's primitive urges and attempts by the individual to overcome his or her childish fears of helplessness in the face of an overwhelming parent figure. This was the view expressed in Freud's *Future of an Illusion*. However, more recently, Gay[11] contends that in Freud's very first writing on religion (supernatural belief systems) in his 1907 essay, "Obsessive Acts and Religious Practices'" Freud had a somewhat more neutral view of a supernatural belief system, seeing it as a process of suppression whereby the ego's attempts at suppressing disruptive or dangerous id impulses were aided, thereby furthering adaptation.

Freud's early statement (which he apparently later discounted), that such a belief system could be adaptive, finds support in some of the more recent coping studies and case studies of supernatural belief systems and mental illness. For example, Cavenor and Spaulding[6] found that in cases if diagnosed depression with hysterical features, a conversion to a supernatural belief system appeared to lead to a complete resolution of depressive symptoms. They concluded that such a conversion strengthened repression in depression with hysterical features. It is also possible that the conversion experience furnished the ego with more controls with which to suppress and control hysterical reactions.

Similarly, two more recent anecdotal reports[17,27] also seemed to suggest that a supernatural belief system had a positive impact on a depression with hysterical features. In both cases, the cognitive knowledge of God's acceptance seemed to lend the individuals strength to admit to their own feelings of nonacceptance, which in turn decreased the needs for somatization. In all cases, the ego's cognitive tools were strengthened, not weakened.

The contribution of a supernatural belief system or conversion to adaptive coping seems to be borne out by a few scattered references to supernatural belief systems in the coping liturature. Thus, for example, Bulman and Wortman[5] found that individuals who had been paralyzed in a serious accident frequently expressed the belief that God had had a reason for the accident, while Dimsdale[7] found that survivors of a Nazi concentration camp reported surviving by mobilizing hope, often with philosophical or transcendent content.

More recently, a study to determine whether a supernatural belief system was used as a coping mechanism by poverty-level rural elderly ethnic groups residing in the Bible Belt found that 40 percent of the elderly spontaneously reported using these beliefs to cope, especially during adversity, while 26 percent used it with feelings of depression and for raising the morale.[24]

The mobilization of hope suggested by the concentration camp study has been a crucial ingredient in psychotherapy and healing, according to Jerome Franks. This may partially explain the positive effects of a transcendent belief system whose function it is to increase individuals' expectations and hope for a better life. Indeed, Franks cites numerous incidents in his book, *Persuasion and Healing*,[9] of the individual's belief in the efficacy of a technique or ritual as being productive of the actual therapeutic efficacy of the technique or ritual. Thus, the hope engendered by supernatural belief systems may not be unlike that hope necessary in the client for successful psychotherapy. It may be, in fact, that for some clients, for whom a transcendent or supernatural belief system is the primary channel by which hope and expectations for healing is advanced, that only use of these belief systems will lead to psychological healing. Thus, it may be necessary for the psychotherapist to consider how he or she might encompass these belief channels within the therapeutic process itself.

Thus far, there have been only two attempts to actually examine whether or not actually putting the hypothesized ingredients of therapeutic change into transcendent or supernatural belief system channels by using the individual's values and language is more effective than not doing so. One study by Swenson, Brady, and Edwards[29] examined the effects of attitude pretraining, geared to the value system of the individual, on the efficacy of assertion training. Prior to assertion training, they met with participants and discussed with them the value of assertion and asked the clients themselves to state why assertion was good. One treatment emphasized the compatibility of assertiveness with Christian values while the other treatment merely focused on the intrinsic benefits of assertiveness. Participants were from a small Christian college. The post-test results indicated that the clients in the Christian values pre-training group were more assertive both on a behavioral measure tapping *in vivo* refusal of an undesirable request and on a self-report semantic differential measuring a subject's response and feelings about both assertive and nonassertive behavior than those in the secular values pre-training group. Out of all the students in the biblical pre-training group (those given a religious rationale for assertion) 35.7 percent were given a maximum assertive rating of five, constituting an unqualified refusal to an undesirable response. Only 12.5 percent of students in the secular pre-training group, and no students in an assertive training group only (no attitude pre-training) responded with an unqualified refusal.

The only problem with this study was the brief length of the attitude pretraining (one session) and the assertion training (only two sessions). Had such training been longer, it is possible that the differential effects would have been even greater.

A previous study by the author of this chapter[23] also attempted to put the active ingredients of a therapy into the framework of the clients. This work examined the efficacy of a cognitive treatment using a supernatural belief system for those individuals who claimed to believe in such a system, and who were mildly depressed. This study was the first controlled psychotherapy outcome study reported in the literature that used a supernatural belief system as a component of psychotherapy and evaluated the efficacy of that component. In this study, 44 mildly depressed individuals, selected on the basis of self-reported mood over a period of two weeks and on the basis of some standard self-report measures of depression, were randomly assigned to one of the following treatments: (1) a non-religious imagery (secular) treatment patterned after Goldfried's[12] self-control version of systematic desensitization; (2) a religious imagery treatment (making use of a supernatural belief system) that exactly paralleled the first treatment except that participants used cognitions and images with supernatural and transcendent content to modify their depressive cognitions and images, (3) a therapist contact and self-monitoring treatment only, in which each participant merely recorded his/her daily mood and met with a therapist each week in an instructed discussion situation; and (4) a waiting list control, in which participants merely monitored their moods throughout the duration of the study.

Participants were assessed at pre-, post-, and follow-up sessions on a variety of self report measures and a behavioral measure.

Results revealed that the transcendent religious imagery treatment showed significantly more treatment gains than the self-monitoring or non-transcendent imagery treatments on both the self-report and the behavioral measures, while the self-monitoring plus therapist contact treatment was intermediate in effectiveness.

A six-week follow-up revealed a tendency for the religious imagery group (transcendent) to show less depression. However, the obtaining of further differences may have been precluded because the mildly depressed participants may have reached the lower limits of the measures.

One other area of work relevant to transcendent values should be briefly mentioned, that of the research that has looked at the effects of meditation (TM or otherwise) on stress and mental health. The value of this research is that it has attempted to make use of techniques outside the realm of traditional psychotherapy to aid people in coping. A brief inspection of this literature reveals a variety of results. What all of the literature seems to have in common, however, is the notion that participants' expectations and beliefs about the treatment play a crucial role in their success. Indeed, a review of the literature by Smith[28] concluded that often participants' expectations and beliefs were not controlled for, and when they were, they were highly predictive of symptom improvement.

A COMPONENT MODEL FOR A THERAPY USING TRANSCENDENT OR SUPERNATURAL BELIEF SYSTEMS

Recently, cognitive therapy theorists such as Kazdin[15] have defined the term "placebo reaction" when applied to psychotherapy as something that may increase the patient's expectations and hopes of a successful treatment. These increased expectations may not only induce client's to think differently about their problems (actually an active ingredient in cognitive therapy) but may also induce them to put more effort into therapy homework or to try new behaviors (an active ingredient in behavior therapy).

Increasing the positive expectation value of a treatment is not always easily done, however. Jerome Franks contends that the individual's expectations are largely a by-product of his or her assumptive world (belief system). For example, if an individual has the assumption that a certain ingredient is necessary for healing, then the expectation that something will happen will not be induced until he or she perceives the ingredient to be present.

That expectations should play an important role in psychotherapy is not surprising given the contention by cognitive psychology that information processing is not only data-driven via incoming sensory information, but that it is conceptually driven in that the perceiver imposes knowledge and conceptual structures on the environment.[1] That is, information is classified according to prior information or prior categories. Our knowledge of particulars depends upon a prior, more abstract classification rule. Information that does not fit easily into the classification system may not be understood. Thus, an individual with a transcendent belief system will attempt to fit events, explanations, and personal problems into that framework.

Thus, the contention of the present paper is that therapeutic expectations are made more powerful if the active ingredients of a psychotherapy are translated into the language and belief structures of the patient. Indeed, Rush and Watkins,[2,5] associates of Aaron Beck, have been doing just this with lower class, naive, depressed clients. They have suggested, and are conducting, a pre-therapy program, aimed at correcting patients' erroneous cognitions about therapy by trying to guess what the patient may think about certain aspects of treatment and beginning to challenge these thoughts. They have suggested that attitudes be confronted with cultural appropriate analogues and arguments.

In the framework of cognitive therapy, the focus is on changing the irrational assumptions and distorted perceptions of the individual as the active ingredient of change. The challenge to these irrational assumptions and impetus to reexamine the distorted perceptions must come from within the belief structures and classification systems of the patients themselves. For clients with a transcendent or supernatural belief system, the context, language, and content of the challenges must be translated into the language of that belief structure.

COMPONENTS OF TREATMENT INTERVENTION

This section examines the use of transcendent religious techniques within a cognitive restructuring framework. (This is based on some previous work by the author.) We will first examine each of the components of the cognitive restructuring paradigm separately, indicating how the present treatment suggestions, which make use of the client's personal belief structures, may approach each of these components differently than the more traditional treatment. The components of cognitive therapy discussed here are those proposed in Goldfried and Davison's[13] cognitive restructuring paradigm for anxiety.

The first task of cognitive restructuring is to help clients recognize that self-statements mediate emotional arousal. There are really two aspects to this component. Clients must be taught to begin to monitor their own thoughts and self-statements in emotionally arousing situations and they must also be given a credible theoretical framework that asserts the relationship between self-statements and emotional arousal. This framework should be able to set the context for the "why" of each of the treatment components they will undergo. Meichenbaum,[18] in his earliest treatment manual, gave one of the clearest explanations for why the therapeutic process should be explained to the individual. Essentially, the reason is "expectations." The client and the therapist must have a common conceptualization with common expectations as to what should happen in therapy. The rationale gives the client a set as to what he or she should be focusing on and guides his/her behavior in therapy. According to Meichenbaum, the exact rationale need not be exactly scientifically correct, but it must have face value. He has also suggested that it could easily be fit in with the perspective of the therapist. It is the contention of this chapter that the rationale for the treatment should also be adapted to the conceptual world of the client. Thus, for example, in clinical practice by this author, Christian clients were given a rationale partially based on cognitive theory and partially based on Psalm 42 in the Bible ("Why are you cast down oh my soul . . ."). In that particular passage, the Biblical writer was portrayed as talking to himself and attempting to understand what kind of self-statements he was making to himself to make himself depressed.

Secondly, as clients are encouraged to *become aware* of their self-statements, they are encouraged to ask God to help them become aware of their thoughts. They may be given, for example, Psalm 139, verses 23 and 24 from the Bible, which states, "Search me, oh God, and know my heart. Try me and know my anxious thoughts, and see if there be any hurtful way in me." *Hurtful* was defined as one's pain and the theme was stressed to the clients that the beginning process of healing is always a painful process of allowing one to be made aware of one's depressive or anxious thoughts.

For Christian clients, the treatment is usually outlined with the rejoinder that all thoughts should be brought in line with what Christ would have one think. This means not only evaluating one's thoughts in light of their belief system, but also determining whether one's perceptions were indeed accurate perceptions of the world rather than distortions.

As has already been suggested, the language for the treatment rationale may be substantially different than that associated with Goldfried or Meichenbaum's paradigm. The basic components of the rationale are the same, however. They are merely justified via the patient's transcendent belief system. An analysis of self-statements is seen as a self-analysis of the heart done in a prayerful attitude. The transformation of self-statements is seen as being transformed by Christian perspective rather than being conformed to the surrounding circumstances and the hurtful self-centered thoughts that have arisen from that perspective.

Even though the rationales and set for the procedures may be different in this paradigm from Goldfried's more traditional approach, even greater differences in approach are obvious when the patient is asked to *modify* her or his self-statements (*third component of Goldfried's paradigm*). The coping statements that clients with a transcendent belief system may be encouraged to develop and the examples of coping statement supplied to them are derived right out of the healthy components of the clients' belief systems.

There are at least three variations in practices which the author has pursued in teaching these clients to modify their self-statements.

One procedure, based upon that of Beck *et al.*[2] and Meichenbaum[18] has been to first make clients aware of their self-statements and then, for depressed clients, to give them coping statements or images directed at one aspect of Beck's depressive cognitive triad. For example, to confront and handle feelings of low self-esteem, the depressed person may be given the following thought: "Am I jumping to conclusions that I am incompetent or ugly or that no one likes me and forgetting that I am made in the image of God?" For images, the following image may be suggested to the client. "I can see the Holy Spirit filling me so that I feel a sense of God's presence and power and am able to go back into a situation and correct a mistake." These procedures were used in the 1980 study by this author.[23] Clients were taught to produce images of a depressive situation and then to modify those images using their religious belief system.

A more recent procedure has paralleled that of Goldfried, Decenteceo and Weinberg.[11] After clients had learned to check their perceptions of anxiety or depressive situations and have learned to monitor their self-statements in such situations, they were given Ellis' list of irrational ideas[8] and asked to argue with each of them using their transcendent religious beliefs. After they had produced some arguments of their own, the therapist gave them some additional arguments (Table 5-1), which they were encouraged to use. (For depression, they were asked to relate Ellis' ideas to Beck's cognitive triad.[2]) Clients then classified each of their prerecorded thoughts as examples of Ellis' statements. Finally, the depressive situations that clients had listed were arranged in an ascending order of coping difficulty for the patient. Clients were then taught to apply their coping statements to the depressive or anxious situation via the imaginal presentation procedure of Goldfried and Davison.[13] Stress situations were arranged in

TABLE 5-1. Coping List Excerpt: Religious and Non-Religious Arguments Directed to Ellis' Irrational Beliefs.

I. The idea that it is a dire necessity for an adult human being to be loved and approved of by virtually every significant other person in his community.

    A. There are so many different types of people we run into that it is impossible for us to be loved by all of them.

    B. Actually, sometimes to be disapproved of may mean we are doing something that is worthwhile ("Blessed are you when men hate you," Luke 6:22*).

    C. It is most important to have God's approval, not people's approval. We should not be that concerned about what others think. (The scripture says do work not to please people, but to please God. Also, Matthew 6:2-6 talks about not doing things to be seen of men.)

II. The idea that one should be thoroughly competent, adequate, and achieving in all possible respects if one is to consider oneself worthwhile.

    A. One's worth as a person is not dependent upon doing something. We are valuable just because we are human beings.

    B. To be important to God one must simply exist. God doesn't love you because you are important, God loves you simply because He wants to – and that makes you important.

    C. Sometimes it is okay to fail and be weak, because then we are strong (2 Corinthians 12:10).

III. The idea that human unhappiness is externally caused and that people have little or no ability to control their sorrows and disturbances.

    A. Often it is not events that cause us problems, but our attitudes toward those events.

    B. 2 Timothy 1:7 says that God has not given us a spirit of timidity, but of power and love and self-control. Somehow, God is implying that we have some internal influence over our feelings.

    C. The scripture contains a direct statement of our influence on our feelings in Proverbs 23:7. As a man thinks in his heart so he is.

*The numbers signify a reference to an old testament or new testament Biblical passage. The first number after the title of the book is the chapter and the number after the colon is the verse. These abbreviations are usually familiar to religious clients.

an ascending order of difficulty so that clients could learn to handle the less difficult situations before being required to face the more difficult ones. A relaxation component, based somewhat on Christian meditation procedures, was an additional component for stress and anxiety reactions. Essentially, this component parallels traditional relaxation techniques of clinical behavioral therapy (e.g., Goldfried and Davison) except that it also has blended with it some procedures from Christian meditation, especially those of the inner healing movement of Agnes Sanford.[26]   Thus, using the self-control method of Goldfried, clients are encouraged to focus on God and imagine themselves in God's presence and being filled with the warmth of God's spirit. In the author's previous clinical experience, such a rationale has made many religious clients much more trustful of the relaxation procedure and much less afraid of letting go.

Finally, it is important for the therapist to model the coping procedure for the clients, being careful to use some of the statements or images the clients themselves have suggested from their value systems. An example of therapist modeling encompassing both the RET procedures of Goldfried, Decenteceo, and Weinberg[14] and the meditation suggestions of the inner healing movement is as follows.

I am sitting here and trying to talk to this individual and I feel myself getting tense. I can feel my muscles getting tense and the back of my neck getting tight. I am up to about a 60. So I will stop myself and first tell myself to relax by letting my muscles go just as I learned in the relaxation exercise. They are already tensed up, they just need to be relaxed. I will concentrate on my neck and just let go, letting out as much of the tension as possible. Now I say: "What must I be telling myself that is creating this anxiety?" Well, I think I am worried that I am not making a good impression as I am unsure of what to say. Why does that bother me? Well, I am afraid this person will think badly of me, and maybe even make fun of me. But wait a minute, that's a pretty stupid idea. So what if this person is not impressed with me. It is impossible to impress everyone. It might be nice to impress everyone, but that is impossible. It won't be a disaster if I do not impress this individual. Besides it is more important to have God's approval than anyone else's approval. At this point I can really relax because I know I have God's approval. Do I really let my muscles express that? Can I allow my stomach to relax. There is really nothing for me to be uptight about. How sure am I that I am making a bad impression. Well, actually I do not have any evidence that I am making a bad impression and that I do not have good conversational skills. He seems to be listening intently, but just the same, what if I am making a bad impression? So what, it's not a diaster.
[Another alternative would be], Well, I can see he is not too impressed with what I am saying, but one cannot impress everyone and I am saying what I think is important and must remember that not even Jesus impressed everyone. In fact, there were many people that were unimpressed with him and even hated him.
In thinking about the situation a little bit more rationally, it does not seem to upset me so much. I do not feel as nervous as I did before; perhaps I am only at a level of about 20.

After the therapist has modeled an example, he or she will work with each participant and review with them the situation, their thoughts, and their coping statements, and then ask them to close their eyes and imagine themselves in the situation and using what he has said as a model, imagine their tension, and their thoughts, and then argue with them so they tell themselves to relax. The client will be reassured that whereas the task may seem somewhat deliberate and tedious at first, individuals utilizing this procedure have reported that, with practice, each step becomes easier to carry out. Learning to rationally argue with oneself becomes less deliberate and more automatic, like learning to drive a car.

One final technique, which has been used in several pilot studies, is symbolic imagery. In this particular procedure, the client is asked, after a period of thought-monitoring, to transform those thoughts into a symbol of himself or herself. Here it is stressed that such a symbol need not be realistic, but should merely reflect the clients' thoughts about themselves. One client, who was a student who had been unsuccessful in an honors tutorial program, pictured himself as an ant, someone who was insignificant and might be stepped on. He was then asked to bring his concept of God into the image in some symbolic way. He proceeded to view God as a smiling face, who seemed interested in him even though he was an ant. Apparently, the experience had quite an impact on him, as he brightened up and began to speak of other ways in which he was significant. He also stopped by the author's office more than a year after the pilot study had been completed to reiterate how important the experience had been to him.

The method of symbolic imagery seems to the author to include elements of both the cognitive restructuring paradigm, especially in the thought-monitoring state, and also elements of some of the more esoteric imagery techniques, especially those of active imagination (Jung) in which the individual is encouraged to work with more symbolic representations of his/her thoughts or dreams. It is possible that the impact of the symbolic imagery may arise from allowing the client to work with symbols that represent underlying assumptions and associations of which he or she is not fully aware. Indeed, Mahoney,[16] in his recent book, *Psychotherapy Processes*, suggests that cognitive therapists should not be too quick to discard the possibility of unconscious processes and associations, as humans are often incapable of expressing all of the nuances of a situation verbally (i.e., by becoming aware of self-statements associated with that situation). Symbolism may pick up the nuances of an idea or a construct that one cannot verbally express.

One additional uniqueness the present procedures present to the paradigm of cognitive restructuring is in the area of follow-up and maintenance of treatment gains. Usually, once the client becomes acquainted with thought-monitoring and modification, it is imperative that he/she remain vigilant of thoughts and develop habits of challenging the maladaptive ones. This change in behavior has often been difficult to achieve, as it essentially involves a more self-aware approach to living. One mechanism we have found helpful in this regard is the daily devotional period, which may already be part of the life of a client with a transcendent belief system, especially in the lives of fairly devout Christians. For many of these people, this daily period consisted of reading scripture and then evaluating one's life in light of the concepts of scripture. We have found that the technique of thought-monitoring fits in well here. Clients are merely encouraged during their devotional period to analyze their self-statements and challenge the dysfunctional ones in light of the healthful concepts of their faith.

The validity of using such a procedure for treatment maintenance is an interesting research question.

ADDITIONAL CONSIDERATIONS

One of the difficulties in this area of work is the suspicions of the mental health community toward transcendent or supernatural belief structures.

Because many therapists do not hold such a belief system,[3] most of their impressions of such belief systems come from those beliefs of the emotionally disturbed religious clients they see. Having only seen those belief systems in the context of emotional disturbance, they may have a tendency to regard such belief systems and emotional disturbance as causally linked. This suspicion has prevented mental health professionals from considering the potential coping value such a faith may provide. Only recently, as there has been increased focus on the value of interpersonal support systems, non-professional helpers, and the actual cognitive constructions of the individual, has there been any attention given to the role a religious community and faith may play in coping. There has not, however, been any substantial research in this area, perhaps because, as Franks[10] suggested, it is difficult to get funding in this. Also, Kuhn pointed out in *The Structure of Scientific Revolutions* that a scientist only scientifically investigates answers that she or he already suspects to be answers.

Bergin and Strupp[4] long ago said that we should examine natural healing processes in the world because they may provide clues to useful techniques to be used in psychotherapy. The whole area of transcendent belief systems and healing might be a subject for such examination. It is possible that such an examination would provide us clues not only to the components of the healing processes but, more specifically, provide us with a greater understanding of the role of expectations and hope in emotional healing. There may be powerful therapeutic factors in such belief systems.

It is obvious, for example, that a supernatural belief system gives one a competing system of beliefs that claim to originate from outside any structures with which the individual may be contending. Such a belief system always gives the individual a set of beliefs with which to challenes more immediate perspectives engendered by the environment. Such a system also gives one a much stronger concept of the self (i.e., one is defined as being the image of God in such systems); thus, the self is not defined or limited by circumstances or current social definitions.[19] The psychotherapeutic efficacy of such ideas must be researched.

Another issue of importance in this area is the problem of examination and changing therapists' attitudes toward their clients.

Rush and Watkins[25] provided us with a clue in their work with psychologically naive clients. They attempted to probe clients for any clues as to their self-statements regarding therapy. They then attempted to either adapt their presentation of therapy to the particular client's self-statements or change the self-statements of the client.

It is imperative that one begin to be sensitive to the covert self-statements clients with transcendent or supernatural belief systems may have concerning psychotherapy. Based on the writer's experience, the following are some of the typical questions and thoughts such clients may bring to therapy.

1. What is the therapist's personal beliefs? Will he/she understand me if I hold different beliefs?
2. Why do I have emotional problems if I am a Christian (or other sectarian label)? If I were a good Christian, I would not have such problems and would not have to go to a therapist.
3. The therapist is like a doctor and will cure me. I need only sit here. (Many clients, with many different belief systems, have this belief.)
4. Am I using worldly wisdom by consulting a secular therapist? (Here it is essential for the therapist to be aware that many belief systems are counter-cultural and consider contacts with the predominant culture as evil or a cop-out, just as was the case with the counter-cultural movement of the sixties.)

It is apparent that some of these beliefs may be answered by some of the religious answers to Ellis' irrational ideas. The best rule of thumb is that is is usually good to answer some of the questions with answers arising from the client's perspective if possible and to also remember that not all questions are examples of resistance but rather responses of uncertainty and distrust, much as if a psychotherapist raised within a humanistic-scientific culture was being asked to trust his/her heart condition to an Indian Shaman.

This author has found that it is most helpful to portray oneself as a teacher who attempts to help clients make use of their beliefs in a way they haven't adequately learned in the past.

It is usually best for a therapist to be honest about his or her own personal belief system while at the same time asserting willingness to treat with respect the client's own beliefs and aid the client in living more consistently with them.

It is also helpful for a therapist working with a client holding a different belief structure to be aware of his or her own self-statements concerning that individual's beliefs. It may be helpful for perspective therapists to ask themselves the following questions.

1. What are my personal beliefs regarding a supernatural or transcendent belief system?

2. Would my belief structure on this issue allow me to accept the coping potential of my client's supernatural or transcendent belief structure?
3. What specific aspects of my client's belief system do I see as most objectionable?
4. Is there an alternative scheme I may use that would allow me to accept or make use of these objectionable beliefs?

It is the author's contention that such a self-analysis will enable the therapist to react more sensitively to clients with transcendent belief systems. More important, it may enable them to actually use those beliefs in the therapeutic relationship. Such a self-analysis of perspective and bias is necessary for anyone doing cross-cultural counseling.

While acknowledging that the client's belief system and concerns in therapy are legitimate, one must not also err in the other direction (especially if the therapist him/herself does not have a transcendent belief system) and over-accept the client's beliefs, especially the dysfunctional aspects of the beliefs. It is the author's contention that belief systems such as Christianity provide a healthy belief structure for coping. It is possible, however, that a dysfunctional client may distort some of those beliefs to fit his or her neurosis. It may be necessary, at times, to challenge a client's beliefs, but this may be most profitably done by asking the client to bring to therapy a statement of beliefs of the religious body and use that as an instrument for such challenging. Similarly, using religious beliefs to avoid issues is also possible. However, this is much more likely after the therapeutic relationship has been established and the client has come to trust the therapist. At that point, the sudden appearance of religious issues when a delicate subject is approached may be an avoidance. The sensitive therapist will realize a sudden withdrawal as an avoidance or resistance. Suspicions and emotional closeness on the part of a client before a therapeutic relationship has been established are better labeled cultural alienation.

REFERENCES

1. Anderson, J. *Cognitive Psychology and its Implications*. San Francisco: W. H. Freeman (1980).
2. Beck, A., Rush, A., Shaw, B., and Emery, G. *Cognitive Therapy of Depression*. New York: Guildford Press (1979).
3. Bergin, A. Psychotherapy and religious values. *Journal of Consulting and Clinical Psychology* 48:95–105 (1980).
4. Bergin. A. E. and Strupp, H. H. *Changing Frontiers in the Science of Psychotherapy*. Chicago: Aldine-Atherton (1972).
5. Bulman, R. and Wortman, C. Attributions of blame and coping in the "real world": Severe accident victims react to their lot. *Journal of Personality and Social Psychology* 35:351–363 (1977).

6. Cavenar, J. and Spaulding, J. Depressive disorders and religious conversions. *The Journal of Nervous and Mental Disease* 165:209–212 (1977).

7. Dimsdale, J. The coping of Nazi concentration camp survivors. *American Journal of Psychiatry* 131:792–797 (1974).

8. Ellis, A. Rational-emotive therapy and cognitive behavior therapy: Similarities and differences. *Cognitive Therapy and Research* 4:325–340 (1980).

9. Franks, J. *Persuasion and Healing*. New York: Shocken (1974).

10. Franks, J. Nature and functions of belief systems. *American Psychologist* 32:555 (1977).

11. Gay, V. *Freud on Ritual: Reconstruction and Critique*. Missoula, MT: Scholars Press (1979).

12. Goldfried, M. Systematic desensitization as training in self-control. *Journal of Consulting and Clinical Psychology* 37:228–234 (1971).

13. Goldfried, M. and Davison, C. *Clinical Behavior Therapy*. New York: Holt, Rinehart and Winston (1976).

14. Goldfried, M., Decenteceo, F., and Weinberg, L. Systematic rational restructuring as a self-control technique. *Behavior Therapy* 5:247–254 (1974).

15. Kazdin, A. Non-specific treatment factors in psychotherapy outcome research. *Journal of Consulting and Clinical Psychology* 47:846–851 (1979).

16. Mahoney, M. *Psychotherapy Process*. New York: Plenum (1980).

17. Mallory, M. *Christian Mysticism Transcending Techniques*. Amsterdam: Van Gorcum Assen (1977).

18. Meichenbaum, D. *Therapist's Manual for Cognitive Behavior Modification*. Unpublished manuscript (1973). Available from Donald Meichenbaum, University of Waterloo, Waterloo, Ontario, Canada, N2G 3LI.

19. Niebuhr, R. *The Nature and Destiny of Man*. New York: Charles Scribner's Sons (1941).

20. Oden, T. *Kergina and Counseling*. New York: Harper & Row (1966).

21. Prince, R. Mystical experience and the certainty of belonging: An alternative to insight and suggestion in psychotherapy. *In*: Cox, R. (Ed.). *Religious Systems and Psychotherapy*. Springfield: Charles Thomas (1973).

22. Prince, R. Variations in psychotherapeutic procedures. *In*: Triandis, H. and Draguns, J. (Eds.). *Handbook of Cross-Cultural Psychotherapy* 6. Boston: Allyn and Bacon (1980).

23. Propst, L. R. The comparative efficacy of religious and non-religious imagery for the treatment of mild depression in religious individuals. *Cognitive Therapy and Research* 4:167–178 (1980).

24. Rosen, C. and Balkwell, C. *Do Impoverished Ethnic Elderly Use Religion as a Coping Mechanism?* Paper presented at the meeting of the American Psychological Association, Montreal (September 1980).

25. Rush, J. and Watkins, J. *Specialized Cognitive Therapy Strategies for Psychologically Naive Depressed Outpatients*. Paper presented at the meeting of the American Psychological Association, San Francisco (August 1977).

26. Sanford, A. *The Healing Light*. New Jersey: Logos (1972).

27. Smith, N. *Barren Winter, Fruitful Spring*. Downers Grove, IL: Inter-Varsity Press (1977).

28. Smith, J. Meditation as psychotherapy: A review of the literature. *Psychological Bulletin* 82:558–564 (1975).

29. Swenson, G., Brady, T., and Edwards, K. *The Effects of Attitude Pretraining on Assertion Training with Christian College Students*. Paper presented at the meeting of the Christian Association of Psychologists, Chicago (April 1978).

In the next chapter, logical learning theory is introduced as a form of logical phenomenology. The concepts of telosponsivity is presented in contrast to the responsivity conception of traditional learning theories. An overview of logical learning theory is then provided. The chapter moves on to consider the three motives to psychotherapy for both client and therapist; i.e., scholarly, ethical, and curative. An interpretation of mental illness in terms of telosponsivity is then provided. Mental health is shown to be the result of satisfactorily helpful precedent premise affirmations, which in turn allow for a more stable and productive lifestyle. Insight is seen as the person's recognition that he/she is an agent personally responsible to some extent for what will occur in the lived future. The last half of the chapter takes up five therapeutic techniques that have been used by logical learning theorists to promote productive changes (re-premisings, re-predications) in a client's telosponses. The techniques of dialectical interpretation, creative grounding, teleological structuring, phenomenal elaboration, and grounds challenging are presented with a typescript excerpt exemplifying their use. The chapter closes with a note on working with children.

6

Logical Learning Theory Applications to Psychotherapeutic Practice

Joseph F. Rychlak, Ph.D.

THE MEANING OF PHENOMENOLOGY

Phenomenology is a "fancy word" to many psychologists, and they often misunderstand. Taken literally, it refers to "the study of phenomena," but then we have to appreciate what "phenomena" means. In a nutshell, phenomena (the singular is "phenomenon") refer to the unique points of view that people hold as they come at their personal world of experience.[5] In a psychotherapy contact, we would have the viewpoint of the client who is seeking help or having trouble, and the viewpoint of the therapist who comes to the therapy sessions with certain premises (beliefs, attitudes, etc.) concerning what it means to be maladjusted, and how therefore to go about helping to correct an unhealthy (unhappy, unrewarding) lifestyle.

This is pretty simple. Everyone has a veiwpoint or "slant" on life. What is so important about this? Well, the very heart of phenomenology as a viewpoint, slant, or "philosophy" is that we must always make an honest effort to see what is going on from the perspective of our client in psychotherapy. Behavioristic therapists usually do not take into consideration the premises (outlooks, veiwpoints) of the client *directly*, though they may do so on a informal basis. Such "verbal reports" have been dismissed as either irrelevant to behavior or of decidedly secondary importance. Admittedly, this attitude is changing with the rise of so-called cognitive behaviorism, but there is still a general presumption that behavioral techniques act "on" the client rather than the client acting "on" the behavioral techniques — or in conjunction (cooperation) with the behavioral techniques — to make them "work" as they do quite intentionally.

The traditional "insight" therapies of a Freudian, Adlerian, Jungian, etc., orientation take a client's viewpoint into consideration but they also have a preconceived theoretical system within which such understanding must be couched. The unique aspect of phenomenology is that it proposes to find out what the *client's* theory about life is, accepting his or her outlook as the most important "determiner" of what will take place in the future. People are seen as agents — freely-willed self-determiners — in most phenomenological theories, at least those which follow a *logical* phenomenology.

We can break phenomenology down into two wings — *sensory* phenomenology and *logical* phenomenology. Sensory phenomenology is the approach that the gestalt psychologists Wertheimer, Köhler, and Koffka advocated. These men were trying to counter what they took to be an *ingenuine* presentation of human experience, as reflected in the mechanistic psychology of their time (see, e.g., Köhler,[7] p. 210). Rather than describing people in terms of antecedents impelling (pushing) consequents across time in a stimulus-response (efficient-cause) sense, the gestaltists proposed spatial conceptions in which the whole (figure-ground) pattern was said to be determining behavior "all at once" *sans* time considerations (i.e., via formal causation; see Rychlak,[13] Chapter 12).

When later these sensory-laden theoretical constructs (laws of organization) were analogized to personality by people such as Lewin and Rogers, we had the person or self described as a *figure* on the grounding *phenomenal field* or *life space*. The self is either organized as a sort of "good gestalt," or as out of whack with the needs of the biological organism. Psychotherapy is concerned with helping the individual regain that sense of internal consistency that a "good gestalt" would imply. Many of the self-contemplative and focusing techniques of today continue in this tradition of sensory phenomenology.

Logical phenomenology does not use the figure-ground conception as a basis of explanation, but rather views the human being as a premiser who affirms meanings and then behaves for their sake by extending the implications of these meanings onto life as it continually arises. Kelly's[6] "psychology of personal constructs" typifies a logical phenomenology, for it takes the person's unique slant into consideration at all times. Note again that the person is an agent who "makes things happen" in his or her life depending upon the conceptualization of events in that life. Here the passage of time is not itself important to the explanation. People enact over time what they have affirmed as a personal construction of their lives to begin with.

LOGICAL LEARNING THEORY VERSUS "OTHER" LEARNING THEORIES

Logical learning theory is a logico-phenomenological approach to the explanation of behavior. All other learning theories in psychology approach the explanation of behavior in the tradition of so-called natural science. This means they try to "account for" behavior by emphasizing what are technically called (via Aristotelian terminology) the *material* and *efficient* causes of things and/or events. If you believe that mental illness is due to the genetic substance transmitted to a person through heredity, you are advancing a material-cause explanation of abnormality. If you believe that people are "shaped" by external influences alone, and that they are only capable of influencing their present behavior thanks to earlier shapings (mediators) which "interact" with external influences today, then you are advancing an efficient-cause explanation of abnormality. These are the two major explanations in psychology today, issuing from the medical model but also from the mechanistic learning theories of classical psychology.

Logical learning theory makes great use of formal-cause description, as do all phenomenologies (refer above), by suggesting that behavior always involves a pattern, style, or "logos" (rationale) in its enactment. People are never pushed along over time but rather "come at" their future lives from moment to moment based upon the patterned meaning of "game plans" or "world views" or "personal constructs." All such concepts get at the beginning premises in a course of behavior! Know the person's patterning of "what leads to what" in life and you will better understand his or her behavior as it unfolds. But now, only through a phenomenological examination from the point of view -- the *introspective* slant (see Rychlak,[14] p. 27) -- of the person can we really know "what leads to what?"

Logical learning theory also places emphasis on the final-cause description of behavior. When we begin talking about a person's premises, his or her slant on the world, we are effectively speaking of the *reasons* for a person's behavior. Traditional learning theories do not accept such explanations because people are not seen as originating sources of control in their behavior. Behavior equals "response(s)," and all responses are themselves the (efficiently-caused) "effects" of antecedent events impelling the person along. Logical learning theory, on the other hand, describes behavior as *telosponsive* rather than merely being responsive. A *telosponse* is the person's taking on (predicating, premising) of meaningful items (images, language terms, comparative judgments, etc.) relating to a purposive referent ("reason") *for the sake of which* behavior is then intended (see Rychlak,[11] p. 283).

The observed motions of efficient causation as we see people "doing things" overtly become instrumental and secondary in this account. We cannot "reduce" formal/final causation to underlying material/efficient causation in this account, because it is the patterning of meaning-extension that determines behavioral motility and not *vice versa*, as is held to be the case in behavioristic learning theories. Rather than being "effects" or "mediators," the meanings encompassed as premises ("reasons") for behavior serve as "causes" of the behavioral action to follow. Premised meanings act as *precedents* (*pre*-cedents as opposed to *ante*cedents), i.e., "coming first in order or arrangement *sans* time considerations.' For example, the precedent meaning in the major premise of a classical syllogism (all men are mortal), when extended to the minor premise (this is a man) results *necessarily* — determinately — in the conclusion (this man is mortal). The logical necessity here is accomplished as a *sequacious* extension of meaning — i.e., 'being slavishly compliant upon" what has gone meaningfully before in order. So, rather than a stimulus-response affair, logical learning theory contends that behavior is a precedent-sequacious affair in which the phenomenal premise of the person is what makes things "happen." Unlike other learning theories, which are mechanistic explanations, logical learning theory is a teleological explanation. Teleologies accept final-cause description (*telos* is the Greek word for "end" or the "reason" that something exists or is taking place).

As a teleology, logical learning theory accepts the validity of free will and personal responsibility.[12] How is it possible for a person to be free of the input coming in from experience, and supposedly being mediated in that efficient-cause fashion so popular today in modern cognitive/behavioristic theoretical accounts? At this point, logical learning theory relies upon the vast history of dialectics.[10, 11] Thanks to the dialectical reasoning capacity human beings enjoy, it is always possible to think oppositionally, to get the implications *not* intended by a message but necessarily implied due to the bipolarity of meanings encompassed in that message, and, through the negation of what is known, turning what "is" into what "is not" or "is not yet, but may be possible." Thus, whereas traditional learning theories are based exclusively upon demonstrative logic (unipolar meaning, linear arrangement, law of contradiction, etc.), logical learning theory adds a dialectical interpretation of logic bringing out the uniquely human side to behavior.

Due to the transcendence made possible by dialectical reasoning, the human being comes to "know that he/she knows," and furthermore, that he/she could be "knowing otherwise" (oppositionally, contradictorily, etc.) that what is currently presumed, assumed, believed in, and so forth. This includes self-doubts, of course. We as humans are constantly faced with the task of having to "take a position" on life. Sometimes it is not easy knowing what to believe about ourselves or about others. It is important to stress that logical learning theory does not posit a self as agent (self-director) "first," and then derive telosponsivity 'second" as the creation of this determining agent. Agency is encompassed in telosponsivity, which, as it begins from birth, takes place "with or without" self-identy (knowing that "we" exist). Dreams are often examples of selfless telosponsivity.

Of course, whether we have self-awareness or not, we seem to need a sense of awareness in our patterned behavior before we can be conditioned. We have to know the (patterned) relationship between the conditioned and unconditioned stimuli or the operant response and the contingent reinforcer before we "get" classically or operantly conditioned.[3] The fact that subjects can manipulate the outcome in reinforcement experiments, *intentionally* subverting the "game plan" (experimental design) of the experimenter,[9] lends credence to the concept of telosponsivity. Rather than undirectionally under the control of an experimenter, subjects as clients in psychotherapy are conforming to what is implied by the patterned meanings of life or dialectically countermanding such implications in their behavior altogether.

MOTIVES TO PSYCHOTHERAPY AND
THE NATURE OF MENTAL ABNORMALITY

Advocates of logical learning theory recognize that there are more than one set of grounds motivating a person *or* a therapist to enter psychotherapy. Aside from economic considerations on the part of the therapist, either role in the therapy contact — therapist or client(s) — can be predicated on three somewhat different intentions (grounding reasons): (1) *scholarly motive*, (2) *ethical motive*, and (3) *curative motive* (see Rychlak,[14] pp. 171-191). The latter (curative) motive is doubtless the most common in that ordinarily there is some complaint about adjustment leveled by or "at" the client, and the therapist frames his or her role as that of a helper, facilitator, modifier, and so forth, in hopes of correcting the situation. Quite often, however, people enter therapy for a self-improvement goal, a desire to know more about themselves in what can only be termed a scholarly sense, for they do not consider themselves to be abnormal in any way. Many therapists enjoy the therapy contact out of a comparable desire to understand others — normals as well as abnormals. The founders of psychoanalysis, Freud and Jung, were moved primarily by scholarly motivations (see Rychlak,[13] Chapter 4). Finally, there are ethical motives to therapy in which mental abnormality is traced to moral infractions, ingenuine interpersonal relationships, or social forces of a repressive nature. The implication drawn here by therapist and client alike is that through non-predatory interpersonal relations both inside and outside of therapy, an improved, more spontaneous lifestyle can be achieved. Traditional Rogerian therapy falls under this latter (ethical) designation (see Chapter 12 of Rychlak[13]).

Each of these motivations must be taken into consideration in working with clients. According to logical learning theory, a therapist who construes his/her role in some one or two of these three motives and disregards the alternative motive of the client is not fulfilling a complete professional role. The client who premises therapy in strictly curative terms and is thrust into an expensively long, scholarly analysis which he or she does not appreciate the reason (intent) for is *not* being served well. The behavior modifier who construes the relationship in exclusively curative terms, disregarding the client's repeated expressions of guilt over some past misbehavior (ethical motive) is needlessly dismissing an opportunity to "treat" the total person.

So, the first thing we want to do as therapists is to be clear on what the motives to therapy are for our clients, and, thereby, to tailor our treatment program according to these phenomenal assumptions. This would seem to imply an *eclectic* approach to therapy, and in a true sense logical learning theory does mesh well with eclecticism in technique and even in theoretical accounts. However, it should be understood that logical learning theory is a highly abstract formulation in which it is possible to subsume and thus account for the workings of *all* psychological forms of psychotherapy. Physical causes of mental illness, stemming from material/efficient-cause functionings are obviously beyond the realm of logical learning theory, except only in the sense that not everyone predicates physical states the same. As a telosponding organism, the human being contributes to all aspects of behavior, including the reactions to foreign agents (drugs, infections, etc.) or the actual loss in biological organs (brain damage, etc.). Such predicational factors should not be lost sight of, even as we should avoid the temptation to claim that "everything" is psychological. Obviously, certain types of maladjustment issue from purely "responsive" reactions to biological/hereditary handicaps.

Coming down now to what mental abnormality, mental illness, or personal maladjustment "is," logical learning theory suggests that the problems stem from inadequate, incorrect, or (self/other) destructively framed premises regarding life. We have shown empirically that hospitalized patients of mixed diagnoses (primarily schizophrenics) tend to learn — to enrich meaningfully — material they fundamentally *dislike* more readily than material they have a liking for.[16] This tendency can also be seen in normal children and young adults who have weak self-images (low ego-strengths, negative self-appraisals).[1, 15] The point is that people who frame life with negative precedent meanings bring these meanings forward sequaciously as they telospond, thereby literally *creating* or *determining* to some extent the circumstances that bring them ultimately into therapy.

This does not mean that abnormals *intend* to become maladjusted, although some probably do this as well. It is just that when the grounding premises for the sake of which behavior is enacted encompass what the person takes to be a negative, disliked, harmful, fearful (and so forth) meaning, it is *this* (negative) meaning that is most probably going to be extended in the future of that life experience. A simple example here would be the party a person goes to expecting to have a miserable time. Though this outcome is not certain by any means, it is probable that this person will fail to consider those steps that might head off a boring or embarrassing evening. As no preparation is made to improve chances for a pleasant evening, the likelihood that the negative expectation will be realized increases. As we get to the more involved problems of life, the so-called neurotic indivdual has many of these attitudes, outlooks, "fears," and so on, and because they more often than not "come true," they are accepted as inevitable curses, certainties, or "sicknesses," which now take over the person's life.

It is not necessary to believe in "the" unconscious to be an advocate of logical learning theory. Surely this is a difficult conception for psychologists to confront. However, to the extent that the logical learning theorist entertains a construct of unconscious behavior he/she approaches the topic in terms of dialectical reasoning. That is, as Jung has taught us (see Rychlak,[13] Chapter 3), a principle of opposites holds sway in the mind, so that meanings (ideas) that might have been affirmed, or the other side of meanings that *were affirmed* in consciousness do not simply "go away." These incidental, contradictory, "incorrect," meaningful implications are likely to be retained in mind even though they may not emerge as full-blown memories. Logical learning theory has taken as an initial assumption (premise) the likelihood that what we call "the" unconscious is a loosely patterned (formally-caused) collection of such meanings (Jung's complex; see Rychlak,[11] p. 357). The human being always has a capacity to shift from one set of premises to another, and, given the prompt of a hypnotist or presumably the emotional impact of certain life traumas, the normal person and hysterical neurotic alike seem capable of bringing to bear these unused and unrecognized premises from out of a "region" of mind seeming to have a life of its own.

It follows from all of this that the thrust of logical learning theory in the consulting room is in the direction of changing and improving a client's life premises or predications. After we are clear as therapists why we are "in" the therapeutic relationship, and after we have satisfied ourselves on the matter of why our clients are "in" the therapeutic relationship, we project our course of treatment in the following steps: (1) Alert the client to his/her telosponsive nature by showing how premised meanings are what life adjustment always depends upon. (2) Give the client practice in framing grounds for life premises, thereby demonstrating the role the client plays in his or her life circumstances. (3) Begin projecting scenarios for life based on these various groundings. (4) Gradually shift the locus of responsibility for these scenarios from the therapist to the client. (5) In more involved cases, supplementary assistance may be required from halfway houses, Alcoholics Anonymous, *in vivo* arrangements with family members, and so on.

The logical learning theorist therefore begins from the (precedent) assumption that, as telosponders, what people need is a responsible, self-accepted premise or system of premises on the basis of which to behave. This is what *insight* amounts to — a recognition of one's own agency and a willingness to accept responsibility for one's life. Too many current insight therapies begin from the assumption that there is "a" reason issuing from the past which is "the" cause of the illness manifested, and, unless this "given" cause is dealt with, a cure will not result. This forces such approaches to concoct an ideological "school of thought," which we know of as Freudian, Adlerian, Rogerian, and so on. According to logical learning theory, each of these schools merely reflects a different set of premised meanings regarding the nature of human experience. Any one of them or some combination could serve to frame a given person's life adequately — or the person might concoct a suitable premise system entirely his or her own.

It is the logical learning theorist's position that even in behavioristic techniques this kind of insight arises. In what is clearly a teleological fashion, clients are instructed to carefully outline a symptom picture, and, based on this study, to arrange a sequence of graded steps (formal-cause plan) aimed at solving a specific problem; and then, they carry out this plan by behaving for its sake (final cause). Though behaviorists overlook this telic side to their work, as phenomenologists we would want to know just how relevant this ("insightful") *schematic for problem solving* is to the actual therapeutic outcome achieved. Behaviorists are as glued to the past in trying to find "the" shaping (efficient-) causes of the present adjustment problem as are the traditional insight therapies. In doing so, they overlook the equally plausible suggestion that it is not the so-called reshaping that effects the cure in the present but the more satisfactory premise "for the sake of which" the client begins to behave once a "program" (formal-cause plan) is put into effect.

THERAPEUTIC PRINCIPLES AND TECHNIQUES

As noted above, logical learning theorists are eclectic when it comes to the use of techniques in the therapeutic relationship. The single, unifying conceptualization guiding our work is that we continually look at the therapeutic process through the eyes of the client, trying to understand the client's phenomenal perspective and in the process, encouraging the client to appreciate his/her telosponsive human nature. We consider the therapist to be an expert in teleology, and expect him/her to behave in ways that will promote client insight of the type mentioned above — i.e., acquiring an appreciation of one's personal, albeit frequently limited, responsibility in the course of life events. To this end, the following five techniques are likely to be employed.

Technique of Dialectical Interpretation

Clients are never led to believe that there is one and only one "answer" or "explanation" for their difficulty. If they arrive at such a position in time, we make no effort to attack their conviction. Our point is merely to provide the client with an open intellectual climate concerning the possible causes of his or her difficulty. As a general practice, whenever an interpretation is made, the therapist offers — to the best of his/her ability — an alternative explanation of what might be involved in the case. Since all alternatives begin in seeing dialectical opposites to what "is," we have called this technique a strategy of dialectical interpretation. The client is led in this way to appreciate that psychotherapy need not result in a "final word" concerning his/her problem, but that what *is* essential is that a suitable framework of meaning be devised that makes sense to the client.

Problems of *resistance* are reduced in this approach, but, of course, they are never completely avoided. There will always be disagreements between therapist and client, and as the client is the person "on the spot" in most of the therapy discussions, it is probable that he/she will reject certain interpretations even when the evidence for making them is sound. The logical learning theorist is never insincere in leveling interpretations, of course. If a good deal of evidence supports one interpretation over another, the logical weight of such arguments must be presented openly. Invariably, they will have their impact no matter what either client or therapist thinks about them as a desirable account or explanation. Signs of resistance are often merely signs of recognition and the affirmation of meanings that are distasteful. It serves little purpose to press the client in hopes of getting him/her to state aloud what is surely being registered mentally. An example of dialectical interpretation might be:

> *Client:* I had this "funny" feeling toward my father at that time, sort of a mixture of disgust and fear. I suppose I resented him for not letting me handle that sale myself. I could have done it.
>
> *Therapist:* Yeah, I suppose there's grounds for resentment, all right. Of course, that fear you felt might just suggest you were less sure of making the sale than you thought.
>
> *Client:* (Resisting) No, I could have done it. I think he scared me out of being more insistent right from the start.
>
> *Therapist:* Well, maybe so. I was just . . .
>
> *Client:* (Interrupting) Of course, I admit to some relief in not having had to handle the sale.
>
> *Therapist:* Right. But, in any case, your father could have given you more freedom there to develop the sale, surely . . .

Note how, in this instance, the therapist begins by questioning the client's assigning of complete responsibility to the father's domination. When, however, the client recognizes his personal trepidation about having to make the business deal, the therapist returns to the client's initial claim against the father's domination. The effective therapist need not "know" which of these interpretations is correct. He/she merely uses the client's own words to explore the bipolarities they always contain, encouraging or inviting the client to look at all sides. Thus, as the client is saying one thing, the therapist strives to see the opposite implication in this statement, and then to incorporate both what the client has claimed (thesis) and the opposite (antithesis) in his/her (the therapist's) understanding, never fixing for all time on one side or the other. If the client spontaneously incorporates *both* implications (synthesis), then this is usually considered a forward movement in therapy. For example, the client above might have synthesized things by saying: "I guess some of the fear I thought I had of my father, and some of that disgust too, was actually meant for myself."

Technique of Creative Grounding

If it is true that all behavior is predicated in the act of telosponsivity, then what we must hope to do is perfect the client's ability to ground his/her behavior *from this time forward* in life because that is what a "cure" always comes down to. We try to help the client to think about the grounding *reasons* that are manifested or enacted in his/her behavior. In traditional psychotherapy, a knowledge of such groundings is acquired through examination of the client's childhood. The logical learning theorist may follow this tactic if it is suitable to the case in question. However, some clients prove to be unwilling or incapable of exploring their life history; or they find it pointless to examine their dreams, daily fantasies, and so on. In such cases, the writer has often used the device of taking specific, concrete examples from the past week of a client's life and asking him/her to find *reasons* for the behavior. It is especially helpful to take up "problem" behaviors and then refer to this as an "excuse-making" exercise, as follows.

Therapist: (To male client) You know, when you come right down to it, it isn't what we "do" in life that gets us into trouble, it's the *reasons* we can give for doing what we do. If you have a good excuse, you can usually be forgiven or at least "understood." Now, about this "row" you had last week at work, what is your excuse for having it? In fact, I am going to ask you to think up at least two excuses.

Client: Whattaya mean, "excuses?" I don't need no excuse. That guy is a punk! Everyone knows that. When he took that wrench from my tool kit, I decked him.

Therapist: So, your excuse for decking him was — what? "Straightening out" a punk, or punishing a theft?

Client: (Resistively) Come on! You know how it is!

Therapist: Yeah, I know how it is, but do *you* know how it is?

Client: Whattaya mean?

Therapist: Let's "level" and admit that there was more than one excuse for slugging that guy going on here in your mind — the one you gave to the boss, and the other one you didn't bother to mention. Could there be yet another excuse for your decking this guy?

Gradually, the therapist would begin to — in the language of the client — bring home the fact that excuses are like reasons, and reasons are the meanings we always try to create in our lives as we go along. The problem with an excuse is that it is a reason made up after the fact, after out behavior is over. As a result, excuses are like interpretations — they might be true or half true, and they might be false or half false. We will never know for certain, because the past is past. We can only be certain about our futures, because we always make our futures "happen." So, the trick is to turn our excuse-making exercises into a future-oriented plan to ensure control and, even more important, to arrive at some end-point of our own choosing. The therapist would structure this as follows.

Therapist: (To same client as above) Well, now that we've had some practice making up excuses for your behavior, and we agree that there are always a lot of them around to use as we prefer, suppose we begin doing the same thing about the future?

Client: How so?

Therapist: Well, I don't think we've been trying here to learn how to lie to ourselves. I mean, people make excuses all the time after they have done some damn fool thing. The question is: Do you want to go on playing these excuse-making games with yourself, or do you want to try and figure out some clear reasons for your behavior even *before* you act, and then try to make them "happen?"

Client: Get the excuses first . . . the reasons . . .

Therapist: Get them worked into a plan.

Client: Sort of a "game plan" on life, huh?

Therapist: Yeah, sort of. You can be your own Vince Lombardi and write your own plays.

Client: Well, naturally, I'd like to have my head on a bit straighter. That's why I'm here, doc. So, let's see what "gives."

At this point, the therapist could use any of a number of traditional devices to engender a sense of grounding in the client — role play, laying out a behavior modification program, contractual commitments, and so forth. The fundamental difference between a logical learning theorist's approach in the use of these techniques and other approaches is that we always frame the course of events in light of the client's perspective (introspectively), pointing out again and again that the nature of the client's future is always potentially far more certain than the nature of the client's past, because it is the client who always *creates that future.* On what basis will that future be built? Therapy is aimed at helping the client to build a future of personal satisfaction.

Technique of Teleological Structuring

Occasionally, particularly with rather maladjusted (psychotic) individuals, a very concrete technique is employed to structure the telic nature of mental life and the problems in living that result when this is not properly appreciated. A common structuring of this type would be as follows.

> *Therapist:* (To client) You know, most of us, when we get emotionally "sick," think that this is like our other illnesses. I mean, if you get measles, something happens to you "yesterday," a bug infects you or something, and then "today" you are sick. Well, mental illness is really not like this. Mental illness is more like a "sickness tomorrow." We can maybe find the reasons for why we got mentally or emotionally sick by looking around in the past, but when it comes right down to it, we are presently sick because of how we are facing up to life "from now on." We have to begin working to make our tomorrow a healthy one.

Often it is necessary for the maladjusted individual to affiliate with a group — a halfway house, community organization, church group, etc. — in order to assist in the realistic planning of future steps toward total recovery. A structuring along the lines of the above helps the client to frame his or her problem teleologically. It can be given preliminary to the working out of a desensitization program. Wolpe[18] instructs his clients preliminary to reciprocal inhibition a procedure readily framed in a dialectical fashion, incidentally! — in terms of the stimuli that supposedly "evoke" the neurotic response. He uses as an instructive vignette the "big, black stove" story in which a child may be burned by this household item only to be fearful of this as well as other such objects from then on. Although a logical learning theorist might use Wolpean relaxation techniques to counteract a symptom, the structuring of therapy in this case would be quite different. Rather than being conditioned to events without intention, the client would be instructed as follows.

> *Therapist:* (To client) We are going to help you break up a pattern of understanding that you now have about what it means to be in high places [phobia]. We begin on the assumption that some time ago — maybe in your childhood — you convinced yourself that you could not survive in some spot where you were at the time that was "high up" — at least to you. It could have been on a tabletop in your childhood. We don't have to figure out exactly when this took place, but if we get an idea about when it did happen as we go along, that would be just fine. But what is important is

that once you decided [premise affirmation], "I'm gonna die up here," that meaning was formed [formal cause] into the meaning of height. Maybe the meaning wasn't "dying" but some other fear, like "being caught" or even "being punished." Then, just like when we go to a party expecting to have a lousy time and, sure enough, we have a lousy time, you expected to have that same old feeling about height and high places – and, sure enough, you had it. In fact, it got progressively worse over time. This is all a perfectly understandable thing. Human beings are like this. We continually try to anticipate what might happen in our lives, and our fears go forward in time this way too. In fact, it isn't wrong to say that emotional sicknesses like yours are always "sicknesses tomorrow." They are always being made possible in our future because of our present expectations.

From this point forward, what the logical learning theorist does to reciprocally inhibit symptom manifestation may be exactly the same as what Wolpe does. The point is: We do not have to accept the mechanistic interpretation of the empirical data on which reciprocal inhibition has been based in order to make use of this clinical tool. As we have noted above, the more we learn about the nature of reinforcement and its accompanying phenomena such as generalization, extinction, and inhibition, the more we are convinced that the person's awareness and intentionality play a central role in all behavioral techniques of therapy.[3] Why not make use of this empirically-based knowledge by assigning more responsibility to the client from the outset of therapy?

Technique of Phenomenal Elaboration

Each of the complex patterns of stimuli (formal cause) encompassed meaningfully by a client's predications for the sake of which behavior is intended (final cause) can be phenomenally examined. Clients are not merely "inputting" information, they are framing it, evaluating it, and then affirming that which they find meaningful and most advantageous. This implies that everything that takes place in therapy, including the actions of the therapist, the therapeutic program that has been laid out, and even the ultimate results achieved in helping a client to better adjustment can be examined phenomenally by that client. A logical learning theorist who had just worked out a behavior modification program with a client would therefore encourage the client to give his/her personal phenomenal understanding of what is taking place. Not only might we find (in the spirit of dialectical interpretation; refer to the above) that such spontaneous commentary would lead to an alteration in therapeutic planning, but the relationship would be strengthened in that we would be essentially validating the client as an independent identity and an agent in the process of change.

Such phenomenal commentary by the client — saying what he/she spontaneously thinks, feels, fears, etc., about the total procedure — is encouraged by the logical learning theorist at all times. It is viewed as an antidote to the development of resistance as well as a positive cultivation of the relationship. On the other side of the coin, the therapist can also step out of his/her role and express a personal opinion, a vague feeling of apprehension, or whatever seems troubling or reassuring at any point in the therapeutic contact. At times, role-playing may be used to facilitate understanding of the therapist-client relationship, in which a reversal of roles is attempted. Following such brief enactments (lasting no more than a few minutes), an examination of the relative contributions of each person "in role" and "out of role" to what just took place can be effected. One of the more interesting uses of phenomenal elaboration takes place after some definite step toward improvement has occurred. The following excerpt is from a therapy series in which a male client had in the *previous* session effected a successful flooding/implosion,[17] extinguishing a mock heart attack with extreme death fears as anxiety drained from him. The therapist invites the client to phenomenally elaborate on what took place in the previous session, as follows.

Therapist: Well, I'm glad to hear that you have had so much noticeable relief . . .

Client: No kidding, I haven't had *one* episode [anxiety attack experienced as an impending heart attack] this past week.

Therapist: Great.

Client: Do you realize that's the first clear week in over six years?

Therapist: Tremendous. That's great. But, now . . . I wonder if you could sort of "go back" to last week and tell me as best as you can what was going through your mind as we lived through those three episodes [i.e., three implosions of anxiety, fear of heart attack, death].

Client: What?

Therapist: Just like in the past, when we tried to see how each of us "makes things happen" in our lives, I now want you to kind of "fill me in" on what you were mentally going through as I encouraged you to "let go" in those attacks last week.

Client: Funny, I never thought of that. That never would have occurred to me. Let's see . . . I know that I was scared as hell. Lucky I was so tired, or I don't think it would have worked.

Therapist: Why not?

Client: Because I just had this "oh, hell" or "I don't give a damn" attitude. I just figured when you asked me that stuff —

Therapist: To let the feelings come and learn "once and for all" that you wouldn't die?

Client: Yeah, I had this feeling of "who cares?" Then I began to kind of sense that it was coming — the feeling . . . Kinda scares me now to think of it, but I'm okay. I know I started to sweat . . . breathe heavy.

Therapist: You sure did. To be honest, I got sort of scared myself just before the first release you experienced. I kept telling myself the [medical] doctors had cleared you [i.e., no heart problems].

Client: (Laughs) Well . . . then it all came. I kind of had this feeling of "isn't this nuts?" It all took place so fast I can't be sure, but that kind of feeling was there too — "isn't this nuts?"

Therapist: I wonder what the "this" referred to — your feelings of anxiety or the things we were doing?

Client: I honestly don't know, but right now my feeling is it was meant for the feelings, the fears . . . that shuddering or whatever it was that I came out with. Anyhow, when you got two more of those shudders and gasps out of me I was thinking, "This can't go on" or, "How many times can this go on?" or something like that. I guess I was just surprised or shocked or something like that.

Therapist: You really had a sense of "watching" yourself [transcendence] like that?

Client: Well, I didn't set out to. Like I say, this never really would've occurred to me — to rehash things like this. But, yeah, I think I did have a sense of watching myself go through it [transcendence].

The therapy session continues from this point forward, in which it is made clear to the client that we human beings do have this transcendent capacity to "watch" ourselves behave, to "know that we are knowing," and it is through such understandings that we probably effect our changes in behavior. Rather than using some form of "dammed-up" libido, drive, or tension interpretation of behavior, the logical learning theorist contends that it is the premised expectation (assumption, belief, fear) that is of primary fault in literally generating the physiological reaction (heart attack/anxiety) as a sequacious meaning extention. The client anticipates the worst, is sensitized to expect the worst, and, invariably the worst takes place. Earlier interpretations that have traced the probable reasons for why the original pseudo-heart attacks occurred have already been made. The client has this understanding, but the anxiety attack *per se* has become functionally autonomous of such "dynamics" and hence must be dealt with in its own right. The technical terms telosponse, precedent, sequacious, etc., need not be used to explain symptom manifestations such as these, but with certain clients who choose to read on the topic in any case, the interpretations actually encompass the terminology of logical learning theory.

In knowing that he could call into question the number of times a symptom might be encouraged (by the therapist) to appear, the client discovered at first hand that even he did not phenomenally believe that it was *inevitably* his fate to suffer the anxiety attacks. Coupled with the earlier interpretations mentioned above, and confronted with the fact that he was not dying, the further interpretation was rather easily made that he had probably *at that very point in therapy* re-premised (re-predicated) things: "I don't *have* to have these attacks. They do *not* lead to death." It is our feeling that Frankl's[4] technique of paradoxical intention worked precisely this way — i.e., due to the dialectical transcendence made possible when the client recognizes his personal role in symptom scheduling. Knowing that one can direct the symptom's occurrence leads to a changed attitude *vis a vis* the inevitability of its appearance.

Technique of Challenging the Grounds

The last technique we will consider is usually employed late in therapy, after a client has been accustomed to recognizing his/her telosponsive nature, and has settled on some grounds (life plan, philosophy of life, religious orientation, etc.) for the sake of which life will be carried forward. Considerable time is devoted to a review of these grounds, because unless the client is totally confident and prepared to put up with criticism for holding to a valued position, the likelihood of therapy succeeding is greatly diminished.

It is quite popular today to stress egalitarian values in behavior, suggesting that everyone do what he or she finds personally satisfying: "Let everyone decide personally how to behave." Though such statements are reassuring to many who express them, the truth is that even when a hundred different people each personally decide for themselves how to behave, what to seek in life, and so forth, there are *never* a hundred different groundings being affirmed as the "that" (reason) for the sake of which such decisions are being rendered. People are a lot more alike than different and for any facet of life one can care to name there are usually only a handful of grounding assumptions that logically relate to the point at issue. What is most dangerous is when a person who says, "Let everyone decide for him/herself," actually employs this dictum defensively, to *avoid* looking at such grounds.

The person who is tugged from one stand to another on life, shifting the grounds for the sake of which his/her behavior is being intended is the person who complains of being *in conflict* with the confused pattern that such inconsistency always generates. Or, we have the totally demoralized person who is completely without a grounding set of values, commitments, or ambition for the future. Sometimes the person has a clear life plan, but knows full well that it is grounded on a narrow, selfish, or harmfully predatory approach to others. The resultant confusion, conflict, sense of boredom, self-hatred, and desperation is then laid at the foot of circumstance, the sins of others (parents, teachers, etc.), a heartless society, and so forth. Without denying the truth or partial truth of such claims, the greater truth is that at present the individual is still excuse-making (refer to the above) and a more creative grounding is called for. That is, there is absolutely no evidence in psychological research to suggest that such past wrongs against the person cannot be overcome. Indeed, if *any* psychotherapy is to succeed, they *must* be overcome.

In the typical encounter group, or the meetings of various "anonymous" organizations (alcoholics, drug-abusers, over-eaters, etc.), or even the expiation exercises of religion (confession, giving witness, etc.), the basic vehicle of change is always an open admission of the sincere, true, honest grounds for behavior. Mowrer's[8] integrity therapy has emphasized this side to abnormal behavior. In a more directly religious context, Bergin[2] has recently begun to stress this aspect of effective psychotherapy. In the logical learning theory application to psychotherapy, this matter of defending one's grounds is approached in the last phase of a therapy series, and the extent to which this becomes a full-blown "philosophy of life" examination depends upon the nature of the presenting complaint. A typical excerpt from such a discussion follows.

Therapist: (To female client) So you think you can begin managing things alone pretty soon?

Client: Yes, doctor, I don't think I'll be having those depressions anymore . . . at least, not the bad ones. I'll have my ups and downs, of course.

Therapist: And the difference being?

Client: Difference?

Therapist: Between now and before you came in?

Client: Well, I known that I was setting myself up for a fall all of the time, before . . . you know, what we talked about!

Therapist: Yeah, I probably know. But I want to be sure you know and that you aren't just saying nice things now because you are feeling better. If I asked you a question like, "What makes you think you won't set yourself up again in the future?", what would you say?

Client: I'm not going to do that because I'm not going to expect as much from myself. If the kids don't do as well in school, I'm not going to be so guilty. I'm going to do my best, but then it's up to them.

Therapist: Come on, you're human . . . you'll start thinking again, "Where have I failed?"

Client: Oh sure, but I will also say, "What purpose does that "Where have I failed?" question serve?" — just like you taught me to do. Then,

I'll see what we've seen here so many times — my self-doubts were due to my negative assumptions about myself.

Therapist: So, you've changed your assumptions about yourself, have you?

Client: Well, I hope so. Are you kidding me or something?

Therapist: No, but I imagine in the future you will have failures, or someone will start getting on your case, pulling you down.

Client: Well, sure . . . we have to expect those things. But I think I have a better understanding of all that now. People sometimes do that because they are trying to go "one up" on you for their own reasons. I'm not going to let them use me that way.

Therapist: That's very good, Irma, but now suppose you run into a situation like this: Suppose I'm a teacher, and I call you up on the phone and say something like this . . .

At this point, the therapist frames a brief, spontaneous role-play in which this overly scrupulous mother is pressured to feel responsible for a problem one of her children is having in school. How will the client react in the role-play? Will she be clear enough on her grounding assumptions (self-definition, personal values, etc.) to deal with the implied threat? Can she admit to some shortcoming but also see the other side of the coin and perceive her child's and the teacher's possible contribution to the situation? These kinds of issues would be developed and the point of the technique of challenging the grounds held by the client would be to see if they are genuinely held, and firmly based. In effect, the issue comes down to one of being non-defensive, self-accepting, and then also being sufficiently aggressive to present arguments favoring oneself in life. So long as the client lacks deception and is trying to do the best she is capable of, and accepts this as genuinely her level of competence, there can be no vulnerability in the sense experienced before therapy when she was carrying the weight of the world on her shoulders. Whenever possible, in such closing exchanges with a client, the use of humor is employed. A certain joking banter at this point helps the client obtain a sense of perspective, an expectation that all will not go perfectly in the future, but that life plays tricks on everyone and sometimes it is best to laugh these setbacks off.

It is true that in a more complex case these examinations of grounds can prove very time-consuming, and it is not advisable to become enmeshed in a morass of self-examination. There is no formula that can be written here, but by and large it is the logical learning theorist's intent to focus therapy directly on the person's actual life experience. We are not seeking to play the role of philosopher, theologian, or guru. If a grounding assumption concerning life cannot be aimed specifically at some lived experience (as, at Irma's self-doubts over her competence as a mother), then it is probably not helpful to engage in such exercises. That is, anyone of us could spend hours and hours discussing the meaning of life, basic assumptions regarding why we are on this planet, where we may or may not be heading, and so forth. But such issues are rarely directly tied to the client's presenting difficulties (curative motive) even though they may be tangentially connected to them (scholarly motive).

As a rule of thumb, the logical learning theorist focuses on the presenting complaint and/or other problems in living as likely candidates for grounds challenging. Since we take money from clients for such help, we focus on the curative motive in this context above all. However, our scholarly motives play a close second because we believe that it is essential for human beings to recognize their telosponsive nature if a continuing adjustment to life is to be effected. Ethical considerations are brought in quite naturally as an extension of our telosponsive construct. If behavior is grounded as telosponsivity requires, then we must consider the goodness or badness of such grounding. Put another way, grounds must invariably take us to the realm of values. Values are those most abstract (hence, basic) of all assumptions made by the individual, encompassing meanings that are never challenged. But, in so recognizing the role of values in behavior, logical learning theory does not defend "a" system of values (except only those which frame the approach to the client now being elucidated, of course). We might at this point paraphrase Kelly's[6] familiar "psychology of personal constructs" and say that logical learning theory is a "psychology of personal values" in which each person is given the integrity to frame his or her own beginning assumptions (i.e., values) in life. This integrity is not easily appreciated by the client, and once it is pointed out the responsibility to examine one's values becomes awesome. But if a client comes to defend values which the therapist cannot espouse, so long as these groundings lead to a more suitable adjustment in the client's estimation, the logical learning theorist does not consider this outcome a failure.

A NOTE ON WORK WITH CHILDREN

A closing note on work with children seems in order. We have not used examples from child therapy, but it should not be assumed that an examination of life premises is impossible to accomplish with children. We have found that, if handled properly, it is possible to do phenomenal elaboration with even quite young children. Of course, the language level must be very simple, and the elaboration can be conducted in a playful way, occasionally through the use of dolls portraying the family milieu within which the child is being administered an operant-conditioning "program" of behavioral manipulation. We are likely to assume that the child is unaware of this environmental intervention simply because we never test for it. However, dream analysis or doll-play techniques very often provide us with quite the reverse impression. Often, older children can state clearly what is taking place in their "programs" of reinforcement, which are, after all, formal-cause patterns for the sake of which the child behaves. The logical learning theorist discusses telosponsivity with the parents of a child in therapy, and tries to promote an understanding of the child's behavior in light of such telic considerations even as the parents are being instructed in how to carry out the schedule of reinforcement/non-reinforcement.

Here again, we must recognize our ethico-scholarly biases. We draw these conclusions, we make these affirmations concerning human nature *not* on the basis of some non-scientific ideology, but rather on a careful examination of the research literature.[11]   As teleologists, logical learning theorists continually guard against conveying a machine-model of human nature, knowing as we do that this model simply fails to meet the empirical facts! Moreover, it is our feeling that a machine-model of behavior is detrimental to mental health — at least in the sense of ascribing all problems in living to the breakdown of a machine, or to inadequate adjustments of a machine-like apparatus in which the person has no role to play except as a "responder" to initial inputs and then a mediator of later interactions. The logical learning theorist believes that to further mental health it is essential that we appreciate the teleological nature of human beings, and, to this end, he/she will continue to work both inside and outside the consulting room.

REFERENCES

1. August, C. J., Rychlak, J. F., and Felker, D. W. Affective assessment, self-concept, and the verbal learning styles of fifth-grade children. *Journal of Educational Psychology* 67: 801–806 (1975).
2. Bergin, A. E. Psychotherapy and religious values. *Journal of Consulting and Clinical Psychology* 48:95–105 (1980).
3. Brewer, W. F. There is no convincing evidence for operant or classical conditioning in adult humans. *In*: Weimer, W. B. and Palermo, D. S. (Eds.). *Cognition and the Symbolic Processes*. Hillsdale, NJ: Lawrence Erlbaum (1974).
4. Frankl, V. Paradoxical intention: A logotherapeutic technique. *American Journal of Psychotherapy* 14:520–534 (1960).
5. Husserl, E. *Phenomenology and the Crisis of Philosophy* (translated by Q. Lauer). New York: Harper & Row Torchbooks (1965).
6. Kelly, G. A. *The Psychology of Personal Constructs*. New York: Norton (1955).
7. Köhler, W. Psychological remarks on some questions of anthropology. *In*: Henle, M. (Ed.). *Documents of Gestalt Psychology*. Berkeley, CA: University of California Press (1961).
8. Mowrer, O. H. *The Crisis in Psychiatry and Religion*. New York: D. Van Nostrand (1961).
9. Page, M. M. Demand characteristics and the verbal operant conditioning experiment. *Journal of Personality and Social Psychology* 23:372–378 (1972).
10. Rychlak, J. F. (Ed.). *Dialectic: Humanistic Rationale for Behavior and Development*. Basel, Switzerland: S. Karger AG (1976).
11. Rychlak, J. F. *The Psychology of Rigorous Humanism*. New York: Wiley-Interscience (1977).
12. Rychlak, J. F. *Discovering Free Will and Personal Responsibility*. New York: Oxford University Press (1979).

13. Rychlak, J. F. *Introduction to Personality and Psychotherapy: A Theory-Constructed Approach* (2nd Ed.). Boston: Houghton Mifflin (1981).

14. Rychlak, J. F. *A Philosophy of Science for Personality Theory* (2nd Ed.). Huntington, NY: Krieger (1981).

15. Rychlak, J. F., Carlsen, N. L., and Dunning, L. P. Personal adjustment and the free recall of material with affectively positive or negative meaningfulness. *Journal of Abnormal Psychology* 83:480–487 (1974).

16. Rychlak, J. F., McKee, D. B., Schneider, W. E., and Abramson, Y. Affective evaluation in the verbal learning styles of normals and abnormals. *Journal of Abnormal Psychology* 77:247–257 (1971).

17. Stampfl, T. G. Implosive therapy: The theory, the subhuman analogue, the strategy, and the technique. *In*: Armitage, S. G. (Ed.). *Behavior Modification Techniques in the Treatment of Emotional Disorders*. Battle Creek, MI: Veterans Administration (1966).

18. Wolpe, J. *Psychotherapy by Reciprocal Inhibition*. Stanford, CA: Stanford University Press (1958).

The transpersonal orientation in psychotherapy is defined by the context, the content, and the process of therapy. The context is established by the beliefs, values, and attitudes of the therapist. A transpersonal context emphasizes the centrality of consciousness and self-awareness in shaping experience. The content of therapy is determined by the client, and consists of anything in the client's experience that he or she brings to therapy. A transpersonal approach seeks a balanced integration of physical, emotional, mental, and spiritual aspects of well-being, and values transpersonal experiences as potentially healing and contributing to human growth and development when appropriately integrated.

In the following chapter, specific techniques that may be employed in addition to traditional therapeutic approaches are discussed; these techniques emphasize training awareness and expanding self-knowledge. Specific clinical cases are given to illustrate some of the techniques described, and instructions for developing awareness of context and facilitating disidentification from constricting self-concepts are provided. Finally, the limitations and potential applications of transpersonal psychotherapy are reviewed.

7

Transpersonal Psychotherapy

Frances Vaughan, Ph.D. and Seymour Boorstein, M.D.

By their own theories of human nature psychologists have the power of elevating or degrading that same nature. Debasing assumptions debase human beings; generous assumptions exalt them.

Gordon Allport

Transpersonal psychology can be defined as the study of human consciousness. It is that branch of psychology that includes the realm of the human spirit, and attempts to integrate physical, emotional, mental, and spiritual aspects of well-being in a holistic approach to health maintenance. Transpersonal psychotherapy is growth-oriented and can be considered an open-ended endeavor aimed at facilitating human development toward wholeness and expanding awareness beyond the limits implied by most traditional Western models of mental health. In the process of therapy, a transpersonal therapist may employ traditional therapeutic techniques as well as innovative methods for training awareness derived from Eastern consciousness disciplines. Such methods may include meditation and other exercises for developing self-knowledge and training attention. However, transpersonal therapy is not defined only by techniques. It is also defined by the beliefs and attitudes of the therapist, which establish the *context* of therapy, as well as the *process* and *content* of specific therapeutic sessions.

A transpersonal approach to therapy presupposes certain values and attitudes on the part of the therapist that are based on a view of human nature that considers human beings to be capable of sustained psychological development throughout life, and holds impulses toward spirtual growth to be basic to full realization of human potential. It is assumed that a healthy person is capable of experiencing the full range of emotions while remaining relatively detached from those aspects of personal melodrama that contribute to neurotic disorders. It is also assumed that, in addition to satisfying basic needs for physical survival and emotional needs for healthy psychological functioning, higher needs for self-realization and transcendence must also be met for full functioning at optimum levels of health. Beyond self-actualization, as described by Abraham Maslow,[14] lies the potential for self-transcendence, and questions of identity and self-concept may be central issues in transpersonal psychotherapy.

From a transpersonal point of view, every client has within him or her the capacity for self-healing. One of the aims of therapy is to enable the client to take responsibility for himself or herself in the world, and learn to take charge of the continuing process of growth and development in an optimum way. This implies the conscious acquisition of skills as well as self-awareness and self-determination. The client may thus be empowered to meet his/her physical, emotional, mental, and spiritual needs appropriately. A transpersonal approach does not espouse a particular religious belief, but emphasizes the importance of questioning beliefs and recognizing the fundamental role of beliefs in shaping experience. Unconsciously held beliefs about the nature of self and reality may not only contribute to pathology, but may also contribute to reestablishing inappropriate habits of response even when behavioral treatment may prove successful. While acknowledging the influence of enviornment in addition to intra-psychic factors contributing to disturbance and pathology, a transpersonal approach encourages the recognition that the person also shapes the environment, and that it is possible to transcend conditioning and attain the state that, in Eastern spiritual traditions, is called liberation. Recognizing the subjective nature of limiting beliefs, the client may be enabled to let go of constricting identifications and thus accelerate the process of healing psychological conflicts.

CREATING A TRANSPERSONAL CONTEXT

A transpersonal context in psychotherapy can be established by any therapist who regards him/herself as having a transpersonal orientation in life. The therapist who has personally explored the transpersonal domain will undoubtedly be influenced by whatever views of reality and human beings he or she holds to be self-evident. These are precisely the beliefs that need to be brought to awareness and questioned in attempting to establish an optimum context for psychotherapy. A therapist who held the assumptions outlined above to be self-evident could investigate the foundations of those statements, thus recognizing the relative nature of any position, and acknowledging his or her own part in creating the world view that colors his or her own experience. If a therpist does not sub-scribe to such assumptions, he or she would probably not choose to work as a transpersonal therapist.

A transpersonal orientation does not seek to invalidate any other approach, but simply to emphasize the importance of being aware of the underlying values implicit in any therapeutic approach. As Wilber suggests in *The Spectrum of Consciousness,*[21] different therapeutic appraoches are addressed to different levels of the spectrum, and are therefore appropriate at various times for various people, depending on the particular problem in question. The appropriateness of specific techniques for different levels of consciousness will be discussed in greater detail in the section on content. A transpersonal context, however, pre-supposes the inclusion of all other levels, rather than exclusion. A transpersonal approach is, by definition, an *expansion* of the field of psychology to include spiritual concerns. It is not an attempt to provide a substitute for other dimen-sions of psychotherapy.

A transpersonal context suggests that we limit ourselves by our beliefs, and that we live in a very restricted circle of our potential being. We are in the habit of using a very small portion of our possible consciousness, and optimum health and well-being requires a larger context than that which we usually construct for ourselves.

How can we expand our vision to allow it tc be more inclusive? One way is to look at what some of the spiritual traditions offer as possible points of view regarding what can be expected from training awareness. The power of the mind to create experience cannot be overestimated. A saying of the Buddha illustrates the point: "We are what we think. All that we are arises with our thoughts. With our thought we make the world."[8]

It is common knowledge that as clients improve in psychotherapy they are better able to take responsibility for themselves and their lives, and they shift away from blaming and feeling victimized in the direction of self-determination. The ability to take responsibility for one's thoughts and feelings as well as behav-ior appears to be a further step in the direction of heath. A transpersonal context might be expressed as follows.

I am responsible for what I see.
I choose the feelings I experience, and I decide
upon the goal I would achieve.
And everything that seems to happen to me
I ask for, and recieve as I have asked.[1]

A clinical case of Boorstein's that illustrates working in this context is that of Linda, a 36-year-old housewife who came for treatment because of frequent epi-sodes of crying over almost anything (especially slights).

She had no conscious awareness of how angry she was toward her mother, who had given her "room and board, but little else." She was in terror of displeasing any possible source of affection and caring and therefore was always "nice." Her crying and feeling sorry for herself protected her from being aware of how angry she was, and was also a partial release of her aggression, although disguised. I felt it was necessary to resolve the infantile fears that kept Linda from letting herself feel her anger. Toward this end, the traditional psychoanalytic approach was used, in which the patient's defenses against the repressed transference rage were interpreted. Linda then was able to begin to express her anger outwardly and was therefore able also to stop the crying. As Ken Wilbur[22] would explain this, she expanded her conscious boundaries to include those aspects of her unconscious or shadow that she didn't like or was frightened of. In traditional therapy, once Linda had become aware of the infantile rage and expressed it in the transference for a while, "working it through," she eventually (it was hoped) would come to see her mother in a more reasonable light as having done the best she was able to do under the circumstances. However, I felt that with Linda, once the affect became conscoius, a lighter transpersonal approach permitted the rage to be metabolized more rapidly and in fact gave further impetus to continuing work in a transpersonal mode. At some point, while Linda was raging about her anger toward her mother, I was able to quietly ask, "Then why did you pick her for your mother?" This seemingly preposterous remark was greeted with some minor protestations, then laughter, then the ability to at least begin to accept the responsibility and then the willingness to at least consider reevaluating her relationship with her mother from other than her usual stance of that of helpless victim.

From a technical point of view, the protestations of patients that they couldn't possibly be responsible for choosing their life situations are similar to protestations encountered by traditional therapists who point out to patients that the patients themselves arranged for something unpleasant to happen in their dream, which they then purport to be upset about. The transpersonal view, which on some level makes it possible to see life as a dream that we imagine to be real, can make the same point.[5]

Although few therapists may be willing to make such a blanket assertion based on personal experience, acknowledging this possibility can expand the context in which therapy is conducted. If we, as therapists, do not experience ourselves as victims of the world we see, we can be more effective in enabling clients to see themselves as capable of exercising choice and responsibility in their lives.

Recognizing the power that each person has for creating his or her own experience is a basic premise for establishing a transpersonal context. The issue of responsibility pertains not only to making personal choices about vocation, relationships, and other practical matters in everyday life, but also to the domain of choosing beliefs. It is common knowledge that a teacher's negative beliefs about a child in school are likely to become self-fulfilling prophecies. Likewise, positive expectations also tend to be met. A transpersonal therapist needs to be willing to examine his or her own assumptions about the people he or she works with, and to be aware of how these expectations may affect the outcome of therapy. We know that clients in Freudian therapy tend to have Freudian dreams, while clients in Jungian therapy tend to have Jungian dreams. Likewise, the definition of successful outcome in psychotherapy held by the therapist is likely to be what his or her clients attain under optimum circumstances. Those who fail are said to be resistant or otherwise unmotivated or intractable. If a client does not improve, the therapist may question his or her own competence in the area of technique, but rarely does a therapist examine or question the beliefs he or she holds as a possible barrier to effective treatment. While change in content does not alter the context, the therapist is always responsible for establishing the context, and the broader the context, the more possibilities for growth and development. Ericson and Rossi[10] say:

> ...Patients have problems because of learned limitations. They are caught in mental sets, frames of reference, and belief systems that do not permit them to explore and utilize their own abilities to best advantage....The therapeutic transaction ideally creates a new phenomenal world in which patients can explore their potentials, freed to some extent from their learned limitations.

But how does the therapist free him/herself from learned limitations? This is the question that is addressed by the conscious recognition that a therapist can, by choice, establish a transpersonal context or any other context for the practice of therapy.

For example, one psychologist noted a significant change in his own style of work as a result of his personal therapy and transpersonal exploration. As a 50-year-old psychologist, he had lifelong anxieties relating to performance and shame. Many of his anxieties were expressed in his (1) hard-driving nature to accumulate sufficient money so that he could feel secure and in (2) a generally picky, sarcastic, and angry style. Although he was professionally and financially successful by the usual standards, his anxieties persisted and were often manifested by a timid style toward life. Despite a long and successful analysis with Boorstein,[4] which brought to the fore the Oedipal rivalry with a weak and passive father, some of the aforementioned anxieties persisted. Some of these anxieties could be traced back to pre-Oedipal fears of dying and seemed to be related to a mother-child separation early in the first year of life. However, it was only with the exploration of the issue of death and possible survival that these earlier anxieties subsided.

Perhaps as a result of the later work, he began studying and practicing Zen Buddhism, which further focused on the issues of impermanence and the fear of death. Whereas formerly he would get angry when he felt his security was threatened (e.g., the family spending money, household things breaking, etc.), he was now able to automatically and immediately go to the fear that was at the source of his anger and be calm internally and externally in the face of these adversities while doing what the situation required. It was interesting to note that his favorite boyhood and adult movie was "Lost Horizon," which focused as one of its main themes on the issue of avoiding death by living for hundreds of years in Shangri-La.[4]

In examining the context of therapy — or life, for that matter — the beliefs one has learned about who and what one is are subject to question. Establishing a transpersonal context often implies a radical redefinition. The freedom glimpsed in transpersonal experiences in which ego boundaries dissolve can be both exhilarating and terrifying. If a therapist is not at ease with his or her own transpersonal process, it is not possible for him or her to facilitate transpersonal experiences for a client or to assist in the process of subsequent integration in a non-pejorative way. The therapist cannot provide a safe space for a client if he or she does not feel safe with such experiences. A transpersonal therapist would regard such experiences as potentially healthy and contributing to human growth.[19]

While such experiences are not sought as ends in themselves, establishing a transpersonal context in psychotherapy implies the ability to work with such experiences and to integrate them in an overall model of optimum health and wholeness.

Being open to the inclusion and integration of transpersonal experiences does not imply working only with such experiences or neglecting other aspects of psychological health. A transpersonal approach would simply attempt a balanced integration of inner and outer awareness, emphasizing the value of congruence and consistency between thoughts, feelings, and behavior. Such consistency would necessarily be based on self-awareness and some degree of self-mastery. One of the contributions of Eastern disciplines to Western psychology has been instruction in methods of voluntary control of internal states. The practice of meditation, for example, in addition to being a path of sustained development in the natural evolution of consciousness,[23] also enables advanced practitioners to exert a remarkable degree of control over what are ordinarily involuntary physiological processes.[11, 17]

While the transpersonal therapist may not be an expert at such feats of self-mastery, he or she may be expected to exhibit balance and congruence in his or her own behavior and acknowledge the range of possibilities that are known to exist as part of developing the potentials of consciousness.

A transpersonal therapist thus may be both a "competent" model (i.e., one who is fully competent in what is taught) and a "learning to cope" model for the client who is attempting to gain a new perspective. Studies of modeling have demonstrated that the learning to cope model is frequently more effective than the competent one.[2] A transpersonal therapist, then, need not be an expert or a master of spiritual disciplines, but the context established by the values that he or she espouses will undoubtedly determine whether or not the client can freely explore the transpersonal domain in psychotherapy.

> If our science of mental health is to become more effective, psychotherapists will have to balance their knowledge of psychological concepts and techniques with a contemplative awareness.[7]

A final consideration for establishing a transpersonal context is the attitude the therapist holds regarding his or her role as a therapist, or, for that matter, as a human being. A transpersonal orientation values the concept of selfless service, suggesting that after self-actualization and self-transcendence lies the possibility of selfless service in the world. This does not imply that a therapist need be an exemplary enlightened being, but rather that he or she remains open to the higher potentials of self-realization, which tend to manifest as a form of service in the world.[20]

For example, if a therapist holds that every experience in life is a learning experience rather than something to be either sought after or avoided, the client's experience may also be reframed in such a way as to allow for optimum learning.

For example, Claire is a woman who was brought up a Buddhist. As part of a generalized adolescent rebellion, she rejected all of her parents' and priest's teachings. She came to see Boorstein because of a very difficult marital situation toward which she reacted with severe depression and suicidal ideation. Her previous Buddhist background permitted patient and therapist to quickly incorporate into their work the ideas of attachment as a cause of suffering. The most dramatic changes came about, however, when the therapist responded to her descriptions of her difficult relationship with her husband as "marvelous!" — a normally preposterous response in traditional psychotherapeutic situations. He would go on to talk about what a unique opportunity this gave her to focus on her generally negative personality style. This personality style had been marked with bitterness, anger, pouting, and an unappreciative and unkind approach toward her husband. She began to see that her recognition of her own style, which had been greatly influenced by an identification with an angry and bitter mother, and her subsequent ability to begin to change that style, represented a great victory over her former negative self. She then began to be able to respond to her husband with loving feelings despite his continuing actions, which at that point largely stemmed from his desire for revenge over her formerly negative behavior. Claire was beginning to see that as a result of her difficulties she was becoming a nicer person to be with, a benefit that would be hers whether or not her husband elected to continue to stay with her. Claire's husband became more and more perplexed because she was no longer responding to his desire for a rejecting and angry wife (representing a material transference situation to his own angry mother). Gradually his more adult personality components came to appreciate his wife's "new personality" and an impending divorce was avoided. It became clear ultimately to both partners that their marital problems, seemingly something one would ordinarily want to avoid, were in fact a "marvelous" opportunity for each of them to achieve considerable personal growth.

It often appears that it is not only easier to be light-hearted than to be grim but also that is is therapeutic. Those interventions that seem to be particularly "light-hearted" are direct reflection of a transpersonal orientation. These techniques do not replace traditional psychotherapy but rather catalyze it and make it more effective.[5]

What then are the ways in which a therapist can establish a transpersonal context? Answering the following questions is one way to start the reflection process.

- Who are you?
- What are you doing here?
- What do you believe to be true about human nature?
- What is the role of consciousness in your experience?
- Who is responsible for your life and state of mind?
- What do you believe to be true about reality?
- Are you comfortably familiar with altered states of consciousness?
- How important is the spiritual dimension in your life?
- Are you open to further exploration of the transpersonal domain?

Familiarity with a growing body of literature would certainly be desirable, as well as direct experience of expanded or higher states of consciousness. Higher states are defined as those states that have all the attributes of the normal waking state plus some additional ones. As the transpersonal dimension of experience becomes meaningful and important to him or her personally, a therapist will naturally bring this expanded awareness to bear on clinical practice. A transpersonal orientation presupposes that we exist in a web of mutually conditioned relationships, in which the illusion of separateness prevents us from recognizing our connectedness with everyone and everything. Therefore, whatever changes occur in a therapist's life as a result of spiritual or transpersonal practice will automatically contribute to creating this context in therapy.

CONTENT OF TRANSPERSONAL PSYCHOTHERAPY

The content of transpersonal practice is nothing other than life experience. The specific problems that a transpersonal therapist may be called upon to handle may be identical with those brought to other therapists. The content of therapy is whatever the client presents to the therapist. Therefore, while the beliefs, values, and attitudes of the therapist determine the context of therapy, the content is determined entirely by the client.

The content of therapy, though as varied as life itself, can be differentiated according to whether it is predominantly concerned with personal, existential, or transpersonal problems. Transperonal therapy is characteristically person-centered rather than problem-centered, attempting to teach the client the skills that will enable him or her to cope more effectively with any problem, rather than to solve any particular problem *per se*. However, the content of therapy may vary according to what the individual client is attempting to achieve.

Frequently the change may be a shift in attitude that may subsequently be manifested in behavior, rather than a direct change in behavior.

For example, Rebecca, a 65-year-old retired child care worker, came to Boorstein for help for assorted psychosomatic symptoms accompanying her depression of five years. She had always been overly harsh and critical of herself, resulting in her feeling that she didn't do enough for her children, her husband, and her co-workers. In part, this resulted in her being unable to even ask for things for herself from others. She always felt unworthy. Using the Vipassana meditation approach of dispassionately noting what is happening from moment to moment, the therapist would comment, "condemning," whenever she would begin to be unduly harsh or self-critical during the sessions. She became interested in watching for this style in herself and would begin to catch herself criticizing, saying, "condemning, condemning," and she would laugh. It was necessary for the therapist to point out at times that she was often condemning herself for being condemning. She began to sense after a while that she need not be judgmental about her condemning style. Boorstein felt that, with Rebecca and with other patients with similar problems, this technique brought considerable relief since at least one part of the mind was being nonjudgmental. Boorestein believes the relief also reflects the patient beginning to internalize the therapist's nonjudgmental stance. This is, of course, true in a traditional psychotherapy as well, but by using mindfulness of the Vipassana approach mentioned above, the process of identification with a nonjudgmental therapist is greatly speeded up. This is probably related to the therapist taking a direct stand in this matter, saying that something was not condemnable. As Rebecca became less judgmental, she was able to speak more openly of her needs to her family, her friends, and her therapist. Her depression periods became rare, and most of the time she felt happy and free. In addition, she was able to discuss things that she had felt were too shameful. Once she had developed this capacity to observe herself, the therapist would need only to lightly say, "condemning," and she would begin to laugh at her own process, even if she were in the midst of crying.[5]

At the interpersonal level, the content of therapy is predominantly concerned with resolving conflicts and infantile fears leading to blockages. It also includes improving coping skills, taking responsibility for one's own life, and learning to satisfy basic needs and desires. This level is characterized by deficiency motivation[14] and is concerned with owning projections and integrating the persona, or social facade, with the shadow, or rejected aspects of the self.[22] Wholeness at this level is described in terms of ego strength, and the capacity to establish and satisfy personal goals. Self-acceptance, self-determination, and better communication in interpersonal relationships are typical goals at this level of therapy.

The existential level of therapy is likely to be precipitated by an existential crisis, frequently, but not necessarily, occurring in mid-life. At this level, the individual no longer finds satisfaction in the attainment of ego goals, and what was formerly satisfying may appear empty and meaningless. Content at this level is characterized by disappointment, either disappointment in oneself if personal ambitions have not been attained, or disappointment in the world, if they have been attained. Thus, a successful business man with a devoted wife and healthy children may find himself facing despair and loss of meaning just as readily as one who has not succeeded in actualizing the all-American dream. Existential therapy is typically concerned with deeper questions of meaning and purpose in life, the inevitable confrontation with death and aloneness, and the struggle for authenticity. It may also include an identity crisis. At this level of consciousness, the person experiences him/herself as a separate, self-contained organism, along and alienated in the world in a "no exit" situation.

The way out of the existential impasse as taught by the Buddha has been the subject of many spiritual disciplines. When life is perceived as empty and filled with suffering, a total reorientation of values may be necessary. The first noble truth of Buddhism asserts that all life is suffering. The next three noble truths assert that the cause of suffering is desire and attachment, that relief of suffering comes from cessation of attachment, and that this can be achieved through following the eightfold path of action and mental training aimed at liberation or enlightenment. Release from existential hopelessness in the face of absurdity is not to be found in the ordinary pursuit of worldly desires or ego goals. Only by awakening to another level of consciousness, a radically altered sense of self, can one begin to glimpse the possibility of transpersonal realization in self-transcendence. The transformative process at this level is often experienced as a death and rebirth.

It is at this point that the Eastern consciousness disciplines have something to teach us. According to Washburn and Stark:[21]

The Eastern view holds that (1) attachment to a separate self or ego is one of the main roots of human misery, ignorance, rebirth, etc.; (2) this ego can be transcended; (3) to transcend is to awaken to the illusion that sustains it;

and (4) consciousness thus divested of the ego illusion is experienced as "empty" or "void" and for that reason open to attunement with God, reality, the Tao, and so forth.

Christian mysticism holds a similar view in the emphasis on giving away possessions (attachments). Meister Eckhart,[15] in a sermon on "Blessed are the poor in spirit, for theirs is the kingdom of heaven," says the poor man is he who wills nothing, knows nothing, and has nothing. To be devoid of personal goals, desires, and images is, in all mystical traditions, said to be the necessary condition for grace, liberation, or enlightenment. The transpersonal awakening, then, may occur as a direct result of letting go of attachment to those very goals whose loss was experienced as devastating at the existential level.

At this stage, exercises in disidentification may be particularly useful. As a person learns to disidentify from whatever he or she thinks defines who and what one is, he/she may grow to recognize the freedom inherent in self-transcendence. A useful exercise to initiate the disidentification process is the following.[18]

Take some time to write down nine words or phrases that define you. Put each one on a separate piece of paper and arrange them in order of importance. Stack the pieces of paper with what you consider the essential definition of who you are on the bottom, and the one that seems least important on the top. Be prepared to take your time with this exercise. You can do it alone, but it may be helpful to work with a partner or a group with whom you can share your experience.

Take a few moments to relax your body and clear your mind. You may wish to sit in meditation posture with your spine straight to stay wide awake and keep your attention focused. Look at the words that define you on the first piece of paper at the top of your list. Allow yourself to experience fully what this means to you and how it feels to be you, when defined by this. Take it in, experience it, be it, for a few minutes. Take enough time to acknowledge all the ramifications of this particular self-identification. Now turn that piece of paper over, and imagine how it would feel to be you without that. Who are you without that particular identification? How would it feel to give that up? Allow yourself to experience letting it go as completely as possible. When you feel you have let go, look at the next piece of paper and think about the meaning the second definition has for you. Be aware of all the sensations, feelings, and thoughts associated with this particular identification and experience it fully, as you did the first one. When you are satisfied that you have experienced it fully, turn this piece of paper over and let it go. How would it feel to be you without that? Who are you without that? Repeat this process with each of the pieces of paper, giving each identification enough time to be completely experienced and relinquished. Notice how difficult it may be to give up something even in imagination. Don't be discouraged if you find yourself resisting this process. Just be aware of your resistance and let it be.

Do the exercise according to the directions with as much depth of feeling as you can give it. No one will judge your performance. It is simply a way of learning something about yourself and who you are. When you have completed the process with each of the pieces of paper and you have turned over the last, most essential identification and let it go, take some time to experience how it feels to be you without any of the identifications you have given yourself. Who are you without those roles or attributes? Continue to meditate on the question, "Who are you?" without attempting to find any answer. Let the experience be silent, nonverbal.

After a period of time that can be as long as you like, turn your attention back to the pieces of paper and turn over the last one you let go of and imagine that you are putting it back on. Take this definition of yourself back and be aware of your feelings as you do so. How do you feel about this particular identity? Very slowly, allowing plenty of time to experience each one, take back all of your identifications in reverse order. Notice how your feelings change as you take back each one. When you have put them all back on again, reflect on your experience of letting them go and taking them back. Who were you without them all? How were you different from who you are with them all? There is no right way to experience this exercise. It is simply an opportunity for you to discover who you are behind all the masks and definitions that you create for yourself in the world.

Transpersonal content in psychotherapy is certainly not limited to experiences of awakening to the illusory nature of ego and its insatiable desires. Furthermore, a glimpse of transpersonal realization is by no means a guarantee of psychological health. Carl Jung was probably the first Western psychotherapist to recognize the potential value of transpersonal experience for mental health. He wrote that the main thrust of his work was the approach to the numinous dimensions of experience: ". . . the fact is that the approach to the numinous is the real therapy and inasmuch as you attain to the numinous experience you are released from the curse of pathology."[13]

Today we know that while such experiences are potentially healing in nature, their effect is likely to be temporary unless a sustained effort is made to stabilize such insight into an abiding awareness that is manifested in daily life. For this, additional work may be needed at the personal level, specifically with respect to interpersonal conflict resolution. Training in a spiritual discipline such as meditation may be an appropriate method for integrating transpersonal insight with ordinary reality. Once this type of awakening has occurred, however, denial, neglect, or repression of this awareness can be detrimental to psychological health. Under such circumstances, it may be vitally important for the individual who seeks psychotherapy to identify and find a transpersonal therapist in order to optimize the potential benefit of such experience and integrate it successfully into the circumstances of his or her life.

The path of psychological and spiritual development that may ensue from this point is described in different terminology in each of the mystical traditions, and is beyond the scope of this chapter. However, when a person who has embarked on a spiritual path seeks psychotherapy, and it may indeed be indicated at various stages on the path, it is appropriate for him or her to work with a therapist who has some experience in this endeavor.

TRANSPERSONAL PSYCHOTHERAPEUTIC TECHNIQUES

A considerable body of literature already exists delineating and explaining a wide variety of transpersonal psychotherapeutic techniques. This paper will be limited to listing and commenting on some of the major approaches. For more details, readers will be referred to original sources.[6]

Meditation

Just as there are differences between psychotherapies (depending on the theoretical framework, therapist, etc.), there are differences between meditations. Books such as Carrington's *Freedom in Meditation* and Goleman's *Varieties of the Meditative Experience* suggest the complexity of the subject. Goleman points out that notwithstanding the surface differences between various meditational practices, all meditations fall into one of two major categories. The first of these categories is that of concentration meditation. These meditations stress techniques of focusing the mind on a single meditation objective such as a mantra (sound) or visual image. These techniques often lead to relaxation and even states of happiness.[3] TM, probably the most widely publicized concentration meditation in this country, is an example of this approach. The second category is that of awareness or insight meditation. Awareness meditations focus attention on present inner and outer experience, fostering a capacity for increased self-awareness. In the Buddhist tradition, this is called mindfullness meditation. In other traditions, this same technique may be referred to by different names such as developing the watcher and awakening the witness, or choiceless awareness. Deatherage delineates the use of this form of meditation for both inpatient and outpatient psychotherapy in his article, "Mindfulness Meditation as Psychotherapy."[6] In addition to the basic practices of concentration and awareness training, specific guided meditations may be used with certain clients to promote disidentification, and growth practices such as psychosynthesis make extensive use of guided imagery, which is sometimes referred to as guided meditation.

Biofeedback Training

Biofeedback is a particularly Western technique in which a monitoring device (EEG, EMG, GSR) conveys ongoing information about particular physiological processes to the patient. For example, the EEG measures brain waves, the EMG measures muscle tension, and the GSR measures skin reponse. A variety of functional, psychosomatic, and other stress-related disorders can often be helped as the patient uses amplified feedback for developing awareness of inner states in order to develop mastery over them. Alyce and Elmer Green have been pioneers in this field.[11]   Also, Fehmi and Selzer have developed an effective treatment method using a combination of biofeedback and Open Focus Training, which resembles awareness meditation.[6]

Dream Work

Because of the emphasis on dream work by classical Freudian and neo-Freudian analysis, it is often easy to forget that dreams can be the royal road to the transpersonal unconscious as well as the personal unconscious. Carl Jung was one of the foremost pioneers in using the dream to reach transpersonal realms. Many cultures, past and present, have seen the dream as a window into the transpersonal, and the literature on this is almost universal (e.g., the Old Testament, shamanic texts). Montague Ullman, a classically trained psychiatrist, describes his transpersonal approach to dream work with workshops and patient groups in "Dream Workshops and Healing."[6]

Mind-Altering Drugs

The use of drugs to alter consciousness in order to reach transpersonal realms is as old as recorded history. LSD has been the most extensively researched psychoactive drug. Stanislav Grof has spent much of his professional career using LSD as a research and therapeutic tool. His work gives a good overview of some of the complex issues involved.[12] Since LSD research is no longer permitted in this country, this particular method for examining the transpersonal realms of the mind is not currently available.

Transpersonal Bibliotherapy

Transpersonal Bibliotherapy, or the recommendation that the patient read certain books, is often an effective aid in psychotherapy. Books such as *Life After Life* by Raymond Moody[16] and *No Boundary* by Ken Wilbur[24] can begin to loosen the attachments that most Westerners have to what is popularly called "reality." In particular, obsessional patients tend to clutch at "things," such as power, money, and personality image, for their happiness and security. Frequently, fear of death is an important issue, and here books such as *Life After Life* begin to raise the possibility that consciousness may continue in some form.

For some more scientifically-oriented patients, books such as Capra's *The Tao of Physics*[9] and Zukav's *The Dancing Wu Li Masters*[25] are helpful to the process of letting go of traditional Newtonian ideas and the opening up to new paradigms of viewing life and the universe. These books point in the direction of a common meeting place between mysticism and quantum physics.

PROBLEMS AND LIMITATIONS OF TRANSPERSONAL PSYCHOTHERAPY

In general, a transpersonal approach is most suitable for healthy, growth-oriented clients, and for those suffering from various types of neuroses and some narcissistic disorders. Certain of the narcissistic disorders can be helped when the individual, with the aid of certain transpersonal techniques, can get in touch with the transcendent aspects of consciousness. As an individual becomes aware of a "higher" or "spiritual" part of his or her nature, a type of "feeding" or inner nourishing takes place.

Certain psychotic and other severe disorders might be benefitted by a modified transpersonal approach.[6] With these very disturbed patients, it is not necessary for the patient to even be aware of the transpersonal background of the psychotherapeutic technique being used.

With individuals who are suicidal, it is often necessary to do preliminary work in order to stabilize the situation before some of the aforementioned techniques can be applied. Sometimes severely disturbed individuals may come into therapy already using certain transpersonal practices such as meditation, mind-altering drugs, fasting, etc. In these cases, the therapist may decide to counsel against these practices in favor of manual labor, exericse, etc., in order for the patient to become more grounded and balanced. In some extreme situations, the initial use of tranquilizers may be warranted in order to stabilize the situation.

As more people in the West turn to meditation and other spiritual practices and relationships with a spiritual teacher become more common, the transpersonal psychotherapist must learn to discriminate between the uses and abuses of transpersonal experiences.   Any technique may be misused by neurotic or psychotic trends in the personality. To consider spiritual practice as necessarily free of individual pathology is as blind a view as the rigidly orthodox position that considers all spiritual practices as merely symptomatic.

An objective and experienced therapist needs to discriminate, letting go of preconceptions in favor of looking at what is actually happening in each particular circumstance. For example, meditation can put one in touch with a fine and essential part of oneself; it can also be used to rationalize compulsive withdrawal in a family power struggle, or symbolically to blot out a hated world. The relationship to guru or guide can be a lifesaving orientation but it can also be distorted with transference gratifications. Altered states of consciousness, produced by concentration and breathing practices, may help free a person from constricting linguistic schema, or they may feed paranoid ideation, accentuate schizoid trends, and be used in the service of resistance. The initial glow and romanticism of inexperienced mediators may be useful for the modification of destructive habits; but it may also be used to avoid life's problems, including therapeutic transference reactions.

In working on such areas as anxiety, depression, sense of identity, and reality testing, traditional psychotherapy attempts to strengthen the ego so that it can endure the human condition. Although meditation or other specifically transpersonal practices used alone might eventually unravel a modern anxiety neurosis or depression, therapeutic techniques are more specifically designed for these problems and the settings in which therapists work. The therapist can greatly hasten transpersonal processes by first using ordinary methods to bring into the patient's consciousness what has been repressed. For example, beneath a depression, a patient may be unconsciously clinging to the idea that his mother should "make up" to him all his previous deprivations. By working with the transferences in the traditional fashion, the therapist can help the patient bring this to awareness and work through the feelings involved. It might then be appropriate for the experienced therapist to offer certain meditative techniques to facilitate letting go of the ideas and feelings.

There are possible dangers in working with the spiritual and psychological domains simultaneously. Can therapists be adequately competent in both areas, sufficiently certain to avoid the pitfalls of their own countertransference traps and spiritual biases? Can therapists work in areas beyond those to which they have personally progressed? Many classical therapists who are atheists or agnostics implicitly endorse their own belief systems by the lack of attention they give to the religious aspirations of their clients. Will the transpersonally-oriented therapists be guilty of the same kind of suggestion, albeit in the opposite direction? What are the implications of prescribing meditation practices or other techniques derived from spiritual traditions as adjuncts to treatment?

Clearly, the practice of transpersonal psychotherapy requires the very best of which the therapist is capable: Experiential knowledge rather than opinion; attention instead of preconception; and certainty in place of theory.

Without the transpersonal perspective, traditional psychotherapy gives an implicit message of pessimism, which might be stated without too much exaggeration as, "Know thyself and adjust to the absurd!" The transpersonal ingredient alters this implication to, "Know thyself, transcend defenses, transferences, projections, and even beliefs, and attain the station of one who has outgrown the need for such childish things, as the great human beings of all times and places have done!" It might be added that this station involves the full realization of human possibilities; it is in no way connected with schizoid withdrawal, megalomaniacal delusions of grandeur, or flashy demonstrations of parapsychological prowess.

The ultimate goal of the spiritual quest is the experience of oneness with the universe. As Ken Wilber points out in the *Spectrum of Consciousness*,[22] humanity's task is to remember or become aware of those aspects of itself which it has forgotten or repressed. Thus, different parts of the spectrum are remembered or made available by different approaches. For example, the psychoanalytic approach will permit one to remember and accept as part of oneself that which has been repressed in the unconscious; body therapies such as Reichian Therapy, bioenergetics, and Rolfing permit one to become more aware of unconscious aspects of the body. Other aspects of the unconscious, such as archetypes, are elicited in Jungian work. Other approaches work on the subtle energy fields, and these, too, can become part of our awareness. Finally, through various meditational or contemplative approaches, direct awareness of unity with the rest of the universe can also be attained.

Working in the transpersonal area, it is well to keep in mind what the Buddha said in the Kalamas Sutra:

Do not believe in what you have heard; do not believe in traditions because they have been handed down for many generations; do not believe anything because it is rumored and spoken of by many; do not believe merely because the written statement of some old sage is produced; do not believe in conjectures; do not believe merely in the authority of your teachers and elders. After observation and analysis, when it agrees with reason and it is conducive to the good and benefit of one and all, then accept it and live up to it.

REFERENCES

1. Anonymous. *A Course in Miracles*. New York: Foundation for Inner Peace (1975).
2. Bandura, A. *Social Learning Theory*. Englewood Cliffs, NJ: Prentice Hall (1977).
3. Benson, H. *Relaxation Response*. New York: William Morrow (1975).
4. Boorstein, S. Anger and the fear of death. *In*: Boorstein, S. (Ed.). *Transpersonal Psychotherapy*. Palo Alto, CA: Science and Behavior Books, p. 372 (1980).
5. Boorstein, S. Lightheartedness in psychotherapy. *Journal of Transpersonal Psychology* 12(2): 105-115 (1980).
6. Boorstein, S. (Ed.). *Transpersonal Psychotherapy*, Palo Alto, CA: Science and Behavior Books (1980).
7. Boss, M. *A Psychiatrist Discovers India*. London: Oswald Wolff (1965).
8. Byrom, T. *The Dhammapada: The Sayings of Buddha*. New York: Vintage (1976).
9. Capra, F. *The Tao of Physics*. Berkeley: Shambala (1975).
10. Ericson and Rossi. *Hypnotherapy*. New York: Irvington, pp. 1, 2 (1979).
11. Green, E. and Green, A. *Beyond Biofeedback*. New York: Delacorte (1977).
12. Grof, S. *LSD Psychotherapy*. Claremont, CA: Hunter House (1980).
13. Jung, C. G. *Letters*. Adler, G. (Ed.). Princeton, NJ: Princeton University Press (1973).
14. Maslow, A. *The Farther Reaches of Human Nature*. New York: Viking (1971).
15. *Meister Eckhart: A Modern Translation*. Translated by R. B. Blakney. New York: Harper and Row (1941).

16. Moody, R. *Life After Life*. Covington, GA: Mockingbird (1975).
17. Shapiro, D. *Meditation: Altered States of Consciousness and Self-Regulation Strategy*. New York: Aldine (1980).
18. Vaughan, F. *Awakening Intuition*. New York: Doubleday/Anchor (1979).
19. Vaughan, F. Transpersonal psychotherapy: Context, content and process. *In*: Walsh, R. and Vaughn, F. (Eds.). *Beyond Ego: Transpersonal Dimensions of Psychology*. Los Angeles: J. P. Tarcher (1980).
20. Walsh, R. and Vaughan, F. (Eds.). *Beyond Ego: Transpersonal Dimensions in Psychology*. Los Angeles: J. P. Tarcher (1980).
21. Washburn, M. and Stark, M. Ego egocentricity and self-transcendence: A Western interpretation of Eastern teaching. *In*: Welwood, J. (Ed.). *The Meeting of the Ways*. New York: Schocken (1979).
22. Wilber, K. *The Spectrum of Consciousness*. Wheaton, IL: Theosophical Publishing House (1977).
23. Wilber, K. *The Atman Project: A Transpersonal View of Human Development*. Wheaton, IL: Theosophical Publishing House (1978).
24. Wilber, K. *No Boundary*. Center Press (1979).
25. Zukav, G. *The Dancing Wu Li Masters*. New York: Morrow (1979).

Ego-state therapy is the application of techniques of group and family therapy for the resolution of conflicts between the various ego-states which constitute a "family of self" within a single individual. It is based upon the concept that personality is not a unity but is composed of various subentities or organizational patterns of behavior and experience called "ego-states." When these ego-states are cognitively dissonant with one another or with the entire person, anxiety and other symptoms are created. By activating each state separately to determine its needs and goals, conflicts can be resolved and internal harmony promoted.

Any of the usual procedures of psychotherapy, such as suggestion, support, desensitization, reinforcement, abreaction, re-education, or analytic interpretation, may be employed by the practitioner as part of a program of internal ego-state diplomacy. These may be carried out with certain techniques while the patient is fully conscious but can be better achieved through hypnosis. Accordingly, ego-state therapy in its most sophisticated practice is a form of hypnoanalysis.

The therapeutic goal is a reintegration of the entire personality by reducing dissociation of the various ego-states from one another. Through their mutual cooperation, neurotic symptoms and maladaptive behaviors tend to be eliminated, and general well-being of the individual promoted.

8

Ego-State Therapy

John G. Watkins, Ph.D. and Helen H. Watkins, M.A.

THE THEORY OF EGO-STATES

The idea that humans do not function consistently but demonstrate a wide variability in behaviors at different moments is not new. However, Paul Federn[4] was apparently the first to formulate the concept of "ego-states" as organized sub-patterns of the ego. He claimed that each was experienced as "self" but that they were separated from one another by boundaries which were more or less permeable. Other psychoanalytic writers, such as Hartmann[7] and Kohut,[10] have also described these ego entities but have not assigned to them the importance that Federn did.

The separation of ego-states had been described[19, 28] as a kind of relative dissociation determined by the degree of rigidity or permeability of the boundaries between them. Thus, the Watkins[25, 28] hold that dissociation, like many other psychological processes, lies on a continuum. In normal dissociation, we see the ardent baseball fan who screams at the umpire but who becomes passive and compliant when at home. The extreme end of the dissociative continuum is represented by the true multiple personality case, where the various sub-entities are apparently not even aware of one another's existence.[12, 14, 16, 23] In between, there is a wide range of personality organization in which unconscious ego-states can be hypnotically activated. These act as "covert" multiple personalities.

We have some evidence (not yet published) that, following successful treatment of a multiple personality case, the sub-entities continue to exist in this covert form. Even after the various personalities are apparently integrated, they can still be hypnotically activated and will report on their unique identity and characteristics. Although no longer in severe conflict, and no longer emerging spontaneously, they describe themselves like the ego-states we have found in normal individuals who volunteer for experiments in psychology classes.[26] Their contents are still in existence, but their conflicts with one another are reduced or eliminated. The boundaries between them have become relatively much more permeable, thus permitting the exchange of memories and perceptions. The personality of the entire individual has become a coherent "family" of mutually supportive members, rather than a battleground for warring ego-states.

HYPNOSIS AND EGO-STATES

Hypnosis has been described as a state of suggestibility,[3] an altered state of consciousness,[15] and a regression in the service of the ego.[6] However, in ego-state therapy, hypnosis is best characterized as a controlled dissociation. In fact, Hilgard[8] has proposed a "neo-dissociative" theory of hypnosis.

Hypnosis is especially useful in the analytic therapies because, within its modality, unconscious and preconscious elements of the personality can be made more visible, alterations of perception can be induced, and constructive behaviors can be suggested. Under hypnosis, it is also easier to manipulate "self-energy" — what Federn[4] called "ego cathexis." He held that any physical or mental element that was invested with this energy was experienced as subject, as "I" and as a part of "my"self. Parts of the body or mental processes that can be sensed but are not invested with ego cathexis are experienced as ego-alien; hence, as objects, as "not-me." An introject is an internal object and experienced, usually unconsciously, as a "not-me."

Because of the suggestive influence that is possible in hypnosis, care must be taken that the therapist activate only those ego-states that are actually present within the personality. He/she must not merely create artifacts. A number of writers[11, 13] have pointed to this source of contamination in both research and therapy. We agree with the need for this precaution but feel that this factor has been overemphasized. With proper recognition and control, it can be minimized if not eliminated. However, hypnosis does enable a therapist to focus upon a certain aspect of the personality by separating or dissociating it from other segments. This permits the therapist to activate in relatively pure form various sub-parts of the personality. In this respect, it is not unlike the initiating of transference reactions in traditional psychoanalytic therapy. Underlying organizational patterns are made more observable and subject to correction or control.

When so activated, each ego-state exhibits the characteristics of a "person," albeit a "part-person." It claims for its self identity ("I" or "me"), and it reacts to the entire individual and other ego-states as objects ("he," "she," or "it").

It should be noted that hypnosis is itself not an "either-or." It is a matter of degree, ranging from hypnoidal relaxation, through states of light and medium trance, to the deep somnambulistic condition in which a subject can perform many behaviors that will not be remembered on returning to conscious awareness.

Despite Freud's relinquishment of hypnosis, most hypnoanalysts would hold that the relaxed state of concentration for purposes of free association in the psychoanalytic patient is actually a light hypnotic trance achieved without a formal induction. There is a partial relaxation of the ego and some dissociation, thus permitting regressed states to rise and become manifest.

Not only do ego-states experience themselves as "I," but, like any person they jealously guard their own existence as unique and individual "selves." Great resistance is encountered by a therapist who sets out to eliminate one of them (see Watkins,[19] pp. 399–454). A real therapeutic problem is posed when the ego-state is a malevolent one.

We find that ego-states are created to provide certain specific adaptive and defensive functions. Thus, the "Dark One" (see Watkins,[19] pp. 360–398) informed us that he originated when the patient was sexually molested. It was his job "to protect her from men." For many years he had been accomplishing this by getting her to overeat so as to become fat and unattractive. He also caused her to become schizoid and anti-social. When his trust and cooperation were secured, he relinquished this protective function to the therapist, who helped the patient to mature as a woman and deal with men. Ultimately, the Dark One became an assistant therapist. After being taught Wolpian desensitization techniques,[29] he was able to reduce a phobia in another ego-state, Little One. This infant state had been frightened ever since the patient had been placed in a hospital oxygen tent at the age of 18 months. Through this ego-state manipulation, an anachronistic and reconstructive ego-state was turned into a therapeutic asset.

Most ego-states can describe where, when, and under what circumstances they first came into being. We have found that they usually stem from one of three sources:

1. They split off at the time of a great trauma and serve as a defense.[21] (Such splits are especially true of those ego-state problems that could be diagnosed as true multiple personalities.[23] In such cases, the different personalities (ego-states) emerge overtly, spontaneously, and without hypnotic activation. An unhappy condition may serve to initiate the split as well as a specific trauma. For example, lonely children often create imaginary playmates.[23] In most cases, they are repressed or disappear as the social experiences of school fulfill their needs. However,

we find that often, years later, the imaginary playmate can be reactivated under hypnosis. It then may describe to us its continuing but unconscious role in influencing present behavior. It continues to exist, but now only as a covert ego-state.)

2. Ego-states may also come about through normal development. Every human society has found that it can function best if there is some degree of specialization among its members. One person becomes a teacher, another a merchant, etc. Likewise is it in the "society of self." Various clusters of behaviors and experiences are dissociated from one another by semipermeable boundaries so that the individual may concentrate upon the requirements of each situation (play, work, etc.) without interference from nonrelevant elements of the personality. Accordingly, ego-states with different specific functions are developed. "I am the one who makes him study." "It's my job to see that she behaves like a lady." "I give him headaches whenever he does what he's not supposed to do." Ego-states can be organized around functions ("I'm the one who protects Willie"), around periods in a person's life (e.g., a six-year-old state activated under hypnotic regression), or even around an attitude ("I keep him on guard against his enemies").

3. Finally, ego-states may be built around introjects, often of parents. When Debbie was a child, her mother was rather unaffectionate and did not approve of any angry or hostile behavior. Now in her thirties, Debbie suffers frequent and severe headaches. When her mother-introject ego-state was hypnotically activated, her "mother" said, "She has no business getting angry. I punish her by giving her a headache whenever she has angry thoughts. Little girls are not supposed to be angry."

Battles between states seeking to become executive are often experienced by the patient as "migraine" headaches. We have found this both in normal ego-state problems and in true multiple personalities, where an underlying personality struggles to emerge and the usually normal state strives to repress it. Such was the case of Kenneth Bianchi (the Los Angeles "Hillside Strangler") whom J. G. Watkins[22] examined for the court. Steve, the underlying personality who committed the murders, would often emerge only after Ken had suffered a severe headache. During one of the interviews, Ken complained of not feeling well. Steve soon emerged and angrily exclaimed, "He wouldn't let me out, so I gave him a fuckin' headache." Dissociated ego-states and multiple personalities are more prominent in the commission of violent crimes than has previously been considered.

Ego-states may identify themselves as either male or female. It is not at all uncommon for a male state to appear with a female or *vice versa*. These seem to be organized around the stereotypes of maleness or femaleness. Thus, an ego-state designed to protect a little girl may describe itself as "a boy because boys are stronger than girls." Normally, we do not find a strictly sexual function in such states. However, it is possible that women who are very masculine or play an active lesbian role may do so because of the dominance of a male ego-state. Their female states may be weak and frightened. Ego-strengthening of these female states may result in changes in the individual's interests and behavior. The whole area of sexual identity needs to be studied from an ego-state viewpoint.

Ego-states generally give themselves names. They may simply be names other than those of the individual (Sam, Mary, Jennifer, Bill, etc.) or descriptive (Evil One, Medusa, Love, The Old One, etc.). Or they may relate only to a function ("I'm the one who makes her study"). We make it a point never to suggest a name. The ego-state itself tells us whether it has a name or not. However, when a new state emerges, often spontaneously, we will ask, "Whom am I talking to?" It is best to be as non-directive as possible to avoid the chance of suggestive creation or influence of an ego-state. However, ego-states, since they have an individuality of their own, will often contradict us or present surprising and totally unexpected reactions.[26, 27]

When an ego-state becomes dominant and emerges overtly, we say that it is now "executive." Most underlying ego-states (except in a few cases of multiple personality, where the boundaries are very impermeable) are aware of the thoughts and behaviors of that state which is normally executive. However, they are sometimes not conscious of one another until they have been hypnotically activated. For example, a four-year-old boy state, Sandy,[27] spontaneously and unexpectedly emerged while the therapist was talking to "The Old One," a kind of demanding father entity. When The Old One was reactivated, he was unaware of this existence of this playful child state who was making Ed (the name of the whole person) unable to concentrate on his lessons. Compromises had to be worked out between Sandy and The Old One before Ed was able to study again and secure his usual excellent grades.

The individual generally engages in constructive behavior if his or her normal executive ego-state is strong and mature. Destructive acting out occurs when a more immature state overthrows the constructive one and becomes temporarily executive.

Transactional analysis[2] also uses the concept of ego-states, and both approaches stem from the theories of Federn.[4] However, ego-state therapy does not posit the existence of three basic states — parent, adult, and child. We let the patient tell us what his/her ego-states are. Sometimes they do fall within the categories above, sometimes not. In one patient, an ego-state was activated, to his considerable surprise, which was "The Devil." It proved to be the remnant of an entity that had been created during the individual's adolescence, when for a period he had forsaken God and had engaged in devil worship. The influence of this state had continued to manifest itself in the present only by causing him (a professor) to enjoy especially the teaching of Faust to his classes.

The Hilgards[8, 9] have published considerable research on the "hidden observer" phenomena. They found that sound and pain, when hypnotically dissociated, are still perceived at covert levels by a "cognitive structural system." We have replicated some of their experiments[26, 27] with patients who had previously been treated with ego-state therapy. When "hidden observers" were activated using the same words as the Hilgards', they proved to be one or more of the ego-states that had been dealt with a year earlier in therapy. We believe that these underlying personality "cognitive structural systems," or hidden observers, are actually dissociated ego-states; hence, part-persons. They have both behavioral and experiential content, and are more than merely an abstract process that perceives dissociated sound or pain.

We also believe that there are many more true multiple personalities than are diagnosed. Psychiatric classification systems such as the DSM III[1] describe these conditions as extremely rare. Since the textbooks teach clinicians they are so rare, they are not considered as a possibility during evaluations. Accordingly, multiple personalities walk through clinics undiagnosed or misdiagnosed, because they do not clearly demonstrate a change of state spontaneously during the examination hour. Unless periods of amnesia are carefully investigated (generally requiring hypnosis), the underlying personality is missed. It may even be that hallucinatory voices can come from dissociated personalities as an underlying state "speaks" to the executive one. In such cases, the diagnosis of schizophrenia is usually given. Ego-state theory thus represents a personality conceptualization that is relevant in understanding normal change in mood, many neurotic and psychosomatic symptoms, to the severities of true multiple personalities, and perhaps even some psychoses.

EGO-STATE THERAPY

The principles of good psychotherapy apply at all levels of human organization, whether we are dealing with ego-states within a single individual, individuals within a family or group, or groups (nations) within an international community. In ego-state therapy, the emphasis is on "intrapersonal" relationships — hence, the self and its various segments — rather than on "interpersonal" relationships, as in ordinary group and family therapy. The "self" is formed by the impact of outside relationships, but once constructed, it acts back upon others either destructively or constructively. Ego-state therapy aims at changing the self's internal structure as a way of mitigating painful symptoms and maladaptive behavior.

The treatment we have been practicing from the standpoint of ego-state theory has ranged from smoking and weight reduction problems through the milder and more severe neurotic syndromes, up to and including multiple personalities. When first approaching a new case in which ego-state therapy might be useful, we are concerned with reports of conflict, inconsistent behavior, or the existence of moments of amnesia. If the patient insists that he is "compelled" to smoke or overeat, we may inquire under hypnosis whether there is "some part" of him that knows more about why he is under this compulsion; and if this is true, he is to let the index finger lift itself. If a positive response is secured, we try to communicate with that "part." ("Part, will you please come out and say, 'I'm here.' ") Frequently, an ego-state will emerge which claims "credit" for the problem. Interviewing it under hypnosis then discloses that the state has some grievance, motive, or purpose in compelling the maladaptive behavior or causing the symptom. It may describe to us its conflict with another ego-state, and we then become aware of the existence of that other state.

Each ego-state that is a party to the problem is interviewed, and attempts are made to work out a resolution or a compromise — as might be done in family therapy. We have found it important to avoid making an enemy of any ego-state regardless of how malevolent or unconstructive it appears to be in the patient's psychic economy. It is very helpful to try to meet the needs of each state to the greatest extent possible. Unless an ego-state is treated with respect and courtesy, strong internal resistance to the treatment may be mobilized. An affronted ego-state, like an insulted individual, becomes uncooperative and obstructive.

Any of the usual therapeutic techniques, behavioral, cognitive, humanistic, or analytic, may be employed to change the perception and behavior of each state. However, in this case, they are focused specifically on the ego-state that needs that particular procedure rather than on the whole person. For example, positive reinforcement or encouragement might be applied to a weak but constructive ego-state. A more destructive one, on the other hand, may be induced to meet its needs in less harmful ways.

We have found that most ego-states were constructed for some defensive or adjustive need. However, ego-states, like children, think concretely, and what was adaptive at the age of five may now be a real burden to the patient. We treat the "bad" one with care, calling attention to its original good purpose and suggesting ways that it can now be even more helpful by modifying its behavior. Such an ego-state might be approached as follows: "You were born out of desperation to protect her, and that was a good thing. But now she is in a real struggle because of your voice. She listens to you, and you make her afraid to lose weight. I'm wondering if you would be willing to give her strength and the ability to stand up for herself, and to allow me to take over her growth as a woman. In that way you could really be of help now." It is amazing how "human" and cooperative unproductive ego-states can be when approached with respect for their integrity and treated as "important parts" of the entire person.

Interaction exchanges are not exclusively between ego-states and the therapist. Internal dialogues between different states often encourage them to work out their differences. We have made a practice of recording many sessions of ego-state therapy, some of which have been published.[18, 27] The specific therapeutic techniques can best be learned from these tapes.

Although hypnosis appears to be the best modality for activating and influencing ego-states, other approaches can also be used. H. H. Watkins has developed a "chair technique," which is somewhat different from approaches used in gestalt therapy. Five or six chairs are placed in a circle. The therapist then proceeds as follows.

Initial Ego-State Session

Part I — Discovering of ego-states on specific problem
  1. Setting the stage — mixed emotions, different parts of us feel differently, etc.
  2. Decide on a topic to which each ego-state can address itself with an "I feel . . ."
  3. Have each ego-state express *its* position on the topic while you record verbatim as much as possible.
  4. Have the client move from chair to chair until the client cannot find another feeling state inside.

Part II — Delineating the characteristics of each ego-state
  1. Read off the transcript of each ego-state with an appropriate resonant voice.
  2. Have the client give a description of each personality. (Don't allow negative labeling.)
  3. Ask for a title or a name that encapsulates that ego-state for the client.
  4. Ask, "How old does he/she feel? — older, younger, or contemporary?" If the client gives a non-contemporary age, then ask, "What do you think about when you think of that age?"

Part III — Co-therapist step
  1. Review the name, age, and brief description of each ego-state as given by the client.
  2. Ask, "How do you see what's going on here?" (or words to that effect).

Part IV — Therapist input
  1. Therapeutic interventions following the lead of the client. First follow, then lead in the direction the client seems to be going, but stay *together.*
  2. Obtain some closure, some resolution to the conflict. Move chairs, as appropriate, to line up allies opposite to antagonists. Have the patient move from one chair (ego-state) to another to work out the conflict.

Fortunate indeed is the person whose introjects are supportive and approving. Many people have constructed ego-states within themselves built around the introjects of critical, demanding, or unloving parents. These individuals may go through life chronically depressed as their internal parental ego-states continue to berate them. Such was the case of the following patient, Pat. Her treatment was tape-recorded.

To illustrate how a session of ego-state therapy proceeds, we will present the script of one session. The patient was a 35-year-old divorcee who came to treatment suffering from depression and fluctuation of moods, and given to occasional bouts of drinking. Although she usually exhibited nurturance and maturity in her relationships with others, it was clear she suffered at times from self-defeating behaviors that were dissonant from her predominant personality characteristics. Under hypnosis, two ego-states emerged, one a three-year-old who was distant and angry, and a "Witch Mother" (so named by the patient), who seemed to be causing trouble. The recording was started after a hypnotic induction and deepening. The therapist (H. H. Watkins) has just activated the "Witch Mother" ego-state, which the client reported as sensing inside herself. Witch Mother has been asked to look into a hallucinated room to see who is there.

WITCH MOTHER AND THREE-YEAR OLD: AN INTROJECTION OF THE DRAMA*

Therapist's Notes

T: There are five of them, you say.

P: Yes

T: What are their names?

P: Susan, Jane, Joanne, Mary, and Pat.

T: Oh, I see. What about Pat?

P: (Sigh) I always feel guilty about her.

T: Why?

P: I don't know why. She just ... something about her makes me feel guilty.

T: Did you do anything that you feel bad about?

P: I didn't want her.

T: Do you sense that she knows that or not?

P: She knows.

T: She knows. What do you think she feels about you?

P: She doesn't understand why I feel like I do. She's a child.

T: What do you mean she doesn't understand that you feel like you do? What doesn't she understand?

"Witch Mother" is an introject of Pat's mother — that is how she perceived her mother. These are the patient's actual sisters, so I'm a bit confused. Patient is taking the role of the actual mother.

Pat sensed that her mother didn't want her and built her introjection of that mother around such perceptions.

The introject of the tired mother is itself tired since it is a replica of the patient's perception of her mother when she was a child.

*T = therapist (H. H. Watkins); P = patient.

P: She doesn't understand why I feel like I do.
    She doesn't understand that I am tired.
    Tired of babies, tired of kids.

T: That you are just too burdened?

P: Yes. She always wants attention.

T: I wonder why she wants attention?

P: Just like a puppy. She always wants her
    head patted, she always wants to come and
    hang on my leg, always wants me to hold
    her or something.

Patient is now telling us
through a reversal of subject-
object how she felt her mother
perceived her.

T: What do you usually do?

P: Sometimes I can't. Sometimes I'm just ir-
    ritated with her for hanging around.

T: I can understand that you would be tired
    and kind of worn out. But maybe you
    don't realize that perhaps the reason that
    she is so hanging on to you is that she
    senses that you don't want to hug and
    hold her, and so her need becomes
    greater, that perhaps if you met her
    need and really felt that, then she may
    not hang on so much. And then you
    would get . . .

Therapist is trying to restructure the introject's understanding of the child.

P: She is three years old, she's a girl. I
    feel funny loving her and kissing
    her.

T: Could you tell me more about that.

P: It's like perverted and like women
    don't do that with one another.

T: Oh. A three-year old girl you see as a
    woman.

P: Well, she is growing up.

T: You make it sound sexual.

P: She's sexual.

T: A three-year-old?

P: Yes.

T: Is that what she wants from you?

P: No. But you can see it when she sits on her
    father's lap or any of her father's friends
    come. Pat's always crawling all over the men
    and sitting on their laps and she is hugging
    them and oh they love her. But it is sexual.

Mother was jealous of father's
attentions to Pat.

T: It's sexual in your mind. Three-year-olds are not sexual. They just want hugging and kissing and touching.

P: Well, she gets plenty of it from them.

T: But she doesn't get her needs met from her mother.

> A confronting interpretation.

P: I don't know how to love her.

T: Are you saying you never learned to love?

P: I don't think so.

T: What about the other kids?

P: I felt really protective about Susan and I have taken care of all the kids' needs. But Pat makes me feel guilty.

> Pat's mother probably favored her older sister.

T: Because you didn't want her. Because you didn't want another child. Is that right?

P: Yes.

T: And because . . .

P: Because she is so loving. I don't know how to touch people like she does.

T: You make it sound like you wish you could.

P: I am jealous of her.

T: Since she is part of you, perhaps you could learn.

> Therapist wants to switch to the here and now, so that the mother ego can nurture the little child ego-state that feels lonely and rejected.

P: I can now. I couldn't then.

T: It's now that is important.

P: I can kiss her now. And hold her.

T: Will she let you?

P: Yes.

T: Would you let her come near you and can you see her right now?

P: She's a small child.

T: I'd like the Three-Year-Old to come closer to mother and I'd like to hear from the Three-Year-Old so that I can talk to the Three-Year-Old now. And when you are there, just say I am here.

P: I'm here.

> Three-Year-Old ego-state now activated.

T: Have you been listening to what mother and I have been talking about?

P: Yes.

T: How do you feel about it?

P: I know she didn't love me.

T: Must have hurt.

P: I hate her for it.

T: Could you tell me more about that — how
you feel?

P: She thinks that every, every time you touch
somebody or want to love somebody that
it is sexual and then you are dirty. And
you are not nice, not that sweet little girl.

T: I think you and I know different, don't we?

P: That's why she is dumb.

T: But even if she is dumb it's possible for
her to relearn something new, and if you
heard her before she said that she would
like to be able to love and to touch you.

Therapist giving little girl
ego-state hope of change.

P: I know she loves me now. But she still
doesn't like my sex. And she still doesn't
like it when my dad kisses me.

She switches back to the
external mother.

T: I wonder if you would be willing to talk
to her? Can you see her?

P: Yes.

T: Why don't you say whatever it is that you
would like to say to her.

P: I need to know that my dad loves me and I
like to be kissed and held by him. I don't
want him sexually. Couldn't care less. I
need to touch people and you never could.
You never would. And you never, ever
wanted us to touch you. I wonder how
you ever got pregnant. You must have
been horrible.

Resentment is released in direct communication between
child and mother ego-states.

T: Mother, would you answer the little girl
and tell her how you feel?

She is talking as the actual
mother again.

P: I always thought sex was dirty. I never
could enjoy it. I never did enjoy it. And
I never enjoyed any of the touching. It
was always as though there was something
unclean and dirty about it. My mother
never touched me; I didn't have a mother.
And when my dad got married again that
mother never touched me either. And I
just never have thought . . . I have felt bad
about touching people.

Mother ego-state reports she
was not loved by patient's
grandmother, and hence was
not able to love the three-
year-old Pat.

T: Mother, it's so important for mothers to touch their children.

Therapist trying to change her attitude.

P: I love to touch babies now. I love to hold them. I remember Patty's babies.

T: What is important now? Is it you, Mother, the mother inside of Pat, that you would be willing to touch that three-year-old who has a natural need and has a birthright to be touched and to be loved?

Back to mother ego-state of the present.

P: Too ashamed.

T: If you are too ashamed, perhaps you could ask the Three-Year-Old's forgiveness and see what happens.

P: It's all right, Mom. Just don't give me those nasty looks. I know it. I have known for a long time about you. And I kept hoping that I could just make you get over that. It must be really sad when you can't love somebody and touch them. It must really hurt you. Made you a bitch.

Little girl is more understanding and forgiving than the inhibited, introjected mother.

T: Mother, you've heard the Three-Year-Old really understands how you feel and in the understanding there must be a sense of forgiveness. Would it be possible for you, mother, to hold the Three-Year-Old and do what you need to do to help yourself and her?

P: I'll hold her. She's right. I've always been afraid that they would die like my mother. If I get too close to them and touch them too much it would be the same way.

Apparently, the original mother's internal child reasoned this way!

T: I think the Three-Year-Old can understand even more how this came to pass and that the not touching by you is not her fault. And also . . . Yes, it would have helped. But the point of it is you telling her now helped in the here and now. And it is never too late to love.

Therapist trying to resolve present issue of the lonely Three-Year-Old.

P: It was never her fault.

T: It was never what?

P: It was never her fault.

T: She needs to hear that too.

P: I'm sorry, baby. I'm sorry.

T: I'd like to hear from the Three-Year-Old.
    Three-Year-Old, how do you feel?

P: I think she loves me. She just didn't know
    how to show it. She didn't know how to
    show me. She's scared of me.

T: Yes, I think you're right. She loved
    you. She was ashamed that she didn't
    want you. She felt guilty. She didn't
    know how to show you love and she was
    afraid that if she got too close that some-
    how she might hurt you like she was hurt.

P: I think so.

T: But now that the two of you are together,
    you can resolve this difference. And both
    of you can then feel loved.

P: I can.

T: Good. Now, in a moment I am going to
    arouse you and when I arouse you, you
    will be wide awake, fresh, and alert, but
    I'd like the two of you to stay together and
    continue working out this relationship and
    getting to know each other as you really
    are: Both good human beings who have
    misunderstood each other for a long, long
    time even though you are both part of the
    same personality. Coming up now at the
    count of five, and I am talking to the total
    personality, coming up now, 1-2-3-4-5.
    How do you feel?

P: I did know all those things about my
    mother.

T: You said you did?

P: Yes. I have never said them before. I
    don't know exactly when I figured out
    what was wrong with her. I was very
    young.

T: But the point is, you incorporated her in-
    side your head and so she became the
    "Witch Mother" you described.

P: Because she could hurt me so much.

T: With the looks, the nonverbal behaviors.
    The pushing away. And of course . . .

Reconciliation between patient's mother and child
ego-states reduces anxiety
and depression.

Time is needed to mend the
hurt.

Now out of hypnosis.

Child's perception of her
mother — whether percep-
tion is actually correct is
irrelevant. She introjected
perception.

P: I did, I drove her crazy.

T: But you also did it inside your head. You continued. What you did was to introject not only that mother, but the drama between mother and child. And you continued the drama inside your head.

> Patient must take responsibility for her introjected mother.

P: That's true.

T: It has nothing to do with whether your real mother would be alive or dead outside. That's irrelevant. What you came in for was that problem inside of you that you were describing to me and the conflict that you held. And that's what you introjected. So that the three-year-old you were telling me about, who was so angry and so upset and distant and standing in the corner the last time you talked to me, that's because of the relationship with mother, because she was so hurt and so angry because of it.

> Expanding interpretation.

P: Yes, I am sure that's true.

T: But the point of it is you were talking about the "Witch Mother" inside your head. Well, you told me before you had the sense that they were in conflict with one another. That's why I tried to contact both of them and to bring them together so they are no longer in conflict.

P: I really threatened her as a child, I can remember it. Almost as though she was afraid — she was — that I could get to her as a person.

T: Well, you repeated that whole syndrome inside your head.

> The patient has suffered from depression as the ego-state (introject) of her mother berated the child state. This was the drama she perceived as a child. Her real relationship with her mother today is now good.

P: In what way? You mean just telling you?

T: No. The relationship with mother is good.

P: Yes, it is.

T: So what I am talking about is that you introjected in ego-states the drama that you experienced early in life. And you are the one who told me about the "Witch Mother." So I simply contacted that "Witch Mother" under hypnosis.

P: She punished me a lot.

T: But she's not going to anymore. There's no need to. Because she's been forgiven by the Three-Year-Old.

P: All right.

T: Does that make sense?

P: Yes, it does. It makes sense, you know. Lots of sense.   Cognitive understanding

After the foregoing session and a few subsequent ones, the problem between the "Witch Mother" and the three-year-old ego-state appeared to be resolved. The patient's depression lightened and she reported much less self-defeating behavior. When it is possible to discover and focus on a key conflict, an agreement between the significant ego-states often brings dramatic improvement in a few sessions. However, when there are several states involved in the difficulty a number of diplomatic interactions, relearnings, and "working-through" hours may be required before real progress appears.

QUESTIONS REGARDING EGO-STATE THERAPY

A number of issues and criticisms have been raised reagarding the difficulties and validity of this treatment approach. We shall try to answer some of them here.

1.   *How do you know that ego-states are real? Perhaps they are simply artifacts produced by hypnotic suggestion.*

We are fully aware of the influence of operator variables on outcomes, especially in the practice of hypnosis. We try to be as non-directive as possible. These entities often emerge spontaneously and are quite unexpected by us, either in their actual existence or in their content and reactions. Attempts on our part to ignore or dismiss them frequently fail. We realize that only actual experience in working with them or listening to tapes or sessions may be convincing to therapists who are not acquainted with this conceptualization of personality structure.

2.   *If ego-states are real personality entities, why have they not been discovered before by many others?*

They have been. In their extreme form, they are manifested as multiple personalities, a well-validated diagnosis with over a hundred reported cases in the literature. However, when the boundaries between them are more permeable, and they are not so highly energized, they may remain covert. When they are covert, they are not usually observable unless the therapist employs hypnosis to activate them. Even many hypnotherapists, who do not believe in them and are not alert to their possibility, may fail to provide opportunities for them to emerge. Accordingly, they are overlooked. To the accusation that because of our beliefs we suggest their existence as artifacts, we can only reply that operator influence can be negative as well as positive. One should guard equally against the blindness of failing to see what is there because of preconceived views as well as seeing what is not there.

> 3. *Are you not encouraging patients to dissociate when we want to reduce dissociation?*

Uncovering a repression does not increase a patient's repressive tendencies — quite the opposite, if the findings of psychoanalysis are valid. So is it also with the controlled dissociation of hypnotic ego-state activation. As the patient becomes acquainted with his or her various states, more permeability of boundaries and flexibility of personality ensue. Rather than being frightened at having experiences occur over which he or she had no control, and of whose causes the patient was unaware, our patient becomes more comfortable within his/her entire self — even coming to joke about the various ego-states, calling them by name and recounting how each one influenced him or her recently. Through controlled dissociations, we bring the various facets of the personality into consciousness and under better control, thus approaching the desirable therapeutic goal — what Freud meant when he said: "Where there was Id, there shall be Ego."[5]

SUMMARY

Ego-state therapy involves a conception of personality structure as being organized more like a confederation than a unity. There are individual states (comparable to Montana and California) with "local" ego government as well as a "national" (whole person) self-jurisdiction. Partial dissociation is adaptive. It provides the personality with specialized behavior systems and flexibility in meeting different environmental demands. However, extreme dissociation, combined with cognitive dissonance and conflict between the various sub-systems, creates severe physical and behavioral symptoms. When ego-states are highly energized and have very impermeable boundaries, awareness between them may not even exist. In such a case, an alternating multiple personality results.

The ego-state that is most highly energized and is dominant is said to be "executive." It is "the self" in "the now." Ego-states act as part-persons. When hypnotically or spontaneously activated, they experience themselves as subject ("I") and perceive other ego-states as objects ("he," "she," or "it"). They struggle to protect their unique identity just as entire persons do. They are probably the same entities as found by the Hilgards in their "hidden observer" studies.

Ego-state therapy is the application of group and family therapy procedures for the resolution of conflicts between the various ego-states that constitute a "family of self" within a single individual. Such states are usually activated under hypnosis and can then be studied separately by any of the usual evaluative techniques, such as interviews or psychological tests. The conflicts between various ego-states within a person, or the cognitive dissonance between the needs of any state and the entire individual, are handled as one would in group or family therapy. Any of the various therapeutic procedures – behavioral, cognitive, analytic, or humanistic – may be employed. The aim is a kind of internal diplomacy reconciling antagonistic ego-states and finding better ways by which they can meet their respective needs.

As internal dissension subsides, and as the cognitive dissonance between the various states decreases, the boundaries between them become less rigid. Intrapersonal communication and cooperation improve. Anxiety subsides, painful symptoms diminish, and the individual's behavior is more adaptive. He or she becomes less dissociated, more integrated, and better aware of the functioning of the whole self.

Ego-state therapy is itself simply an integration and application of concepts from many fields – behaviorism, psychoanalysis, humanism, hypnosis, multiple personality study, family and group therapy, and diplomacy. Through its theoretical position and application, we have found considerably increased success in understanding and treating many previously difficult therapeutic problems.

REFERENCES

1. American Psychiatric Association. *Diagnostic and Statistical Manual of Mental Disorders (DSM-III)*. Washington, DC: American Psychiatric Association (1980).
2. Berne, E. *Transactional Analysis in Psychotherapy*. New York: Grove (1961).
3. Bernheim, H. *Hypnosis and Suggestion in Psychotherapy*. New Hyde Park, NY: University Books (1965). First published in French (1884).
4. Federn, P. *In*: Weiss, E. (Ed.). *Ego Psychology and the Psychoses*. New York: Basic Books (1952).
5. Freud, S. *The Ego and the Id*. 19 *(Standard Edition)*. Strachey, J. (Ed.). London: Hogarth (1961).
6. Gill, M. M. Hypnosis as an altered and regressed state. *International Journal of Clinical and Experimental Hypnosis*. 20:224–237 (1972).
7. Hartmann, H. *Ego Psychology and the Problem of Adaptation*. New York: International Universities Press (1958).
8. Hilgard, E. R. *Divided Consciousness: Multiple Controls in Human Thought and Action*. New York: Wiley (1977).
9. Hilgard, E. R. and Hilgard, J. R. *Hypnosis in the Relief of Pain*. Los Altos, CA: William Kaufmann (1975).

10. Kohut, H. *In*: Ornstein, P. H. (Ed.). *The Search for Self* I, II. New York: International Universities Press (1978).

11. Orne, M. T. On the simulating subject as a quasi-control group in hypnosis research: What, why and how. *In*: Fromm, E. and Shor, R. (Eds.). *Hypnosis: Research Developments and Perspectives*. Chicago: Aldine-Atherton (1972).

12. Prince, M. *The Dissociation of a Personality*. New York: Longmans-Green (1925).

13. Rosenthal, R. *Experimenter Effects in Behavioral Research*. New York: Appleton-Century-Cross (1966).

14. Schreiber, F. R. *Sybil*. New York: Warner Paperback Library (1974).

15. Tart, C. T. (Ed.). *Altered States of Consciousness*. New York: Wiley (1969).

16. Thigpen, C. H. and Cleckley, H. M. *Three Faces of Eve*. New York: McGraw-Hill (1957).

17. Watkins, H. H. The silent abreaction. *International Journal of Clinical and Experimental Hypnosis*. 28:101–113 (1980).

18. Watkins, H. H. and Watkins, J. G. *Hypnoanalytic Ego-State Therapy* (Audio Tape No. 94). Orlando, FL: American Academy of Psychotherapist Tape Library (1976).

19. Watkins, J. G. *The Therapeutic Self*. New York: Human Sciences Press (1978).

20. Watkins, J. G. The psychodynamic manipulation of ego states in hypnotherapy. *In*: Antonelli, F. (Ed.). *Therapy in Psychosomatic Medicine* II *(Symposia)*. Rome, Italy: Proceedings of the 4th International Congress of Psychosomatic Medicine (1977).

21. Watkins, J. G. Ego states and the problem of responsibility: A psychological analysis of the Patty Hearst case. *Journal of Psychiatry and Law*, pp. 471–489 (Winter 1976).

22. Watkins, J. G. Ego states and the problem of responsibility II: The case of Patricia W. *Journal of Psychiatry and Law*, pp. 519–535 (Winter 1978).

23. Watkins, J. G. and Johnson, R. J. *We, the Divided Self*. New York: Irvington Press (1981).

24. Watkins, J. G. and Watkins, H. H. *Abreactive Technique* (Audio Tape). New York: Psychotherapy Tape Library (1978).

25. Watkins, J. G. and Watkins, H. H. The theory and practice of ego-state therapy. *In*: Grayson, H. (Ed.). *Short Term Approaches to Psychotherapy*. New York: Human Sciences Press (1979).

26. Watkins, J. G. and Watkins, H. H. Ego-states and hidden observers. *Journal of Altered States of Consciousness* 5:3–18 (1979–1980).

27. Watkins, J. G. and Watkins, H. H. *1. Ego-States and Hidden Observers. 2. Ego-State Therapy: The Woman in Black and the Lady in White* (Audio Tapes and Scripts). New York: Jeffrey Norton (1980).

28. Watkins, J. G. and Watkins, H. H. Ego-state therapy. *In*: Corsini, R. (Ed.). *Handbook of Innovative Therapies*. New York: Wiley (1981).

29. Wolpe, J. The systematic desensitization treatment of neuroses. *Journal of Nervous and Mental Disorders* 132:189–203 (1961).

Part II
Therapy With Children

Therapy with children has long been central to American ideals and practice, and the two chapters of Part II examine different facets of thinking and practice in this active area.

Evelyn Heimlich's contribution on paraverbal psychotherapy stakes out a new focus of attention for workers with children. Based on her many years' work at the New York State Psychiatric Institute in New York City, her ideas have the true ring of the innovative. Her chapter is a valuable and insightful illustration of how a creative practitioner, confronted with intractable problems and difficulties, seeks a solution grounded in her own experience and talents.

Ann Jernberg's chapter describes a new form of therapy with children that is based on a replication, within the therapeutic experience, of the original parent-infant relationship. In its extension to other areas of work with children, this new approach lends itself to expression as "family theraplay," in which it focuses on establishing bonding between adoptive children and their foster parents.

The following chapter describes an alternate approach to the treatment of children with communication difficulties. It is called paraverbal psychotherapy, and it uses principally sensorimotor channels for communication between therapist and patient. Through paraverbal psychotherapy techniques, lines of communication have been opened for children who have behavioral manifestations of such pathology as muteness, language disorders, withdrawal, and aggressiveness. Any simple media that provide pleasure are used as tools for communication, including fingerpaints, elastic ropes, soap bubbles, water, and simple string and percussion instruments. Specific application of paraverbal psychotherapy techniques to the treatment of three cases is delineated.

9

Paraverbal Psychotherapy:
A Multisensory Approach to
Communication With
Inaccessible Children

Evelyn Heimlich, B.A.

Paraverbal psychotherapy is a method of treatment in which the therapist communicates with the patient principally through sensorimotor channels. As the name of the therapy implies, sensorimotor communication does not replace verbal communication, but is used alongside it.

Paraverbal psychotherapy has proven to be effective in a variety of situations wherein the traditional forms of communication between therapist and patient have proven inadequate. The rationale underlying the therapy with children is that if the child can be engaged in activity that is pleasurable, and if the child can be made to feel accepted, maladaptive behavior will be decreased and a therapeutic relationship will be established. The child will be able to discharge tension and ventilate ideas and feelings. Amelioration of symptoms will follow.

Communication with the child is established primarily through sound, movement, and touch — the last playing a central role.[7] Accompanying these channels for communication are, of course, visual stimuli and a minimum of words. The techniques used in paraverbal therapy have been organized into maneuvers. Each maneuver has its own channel for communication, as well as ways in which the channel is to be used. Any media that provide pleasure are used as tools for communication. They include nonverbal vocalizations, statements in the form of rhymes, familiar song melodies, miming, and dramatization. The materials used include fingerpaints, elastic ropes, soap bubbles, water, and simple string and percussion instruments. While the materials used are similar to those employed in play therapy or (at times) in verbal therapy, the paraverbal goal is different. Emphasis is on communication and the purposeful attenuation of the disorganizing effects in the child when they are aroused, particularly by verbal therapy. None of the materials requires any great degree of skill. This last feature should not only be reassuring to any prospective therapist; it also has its rationale in terms of the child. For example, it is practically impossible for one to make a mistake when asked to tap a drum or clash cymbals together, and so the child is quickly given an opportunity to feel competent and even successful, always a pleasurable experience.

The therapist maintains control of the situation and keeps the session structured by a variety of strategies. The therapist's facial expressions, body movements, and voice modulations provide structure and also act as stimuli and as a possible model for the child to imitate.[4] Changing the volume, accent, or tempo of rhythmic sound also helps to maintain the session's structure. Sound and movement are intertwined when familiar songs are accompanied by mime, dramatization, and other motor activity.

The maneuvers are dominated by either sound or movement, but incorporate both, and also include visual, verbal, and tactile elements. For example, in a sound-dominated maneuver, a drum may be used at first as a percussive vehicle to present neutral sounds, such as a simple rhythmic pattern, but in the course of the session, it can be developed into a means of communicating fear or anger; it can become part of a percussive dialogue. Later on in the session, it can be used to stimulate verbal comment. It can accompany and intensify body movement, chants, or songs. There are maneuvers with which familiar folk melodies or improvised songs may be used to stimulate mime, dramatization, role-playing, the revelation of hidden feelings, and so on. The same holds true of all the maneuvers.

The voice can be used with or without melody, with or without words, or with improvised rhyme, chanted or sung, according to the communicative needs of the moment. Sessions usually (but not always) start with percussive instruments. These instruments are useful because they are attractive, often familiar, and easy to use. The usual sonorities that they create differ from speech, and are less threatening on this account.

It should be stressed that the maneuvers are often (but definitely not always) used in an established sequence. For example, in dealing with a very young elective mute[5] child, the first problem is to command his or her attention. If, in addition, the child is hyperactive, it is at times necessary to substitute for a percussive approach the penetrating, yet soft and unusual, sound of the therapist's singing voice, using the patient's name and directing the vocal and accompanying string instrument sound directly at the child. Thus, to a familiar tune such as "Frere Jacques," the therapist would improvise, "I like Tom, I like Tom. He is good, he is nice."

Because it is of the essence to create an atmosphere in which the child feels pleasure and acceptance, the paraverbal therapist is constantly alert to the child's responses, tries to anticipate boredom, and is ready to swiftly change maneuvers when the child's interest flags.

The maneuvers employed provide the child with a means of keeping a distance from what is troubling him or her; improvising chants or songs about neutral third parties, for example, is less threatening than a direct confrontation. The sensorimotor approach provides concrete, failure-free opportunities for fulfillment of such basic needs as improved body image, development of identification, sense of mastery, and spontaneity and trust, while enabling the child to perceive and communicate appropriate concrete responses to the various maneuvers. The recognition and success the child experiences through multisensory maneuvers help to command and expand his/her attention, raise self-esteem, and establish rapport with the therapist, as both child and therapist participate reciprocally, synchronously, and pleasurefully throughout the session.

In all maneuvers, whether sound or movement dominated, the child is encouraged to imitate the therapist in order to stimulate reciprocal behavior and ensuing communication. If the child fails to imitate the therapist, roles are reversed. Then the therapist playfully imitates the child, sometimes even his/her slightest involuntary movement. This usually evokes laughter, and a pleasure relationship is begun.[8] Continued, shared joy is a most essential part of all paraverbal psychotherapy sessions. It helps form a basis for the development of a trusting relationship and increases the likelihood of eventual communication on a higher level.[6]

In each case below, excerpts have been extrapolated to illustrate specific uses of the maneuvers.

CASE 1 When P, a well-developed boy of four and a half, was two and a half years old, his mother first noticed his silence and staring. Until then, he had been in the care of the janitor while she worked. With the arrival of a second child, she had to stay home. On the advice of the janitor, she took P to her local hospital for help.

The hospital's findings were as follows: Poor relationships with staff and peers; egocentric play; deviant motor behavior; and severe developmental lags affecting speech, cognition, affective expression, and integrative ability. In American Psychiatric Association DSM III terms, he displayed the behavioral characteristics of autism,[2] which was the diagnosis given by the hospital.

When attempts at traditional treatment were inadequate, he was transferred to the New York State Psychiatric Institute, where he was referred to the author for paraverbal therapy.

He had two half-hour sessions with me per week for two years. (At the end of this period, he was discharged to his home and was able to attend a special education class at the local public school.) The following is a description of his first session.

As soon as he entered the room, I seated him opposite me, knee to knee for intimacy. I tapped a shining metal drum with my fingers, then handed it to him and encouraged him to do likewise. He was intrigued, took the drum, and gave it a good loud bang. He looked at me in pleased surprise at the sound he had made. I smiled back, showing great pleasure and approval, and said, "Good, P, good!" Then I developed this maneuver further by tapping the drum with my hands, knuckles, and fists. P copied me and was fascinated when he discovered the different sounds he could make with the various parts of his hands. He wanted to repeat our little percussion dialogue over and over. But suddenly, without warning and before I had a chance to observe his satiety with this maneuver, he slid from his chair to the floor.

I immediately introduced a maneuver that was movement-dominated, in contrast to the sound-dominated maneuver he had just rejected. This time, his pleasure came through touch[7] and body movement.[11] I grasped both of his legs as he lay on the floor and began to move them back and forth so his knees bent toward his abdomen and then his feet came straight up in the air. This movement was altered with my rhythmically stretching his legs out into a V and moving them together again. In the meantime, I playfully chanted descriptive lyrics, which went as follows: "Pushing, pushing, back and forth, pushing, pushing, out and in." P showed his pleasure by the smile on his face and the eagerness with which he responded to my rhythmic movement of his legs. I continued, introducing a different experience with new descriptive words and movement. I changed the tempo and direction of his leg movement and at the same time chanted the new words, "Up and down," and "Fast and slow." He was particularly amused at my tempo change, and laughed every time I moved his legs from a slow to a fast tempo. Soon he tired of the movement and I felt his legs beginning to go limp. I gently let go of his legs and he promptly stood up.

To maintain his attention and reciprocal,[12] pleasureful involvement with me, I quickly took his hand and, with my free hand, I gave a strum on the autoharp (an 18-inch oblong stringed instrument) that was on the nearby table. He was curious about the new sound and stretched out his hand to touch the strings. I encouraged him. Then I had both of us sit down and I placed the autoharp partly on his lap and partly on mine. This was so we could have the synchronous[12] experience of sharing the vibrations of the strings as we took turns in strumming them. When he lost interest in this aspect of the maneuver, I stimulated him further by adding personal words, chanting his name and strumming (i.e., I chanted his name and a description of what we were doing). The chant went as follows: "I like P, I like P, he is good, he is nice. We strum the autoharp, we strum the autoharp. I like him, I like him." He was particularly delighted to hear his name and his praises chanted over and over again. Every time I sang of him and my liking him, he smiled.

Lest his interest and pleasure wane, I introduced a new body movement that involved intimacy and touch[7] as well as a reinforcement of the slow and fast pleasureful time experience he had had earlier in the session. I gently but firmly put aside the autoharp and set him astride my lap so that we faced each other. I then took his hands in mine and began swinging him back and forth as I chanted, "Swinging, swinging, back and forth." He became mischievous and started leaning back all the way to the floor. I pretended amazement and alarm as he vigorously pulled down and then sprang forward again. We both laughed as he began to feel masterful in his swinging movements. At the height of his pleasure, I stood him up, lest he become overstimulated and out of control. I quietly took his hand and softly chanted, "Goodbye, P, see you some more," accenting the word more. P looked up at me, smiled as we left the room, and said his first word, "More."

The first session revealed that P could be engaged and could be involved in appropriate motor behavior.

CASE 2   Several years after I had developed and refined the maneuvers used in paraverbal therapy, it occurred to me that this treatment approach with its variety and flexibility might have wider application. It might be useful in the simultaneous treatment of a dyad of children, especially if the children were of different ages.

The idea developed while I was on the ward. I was observing an inaccessible eleven-year-old girl tenderly help an equally inaccessible five-year-old boy to put on his shoes and tie his shoelaces. Their mutual satisfaction in the interchange was remarkable. It was the first time either one of them had showed any interest whatsoever in another individual. Accordingly, I decided to pair the older child with the younger one in paraverbal therapy treatment sessions. Many of their problems would be similar, but the older child would act as my "assistant" and help me treat the younger child. S, the older child, entered the New York State Psychiatric Institute when she was eleven. Her younger brother had been treated for autism when he was four, but when he became well, S came to view him as a serious rival for her parents' affection. His excellence in school and the admiration he received from the family were more than S could cope with. She developed problems at school, where her teacher reported the following: She would not speak[5] either to the teacher or to peers; she was rigid and oppositional; and she could not learn. These problems, in turn, were followed by ulcerative colitis that proved unresponsive to treatment. She was admitted to the hospital with a diagnosis of obsessive-compulsive neurosis and ulcerative colitis. It was after six weeks of traditional psychotherapy, in which she remained uncooperative, that she began paraverbal therapy with me. The immediate goals for S, at this point, were: (1) to gratify her childish needs by exposing her, in the service of a younger child, to regressive maneuvers[1] such as rocking, hopping, skipping, creeping, and rolling on the floor (the use of this regressive behavior, it was hoped, would give her such gratification that she could more easily move to a level of more independent activity; (2) to help her to develop greater spontaneity;[11] and (3) to provide her with the means of increasing the repertoire of her behavior.

The younger child chosen to participate in my sessions with S was a five-year-old boy, J, who had many problems similar to hers. He was compulsive, rigid, withdrawn, oppositional, and dependent. In addition, J was mute and had a short attention span. The goals for J were: (1) to capture his attention and thus involve him in the process of therapy; (2) to get him to relate to people;[8] (3) to make restitution to him for his early deprivation; (4) to get him to listen to organized sound[4] as a step toward moving him in the direction of speech; (5) to help him with his problem of oppositionalism; and (6) to help him to overcome his compulsions.

Before beginning the joint sessions, I approached S by telling her that I had observed her on the ward helping J tie his shoelaces and playing with him. I told her of the difficulty I had in involving J for any length of time in therapy. I suggested that she could be very helpful to him as well as to me because of her tenderness for him and her patience with him. She was pleased and flattered, and readily consented to be my "assistant." I then described some of J's needs to her, telling her that J needed "to be part of the real world; to learn to explore sounds as a prelude to his learning speech; and to have the pleasures of childhood, especially the pleasure of movement." Again I shall describe the first session.

Before S and J came into the room, I placed a group of percussive instruments on the floor, where I planned to have the three of us work. It seemed a safe and appropriate place for regressive, sensorimotor, therapeutic experiences to take place. S entered the room with J reluctantly tagging along behind her. I motioned to her to bring him to where I was seated on the floor with the instruments. She coaxed the boy along and then sat quietly and attentively observing. J promptly picked up the bells and started shaking them at random, much as a baby would with a rattle. With this minimal participation on his part, I improvised a rhythmic bell song, trying to structure his random movements into rhythmic ones, but without success. In the meantime, S spontaneously picked up a tambourine and reinforced my rhythmic playing. J looked at her, but was still not caught up in our rhythm. I therefore told S to take J by the hands and gently and rhythmically swing him back and forth as I improvised a song about what they were doing. With this even more primitive activity, which included body contact,[7] I hoped to stimulate both children through synchronous behavior. Since this maneuver, too, produced no rhythmic response in J, I altered it by joining hands with both youngsters, forming a circle with them. The three of us swayed back and forth, and at last, after I strongly accented the words rhythmically, J responded. However, he soon dropped both our hands. He needed to be stimulated still further in order to be re-engaged and maintain his attention. This time I handed S a tape of bells and asked her to pull on it rhythmically with

J. His rhythmic response was immediate; he began pushing and pulling in rhythm with her motions and the improvised song with which I accompanied them. S's apparently keen sensitivity to J's needs was impressive. Without my saying anything, she noticed his waning interest and immediately picked him up and swung him in the air in a rocking rhythm. He was delighted and rewarded her with his first laugh. S looked so proud and pleased with his response that she spontaneously hugged him. However, J's attention was extremely limited, and he left the room before the session was officially concluded.

During this first session, S gave evidence that, in the service of J, she could and would be spontaneous. She observed that the various forms of organized sound, instrumental as well as vocal, in addition to the body movements, served as a bridge for communication, and said, "I hope J will like it even better the next time." Her new role as my "assistant" seemed to begin to provide her with opportunities for independence, spontaneity, and a beginning of trust[6] in me as she saw me work with J and support her in her efforts to engage him. The opportunity for needed regression[1] and motility[11] was a beginning of therapy for both of them.

Part of the "assistant therapist" technique involved having S speak to me at the end of each session about the progress that J had made, and the meaning to her of some of the things he did. These little talks allowed S to develop greater spontaneity and trust.[6] This development, in turn, helped her to feel free to project onto J her own problems and then to verbalize them.

Session No. 13 will serve to show the kind of progress both J and S were able to make.

I felt that S was now ready for a new maneuver that would help to free her from her extreme reserve and rigidity. I therefore rolled out a tall drum into the middle of the room and seated myself astride it, as if I were riding a horse. After a few moments, I said to S, "Now you sit on the drum and get J to hit it while you and I both sing about what he is doing," which she did with absolutely no sign of her usual self-consciousness. Then she got J to imitate her.[10] It seemed wise at this point to extend this maneuver further, and so, with S still mounted on the drum, she and I alternately hit each other's hands[7] and then the drum. S was as delighted as a small child at this rhythmic play. I then directed her to include J in our now more vigorous motor play.[11] To our pleasure, he became so free that, of his own accord, for the first time he walked across the room to bring over another drum. After some time, J became restless and wanted to leave the room. After I had opened the door to let him out, S brought up one of her own central themes — oppositionalism. She projected onto J her own thinking about oppositionalism. She said to me, "Now, don't lock the door. Leave it open a little and see if he wants to come back." She picked up my guitar and seated herself at the open door so that she could observe J and interpret his behavior to me. "You know what he's doing now? He's looking over at me, but when I look at him, he turns his head away." I asked, "Why do you think he does that?" "Well, he's afraid to come in because maybe he'll make a mistake. He likes to do things for himself and not to be told to do them by somebody else. You know, I think his parents must have hit him and not let him do things by himself." Of course, she was talking about herself, her fear of learning, her being told what to do, and her mother's constant demands that she be a little mother to her brother while her mother was away at work. Eventually, when J returned to the room of his own accord, S looked at me triumphantly.

As a result of her work as an "assistant therapist," S became more trusting[6] and less anxious. She developed an improved body image and an improved sense of competence. Increasingly, she was able to accept direct confrontation and then came surcease from her presenting illness. Her affirmative response was evident in a letter she wrote to me two years after her discharge from the hospital. Among other things, she said, "I miss helping you with the kids."

J, too, showed progress. His attention span increased. He related better to peers and adults; he was less rigid, less compulsive, and less oppositional. In addition, he became able to communicate verbally, although only in a limited way.[3]

CASE 3 The third case is representative of a further development in the use of paraverbal psychotherapy and its extension to more than one patient. Currently it is being used at St. Luke's Hospital in New York to serve the needs of adolescent mothers and their children. It evolved in response to the staff's reports that efforts to help these patients were hampered by the inability of the patients to communicate.

E was a sixteen-year-old unmarried mother with two children — one a baby girl, R, eight-months-old; the other a three and a half-year-old boy, K. The mother was a depressed, lonely Hispanic young woman. The baby, R, was listless and did not thrive well. The boy, K, was hyperactive, had language difficulties, and could not be retained in the local preschool.

The treatment goals were to provide: (1) restitution for the mother and children through the pleasures available in paraverbal psychotherapy; (2) to improve communication between mother and children; (3) to develop attachment between mother and children; and (4) to have the mother use the paraverbal therapist as a model for behavior.

The therapist gently placed a plastic circle of wristbells in the boy's hands, who was helped to close his fingers over the circle so he could maintain his grasp. She gave a wristbell circle to the mother as well. To guide them in what to do with a minimum of talk, the therapist began chanting the descriptive words, "Pulling, pulling, back and forth." At the same time, in order to share the circle and help with the pulling, she grasped each of the circles that mother and child held. Simultaneously, she rocked back and forth as she pulled them to and fro. This event provided pleasure in kinesthetic stimulation as well as a feeling of safety and trust, which is attained from synchronous, rhythmic body movement.[12] As they worked together, K began to smile. To maintain interest and to reinforce their pleasure, the therapist now stimulated them with the novelty of a new tempo. She said, with excitement in her voice, "Now let's pull fast, very fast." Both mother and child laughed as they had this new synchronous experience. The therapist followed this with a different movement producing new excitement. Still using the bracelets as a tool, she now had them experience a change of direction as well as of pace. She chanted, demonstrated, and moved their tightly grasped bell circles up and down, first slowly, then fast. This provided still more synchronous experience. At this point, the therapist relinquished the bracelets, and mother and son pulled them back and forth independently without her physical participation. However, to support them, she chanted about what they were doing. As they worked together, the mother began smiling at the boy, who smiled back at his mother in pleasure.

In order to extend this nurturing synchronous experience, an elastic rope was then placed by the therapist around the mother, the son, and herself. The therapist modeled the way they should place their hands on the rope and began to sway as she chanted, "Pulling, pulling, pulling in a circle." She thus provided a means for mother and child to imitate her body movement, and made a beginning effort at incorporating developmental behavior. Both mother and child showed pleasure as their shoulders touched in the synchronous swaying back and forth.

The next event involved the use of three pairs of small cymbals. With the therapist once again acting as the model, she demonstrated and chanted the following, "I tap mommy, mommy taps me; I tap K, K taps me; mommy taps K, K taps mommy." (These words are sung to the tune of "Frere Jacques.") The purposes of this procedure were threefold: (1) to develop communication through reciprocal involvement; (2) to provide mutual stimulation, nurture, and pleasure through a new kinesthetic, auditory, tactile experience; and (3) to reinforce the child's previous impulse control experience in the session.

Now that mother and son had shared joint pleasure in a few simple preparatory experiences, a slightly more complex experience was introduced. For the first time, the baby was mentioned by name and actively included. With accompanying autoharp and with improvised lyrics, the therapist described her feelings of affection and admiration for each one of them, as follows: "I like K, I like mommy, I like R, they are good, they are nice." Both mother and son looked over at the baby when the therapist introduced her name into the lyrics. The mother looked pleased and surprised when the baby was mentioned and even more so when the therapist deliberately included the baby in the event by placing wristbells in front of her. The mother spontaneously picked up the bells, shook them at the baby, and was delighted when the baby reached for them. The therapist then gave additional wristbells to mother and son so they could accompany her while she played and chanted words describing what they were doing. During the chanting, the baby spontaneously turned over on her belly, jiggled the bells, and moved herself toward the group. K patted her on the head. The mother smiled.

To further develop the feeling of mutual relatedness and intimacy, the therapist picked up the baby, put her in the center of the group, and had everyone take hands to form a circle around the baby. Then, with all of them swaying together, she started to chant the following: "Here we are together, all sitting on the floor. We're singing, we're smiling, we're looking at the baby." The baby began to coo, and K said, "She's talking. She's smiling." The mother nodded. When it was time for the session to end, the therapist stood up and chanted, "Good-bye everybody. Come again. It is nice to play with you. Come again." The mother picked up the baby and dressed her while the therapist helped K with his jacket. When the therapist sang, "Come again," K said, "Again." The mother smiled. The therapist opened the door and said, "See you next Wednesday."

The response of this family to the paraverbal therapy maneuvers offered during the first session made me feel that communication could be developed and that there was a possibility for the eventual achievement of some of the goals. The accuracy of this judgment proved valid when, at the end of the thirteenth session, the following results were obtained.

1. The mother was less depressed and more hopeful. She asked to be referred to a school for the boy.
2. She spontaneously introduced new ways of using the materials with both children.
3. She touched and looked at them more frequently.
4. The boy turned more frequently to his mother and occasionally to the baby.
5. The baby started to babble and occasionally reached out toward her mother and brother.

SUMMARY

A description of paraverbal psychotherapy and its rationale was given, with the central role of pleasure and acceptance in the use of the various sensorimotor maneuvers underscored. The theoretical concepts of investigators in the field of child therapy were indicated in support of the multi-faceted, chiefly nonverbal, approach to communication with inaccessible child patients. The specific application of paraverbal psychotherapy maneuvers in the treatment of three cases, with patients having markedly different pathologies, was described.

REFERENCES

1. Alpert, A. Reversibility of pathological fixations associated with maternal deprivation in infancy. *Psychological Study of the Child* 14:169–185 (1959).
2. American Psychiatric Association. *Diagnostic and Statistical Manual of Mental Disorders (DSM III)*. Washington, DC: American Psychiatric Association (1978).
3. Bruner, J. The cognitive consequences of early sensory deprivation. *Psychosomatic Medicine* 21 (1959).
4. Clark, G. The education of noncommunicating children. *In:* Renfrew, C. and Murphy, K. (Eds.). *The Child Who Does Not Talk.* London: The Spastics Society Medical and Information Unit and Heinemann Medical Books (1964).

5. Elson, A. *et al.* Follow-up study of childhood elective mutism. *Archives of General Psychiatry* 13:182–187 (1965).
6. Erikson, E. H. *Childhood and Society.* New York: Norton (1950).
7. Frank, L. K. Tactile communication. *In:* Bosmajian, H. A. (Ed.). *The Rhetoric of Nonverbal Communication.* Glenview Scott (1971).
8. Freud, A. *The Psychoanalytic Treatment of Children.* New York: International Universities Press (1946).
9. Heimlich, E. Paraverbal techniques in the therapy of childhood communication disorders. *International Journal of Psychotherapy* 1(1):65–83 (1972).
10. Hendrick, I. Early development of the ego: Identification in infancy. *Psychoanalytic Quarterly* 20:44–71 (1951).
11. Mittelmann, B. Motility in infants, children and adults. *Psychoanalytic Study of Child* 9:142–177 (1954).
12. Stern, D. The goal and structure of mother–infant play. *In:* Lewis, M. and Rosenblum, L. (Eds.). *The Origins of Behavior* 2. New York: Wiley, pp. 187–213 (1974).

Theraplay is a new form of psychotherapy which replicates the parent-infant relationship. Like a mother with her baby, the theraplay therapist structures, challenges, intrudes, and nurtures (SCIN) and, like the wholesome parent, the therapist does all of this in an atmosphere that is joyful, physical, and intensely personal. The chapter provides a sampling of guidelines for the therapist, describes which kinds of children benefit and which do not, outlines the process of family theraplay, and focuses on theraplay as a method for bonding older adoptive children to their new parents. Included as well are some notes of caution to therapists undertaking to do this form of treatment, and references to the combining of theraplay with speech therapy and with sensory motor integration therapy. The chapter ends on a note of optimism that future developments will offer yet newer ideas and applications, and that future research will yield a yet better understanding of theraplay's effectiveness.

10

Theraplay:
The Nursery Revisited

Ann M. Jernberg, Ph.D.

Theraplay[9] is a psychotherapeutic modality that reenacts the wholesome aspects of the mother-infant relationship.

Every baby needs to receive the kinds of attention that are optimally growth-fostering and enhancing of self-esteem. Given this attention, babies become competent, confident, and trusting. They come to see themselves as special, important, lovable, and worthy; and they come to see their uniqueness and worth reflected in the eyes of those who interact with them. They come to develop a view of their world not only as a secure, trustworthy, responsive, and apprecia-tive place, but as one that is exciting and fun as well. In the absence of these kinds of attention, both their image of self and their view of the world may suffer. The infant so deprived may come to feel empty, alone, unworthy, ugly, or "bad," and to view the world as cruel, cold, withholding, punitive, chaotic, exploiting, bewildering, or grim. We are not surprised when children with these outlooks are referred for help, for, in their effort to fill the void, such children may become withdrawn, aggressive, psychosomatic, addictive, pseudomature, rebellious, or short on temper or attention span.

These disasters are most likely to be absent when bonding and attachment[5] proceed as smoothly as possible. In ideal development, the following conditions will be met: (1) through body postures, gurgles and cooing, and smiles, the infant will invite the mother's engagement; (2) the infant's mother will be alert to her child's physical and vocal cues, and be empathic to his or her underlying emotional state; and (3) she will be ever ready to respond at the level and with the kind of response required by the child. Since both mother and child are involved, it is important that both mother and child be in good functioning order. If anything happens, or has happened, to interfere with the optimal functioning of either, the whole developmental sequence can be thrown off track. Later on, when the child appears for therapy, it becomes the task of the therapist first to assess what has been missing in the way of good mothering and then to remedy the loss. Although several therapeutic schools agree that "failure in mothering can create excessive vulnerability to anxiety and disrupt adequate defensive development,"[17] the ways in which this remediation takes place will vary even among therapies that hold in common the belief that childhood deprivation can produce later disturbances. Variations generally concern not what is missing, nor the conviction that compensation is appropriate, but rather the extent to which the therapy is verbal versus nonverbal and how these primitive needs are to be satisfied. Paraphrasing Kohut, Langs[17] writes, "since many of these problems are pre-verbal, they will be accessible to change largely through non-verbal attitudes in the therapist and verbalizations which are in keeping with the patient's needs as derived from this period . . . " and, paraphrasing Balint, Langs goes on to caution that ". . . gratifications of the patient's wishes that go beyond the appropriate boundaries of the therapeutic relationship make the therapist an indulgent, over-stimulating, over-gratifying mother-figure and thereby a bad therapist-mother . . . Inappropriate gratifications foster regressions for the sake of indulgence and need satisfaction that is malignant regression."

The task of the theraplay therapist, whether working with a six-month-old infant or an adolescent, is two-fold: First, to determine at what developmental stage and on which side of the mother-child equation (if not on both sides) the damage has occurred; second, to fill the resulting void in ways that, although directed to the underlying baby, are neither overstimulating nor overindulging.

There is no better way to determine exactly what has been responsible for interrupting the parent-infant attachment process than through observing parent-child pairs as they perform together. The tasks of the Marschak Interaction Method (MIM)[18] provide just this opportunity. Whether the child is a year old or 21, his or her style and degree of appeal and effectiveness can be clearly seen on the MIM, as can both the parent's capacity for appropriate engagement and empathy and the child's consequent degree of responsiveness to that effort. Observers of the MIM session can pinpoint how satisfying are the interactions between a particular parent-child pair and under what conditions communication and mutual satisfaction break down. When administration of the MIM is not feasible, determination of a child's psychological needs must, of course, be made on the basis of other evidence (e.g., psychological testing, teacher observation, or "trial" or diagnostic theraplay, etc.).

Having made the determination that a parent is too harsh, too rigid, too permissive, too seductive, too ambitious, too indulging, too distant, too clinging, or too exploiting, one formulates a treatment strategy, just as such a strategy can be determined by noting that a child is too tyrannical, too undifferentiated, too accident-prone, too suspicious, too self-effacing, too autonomous, or too dependent. Plans can then be made for helping each of the two individuals overcome his or her "weaknesses," either independently or, in the best of treatment situations, with each other.

Theraplay is designed to set on the "right" course the previously interrupted — or inadequately established — bonding and attachment. Ideally, as stated above, both parent and child are available to participate in the treatment process. When they are not (that is, when, of necessity, as in Head Start programs, for example, the child alone appears for the theraplay sessions) the treatment aim is still one of belatedly allowing the child to become familiar with the joys and security he or she would have known if he/she had had optimal parenting. (Under no circumstances, however, is the treatment aim one of allowing the child to have any and all experiences his or her heart desires.) Normal parenting — that is, normal nursery interaction — if studied closely, contains at least four dimensions, which, alone or in combination with one another, may take center stage at any one moment: Structuring, challenging, intruding, and nurturing (SCIN). In her setting of rules, following of routines, firm holding, and defining of her baby's body boundaries, the mother's activities are *structuring*. In her efforts to help the child expand his/her horizons, she *challenges* the child to stretch, to reach, and to communicate wishes. *Intrusion* characterizes her games of blowing on the infant's eyelids, jumping into view like a jack-in-the-box, gurgling on his/her tummy, or playing peek-a-boo. And finally, in a million and one comforting, feeding, reassuring, and soothing ways, she *nurtures* the child. These same four nursery characteristics — structuring, challenging, intruding, and nurturing — are the basic dimensions of theraplay.

Since it is assumed that the life experience of the child in need of psychotherapy has generally been deficient in one or more of the ingredients of the happy nursery, it becomes the job of the theraplay therapist, always with reassuring firmness and in the spirit of engagement and joy, to provide one or more of these ingredients.

The child's reported symptomatic behavior (if not the observed parent-child interaction) determines whether it is best for the therapist to structure, challenge, intrude, or nurture. Obsessive children, for example, being already too structured and often too challenged, tend to respond well to both intrusion and nurturing. Although the child may appear uneasy and resistant at first, surprising and playful activities,[1] all in a physical, rather than mental, context, soon prove too tempting for even the obsessive child to refuse. The autistic child benefits from the same prescriptions. Being in so many ways even further along the continuum of rigidity, control, and tyranny,[7] he or she requires more intense intrusions yet.

Children who, either motorically (hyperactivity) or ideationally (schizo-phrenia), are overactive, require structuring. To intrude or challenge would only intensify their problem. Challenge, together with structure, is appropriate, how-ever, for the colorful yet diffuse, dramatizing child whose wishful, impulsive denial of fact and avoidance of serious questions have earned him or her the label "hysteric."[21] For the pseudomature child — the boy who boasts and swaggers, the girl who wiggles seductively — nurturing theraplay, generally resisted behe-mently rather than overtly wished for by this kind of child, is aimed at the little baby underlying his or her caricature of the fully grown adult.

Theraplay, of course, is not for everyone. There are children who either should not receive theraplay or cannot make use of it. A child who has suffered a recent emotional or physical trauma, for example, deserves careful understanding, reduc-tion of anxiety, the opportunity to ventilate feelings, and help in coming to realize that, even though he or she may have wished for what happened, there are limitations to the part the child played in its outcome. Additionally, such children must be re-assured as to legitimate expectations for protection in the future. One further group deserves mention: Children classified "sociopathic," even young ones, seem to de-rive no long-lasting benefits from theraplay. Parental commitment to family change, a seeming rarity in these cases, is essential if there is to be change at all. Thera-play, even family theraplay (to be discussed later), cannot usually bring this about.

To the extent that the theraplay session replicates a moment in the nursery, it differs from traditional child therapy. Some of the ways in which the thera-play therapist attempts to be the ideal model of the ideal mother are (1) by focusing exclusively on the child; (2) by being in charge and "running the show," neither asking permission of the client to do, nor apologizing for having done, what the therapist knows will be beneficial; (3) by relating physically and con-cretely rather than verbally and abstractly; (4) by dealing with the here and now rather than with the past; (5) by dealing with reality rather than with fantasy; (6) by being cheerful and optimistic rather than gloomy and sad; (7) by using pri-marily the child's and his/her own bodies rather than using puzzles, dollhouses, or games; (8) by responding to the child's uniqueness, beauty, lovability, liveli-ness, or strength rather than to discrete tasks well done; (9) by attending instantly to physical hurts; and (10) by striving to maintain eye contact throughout a session, whether or not the child "agrees" to it.

The above list covers less than half of all the theraplay "do's and dont's" and it neglects clarification of two additional, very important points: The first concerns a special group of clients, the second a note of caution for the therapist.

Theraplay clients come in all sizes. Even infants and toddlers can have prob-lems. If at all possible, their sessions should particularly include their parents. Given the picture of the wholesome nursery life and armed with the list above, a therapist finds it easy enough to imagine the nature of their treatment. At the other end of the developmental ladder, however, are adolescents. Their physical size, intellectual sophistication, and sexual awareness make it essential to modify the theraplay technique for them. Not that their maturity changes the need for the therapist to remain in charge, to maintain eye and physical contact, to focus exclusively on the client, and to make the sessions cheerful, caretaking, and engaged. The adolescent's heightened self-consciousness and insistence on autonomy, however, present new challenges to the therapist and call for yet greater imagination, understanding, firm support, tolerance, and commitment.

And now, a note of caution: Theraplay, as a therapy technique, offers many more opportunities for the therapist's countertransference acting out than do most other therapeutic methods. Because in its infantile ministrations, it is so deliberately a replication of the parent-child relationship, because it is so physical, because the therapist must exercise so much power in the session, and because it is so often inviting of confrontation, it is a seductive method indeed for the therapist who has his or her own "hang-ups" about sex, control, anger, competition, or regression. Yet the session's fast pace precludes the opportunity to sit back, scratch his/her head, and wonder, "Now what in the world made me do that thing, or behave in (or feel) that particular way, just now?" For this reason, it is imperative that beginning (and to a lesser extent ongoing) theraplay therapists avail themselves of regular on-site or videotape supervision by supervisors or peers who can directly confront the kinds of questions suggested above. Yet even with the best of supervisory provisions, there is one question the theraplay therapist must ask him/herself just as the good parent must ask him/herself also: "Whose need is being met right now? (In whose interest (my own or the child's) am I really doing this?)" There can be only one legitimate answer: "The child's." If the therapist finds him/herself giving any other answer, prompt help should be sought.

Depending on the needs of the child and the availability of resources, theraplay sessions can be arranged to be individual, family, or group. They can be scheduled in out-patient treatment facilities, residential treatment settings, schools, or the child's own home. Individual theraplay is most frequent in school settings, but ideally the family should be included. Family theraplay begins with a few warm-up sessions in which, within the therapeutic relationship, the child develops a new self-image. Meanwhile, the parents, sitting with an interpreting therapist in an adjoining viewing room, are helped to see their child in a new, empathic, and more positive light and to understand both the principles underlying what they see happening and what, in the way of treatment carry-over, they can begin to do at home. Following these early warm-up meetings, the parents are introduced into the therapy room and, with enthusiastic guidance and support by the therapist(s), are included in the theraplay sessions. Although it might appear logically to be the most fitting, home-based theraplay, being by far the most difficult, should be undertaken by experienced therapists only.

In addition to developmentally-delayed children and children with emotional problems, other circumstances bring children into theraplay. Older adoptive children are referred with their new parents, specifically for parent-child bonding. The older adoptive child, having never completed the attachment process with respect to the original parents is often (to compound the child's troubles further) moved from one foster situation to another before landing, finally, on the doorstep of a new adoptive family. By the time the child arrives, he or she is either bitter, suspicious, pseudo-grownup, and intolerant of intimacy, or clinging, demanding, and infantile,[14] hardly the kind of behavior that will endear him or her to adoptive parents, who are hopeful for a reciprocal relationship with a loving, responsive child. Family theraplay allows adoptive parents to come to understand their child and to see from a "safe" vantage point the vulnerability, for example, that underlies the defensively tough exterior. It allows them to watch the kinds of actions the therapist uses to "disarm" the child, to delight, engage him, and take good care of him/her. Finally, their interpreting therapist gives adoptive parents support to counter their own reactively lowered self-esteem. When, a few weeks later, the parents enter the theraplay room to join in the child' session, they are carefully guided through the child's ambivalence toward the phase of reciprocal bonding.[5] Follow-up sessions, weeks or months after termination, assure that the recently established bonds remain strong.

CASE ILLUSTRATION

Dean is a tough-acting seven-year-old boy referred by his teacher for oppositional behavior.

Theraplay Session #1

DEAN	MS. ALLERT
	(Approaching Dean in waiting room) Oh, Dean. There you are! I see that gorgeous golden hair peeking out from behind that chair.
Well, I don't see nobody.	
(Pulling away)	I see your toe is hiding and your ear . . . and your feet! You know what? I'm going to put your feet right here on my feet . . . like this . . . and I'm going to take your arms . . . there we go . . . and I'm going to wrap them right around my middle. Now . . . how's that? We're all set for a nice foot ride down the hall. Oh my, you are a good rider! (The action moves swiftly)

(Dean forgets to protest)

Well, here we are at the end of our ride. Sit down. I'll bet you're just beat. Here, let me blow and cool off those fast-moving eyelids. (Blows)

Get away!

Get away? You mean like this? (Removing her one arm from around his shoulder but instantly replacing it with her other arm)

No. Get away.

Oh! You mean get away and touch your feet like this! (Touching the top of his head)

No! Away!

Well, you've got to push me away if you want me to go away. Here, push hard against my hands. You gotta push harder . . . harder . . . harder . . .

(He pushes her away, hard)

Well, just look at that. You are so strong, you darn near bowled me over (pretending to fall over backwards). Well, if that doesn't just deserve a handshake. Let me have your hand. Here. Shake. (She has his hand and continues to hold it as she pulls him to his feet.) Well, will you look at that! You are just a *perfect* height. Perfect for coming up to right here on me. Let me see. Oh, yes! And perfect for that handsome nose to come right up to here. And, look, looky there! A *beautiful* smile I see . . . Oh, there it went. It went and hid agan. And teeth. Let me count. Oh . . . 1 . . . 2 . . . 3 . . . oh, let me guess what happened here. I'll bet you . . . no, it couldn't be . . . I must be wrong . . . but . . . oh, I *bet* you lost one tooth, right here, just the other day. Right? You know what? I think I've got something that's going to fit right in that mouth just right. Sit down (arranging him so he is cradled in her arms). Open your mouth, here comes a banana slice I saved just for you. Oh, you chew that with such nice squishy noises. (Continuing to cuddle him and looking right into his eyes, Ms. Allert sings to the tune of "Jingle Bells") — Dean's right here, Dean is here. With your eyes of blue, you are such a cuddly dear as you chew and chew . . ."

It can be seen from the foregoing that many elements have been transposed from the nursery. There is structuring (sit here, stand there, "I'm going to wrap your arms right around my middle"), challenging (to stay aboard during the foot ride: "Push me hard, harder"), intruding ("I see your toe is hiding." "Oh, you mean get away and touch your foot like this?"), and nurturing ("cooling off" his eyelids, cradling him, feeding him the banana, singing to him). Like the nursery, these are chattering verbalizations only. No questions are asked that require answers. There is no interview, no history, no interpretation. There are no "reflections," and no rewards are conditional upon task completion or "good" behavior. Like the nursery, the ambiance is personal, cheerful, and physical. The messages are optimistic, not gloomy. They deal with health, not with pathology. Communications are designed to be enhancing of self-esteem ("your gorgeous golden hair," "Oh my, you *are* so strong!", "just a *perfect* height," "that *handsome* nose," "a *beautiful* smile," "you chew with such *nice* squishy noises," " . . . such a *cuddly* dear . . . "). Needless to say, Dean does not hold his grudge for long. The bristling stops and, hard as he may try to prevent it, a smile does slip out every now and then. Soon he stops having to control every interaction, and shortly thereafter he allows expression of the baby needs which underlie his tough facade. If his problem is not of psychotic severity and his parents are cooperative in continuing theraplay with him between appointments, he should be able to terminate his weekly half-hour sessions in just a few months.

Sometimes theraplay is carried out in conjunction with other treatment methods. Speech theraplay[3] combines traditional speech therapy with theraplay; and sensory motor integration theraplay[2, 4, 15, 19] combines traditional sensory motor integration[2] with theraplay. Used not only for developmental delays and communication disorders but also for children with articulation problems,[16] speech theraplay, like other theraplay, replicates pleasurable, meaningful, intensely personal mother-infant interactions, including, particularly in articulation referrals, the gurgling and cooing, blowing, clicking, tongue peek-a-booing, and cheek-popping that occurs in the normal nursery. Sensory motor integration (SMI) theraplay[10, 11] exposes the learning-disabled child to ever-new, deliberately structured, proprioceptive and kinesthetic activities and experiences, always in ways that, like mother with infant, are personally focused, physical, fun, delighting, surprising, nurturing, and totally involving of eye contact. The professionals doing both speech and SMI theraplay generally have their basic training not in psychotherapy but in speech and language disorders, occupational therapy or physical therapy. It is their theraplay work with children, professionals in these fields report, that combines for them a new awareness of psychodynamics and family therapy with their previous training and field experience.

Some research has already begun investigating the effectiveness of the theraplay method.[3, 6, 16, 20] The treatment of a few individual cases has been filmed and the same children re-filmed three years after theraplay termination.[12, 13]

Pre- and post-treatment testing has been compared and reported elsewhere.[9] All in all, however, to the best of this author's knowledge, no large-scale study has been undertaken to date. What is necessary is a comparison of (1) children who have and have not had theraplay and (2) those who have had therapy and those who have had some other types of psychological intervention. Many more studies will be needed before we can be certain of the full limits of theraplay or have an expanded understanding of why it works and with whom it works best. Quite apart from research, although Austin Des Lauriers introduced related concepts as early as 1962,[8] the method is still a relatively novel one. New and exciting modifications on it will surely evolve as imaginative therapists in the future make theraplay a part of their therapeutic armamentarium.

REFERENCES

1. Adams, P. L. *Obsessive Children: A Sociopsychiatric Study.* New York: Grune & Stratton (1978).
2. Ayres, A. *Sensory Integration and Learning Disorders.* Los Angeles: Western Psychological Services (1972).
3. Bligh, S. *et al.* Activating communication skills in autistic children: Five case studies. Unpublished paper available from the author. Elmhurst, IL: Speech Clinic, Elmhurst College (1979).
4. Bourguignon, J. P. Personal communication (January 1981).
5. Bowlby, J. *Attachment and Loss,* 1 – *Attachment.* New York: Basic Books (1969).
6. Brody, V., Fenderson, C., and Stephenson, S. *Sourcebook for Finding Your Way to Helping Young Children Through Developmental Play.* State of Florida, Department of State (1976). Distributed by Pupil Personnel Services Demonstration Project, All Children's Hospital, 806 6th St., St. Petersburg, FL 33701.
7. Clancy, H. and McBride, G. The autistic process and its treatment. *Journal of Child Psychology and Psychiatry* **10** (1969).
8. Des Lauriers, A. *The Experience of Reality in Childhood Schizophrenia.* New York: International Universities Press (1962).
9. Jernberg, A. *Theraplay.* San Francisco: Jossey-Bass (1979).
10. Jernberg, A. *Combining Theraplay with Sensory Motor Integration for Learning Disabled Children.* Paper accepted for presentation at the Annual Meeting of The American Psychological Association, Los Angeles (August 1981).
11. Jernberg, A. Therapeutic uses of sensory motor play. *In*: Schaefer, C. E. and O'Connor, K. J. (Eds.). *Handbook of Play Therapy.* New York: Wiley (in press).
12. Jernberg, A., Hurst, T., and Lyman, C. *Here I Am* (16mm film) (1969). Available from The Theraplay Institute, 333 N. Michigan Ave., Chicago, IL 60601.
13. Jernberg, A., Hurst, T., and Lyman, C. *There He Goes* (16mm film) (1975). Available from The Theraplay Institute.
14. Koller, T. Maternal and paternal re-bonding: The theraplay method applied to incomplete, foster and adoptive families. Paper in preparation (1981).
15. Kowalkowski, D. Personal communication (January 1981).
16. Kupperman, P. Speech theraplay: High impact articulation therapy. Paper presented at the American Speech and Hearing Association, Chicago (November 1977).
17. Langs, R. *The Technique of Psychoanalytic Psychotherapy.* New York: Jason Aronson (1973).

18. Marschak, M. *Parent-Child Interaction and Youth Rebellion.* New York: Gardner Press (1979).
19. Milligan, T. Lecture, Sensory Motor Integration Class, graduate course presented through the Chicago Consortium of Colleges and Universities (November 1980).
20. Rubin, P. Theraplay in the public schools: Opening the door to communication. Paper presented at the Illinois Speech and Hearing Association Convention, Chicago (April 1978).
21. Shapiro, D. *Neurotic Styles.* New York: Basic Books (1965).

Part III
Group Approaches

Six chapters constitute Part III and suggest the wide range of activities that make up group psychotherapy. Such therapeutic activities cover the spectrum of work done with clients who come together to share their own conflicts with members of a group to those whose group membership is defined by their family relationships. In this broad area, many new trends are showing themselves.

Leo Berman's chapter on family therapy is both a treatment of the origins of this fertile area of therapeutic advance and a deeply personal statement — of an autobiographical sort — of why he is involved in family therapy, what its current views are, and what he sees as its prospects.

The second chapter, "A Systems Approach to Group Therapy: Theory and Practice," offers a new group of conceptualizations about group dynamics, individual client participation, and the nature of group behavior — all from the perspective of looking at these as part of a total system which they both determine and are determined by. Exciting new possibilities emerge and new ways of examining and understanding dynamics arise.

Another approach, very different from that set forth in Chapter 2, may be found in the use of photographs, particularly photo albums, in the use of such materials in family therapy to explore intra- and inter-generational views of family relationships. Particularly valuable is likely to be the range of visual representations of interactional patterns that may be uncovered in such approaches to group process.

Poets have always had an uncanny ability to search out all aspects of the human condition, and it is not surprising that their poems may offer a fruitful vehicle for furthering group process in the hands of skillful group therapy leaders.

It is the rich vein of this newer approach that the chapter on Poetry Therapy deals with, and readers may see in it a new dimension of group interaction.

Both Strategic System Therapies, represented by Chapter 5, and Network Therapies, set forth in Chapter Six, conclude Part 3 on Group Approaches. Each chapter, in its own way, illustrates how conceptions of group process, and more specifically interactive strategies of group therapy members, are more fully appreciated and tactically used by group therapy leaders in furthering growth and change among participating clients.

Taken together, then, the foregoing chapters lead the reader into newer main stream and by-ways of on-going group therapy theory, thinking, and practice.

In recent years, family therapy has become a robust tree with strong, far-reaching branches. One of the merits of the chapter that follows is to set forth the historical and theoretical root structure of this flowering tree, and another is to indicate how one of its gifted practitioners and teachers came to embrace family therapy. The story is interesting, and the reader is likely to follow it with full attention.

With ever-changing family patterning, the need for and the importance of family therapy seem assured. The author's own view is indeed optimistic about trends in the field, and we can share his view that family therapy is a specialized discipline and that one requires discipline to practice it fruitfully.

11

Family Therapy

Leo H. Berman, M.D.

Family therapy is not in itself a new therapy, but rather an extension of all that has gone before. It is not merely a new set of techniques, but rather a new way of conceptualizing human interactions, and an approach to producing change.

ROOTS OF FAMILY THERAPY

To clarify this notion, I would like to consider the very many roots which come together to create and nourish this tree of family therapy. First and foremost, I would mention Freud, who, while concentrating on the individual's behavior, recognized the forces of the family in the shaping and processing of the personality and character of the individual. He examined these forces in terms of the molding of character and the development of its pathology. Freud also gave us the technique of psychoanalysis — the mutual and cooperative work to unravel the tangled threads of existence. By a stretch of imagination, his case report on Little Hans is often cited as the first example of family therapy. However, we should remember that Freud really excluded the family and warned against involvement with it. J. C. Flugel, author of *The Psychoanalytical Study of the Family*, is also referred to as the first to integrate psychoanalysis and the family, but that is grossly untrue, as one learns when reading his book.

It was a later psychoanalyst, Nathan Ackerman, who made the fundamental change, which led to the utilization of psychoanalytical principles not only in the understanding of families but also in treating them as a unit. Ackerman was intensely interested in the dynamics of family life, and as part of his growth and development, went to study the effects on the family of a long-lasting strike of mine workers, examining changes in roles and relationships. For years, he was associated with a social service agency, the Jewish Family Service of New York City, and no doubt the basic concern of such an agency had an impact and influence on him. He is considered the father of family therapy, although other analysts, such as Otto Rank, Alfred Adler, Clarence Obendorf, and Bela Mittlemann, made important contributions to the field. Probably Ackerman's influence on the training of others in this area served to set him apart and established him as the founder of a new system.

While Ackerman, a psychiatrist, was being influenced by social workers, a social worker, Virginia Satir, was having to deal with psychiatric issues and problems. The mental illness, schizophrenia, with its mysterious causes, its chronicity, and its devastating effect on family life, had involved social workers who first saw the need to help families deal with this condition. Thus they began to study not only the effect of schizophrenia on the family, but the impact of the family upon the schizophrenic individual. Satir, working at the Chicago Psychiatric Institute, became interested in the families of such patients, and began to see them as units for treatment. She was particularly interested in the concept of self-esteem and saw symptoms as the individual's way of attempting to cope. Her warmth and the high level of her therapeutic interventions brought about growth, not only for the patient, but for all members of the family. Her book, *Conjoint Family Therapy* (1964), introduced others to this approach and brought many others into the field. She sought therapists who thought as she did, and she joined a group in Palo Alto, made up of Don Jackson, Gregory Bateson, John Weakland, Paul Watzlawick, and Jay Haley.

This was a multidisciplinary team, which brought together a diverse group of people and their specialized skills but who were able to merge their talents for extraordinary results. Don Jackson was a psychiatrist who trained at Chestnut Lodge, where he was influenced by Frieda Fromm-Reichmann, a gifted therapist who coined the disturbing phrase, "schizophrenogenic mother." Jackson was also familiar with Harry Stack Sullivan, who had designated psychiatry as the study of interpersonal processes. Here we have the move away from the psychoanalytical intrapsychic concern to that of human relationships. Jackson related how he was puzzled by the repeated relapses of a young woman he thought he was treating successfully. When he accidentally met the woman's family, he came to the realization that to make a real change in the patient, he would have to bring about changes in the family, and he would have to see them all in concurrent therapy.

Jackson was particularly concerned with communications that flowed in the family group, and he was aided in this study by Watzlawick, a linguist; Bateson, an anthropologist who was interested in the various channels by which meanings are conveyed; Weakland, who as a chemical engineer felt himself too removed from human contact and turned to the study of Chinese culture and social anthropology; and Jay Haley, who was also interested in problems of communication but took time out to work with Milton Erickson, the leading hypnotherapist in the States. He became fascinated with Erickson's paradoxical, unorthodox, and dramatic approach to therapy, and began to analyze the techniques in terms of how change was effected.

The concept of family homeostasis and the double-bind theory are two familiar earmarks of this group, but their contributions surpassed these, particularly with Bateson's study of paradox and his discussion of epistemological levels.

It was obvious that communication took place not by spoken words alone. Family therapists became particularly interested in non-verbal communication — in the positioning of people as they took their seats at a session or in how they related kinesthetically. Spearheaded by the work of Ray Birdwhistell, who could, like Professor Higgins, tell from what part of the country a person came from by how much lip he or she showed when smiling; others, such as Jane Ferber and the late Al Scheflen, examined in detail the physical interactions of family members as well as those between therapist and the family. These therapists were able to show how quickly the therapist became part of the family system. Microanalysis of videotapes and motion pictures revealed interactions that were completely outside the awareness of the participants. The Palo Alto group also examined letters written by parents and commented on the specific and differentiating characteristics of such letters written by parents of schizophrenic children.

Satir had been introduced to the Palo Alto group by Murray Bowen, a psychiatrist, also interested in understanding schizophrenia. While at the Menninger Clinic, he set up a cottage where patients and their families could live and be studied together. Not all members of the family participated, but as he moved on to the National Institute of Mental Health, he continued this practice and gradually achieved seeing the entire family together. At first, his interest was primarily research, but this was transformed into a therapeutic experience, and Bowen became one of the foremost theoreticians, with his emphasis on the triangulation process that takes place within the family, and on the multigenerational process involved in the development of pathology, such as alcoholism and schizophrenia.

There were a number of other psychiatrists whose interest in, and study of, schizophrenic patients led them to a greater involvement with the family. Among these is the group at Yale, which included Theodore Lidz, Stephen Fleck, and Alice Cornelison. They made fundamental formulations regarding the family structure that provided the fertile environment for the development of pathology. Lyman Wynne, in his studies with Margaret Singer, explored the thinking styles of family members, and was able to make diagnostic predictions regarding the occurrence of specific forms of mental disturbance in off-spring.

Leaving this group of pioneers, we go back to another set of roots, and these lay in the field of child psychiatry. The format of the Commonwealth Child Guidance Clinics was that of a team approach, with a psychologist administering tests, social workers seeing the family (and almost always that was the mother alone), and the psychiatrist offering treatment to the child. Out of the work of these clinics, certain facts became clear and became fundamental concepts in family therapy. First was the recognition that symptoms were not only to be thought of as aberrations or pathology, but also as the child's attempt at coping with difficulties in the family. This concept was derived from the work of the psychoanalyst Sandor Rado. Second, it was noted that the child, though identified as the patient, was not necessarily the "sickest" one in the family, but somehow was more prominent and noticeable. Third, the experience of the clinic was that, frequently, as the disturbed child improved, someone else in the family presented problems that required attention. As the therapeutic team began to deal with such issues, boundaries of their specialties were broken down, and the work of the psychiatrist, psychologist, and social worker became interchangeable.

Still another line of development was that of group therapy. This had begun prior to World War II, but was rapidly accelerated during the war to meet the special needs of the military. The interest in, and utilization of, group therapy continued to increase and paralleled the investigation of group dynamics. It was easy to move from the study of artificially constructed groups to the study of the natural group, the family. Talcott Parsons, at Harvard, was one of the leading theoreticians in this area and influenced many family therapists, such as, for example, Lyman Wynne.

A foremost proponent of group therapy, but utilizing it in a very special way, was J. L. Moreno, the founder of psychodrama. His was a very active therapy, with people moving about and reconstructing families and having people role-play and reenact scenes of their lives. His techniques were adopted by the psychoanalyst Fritz Perls, the originator of gestalt therapy, who, though working in a group setting, concentrated on one individual at a time. Perls emphasized not the past but the here and now. He also talked in terms of growth rather than dealing with illness. His work became part of the human potential movement and the development of such centers as Esalen. It is noteworthy that Satir became the first director at that institute.

Back-tracking for a moment, we need to be reminded that Freudian concepts developed at the beginning of the twentieth century, utilizing as models the physics of its day — namely, hydraulics and simple electrical concepts. Thus there were the formulations regarding repression and damned-up energies and breakthroughs in the form of symptoms. The familiar models of the twentieth century are computers, and it is understandable that this period has seen the development of cybernetic principles. Instead of reliance on linear causation, there is the study of systems and circular controls. Feedback mechanisms, servo-controls, and positive and negative amplification are ideas now used in explaining behavior.

The work of Bertalanffy in general systems theory has been frequently referred to by the writers in the field of family therapy.

The consideration of working with systems rather than isolated individuals is fundamental to the work of Salvatore Minuchin, who brought to the Philadelphia Child Guidance Clinic, among others, Braulio Montalvo and Jay Haley. They examined and dealt with the structure of the family. Even more involved with systems is the Milan group, headed by Mara Selvini-Palazzoli. She is indebted to Bateson and his formulation of logical types. Her insistence is on systemic thinking and she is ever on the alert for the tendency to slip from this level of dealing with family problems.

This is a rather personal and subjective history of family therapy.* Its purpose is to demonstrate that this therapeutic approach is built upon the psychodynamics of psychoanalysis, the conceptualizations of interpersonal and systems theory, the use of teams, the examination of communication, and of paradox, the emphasis on the here and now, and yet with the knowledge that the dynamics of the family are important in understanding the difficulties of the individual within the family. Co-therapy, family sculpting, modifications of timing of sessions, home visits, network systems, multiple-impact therapy, family reconstruction and family reunions, and many more innovations have been made by family therapists or incorporated by them in their treatment approaches.

PERSONAL HISTORY

Why and how does a therapist come to work in this modality? Here I must become more personal and recount my own odyssey. The importance of my being the first-born son of a Jewish immigrant family cannot be minimized. The role of becoming a helper was assigned to me at a young age, perhaps even before I was born. The strength of family ties, despite the tensions and strains of my parents, established norms and values for me. To become a physician was firmly established by the time I was six years old, although the desire to become a psychiatrist had to await my thirteenth birthday. Medical school in a foreign country served to clarify my own family connections, but since that foreign country was Scotland, I had another exposure to the meaning and significance of clans. In the country of tartans, where the lecturer in anatomy could suggest that a student sit in a particular seat in the amphitheater because that is where his father and grandfather had sat, I could have no misgivings about the forces of tradition.

When my medical studies were interrupted by the war, I turned to what I thought was the closest field to psychiatry — social work. The training reinforced my acculturated sense of the family and gave me a way of dealing with

---

*For a more objective account, readers are referred to Carlfred B. Broderick and Sandra S. Schrader, "The History of Professional Marriage and Family Therapy," in *Handbook of Family Therapy,* Alan S. Gurman and David P. Kniskem (Eds.).

people that I doubt I could have gotten at medical school alone. Medical social work with tubercular patients served again to emphasize family life and how families, as a unit, were affected by the illness of one of its members, and also how the family impacted on the sick one. Experience with the American Red Cross in the South Pacific during the war years centered on family relationships dealing with loss and separation. At the end of that period, I returned to medical school, integrating there the more complete picture of the individual and learning to deal with life and death matters of the patients.

Back in the United States for my residency training, I had a great deal of experience dealing with schizophrenic patients. This kept me involved with families and made me familiar with the work of Frieda Fromm-Reichmann. The search for enhancement of skills, and the unconscious desire to tilt at windmills, brought me into a psychoanalytical training program. Fortunately, this was at a school noted for its ecclecticism, and many of the teachers there stressed the influence of culture on the lifestyle and structure of the individual and the family. Further experience with therapists such as Moreno, Whitaker, Laura Perls, and Virginia Satir, opened up all of the possibilities of helping in creative and new ways. Working in a psychiatric hospital that was experimenting with the concept of a therapeutic community facilitated my working intensively with families, in individual and multi-family sessions.

STYLES OF THERAPY

Family therapy is not just a matter of seeing the whole family in each and every session, but rather reflects a way of thinking in terms of systems. Whitaker prefers to get everyone into the act — children, parents, grandparents, ex-spouses, and all. Bowen can work with a single individual, coaching him/her how to go back to the family of origin and rework the connections and relationships there.

Family therapy is not a matter of how active one is. Peggy Papp can get a family group to create three-dimensional living sculptures all over the place or she can sit quietly with them and write complex prescriptions for them at the end of the session.

Family therapy is not a matter of how manipulative one is. Palazzoli can give detailed instructions for a family ritual, and Whitaker can fall asleep in a session, awakening to speculate about why he dozed off.

One can make detailed diagnostic studies such as those of Ravitch, who utilizes a computerized train game to study interactions, or the therapist can go in cold, to be diagnostic and therapeutic concurrently as he or she becomes part of the family system.

Family therapy tends to be brief and focused on specific problems. However, what frequently happens is that a relationship is established which is utilized by the family, as a family should be. Just as a functional family can be called upon in times of need, so too the family therapist can be involved for retreads as the occasion arises. Family therapy can also be utilized for growth processes and to enhance the richness of living. Many people call upon the skills of Satir in that way, not coming because of "illness," but because of the awareness that life can be even fuller than it is.

VIDEOTAPING

From the very beginning there has been an openness about family therapists and their work. Nathan Ackerman began taking movies of his sessions, which he shared with others. The introduction of videotape was quickly utilized because of the economy and the immediacy of its playback. Ackerman may have been motivated by his desire to keep things as open as possible. Just as he would seek to uncover the secrets in families, so too was he prepared to reveal the magic of his therapy. Films and tapes were shared among therapists and led to a congruency between what a therapist said was done and what was actually observed in the session. This was in contrast to individual therapy, where the mystery of the session was maintained and where there were many discrepancies between the reports of the therapist and those of the patient. Filming also made it possible to analyze and compare the styles of different therapists. Thus, one famous series, "The Hillcrest Family," showed Ackerman, Bowen, Jackson, and Whitaker interviewing the same blended family.

Videotaping was utilized in other ways by family therapists. Ian Alger and the late Peter Hogan utilized a technique of taping a session for a period of time and then viewing and reviewing that segment with the family, searching for hidden meanings in the revelations of the tape. Ian Alger and Milton Berger became most skilled in operating the camera as extensions of themselves during the session so as to add other eyes and ears to the transactions that took place in the room.

At the present time, a great deal of teaching of family therapy is done through the utilization of such tapes. Training institutes have developed well-stocked libraries of such tapes which can be viewed at one's leisure or scrutinized by a group.

WRITING AND TRAINING

There has naturally been a rapid growth of literature on this subject. Works by single authors or multi-authored volumes are announced every month. James Framo and Robert Green have just updated their bibliography, listing 335 books. Ranking these is always a very personal matter, but for me Satir's *Conjoint Family Therapy*,[8] Bateson's *Steps to an Ecology of Mind*,[1] Minuchin's *Families and Family Therapy*,[4] Watzlawick, Weakland, and Fisch's *Change*,[10] Napier and Whitaker's *The Family Crucible*,[5] and Palazzoli, Boscolo, Cocchin, and Prata's

Paradox and Counterparadox[6] are outstanding in readability and stimulation. Gurman and Kniskern's *Handbook of Family Therapy*[3] is an encyclopedian text.

The field has seen within the United States the creation of two professional organizations, the American Association for Marriage and Family Therapy and the American Family Therapy Association, with slightly different aims and goals. There are two principal journals in this country, *The Journal of the American Association for Marriage and Family Therapy* and *Family Process,* though a number of other journals are published here and abroad. Research is conducted in some centers, but my general impression is that most of the writing is clinical in nature and frequently theoretical.

Family therapy currently has an appeal for many in the helping professions. Training programs have been established as part of a university curriculum, such as at Hahnemann Medical College, where a master's degree in Family Therapy is offered, or at free-standing institutions, such as the Nathan Ackerman Institute in New York. However, this appeal also has drawn into the field many fringe elements — people who want to do therapy but who do not have the training, supervision, or professionalism to avoid doing harm. There is a real need for controls and standards, and the American Association for Marriage and Family Therapy is attempting to offer guidelines for such standards of training.

THE FUTURE

What of the future? As new trends affect families, therapists alter their focus and perhaps their techniques. With the dramatic increase in divorce rates, there comes a host of new issues for the family therapist. Marital counseling to help resolve difficulties in the spouse pair, or divorce mediation to assist in working out an amiable, rather than adversarial, relationship when the decision has been made to break the marriage contract, are two important current trends. Also related to the issue of marriage break-up are the problems of the single parent and of blended families where we may find "his children," "her children," and "our children." Wife abuse, child abuse, and incest are other specific issues that seem to be the topics of the moment and have called forth the specialized skills of the family therapist.

CONCLUSION

Therapists frequently consider family therapy with fear and trepidation. Finding individual therapy challenging enough, they wonder how they can ever deal with the larger unit. At the other end of the spectrum are therapists who believe that since they are good individual therapists, they can jump right in and deal with families without further training or the development of new skills. Family therapy is a specialized discipline and needs discipline to achieve it. It is exciting and rewarding for those who make the leap from the individual to thinking in terms of systems. Just as innovators working in this style found stimulation at learning that others had been experimenting with this approach, so too family therapists today find it useful to meet and share. Individual therapists practice frequently in solo fashion; family therapists seek contact with others. Perhaps that is an oversimplistic generalization, but it is interesting that the latest development in the field, pioneered by the Milan group and replicated in the United States by Olga Silverstein, Peggy Papp, and others, utilizes a team working with the family and a team observing behind a one-way mirror, to serve as active consultants to the therapeutic process.

Such an approach may lead to the question of cost-effectiveness. How much should it cost to treat a family or turn around an anorectic child or a brittle diabetic? These are real issues that should not be ignored. Obviously, there are no easy answers. Family therapy has been utilized for every type of psychiatric condition — psychosomatic illness such as anorexia nervosa, schizophrenia, alcoholism, and juvenile delinquency. Its value has been demonstrated in preventive and prophylactic work, such as in helping parents divorce without excessive damage to themselves and their children.

Many of the techniques and approaches of family therapy have altered the styles of other therapists. The avoidance of blaming, each person speaking for him/herself and taking responsibility for his/her behavior, the recognition of the influence of culture, the concern for the here and now, the search for methods of making real change rather than "spinning wheels" — all of these are outgrowths of the work of family therapists. The field will continue to grow, and it will absorb, as it has in the past, all that sensitive therapists have to offer.

REFERENCES

1. Bateson, G. *Steps to an Ecology of Mind.* New York: Ballantine (1972).
2. Framo, James L. and Green, Robert Jay. *Bibliography of Books Related to Family and Marital Systems Theory and Therapy.* California: American Association of Marriage and Family Therapy.
3. Gurman, A. S. and Kniskern, D. P. (Eds.). *Handbook of Family Therapy.* New York: Brunner/Mazel (1980).
4. Minuchin, S. *Families and Family Therapy.* Cambridge: Harvard University Press (1974).
5. Napier, A. Y. and Whitaker, C. A. *The Family Crucible.* New York: Harper & Row (1978).
6. Palazzoli, M. S., Boscolo, L., Cecchin, G., and Prata, G. *Paradox and Counterparadox.* New York: Aronson (1978).
7. Papp, P. (Ed.). *Family Therapy: Full Length Case Studies.* New York: Gardner (1977).
8. Satir, V. *Conjoint Family Therapy.* Palo Alto, CA: Science and Behavior Books (1967).
9. Watzlawick, P., Bedvin, J. H., and Jackson, D. D. *Pragmatics of Human Communication.* New York: Norton (1967).
10. Watzlawick, P., Weakland, J., and Fisch, R. *Change.* New York: Norton (1974).

In her Systems Approach to Group Therapy, the author of the following chapter suggests that the use of a supraordinate theoretical framework, derived from general systems theory, more fully serves to integrate the whole range of conceptually fragmented "group therapies," without in any significant way homogenizing them, than any other available conceptualization.

Within an essentially modern psychoanalytical point of view that relies on ego psychology and object relations theory, she examines both the theoretical and clinical implications of general systems theory for the analytical method of group therapy. It is her contention that reliance on general systems theory thinking not only can make up for current inadequacies in psychoanalytic theory – such as the libido theory, for example – but also that it is useful when combined with other current approaches, such as gestalt, transactional, etc.

It is clear, as one reads on, that general systems theory, properly understood and applied, is a large conceptualizing principle of remarkable integrative power when applied to group psychotherapy theory and practice.

12

A Systems Approach
to Group Therapy:
Theory and Practice

Helen E. Durkin, Ph.D.

My experience in practicing, supervising, and training analytic group psycho-therapists has convinced me that insight into unconscious conflicts, knowledge of the phases of development, and the technique of analyzing transference and resistance are essential to profound understanding and basic reconstruction in group therapy. Nevertheless, I have become increasingly aware of certain theo-retical shortcomings of psychoanalytic theory. For example, it takes insufficient account of ecological factors. And there are consequently deficiencies in tech-nique, such as its failure systematically to turn insight into actual change of behavior.

As Edgar Levinson[11] pointed out, "Paradigms are time and space bound," and time has certainly caught up with orthodox psychoanalytic theory. Although it dominated the field of group therapy for a long time, it began to be challenged, in the fifties, by existential therapy and group dynamics. There followed a pro-liferation of techniques, such as transactional analysis, gestalt, encounter, and existential therapy, which fragmented group therapy theory. During the sixties, a number of us began to search for a way to integrate the most valid of the new ideas into a coordinated group therapy theory, since the conflicting approaches which might have brought about progress to a higher level of organization seemed instead only to exacerbate our dissensions. Marathons became popular as an attempt to solve the problem,[15] but my own feeling was that what we really needed was a supraordinate theoretical framework under which the various new approaches might be reintegrated.

Meanwhile, general systems thinking was making its mark in the new physics, in chemistry, and in the social sciences. General Systems Theory (GST) constitutes one scientific formulation of the new paradigm that has been evolving ever since quantum mechanics and relativity theory changed our views of the phenomenal world. Spurred on by the fact that the communications, or the cybernetic branch of systems theory, had already generated a new systems-oriented family therapy, we formed a task force* to find out if it had the capacity to fill in the gaps left by analytic group psychotherapy.

GST had grown out of many leading scientists beginning to focus on the organization or structure rather than the content of whatever phenomena they were studying. They made an intensive study of those complex phenomena that were the product of the interaction of their parts, and they began to call these "organized complexities" systems, in contrast to the simpler sums and aggregates which interact additively. A system was defined as "an order of parts and processes, standing in continuous dynamic interaction."[1] The systems scientists then went on to make a comparative investigation of the whole range of systems in order to identify their basic structural features and to codify the laws by which they operate. GST became a structural metatheory.

This project produced a whole new order of knowledge about the interrelationships and the interactions among systems. Investigators found that any system is composed of subsystems, and that these can become a part of a number of larger "suprasystems." Thus, systems form a hierarchy of increasing complexities. Living systems from the cell to society are examples. At each new level of complexity, certain new characteristics occur. Thus, living systems have permeable boundaries, and in their transactions they exert a mutual influence upon one another. One of the most remarkable discoveries pertinent to group psychotherapy was the information that all systems are isomorphic. That is to say, they have the same basic structural features. Thus, the group, its members, and their personality structure may be regarded as three isomorphic systems at increasing levels of complexity. Whatever we know about the structure of one of these systems is at our disposal for all three, and this adds significantly to what psychoanalysis has taught us about the content of personality systems. Moreover, the therapist will have at his/her command a single uniform method and will not have to move from psychodynamics to group dynamics. A unified theory of group therapy has now become possible.

---

*Under the auspices of the American Group Psychotherapy Association.

It was to be expected, therefore, that the new information would engender a host of new hypotheses and techniques that could be applied to many fields of science. Why not, then, to group therapy? We were excited by the project and continued our investigations.

We had begun by examining the application of cybernetics to family therapy, but its literature did not have much to say about how individual members form the family, and said still less about the function of the members' personality or character structures. Yet experience in analytic group therapy had already demonstrated that change in these subsystems is of primary importance in changing the other two levels. Moreover, systems family therapy deals mostly with the effect of systems, whereas what group therapists really needed to know was how to *form new* systems. Therapy groups are initially composed of strangers. They begin as "aggregates," and one of the primary tasks of the therapist is to help them organize themselves to form suprasystems which can then serve as valuable partners in the group therapeutic process. Von Bertalanffy's organisonic model of living systems, on the other hand, provides this essential information because it describes exactly how such systems organize, maintain, and transform themselves. It seemed more suitable than the cybernetic machine model as a guide to understanding the living individual and social systems with which we are concerned in group therapy, and we decided to employ it in our application of GST to group therapy.

Von Bertalanffy's new model of living systems is based on extensive embryological research. According to it, living systems are neither vitalistic nor mechanistic. By virute of their structure, they are autonomous, for they are phylogenetically programmed with permeable boundaries and the capacity to open or close them. This enables them to exchange energy and information with one another, so that they can either maintain their organization or restructure — i.e., transform — themselves. By closing their boundaries to exclude new input, they are able to maintain a stable identity. By opening them, they can import new energy and information for the purpose of restructuring themselves. Thus they can also change and grow. Moreover, if the alternating process of opening and closing is carried out systematically over time, living systems develop a hitherto unrecognized phenomenon which von Bertalanffy called Fliessgleichgewicht. It consists of a dynamic, or flowing (rather than a static) equilibrium, and gives rise to a flexible (rather than a rigid) steady state. Thus, living systems are assured of being able to maintain their identity even as they progressively transform their structure. It was the first model that enabled us to define the group therapeutic process as a series of exchanges in which spontaneous emotion conveys energy and tends to open boundaries, while cognitive processes convey information used to draw, maintain, or create new boundaries.

THE APPLICATION OF GST TO GROUP THERAPY

GST is not merely a change of language, nor is it limited to a change in the philosophy of treatment. It gives us a new way of looking at clinical phenomena and puts at our disposal the considerable new information which has been accumulated about their structure.

Perhaps even more important is the fact that it adds to our technical options. Besides the usual analysis of the meaning of the content of the group interchanges, the therapist may use gestalt, humanistic, or encounter technique. He or she does not depend on the techniques of any one of the current approaches. Furthermore, the GST therapist may choose to make structural interventions. In cases where the analysis of content produces only insight, for example, he/she can facilitate boundary opening or closing in the structure of any one of the systems levels and so generate new behavior in the form of new modes of interacting.

As we put the new technical principle of boundarying into practice, we took our lead from the way normal living systems operate. We found that if the therapist assumes responsibility for monitoring the boundarying process as it occurs in the group, he/she can catalyze the dormant potentials of systems that are dysfunctional. Step by step, the therapist can help to bring about transformations by facilitating the opening of dysfunctionally closed boundaries, or increase the stability of dysfunctionally open systems by closing dysfunctionally open boundaries, continuing until the group suprasystem, the individual target systems, and their personality subsystems have achieved a steady state, which enables them to manage their own boundarying process and attain a functional autonomy.

(Exactly how to facilitate their capacity for boundarying is described in several chapters of our forthcoming book, *Living Groups.*[5])

For the present I will attempt only to show the way in which changing the boundary permeability of any one of the three isomorphic systems of a therapy group will bring about a transformation of its structure and its mode of interacting and how this in turn will bring about transformation of the other two levels. I will also show how the expression of strong spontaneous emotion opens boundaries, while the cognitive exchanges create new boundaries or close those that are dysfunctionally open.

One man started to tell about his difficulties with his present girlfriend, whom he perceived as critical and controlling. The women in the group experienced this as a "put down." They became angry with him, but because they needed to avoid personal feelings, they generalized about men's attitudes toward women. The man was irritated but unresponsive to them. Clearly his interpersonal boundaries were even more closed than theirs. As a result, the interaction soon turned into a sociological debate, and two subgroups formed, men versus women. The boundaries between them seemed impermeable. No energy in the form of emotion could be exchanged.

When the intellectual (cognitive) exchanges became repetitive and signs of boredom and restlessness appeared, I decided to facilitate boundary opening by calling attention to their avoidance of their deeper and more personal feelings, which I knew to have originated in their relationships with their parents. As I expected, my comment evoked a variety of spontaneous emotions toward me. It was the man who had started the discussion who became furious with me. He threatened to leave because I was such a terrible therapist.

As expected, his strong spontaneous emotions injected enough energy into the situation to open the subgroup boundaries. The subgroups dissolved. Accordingly, the boundaries of the group as a whole became firmer and the nature of its structure was transformed. It came to life. Now emotions were exchanged again, and the participants began to have a mutual influence upon one another. In other words, the group could again serve as a "nutrient bed" so that its members felt comfortable enough to open their interpersonal and their intrapsychic boundaries.

What happened is that they began to expose their formerly withheld transferential modes of interacting, both to me and to childhood. They worked analytically now and gained a good deal of insight into the relation between their feelings toward the opposite sex and those toward their parents. This experience helped prepare them for further structural interventions that would help them turn that insight into changed behavior. The combination of structural transformations and insight was working in tandem.

Because this new model of living systems is based on the whole range of systems under normal conditions, instead of on patients in treatment, it presents us with a fundamentally different and more robust view of the systems we encounter in our therapy groups. We no longer see them as largely reactive to environmental impact, but as actively able to influence their environments and as creatively able to change themselves. Indeed, patients are more vigorous, resilient, and hardy than we have been accustomed to think they are. They have an extraordinarily high capacity to organize and reorganize themselves.

The implication is that even those systems that have become dysfunctional in the course of their early exchanges with their more powerful parental systems retain their potential for autonomy so that, with some help from the therapist and the group, they will be able to actualize it. This robust view is particularly important toward the last phases in treatment, when the confidence of the therapist and the hope it engenders in patients enable them to overcome their fear of basic personality reorganization.

THE COMPLEMENTARITY BETWEEN PSYCHOANALYTIC AND GENERAL SYSTEMS THEORIES

In general, we found that the two theoretical approaches were not as the systems theorists[19] had reported — contradictory and mutually exclusive. Rather, they supplement each other. For this reason, it was possible, in practice, to combine them by employing GST as an overall theory and psychoanalysis as a critical conceptual subsystem.

Here are some ways of looking at the situation.

1. Psychoanalytic theory is based solely on the study of personality subsystems. It provides essential information about the special characteristics of human individual and social systems. GST is a structured metatheory based on a study of systems in general. It provides additional information about organizational features that such systems have in common. The two approaches together give a more complete view of clinical events.

2. Traditional psychoanalytic theory is based primarily on a study of patients in treatment and accounts very well for the numerous kinds and degrees of pathology countered in therapy groups. But it fails to give us a systematic account of normal behavior. The model of living systems, which is at the heart of our application of GST to therapy, provides this information and permits us to specify precise standards and norms for use by the therapist. We continue to provide a corrective experience which offers insight into the group therapy members' transferential modes of interacting, but we give more time to cultivating their capacity to initiate new, more spontaneous and realistic patterns of behavior.

3. Energy distribution is the *sine qua non* of therapeutic change. Without exchange of energy, no change in structure or behavior is possible. Psychoanalytic theory is generally conceded to have an inadequate theory of energy. Libido theory is expressed in terms of nineteenth century instinct theory. Although it accounts for biological and intrapsychic sources of energy, it fails to take into account its ecological sources. GST fills that gap with its thermodynamic theory of energy. The second law of thermodynamics states that without the application of energy in the form of work, systems are subject to entropy. Their organization will gradually decrease, and they will begin to move toward randomness. But living systems, as open systems, have the capacity to counteract forces of entropy by importing energy and information from each other and from their environment. They are thus negentropic. They can process current sources of energy. In group therapy, therefore, the leader can make excellent use of interaction as an *additional* source of energy to bring about changes in the behavior patterns of the members.

4. Psychoanalysis has clung too long to the notion that man's major motivation consists of need gratification and relies on tension reduction to restore the so-called normal homeostatic condition. GST takes the innovative position that living systems are heterostatic. It accepts homeostasis and tension reduction as consistent sources of stability, but

it considers a certain amount of tension to be essential in their capacity to grow and change. The dynamic equilibrium of a living system may, because of the extra tension it harbors, really consist of a quasi-disequilibrium in which the fluctuating tensions serve as sources of change and growth.

ILLUSTRATIONS OF TECHNIQUES DERIVED FROM GST

Up to this point, we have been examining the way in which the principles of GST may be applied in group therapy and have examined the new technical principle of boundarying in group therapy. It is time now to explore its technical implications a bit further by giving some examples of new techniques that have grown out of our application of GST to group therapy.

The Growth Technique

Our early clinical attempts to apply general systems principles to group therapy provided evidence that human and social systems have an extraordinarily high capacity for change and growth which traditional group therapists have not sufficiently exploited. There has been an unfortunate tendency to put a premium on correcting members' transferential modes of interacting, whereas cultivating growth and generating new patterns of behavior have been a relatively rare occurrence in spite of the fact that ego psychology has long pointed in this direction. GST, on the other hand, is basically a theory providing a model that describes exactly how change and growth can be achieved. For this reason, a number of our task force members initiated new techniques for this purpose. Let me describe my own version of such growth techniques.

While searching for ways to stimulate change and new behavior, I became intrigued by Maruyama's[13] remarks on the development of social systems. He shows how accidental events, such as someone getting stranded near an oasis in the desert, can "kick off" the growth of a whole community. It occurred to me that in the unstructured interaction of the therapy group, similar accidental clinical events, in the form of unintended expressions of usually repressed feelings, thoughts or actions, can lead to forming new systems of communication. They usually go unnoticed in the swiftly moving group exchanges. I decided to keep a sharp lookout for such accidental events, to call them to the group's attention as soon as possible, and to ask for patient associations to them. It meant that I would have to risk interrupting the usually sacrosanct group process and to ask members to hold onto the very feelings they had been avoiding. They would require time and space to process the new input and to take responsibility for the feeling.

William Gray, who works with emotional/cognitive patterns of interacting, which convey energy and emotion across boundaries rather than directly to the boundarying process, would view such unintended feeling and thoughts as "precursors" of new systems of communicating that are developing. He points out that they can be expected to form an "organizing focus" which will then give rise to new functional systems or modes of interacting. Since group members generally respond warmly to such situations, the group may become a nutrient bed in which growth would flourish (see Gray in Durkin[5]).

Illustration of the Growth Technique. Jonathan was well liked by his group although he repeatedly denigrated his own behavior. Group therapy members often took him to task because he refused to acknowledge what they called his "good instincts." In spite of his inability to express, or even recognize, his positive feelings, his strong underlying emotionality got across to them by means of nonverbal communication. One day he seemed to be under great tension. He told them about the painful experience he was having with his unmarried daughter, who had become pregnant during an affair with an "undesirable" married man. The group recognized that he had been extremely helpful to her. Yet he consistently blamed himself for how badly he treated her. He owned up to having "old-fashioned" prejudices and voiced his fear that he had alienated her affection forever. In this case, it was the group instead of me who first called attention to his unacknowledged "good behavior," and it was they who stopped the process to tell him how wonderful he had been. They urged him to own his good feelings and behavior as well as his bad ones. Several women expressed the wish that he had been their father. I asked him if he had ever noticed that he regularly avoided giving himself credit for loving behavior. His breathless laugh indicated the "assent of unconscious" and also some dismay at having been "discovered." This combination of stopping a trend and focusing on an unacknowledged bit of behavior was the beginning of new growth in Jonathan. Usually, I am the one who stops the process when I discover the seed of a long repressed way of being, and the group tills the soil. In this case, the opposite occurred.

In subsequent sessions, the seed began to germinate. The very next meeting he told us, with a big grin, that his wife had given him a birthday party and that instead of being grouchy about it, he had fully participated and enjoyed every minute. Then he became sober and, in a voice shaking with feeling, told us how much he really cared for her. It was the first time he had talked as someone who is entitled to love and be loved. The change in his self-perception registered an inner growth that was to continue the profound changes that were occurring in his personal organization and would continue to influence his future relationships.

Creating Disequilibrium

Another technique is that of creating disequilibrium in systems that seem to be losing liveliness and are approaching stasis. Actually, it is a name given by

George Vassiliou[18] to include a number of nonanalytic confrontative techniques that have, in recent years, come increasingly into practice. They include Spotnitz'[17] technique of "staying with the resistance," the therapeutic paradox used by family systems therapists,[10] and certain more direct forms of confronting, such as I often use. I am likely to say what a traditional analyst would find unconscionable, such as, "I don't believe you."

What these techniques have in common is a powerful emotional shock effect that shatters even tightly bounded sets of interlocking defenses, such as we observe in obsessive/compulsive group members.

In the case of Ann, I took a different tack. She was a very bright, charming, and always "ladylike" young woman who consistently avoided an underlying layer of infantile impotent rage. In the group, she participated actively and successfully in helping other members change. She also talked *about* events and people in her life, but in a quite rational way, without really exposing her feelings. Occasionally, when she actually experienced trouble in relation to the man she was living with, she would open up her genuine feelings, but always managed to restore her composure immediately afterward. She gained insight into the sources of some of her problems this way, but changed her behavior only minimally.

Ann could not seem to give up the myth that she was not entitled to a long-range relationship with a man who would be hers alone. She knew her need to remain celibate had to do with her childhood fear of her mother's jealousy, and her longstanding need to protect her incompetent and often absent father. She could express anger about her mother and guilt about her father, but could not face her infantile wish to take him for herself. Her nonverbal defenses helped to maintain her overtly calm stance. She was always polite, her voice and manners were rigidly controlled, and she never expressed direct feelings to me or to the group members in a real "encounter." Her deep inner tension seldom got out of hand.

One day she came in with a familiar and evidently very painful situation. She had been badly treated by the man she was living with, but she talked about it with incredibly polite reasonableness. Nothing the members said made more than an intellectual dent. I decided deliberately to create disequilibrium by imitating the voice and manner in which she had been talking about the man who had been untrue to her.

Using her tone of voice, I repeated some of the incredibly understanding statements she made about him. She looked startled and then completely lost her cool. She became furious with me, but in the middle of her outburst, she began to experience her hurt feelings and sobbed bitterly. Although she had started with her feelings toward me, she moved quickly to how she felt victimized by "John" and by her mother. Even her usually protected angry feelings toward her father poured out for the first time. I listened intently.

As I was breaking through her boundaries in a quest for a change, the group members were very supportive. Once her feelings broke through, I could sense that she recognized my empathy. The combination of pressure and support enabled her to go through the stress of this disturbing phase of disorientation or disequilibrium. It was the first step toward a basic reorganization of her character structure. Soon after this incident, she gave up John. Her choice of men changed, as did her attitude toward them. She was no longer the "geisha girl," as the group members had dubbed her. It was not long before she found a really caring man of her own. She regressed occasionally, but with the group's help she stayed with him. There was some working through to be done, but in the following year the group members and I agreed that she was ready to leave the group. We were sad to lose her but confident that she was ready to "take charge" of her love life.

When the therapist creates disequilibrium, the patient will respond with global anxiety and/or rage, and it is imperative that the therapist remain quiet and understanding, rather than respond in kind to the strong feelings that are being expressed. If he does so, the raw, unplanned emotion usually releases enough energy to shatter the intrapsychic boundaries to allow the member to process the input he/she had rejected and to draw new inner boundaries. The transformation of the character structure then automatically activates new modes of interacting with others so that they and the whole group are transformed, too. As often happens, the whole group began to question my intervention, but Ann said, "No, actually I'm glad Dr. Durkin did that. I found out that my rage didn't kill her, and I stopped being afraid that I would be attacked for it."

The therapist can help the patient who undergoes this frightening disequilibrium, if he encourages her to "stay with the anxiety," by pointing out that everyone finds it hurts to make a radical change and that, in fact, whether or not she changes is up to her.

When to Create Disequilibrium. Obviously this technique is not to be used with patients whose structure is too fragile to withstand further tension. It is suitable in analytic therapy groups which are presumably composed of persons with a fair degree of ego strength. Because it depends on shock value, it can be used only rarely and is best reserved for dealing with especially intransigent boundary structure. Generally, it is wise not to attempt it until late in treatment, after sufficient trust in the group and the therapist has been established.

But the real value of this technique comes late in treatment, after most of the ordinary dysfunctional transferential exchanges have been transformed and the members have to face a radical reorganization of character structure. The need to destructure the very defensive structures by which they have long managed to cope with the exigencies of reality is very hard for patients to bear. They are apt to resort to desperate measures to avoid the dilemma. They often experience confusion and complain of it enough to frighten off the therapist. Sometimes they become ill, yet the body may only be giving a message such as, "Look what you're doing to me, you bastard!" or, "Please take this cup from me." One of my patients developed attacks of vertigo whenever he found himself contemplating the possibility of real change. It helps when they are able to put into words similar messages that may mean, "I won't change, you can't make me" — or something of that nature.

On the whole, it takes a good deal of courage for the analytically trained therapist to take the risk of creating disequilibrium, but it is of critical importance that he not retreat, as analysts have tended to do, at this crossroad, where basic structural change is within reaching distance. GST eliminates this difficulty.

Some Caveats

1. Obviously, this powerful technique is not to be used with members whose ego structure is too fragile to withstand further tensions. It wouldn't do for borderline patients or those who are still immersed in narcissism. The therapist must be well enough trained to recognize the ego strength of each group member and to distinguish between signs of imminent psychotic break and the wily ploys of patients who want to be delivered from the agony of radical character change.

2. It goes without saying that since it depends on "shock" value, creating disequilibrium can be used only occasionally and for the specific purpose of breaking through a static equilibrium.

3. The therapist who decides to use the technique must be sure that solid support is available to the patient. Usually the group can be depended on for warmth and comfort while the patient is going through this critical phase. Furthermore, although pressing for change, the therapist's nonverbal communications consistently indicate his/her basic acceptance, concern, and support of the patient as a total person.

REFERENCES

1. Bertalanffy, L. von. *General Systems Theory.* New York: Braziller (1968).
2. Blanck, G. and Blanck, R. *Ego Psychology II.* New York: Columbia University Press (1979).
3. Durkin, H. E. Group therapy and general systems theory. *In:* Sager, C. and Kaplan, H. (Eds.). *Progress in Group and Family Therapy.* New York: Brunner/Mazel (1972).
4. Durkin, H. E. The development of general systems theory and its implications for group therapy. *In:* Wolber, L. and Aronson, M. (Eds.). *Group Therapy 1975 — An Overview.* New York: Stratton Intercontinental Books (1975).
5. Durkin, H. E. (Ed.). *Living Groups.* New York: Brunner/Mazel (in press).
6. Fried, E. N. *The Courage to Change.* New York: Brunner/Mazel (1980).
7. Fried, E. N. *In:* Slipp, S. (Ed.). *On Working Through as a Method of Self-Innovation.* New York: McGraw-Hill (in press).
8. Gray, W. Emotional cognitive structure. *General Systems Review* XVIII (1973).

9. Guntrip, H. *Schizoid Phenomena, Object Relations and the Self.* New York: International Universities Press (1969).
10. Haley, J. *Strategies in Psychotherapy.* New York: Grune and Stratton (1963).
11. Levinson, E. *The Fallacy of Understanding.* New York: Basic Books (1972).
12. Mahler, M. *On Human Symbiosis and the Vicissitudes of Individuation.* New York: International Universities Press (1963).
13. Maruyama, M. The second cybernetics. *American Scientist* I (2) (1963).
14. Miller, J. *Living Systems: Basic Concepts.* New York: Behavioral Science Press (1965).
15. Mintz, E. Group therapy and encounter techniques. *American Journal of Psychotherapy* 25 (1) (1975).
16. Schafer, R. *A New Language for Psychoanalysis.* New Haven: Yale University Press (1976).
17. Spotnitz, H. and Meadows, P. *The Treatment of Narcissistic Neurosis.* New York: The Manhattan Center for Advanced Psychoanalytic Studies (1976).
18. Vassiliou, C. and Vassiliou, V. Introducing disequilibrium. *In:* Wolberg, A. (Ed.). *Group Therapy 1976 – An Overview.* New York: Stratton Intercontinental Books (1976).
19. Watzlawick, F., Beavin, J., and Jackson, D. *The Pragmatics of Human Communication.* New York: W. W. Norton (1967).

Family photographs, and particularly photo albums, as the following chapter suggests, provide a very useful intra- as well as intergenerational view of a family and may therefore function as family icons. In the author's hands, these bare facts find fruitful application in family therapy and offer an additional dimension — the visual — to patterns of family interaction. Thus, they are both diagnostically and therapeutically useful and stimulating.

The chapter sets forth the relationships between the theory and technique of family therapy when the dimension of photography is added to the unfolding drama of the family. The reader is likely to find an intriguing experience ahead.

13

Family Icons: Photographs in Family Psychotherapy

Alan D. Entin, Ph.D.

The aim of this chapter is to explore some of the ways that photographs and family albums may be used in family psychotherapy. Photographs are a form of communication that can function to address the question: What does it mean to be a person in this family? They are of importance not only for the individuals depicted in the photographs, but for the family as a whole. They are links from the family's past to the present, and an affirmation of the traditions and ideals for the future. The Bowen family systems theory is a seminal, elegant, and comprehensive conceptual approach to the understanding of people and relationships. The theory emphasizes the importance of returning to the family of origin to establish different personal relationships with family members. The extended family is thus of considerable significance as a potential for individual change and growth. When the theory is used as a framework to guide the observations and interpretations of photographs and family albums, it then becomes possible to understand better one's own personal and family history. Family albums reflect a continuation of generational rhythms in the family life cycle, presenting a recurring pattern of relationships linking people, the passage of time, and the organization of space far more systematically than has generally been recognized. Photographs and family albums function as icons of the family, visually articulating the meanings and relationships of the family, while serving as landmarks for a history of continuity and change within the multigenerational family portrait.

THE RELATIONSHIP BETWEEN THEORY AND TECHNIQUE

In this chapter, we examine how photographs and family photograph albums may help in understanding family processes, relationship patterns, goals, expectations, issues, and three-generational themes, as well as the values, traditions, and ideals of the family. A brief overview of the concepts of the Bowen family systems theory is presented as a background and conceptual tool to provide a way of thinking about the family as a system and to offer a theoretical framework to organize ideas about photographs. The emphasis is on how the principles of family systems theory can be operationalized and applied to the observation of photographs and family albums. My goal as a family therapist is to understand family emotional systems and processes. It is within this context that family albums can have the greatest impact in family psychotherapy.

For a more comprehensive explication of the concepts of the Bowen family systems theory and psychotherapy and discussions of how the therapy is based on the theory, the reader is referred to the writings of Murray Bowen,[4, 5, 6] in particular *Family Therapy in Clinical Practice,*[7] as well as the volumes of the Georgetown Family Therapy Symposia.[8, 17] For a review of the variety of techniques and approaches that clinicians have evolved using photographs in psychotherapy, the reader may consult the literature on phototherapy.[12, 13, 14, 24, 26, 29, 30, 33] For a detailed guide to the analysis of photographs, the reader is referred to *Photoanalysis.*[2]

ABOUT PHOTOGRAPHS: TOWARD A PSYCHOLOGY OF FAMILY PHOTO ALBUMS

A photograph is a form of communication, both *of* something and *about* something, that "can be read as if it were a paragraph or chapter in a book."[19] A photograph is about time; it is a unique, one-of-a-kind experience, a slice of reality that will never again exist. A photograph is about an observation — a remembrance. And it is about space — an organization of people, objects, and their relationships. The nonvisual, metaphorical, and iconographic aspects of a photograph may be their most valued and significant contributions to future generations. Photographs contain a wealth of information: Not only are the images and relationships depicted important; so, too, are the spaces around the figures. The background can be read as information about social-cultural values, traditions, and ideals. Photographs tell not only about what is photographed, but about who is doing the photographing. Photographs are biographical as well as autobiographical. A lot is going on in the photographs, which can be "read" if people pay attention to them. By understanding the language, vocabulary, and syntax of photographs, by learning how to "read" them, and by combining that knowledge with an understanding of the concepts of the Bowen family systems theory, it then becomes possible to approach the study of photographs and family albums, and thus to better understand their meaning for one's own personal and family history.

Photographs and family albums, as well as family movies, provide the richest source of collected memories and traditions of the family. Their richness is in part related to the diversity of visual imagery and information that they are able to record about the individuals photographed, their relationships, and their surroundings. We have accepted the premise that the camera does not lie, and that it is an accurate and objective recording of reality: It captures everything in its view. Susan Sontag[8] declares that "through photographs, each family constructs a portrait — chronicle of itself — a portable kit of images that bares witness to its connectedness"(p. 8).

Photographs are signals of family life cycle ceremonies, rituals, and traditions, all of which are important for the development of the "identity" of the person involved. They indicate the relevance of the photographed event for the development of the whole family (for the "family identity").

As a family therapist, I am interested in who, what, where, when, and how the family chooses to document its existence as a family. This includes a myriad of observations and facts concerning the boundaries of the family system, the events and ceremonies chosen to be preserved, recorded and remembered, and who is the family historian. Given that the camera can capture and preserve a mini-slice of family history, important questions are raised as to the meaning surrounding such activities, as well as the relationships and events selected to be permanent photographic images. What is chosen to be photographed, recorded, and documented for the family album reflects the ideals, traditions, and values of the family. The activities surrounding the photographing of the events become as integral a part of family life as the events they commemorate. The records form the history of the family and present a collective image of the family. The albums are documents that can be studied to learn about what this particular family values and what its commonalities and differences with other families were.

Typical picture-taking behavior in families[2, 14, 18, 20] occurs at important events in the family's life cycle, such as births, birthday parties, weddings, holidays, vacations and family reunions. Conversely, there is a sharp decrease in the number of pictures taken during periods of family stress, crisis, or conflict. Firstborn children are generally photographed more frequently than later children, and most pictures are taken while the children are relatively young and changing. People from all socioeconomic classes own cameras and take, keep, and treasure their photographs. The size and the prominence of pictures and portraits of family members hung in the house also reflect attitudes about the family. Families tend to take pictures when events or changes represent progress (such as moving to a larger home), when a positive change is anticipated (such as cosmetic plastic surgery), or to recapture developmental change (such as loss of a child's baby teeth). Titus[31] suggests that photographs reflect rolelearning behavior for parents. The quantity and proportion of pictures of parents and the development of parental skills through caretaking activities, such as holding and feeding the child, as well as the number of solo pictures of the child, reflect the transition to parenthood. She further suggests that the inclusion of "significant others," defined as grandparents, aunts, uncles, and friends, "provides a break in routine, or becomes an occasion to record the family's continuity through the generations, or reflects wanting to have an economical ongoing record of significant others . . . " (p. 528). Knowledge of these patterns of picture-taking behavior is important because departures from the expected patterns may provide important clues for the therapist and the family about emotional processes operating in the family. For example, if a second child is photographed significantly more often than the firstborn, hypotheses can be raised regarding the child's meeting the expectations of the family in terms of its sex or attractiveness, or because of some family secret such as illegitimacy, handicap, or disfigurement. Issues such as equality and favoritism are also raised when individual family members become adamant about trying to equalize the number of photographs of the first and second child.

Favorite pictures of one's self, spouse, children, and parents are significant in helping to understand each person's view of the emotional process operating at the time within self and family. Favorite pictures are interesting because they have both visual and nonvisual referents. Visually they refer to a characteristic look or expression, while their nonvisual referents are about remembrances of times, events, people, and places. Obviously, there will not be unanimous agreement about which pictures best represent the family, although in highly fused families they may all tend to "think alike" and attempt to agree on their selections. Each person, however, has a unique point of view. The processes of selection of which events to document, which people to include, and which photographs to keep and place in an album are significant indicators of family processes. What is chosen reflects the self-image of the selector, as the family historian, on an individual as well as a family level. It could represent the family as it really is, the family at a transitory moment in family life, or it can represent the family as it would like to be. The photographs may represent characteristic aspects of a family relationship (which can be seen when several photos are examined), a temporary state within the family, or document a momentary aspect of the family's experience. Yoko Ono, for example, observed that a widely published photograph of John Lennon signing an autograph for Mark Chapman, "the man who was to betray John later," was harder for her to look at than the death photo of Lennon. She said it was the only time she had seen her husband "where John's head was bent forward, obviously to sign his name. But it was a strange posture for John to show." In retrospect, she interpreted this momentary state as "signing for the gate of Heaven."[25]

A family photograph album may be examined to determine whether it expresses a singular, unitary point of view of the family or whether it is open to reflect the multiple facets of the family's experiences and events.

THE CASE OF THE PERFECT FAMILY (ALBUM)

A client one day brought in her family album, which depicted what could be best described as an attempt to create a "perfect family." The album was "special," since it had been assembled by her terminally ill mother as a present to the daughter, who was a young adult. It expressed the mother's point of view about the family, indicating those characteristics of the family that she perceived as important. Her choices included pictures of Christmas trees with many, many toys around them, pictures of the client as a young girl, occasionally a picture of her only brother, but only two pictures that included both parents. The album spanned 24 years of development and family life. As a little girl, the client was immaculately dressed, with every hair in place and never a crease in her clothing. She was always standing rigid and posed, never playing with any of the toys surrounding her. During her mid-childhood years, there were photos of her hugging dolls and stuffed animals, but photos with her parents were conspicuous by their absence. In several photographs of her with her older brother, there was a distinct physical distance between them. Although separated by some 20 years, the only two photographs containing all four family members reflected the "special relationship" between mother and son.

The client wrote (interestingly, in the third person) her reactions to the family album. She described her family members as "rigid and uncommunicative. (She) complained of having an unsatisfactory relationship with her older brother and an uncomfortably distant relationship with her father . . . (She) never got along well with her mother as her brother did." She characterized herself as "a very compliant child . . . behaving exactly as she is told." She continued: "There are only a few pictures of the mother, but when the brother is in them, he is usually standing next to her . . . In the picture of the foursome, at some kind of celebration, the children are seated across from the parents. Daughter and father are looking at the camera, smiling. Mother has her back to the camera and is looking at the son. The son, leaning into a corner, away from the sister, is looking at his mother."[1]

Since all these interpretations were made by the client about the photographs and the relationships in the family, I suggested she speak with her mother, remembering the concepts of family systems theory, to obtain her mother's point of view about the relationship processes in the family and suggesting that she might want to review the album with her mother to clarify, confirm, or rethink her previous attitudes and memories about the family. Overall, the client thought that "the photographs were an accurate portrait of the inner lives of her family members." From my viewpoint, although a present from a dying mother to the daughter, the pictures reflected the mother's need to see the girl as "perfect" or "ideal" and "the hidden message" appeared to reflect the relationship between the mother and son, to which the girl was not privileged and to which she remained an outsider despite her desires for closeness with her mother. From a therapeutic vantage point, the album provided clues to where the client could focus in her attempts to alter her relationship with her dying mother.

Family albums typically reflect the positive experiences, happy ceremonies, events, and rituals in the family life cycle. My experience with families and their albums is generally consistent with Albert's[27] observation that "they record only the happy moments . . . (and) highlight all that is life affirming and pleasurable, while systematically suppressing life's pains" (p. 108). Consequently, the importance of photo albums has been dismissed or diminished by some authors, since they suggest that these albums constitute a "fairy tale . . . (a) pseudonarrative"[27] (p. 108), "a form of folklore,"[23] or an artifact of family life. According to the view presented in this chapter, however, such arguments are spurious and miss the significance of the album as a mirror and window reflecting the experiences of the family. The family album communicates the values, tradition, and ideals of the family, indicating the ways in which all families are alike and the ways in which they are different and the variety of ways in which they respond to similar cultural and life cycle experiences.

Family pictures are preserved and shown off in a variety of ways. The family that takes photos and throws them in a bureau drawer or a shoe box is often not as rigid as the family that carefully documents each "special occasion" and preserves it in a gold-bound album displayed on the living room coffee table. Almost universally, however, people indicate that "in case of fire" they would try to preserve the family photo albums because they are irreplaceable and their only link with the past.

The manner in which family photos are displayed may also reveal aspects of the family's attitudes. While families that hang portraits in prominent spots may be proud of their families' ties, or while the people or portraits may have some special significance, the converse is not true. It is important to ask questions to understand how the photos displayed function in that particular family. Kaslow and Friedman,[20, 22] for example, have shown that the size and prominence of family pictures in a bedroom might function to inhibit sexual activity. They ask, "Who's in the bedroom with you?" to shed light on sexual problems in marriages.

THE THEORY: BOWEN FAMILY SYSTEMS THEORY AND PSYCHOTHERAPY

Bowen Theory

The Bowen family systems theory is a conceptual approach that can be applied to a variety of problems and symptoms in the treatment of individuals, couples, and families.[4, 5, 6, 7] Bowen theory is a way of thinking about emotional problems in families. In contrast to individual theory, Bowen theory provides a different view of the human family and emotional disorders, as well as a different concept of change. Emotional disorder is conceived of as dysfunction in the family emotional system. Treatment is therefore directed toward modification of the relationship system among the most important adult members of the family, usually the spouse or parents, and their families of origin; it is a multigenerational approach. If an individual is to change, the context in which he or she lives — the family — must also change. If one individual in the family is symptomatic, all the members of the family are involved in the problem. No longer is a problem viewed as existing within self. Others must be involved. It is a shared family problem.

The goal of Bowen family systems psychotherapy is to change the patterns of relating, the way individual members interact and communicate. The functioning as a family is improved thereby, and the growth and differentiation of all the members of the family are promoted, giving new form and shape to the multigenerational family portrait.

The concept of the "triangle" is essential to Bowen's theoretical system. The triangle, a three-person system, is the "molecule" or building block of any emotional system, whether in a family or a social system. One of the characteristics of the triangle is that it is "the smallest stable relationship system. A two person system is an unstable system which immediately forms a series of interlocking triangles."[4] Bowen's triangle theory is an attempt to conceptualize the way in which three family members, or two family members and an issue (for example, drinking, which takes on the emotional significance of a third person) relate to one another in an orderly series of alliances and rejections within the family. Triangles thus reflect definite relationship patterns that repeat predictably in periods of stress. In periods of calm, there is a close, comfortable togetherness of two people and there is a less comfortable third person outsider. The preferred position is that of the insider. If tension builds in the twosome, one person becomes uncomfortable and initiates a move toward more comfortable togetherness for self, usually by bringing in a third person ("triangling"). In periods of stress, each person works to get to an outside position, the preferred position at that time, to escape the tension from the twosome by "letting the two of them fight it out."

The Bowen theory further conceptualizes the family as being composed of interlocking triangles. The primary triangle is the nuclear family, consisting of father, mother, and children; the extended family, comprising the husband and his family of origin, is another triangle; the wife and her family of origin, another triangle; and the relation of each spouse to his or her in-laws, two additional family triangles. In any family, tensions between parents can be transmitted to their children and become manifest as symptoms. This is predictable in all systems. While conventional theory dictates treating the "sick individual," the Bowen theory postulates that, if you "modify the basic triangle," you will achieve change in all relationships. Thus, treatment efforts are directed toward the heads of the family system.

One of the most innovative aspects of the Bowen theory is the concept of "the scale of differentiation." This concept is important because it attempts to conceptualize all human functioning on a single continuum, avoiding the concept of "normal" in describing the differences in how people are not alike — how they are different. Characteristics of individuals are based on their relative positions on "the scale," and it is a means of making predictions about them. Individuals are characterized according to their orientation to life. People low on the scale live in a feeling world and cannot distinguish feeling from fact. They manifest the greatest amount of emotional fusion or emotional "undifferentiation." This "emotional stuck-togetherness" is sometimes seen as "mind-reading," as when one spouse starts a sentence and the other finishes it. All their life decisions are based on what feels right. They cannot distinguish between a feeling and a thought: The two are fused together.

With increasingly higher positions on "the scale," the "feeling" and "intellectual" systems begin to become more autonomous and there is a growing awareness of the two systems as separately defined: Both systems become free. The thinking system is not reactive to emotional relationships, and individuals are free to choose if they want to have close relationships with others. The concept of "level of differentiation" is useful in understanding people's approaches to life, goals, and relationships because people choose others who function at the same level for friends and marital partners. Therefore, you cannot call your spouse stupid without it reflecting back on you! Psychotherapy is directed toward helping individuals differentiate, establishing an "I" position and changing their level of functioning.

The multigenerational transmission process posits how problems move across generations as parents transmit varying levels of undifferentiation to their children over multigenerations. It provides a way of predicting from past generations the general life course of future generations, all else being equal. An individual's level of differentiation depends in part upon the extent to which he or she is involved in the family emotional process. The term "undifferentiated family ego mass" refers to the degree of fusion in the nuclear family.[4,7] The greater the degree of undifferentiation, the greater the potential for problems. The mechanisms used by the parents in coping with the intensity of emotional fusion are their mirror image patterns of relationships with their families of origin. The three main patterns, which may coexist, whereby undifferentiation is manifest, are (1) marital conflict; (2) dysfunction in either spouse (or both) through physical or emotional illness or social dysfunctioning, such as drinking, acting out, or other irresponsible behavior; and (3) projection of the family problem onto the children, who then are symptomatic. These mechanisms for controlling the intensity of the fusion are present in all emotional systems to some degree. The amount of energy absorbed by any one mechanism generally reduces the amount to be absorbed by the other mechanisms. The more families manifest symptoms in all three areas and the less crystallized the symptoms, the more families are likely to benefit from family psychotherapy.

The concept of sibling position describes personality profiles, expectations, and orientations to life based on one's position in the family. The sibling position is a social role that predisposes an individual in a certain way for permanent social relationships outside the family.[32]

Family systems theory includes other concepts, such as distancer-pursuer, overfunctioning and underfunctioning, functioning at the expense of the other, responsibility for self and lowering expectations of others, consideration of family secrets and myths, and the effects of divorce, legal and emotional, for future generations.[9]

Psychotherapy

Based on my experience with families, emotional problems can be understood best by first placing them in the context of a three-generational emotional process and, second, by realizing that the extended family system of an individual, parents, and grandparents supplies prime resources for the resolution of conflicts and stress within the nuclear family.[10] Symptoms that are shown by an individual can be alleviated most effectively by helping the individual "work on the family" to resolve the "mirror image" patterns of repeating difficulties and long-standing issues that have "funneled down" the emotional-hereditary axis in the parental and grandparental systems. To accomplish this, an individual has to understand the structural and functional laws of family process, to become expert about one's own family system and the parts played in the emotional process and the triangular processes that lead to the stabilization of emotional dysfunctioning, and to work toward genuine person-to-person relationships with one's own parents and other important individuals within the family system. It means finding out about the family and how the generations got programmed to accept the various mythologies, labels, and rules of how men and women and boys and girls should be and should behave in the family. Getting to know one's family is best accomplished through "family voyages" in which the goal is to "differentiate" from, and to review stale or dysfunctional relationships with, parents and grandparents. It means talking about self, always knocking yourself first so as to allow the other person the opportunity to talk about him/herself openly. It means helping to delabel and demythologize parental and grandparental roles to get to the "person" behind the role. It makes the past real and bridges the generation gap. By going back to the family elders (parents, grandparents, aunts, and uncles), the individual restores a sense of continuity with his or her past, a sense of continuity in the present, and a sense of the future for today's children. Grandparents talking about their childhood to both their adult children and to their grandchildren tends to illuminate the emotional processes of a family that have been operating for years, often subliminally, and gives the younger generation a different perspective on their parents and grandparents.[10] It is in this context that photographs and family albums can have their greatest impact.

It is helping to define and realign the interlocking triangles and repeating "mirror image" relationships between the generations that is the clinical frontier in working with individuals and their families. The aim is to give more emotional freedom to intergenerational relationships, so that individuals can relate across the generations without cutting off physical and emotional contact, or adapting in an overly close involvement to maintain a superficially peaceful and harmonious relationship between the generations.

Typically, I define the problem and process in my first contact with the family as a relationship problem. I try to get the parental generation (or couple) to come in without their children, even when their problem is a child. During the course of therapy, I maintain a family systems-oriented view of "the problem" as a relationship problem. At times, only one family member is motivated to see me to work on his/her part of the family process and I will work only with that person, but "my head" is oriented toward thinking in systems terms. If the anxiety about a child is extremely intense, I may see a child or an adolescent for a brief time. Again, however, I direct my thinking and questioning to areas of relationships and patterns of relationships within the extended family, between the child and parents, and between the parents and the grandparents. I thus attempt to defocus "it" as the "child's" problem while continuing to redefine it as a family systems problem. On rare occasions, I have seen various members of the extended family, parents, brothers, sisters, and other significant family members with the individual(s) with whom I am primarily working. My emphasis during these sessions is to delineate the "mirror image" patterns in the family process. The theory organizes how I "think" about people and problems; it does not define who will be included in the sessions. Stated another way, the theory is what is in my head, not how many people are in the room.

I organize my questioning about relationships in the family using the structure of the genogram. The genogram, or annotated family tree, and the family photo album, are portraits of a family system.[11] They present an overview of the family relationship process that provides a time/space multigenerational family portrait — the who, what, when, where, and how of its members. While obtaining the "subjective" perception of the family members about "the problem" during the initial phase of therapy, questions aimed at obtaining "objective" facts (such as names and ages of all family members, exact dates of birth, marriage, separations, divorce, and death) can also be intermingled to complete the picture of the family system. The initial sessions should provide a balance between relieving family distress in a crisis and obtaining information. Agitated families may need to talk about their view of the crisis, which will cool things down, while in other families it may be easier to start with structure and information gathering. As family members define their view of "the problem," family systems theory organizes my thinking. The concepts of triangles, interlocking triangles, repeating mirror image problems across generations, the family projection process, and so on, help keep me, the therapist, focused on the overall pattern. The aim is to obtain a two- or three-generational overview of the emotional process in the family.

ABOUT TECHNIQUE: TOWARD THE APPLICATION OF FAMILY SYSTEM CONCEPTS TO PHOTOGRAPHS AND FAMILY ALBUMS

As a family systems therapist, I find that photographs can have their greatest impact within the context of getting to know one's own self and the relationship patterns in the family of origin. My approach is radically different from that of most practitioners who use photographs in psychotherapy.[14, 15] Clients do not usually bring photographs to the therapy session, and my aim when I do look at photographs is not for them to obtain emotional release during the therapy session.[2, 3, 20, 22, 33] When I look at photographs with clients, the purpose is to understand the message of the photographs in the language and syntax of systems theory and to see the manifold ways that the family process is expressed in the photographs. It is not for ventilating feelings or emotions. Ventilation of feelings and emotions for the resolution of longstanding relationship problems is more appropriately communicated and worked out in the relationship system in which the emotions were initially experienced, within the family of origin. My goal as a family systems psychotherapist is to help individuals obtain and/or maintain contact with their families of origin. The photographs serve to facilitate the process. In family systems psychotherapy, the sessions are used for clients to obtain an overview of the situations and problems, as well as to plan the work to be done outside the sessions with their own families of origin. Clients need to understand the language and concepts of family systems theory, which will aid them in their interpretation of their family photo albums as they embark on the search for self and family history.

A family systems theory approach to the study of photograph albums focuses on the who, what, where, when, and how of the family. It involves speculating about what is happening in the picture at the time (the people, relationships, events, clothing and other items in the pictures), what the people may have been thinking and feeling about the events, and what happened just prior to and following the picture. Significant information is also provided by charting a relationship process through viewing the same people or events in a series of photographs over time, noting changes in who is included and who absent, and observing who stands next to whom and what he is wearing. What events are documented, and how and when the photographs change, are also informative. The dimensions of time and space, the passages and transitions of the family as an expanding and contracting system through births, marriages, separations, deaths, and divorces are all available for observation within the family photo album. Obvious gaps may reveal times of family crisis or distress, or the absence of an expected or significant figure may be attributable to illness or hospitalization, and an inference may be made about the operation of the family emotional process. These assumptions, however, should be validated through discussions with family members. The photographs also reveal the extent of the relationship system of a family by the inclusion of significant others. The rituals, traditions and ceremonies the family values are reflected in the albums. These ideas are not exhaustive or definitive; they are suggestive and offered to stimulate therapists to think of additional ways in which family systems concepts can be applied to the observation of photographs. Some concepts may be easily operationalized, others may not be capable of translation into visual phenomenon, and some may be inferred from photographs.

When individuals are trying to get to know their family, to find out about family myths, stories, events, or history, family members often either cannot or will not talk about their past. As an aid to memory, or possibly to revive feelings which they are unable to otherwise verbalize, I suggest that clients may want to review photographs with their families to augment the verbal discussions and to get clues as to the themes, issues, goals, traditions, and values of their families. This activity has powerful effects, both as a process of reminiscing and talking about memories and previous relationships and as a way of developing renewed relationships in the present. During the course of therapy, I teach the concepts of family systems theory by discussion of clinical examples from clients' own family experiences. When they get stuck in their work with their families of origin, it is sometimes suggested that they may learn more about the family processes by looking at their family albums.

The role of the therapist is to ask questions while family members become experts at understanding the laws of family process that operate in their system. The achievement of these goals is accomplished through their own efforts outside the therapy sessions. Consequently, I do not typically sit down with individuals to look at their pictures. Usually, individuals are urged to do this with their parents, although occasionally they bring their albums to therapy sessions.

The principle that guides my thinking is: "How can the concepts of family systems theory be operationalized and conveyed visually?" In looking at photographs, I am thinking about them in terms of the information they convey about the family system and what the album communicates about the family relationship process. The interpretation and analysis of photographs *per se* is not the main focus of my clinical use of photographs in psychotherapy. The observation of photographs without a theoretical orientation results in mere interpretation, and simply emphasizing what to look for in photographs may, paradoxically, both expand and inhibit one's powers of observation. The Bowen family systems theory is an "open system" model; the technique is, likewise, open. There are no direct translations or correspondences between the theory and the photographs. While there are many clues and hypotheses generated by the theory, it is the family members who must complete the picture and develop additional discoveries and understandings. The "reading" of the photographs is open to multiple interpretations. There is no generalized, one-to-one correspondence between what is present in a photograph and a fact or interpretation about this or any other family. Rather, the observations of what is going on in the pictures should serve as jumping off points to raise questions and start discussions. Photographs can be read many times, and in many ways, to reveal the wealth of information they contain. The client's examinations, interpretations, and experiences of looking at photographs with the family become, in turn, the basis for changing him/herself. Utilized with the family systems theoretical approach, this framework enables the viewer to locate with more precision what is going on in the photographs and within families and to reveal in the language of systems what is implicit in the images of the photographs. When applied to the observation of photographs and family photo albums, the theory provides a framework to guide the formation of questions and hypotheses about individuals and relationships as expressed in the photographs. The goal is working toward changing behavioral patterns and relationships within the family.

The following anecdotes, clinical examples, and case histories are illustrative and suggestive of the manner in which a family systems approach can be applied to the observation of photographs and family albums. They are not definitive or exhaustive. They are offered to stimulate therapists to think about photographs as icons of the family — visual metaphors of the relationship patterns of the family.

Triangles and Interlocking Triangles

Triangles deal with emotional closeness and distance between two individuals and the role of a third person in that relationship. Interlocking triangles refer to the expansion of the system to include more people, but even these can collapse into functional triangles, such as in an "in-law" triangle. These observations can be applied to photographs to observe the closeness/distance aspects of relationships and triangles. The accumulation of repeated images helps to differentiate between more characteristic relationship patterns and more temporary patterns and alliances.

In a three-generational photograph, for example, taken about 18 months prior to discussion, the grandfather-photographer wanted a picture of his son and daughter with their spouses and children. This large family constellation grouped themselves as four separate units. The daughter was photographed with her husband, while their children were with the grandparents. The son formed another unit, with his arms around each small son, while his wife was apart from them, holding the family dog. At the time of the photograph, the meaning was unclear to the family. At the time of the session, the message was clear. The latter couple had been divorced with custody of the boys awarded to the father. The mother got the dog! While pictures cannot predict the future, they may suggest changes that are operating in the family relationship process which may surface in some form later. They can be indicators of the emotional climate in the family. This example also illustrates the role of pets for the family and how they may function as part of a triangle in a family.

In another family, the client, a middle-aged woman, complained of her continuing distance from her husband and her feeling of alienation from her older sister. She perceived her husband and sister as having a close relationship. These feelings were heightened during her older sister's visit (from a distant city) at Christmas. Photographs had been taken during the visit, and the client was eager to show them, because, for a change, she liked how she looked in them ("That was a nice picture of me . . . one of the few . . . I can't believe I said that!"). In a picture taken by her husband, she was sitting on the couch with her sister; she commented about the photograph and the relationship:

> *Client:*   Well, there is a lot of distance between us, except for our knees, isn't there? But we seem to be having a really good time, and I guess that's why I like these pictures . . . and we're laughing a lot, that's real important. I noticed that I have my hands clasped together between my knees . . .
>
> *Therapist:* What does that mean?
>
> *Client:*   I don't know, closed in a way . . . maybe it could mean that part of me is open to my sister and part of me is closed.

She had taken a picture of her husband and her sister, on the same couch — but "I wanted to get the Christmas tree in," she explained, and, in so doing, shifted the vantage point to take the picture. The resulting image reflected the relationship: The arm of the sofa functioned as a barrier between her and them. In the photograph, she created and maintained barriers to mirror the emotional distance she experienced in all her relationships.

Sibling Position

As the family expands from a twosome to a three-person system when the first child is born, the relationship between the spouses changes. How the changes affect the family may be visible in photographs. How the newborn changes the relationship between the parents, and, for example, who may be more emotionally involved or responsible for the caretaking of the child, may be reflected in photographs. The photographic images may be examined to see if and how the relationship pattern changes over time. As the next child is born, the three-person system changes to a four-person system. The photographs then may be looked at to evaluate how the newcomer to the system has changed previously established relationships, as well as how the older child responds to the birth of the new sibling. Who stands next to whom, shifts in alliances, receptiveness, facial expressions, and mannerisms are all signs of changing emotional experiences in the family. These may record and suggest the process of change in the family. By viewing a series of photos, it becomes possible to determine the types and constancy of relationships that have developed between siblings in the family.

Differentiation of Self — "I Position"

Other family systems concepts are not directly visible in photographs, but their operation may be inferred. In a therapy session one day, I was asked if I wanted to see some photographs. Excited that the client unknowingly brought in information relevant to my interests, I quickly assented. The resulting photographs were indeed interesting. The images were of a tie on a dresser (to document how long the woman has complained about her husband's sloppy habits); a black sheet on a window (which had hung there for 25 years to help darken the room since her husband slept during the day and worked at night); and inadequate cabinets in the kitchen, preventing her from functioning effectively. Her aim was to elicit support. The thrust of her argument was that the photographs documented and, in the eyes of any reasonable person, supported her contentions about her husband's unreasonableness. She had not yet learned how to develop responsibility for her own functioning — how to become a self in the marriage.

Working on a Relationship in the Family of Origin

In one family, the client attempted to obtain access to the family albums. The wife's mother, however, vigorously denied the existence of any photographs, although the woman vividly remembered seeing them when she was a child. This suggested that there were some important and intensely emotional issues present, but much ground work relating to her mother had to be done before such issues could be dealt with openly. The process of attempting to attain the necessary information and to change her relationship with her mother by becoming less angry or anxious with her than in previous encounters, for example, could also be interpreted as a successful experience even if the "end products" (the photographs) were not obtained. Her feelings of frustration and hopelessness because the difficulties were significant provided further material for her to work with in her family.

Multigenerational Transmission Process

The multigenerational transmission process explains the generational recycling of relationship patterns. Examining a series of photos over time, or of the same event, such as a wedding, over several generations, may provide clues to the continuity/discontinuity of patterns and relationships over time. The study of generational themes is further enhanced by observing parents and grandparents when they were both younger and at similar ages and/or life cycle stages. These photographs may illuminate the emotional processes of the family that have been operating for years, often subliminally, and give the younger generation a different perspective on their parents and grandparents. As stated by a photographer: "When I saw this photograph of my daughter, I felt as if I were looking at myself in the mirror, but in another time and place."[16]

Like Mother, Like Daughter. The following dialogue provides an example of the multigenerational transmission process.

> *Client:* I did see myself in my mother's pictures. I did! When I was looking at the pictures, I just . . . I realized that there I was. You know.
>
> *Therapist:* What kind of pictures are they?
>
> *Client:* Seductive, you know, type pictures. I could see my self-perception in the pictures because of the way she looked in the pictures. You know? I had a feeling that she perceived herself the same way I am perceiving myself. So . . .
>
> *Therapist:* What kinds of pictures were they? Any kinds of particular images that you saw that —
>
> *Client:* Well, she was, you know, on the beach in a bathing suit. Just very seductive pictures — attractive, that's the way she looked, and that's the way I saw myself in the pictures . . . as being seductive and attractive in that respect. I could relate to my mother at that time.

Therapist: Have you noticed that kind of parallel or similarity between the two of you before — before you looked at the pictures?

Client: No, never. No. Mom now is — you know, as I told you — she has a thyroid problem now and that changed her appearance tremendously. So she doesn't perceive herself in that respect anymore and, you know, I don't relate to her anymore in that sense. But I did in the pictures. I could see that that's the way she was at one time, and I could understand what she must be going through now because of it.

Therapist: Did you ever see her or remember her that way, when you were a little girl?

Client: When I was little, I thought she was very pretty and, you know, I didn't see her very much and I guess that was part of it — that we were away from each other and I had to remember her a lot. My memory of her was her being very pretty as I saw her coming home from work or going off to work or something.

Therapist: There is more than just the separation from your mother during the day that you are talking about, aren't you?

Client: Right, I lived with my grandparents.

Therapist: So that when you talk about separation —

Client: Right in the physical sense.

Therapist: You know, I would wonder if that kind of physical separation between you and her shows up in photographs, as an emotional separation — lots of distance . . . Maybe you have some pictures of the family when you were young?

Client: Could be — I don't know . . . We have lots of picture albums and there were lots of pictures. I want to go to my grandmother's because my grandmother has so many pictures that I remember — pictures of me from the time I was born . . . until I grew up . . . There were less pictures of me, of course, as I got older — just for special times — birthdays, holidays, and that type of thing when I was very small and . . . I thought, well looking back . . . she must have taken these because she didn't spend a lot of time with me . . . she must have taken these — a lot of candids of me as a baby — because she wasn't with me a lot and she needed these because she wasn't with me . . . I could relate to how really important I was in my mother's life . . . but she really had no control over the fact that we were separated. She had to work and the only way they could work things out was for me to stay with my grandmother and be separated at that time. But in the pictures I could see how important I was to her.

Therapist: What about the pictures makes you see how important you were?

Client: Well, being a mother may have something to do with it.

Therapist: That you are a mother now?

Client: Yes. I could see something between her and me when I was like a year old and relate it to how I feel about my daughter.

Therapist: What would you see between you and her when you were a year old and compare it to you and your daughter when she was a year old?

Client: Bonding.

Therapist: What would the bonding look like? That is a crazy question!

Client: But there is something about the image . . . a tremendous amount of — how do you describe it — affection . . .

Therapist: How will it look in the picture?

Client: You won't see probably what I see. I don't know how . . . how to get it across to you.

Therapist: Why wouldn't I see it the way you saw it?

Client: You may . . . it is a lot more emotional what I see — I see emotion . . .

Therapist: How much of what you felt is something you might observe in the photograph and how much of that might have to do with the emotional system or relationship between you and your mother, which somehow has to do more with the interpretation and memory than with the image?

Client: It is very hard to remember . . .

Therapist: I was wondering, did you interpret that picture with the same kind of feeling and emotion, bonding, attachment, affection before you were a mother, before your daughter was born, as after? Did somehow your being a mother have anything to do with it? And your leaving your daughter so that you could work?

Client: Oh, I am sure. I think you become a lot more emotionally aware of relationships after you have a child of your own, as a mother anyway. Of course, it's only been more recently that I have even thought about my relationship way back then with my mother and family . . .

A Wedding Album. An attractive young couple in their late twenties who had been married about a year were experiencing severe marital conflicts resulting in distance and a lack of intimacy. Contrary to my usual practice, I suggested they bring in some photos after I learned that this was the second marriage for each and that they had been college sweethearts before either had married. I was especially curious to see if the lack of emotional involvement they described in their marriage was also present when they had dated many years before. Was this the reason they didn't get married to each other the first time around?

The first photo, taken senior prom night, with her in a formal gown and him in a white tuxedo, revealed a bland, lifeless, nonrelating couple. Each was staring off blankly into the void before him or her, with only a hint of a smile on both their faces, perhaps at the suggestion of the photographer to say "cheese." Their relationship broke up shortly after graduation. While eventually both married, they shortly thereafter divorced. Through a chance meeting several years later, they resumed their courtship. As reflected in the pictures taken at their wedding, they appeared to relate to each other through the wife's four-year-old daughter by her previous marriage — a triangle. The "wedding photo" showed the three principal figures, with the girl in front of and between the bride and groom, arms outstretched in a cruciform. He stood with his hands by his sides while holding the girl's outstretched left hand. By his side was his new bride, holding onto her daughter's outstretched right hand and clutching the groom's right arm with her left arm, their only contact. While generally "corny" and staged, even wedding album photographs can be revealing. In the next photograph, taken on the way to the honeymoon bedroom, upstairs at her parents' previous residence, the couple smiled gaily and eagerly on the bottom step. But as the destination is approached, the relationship pattern emerged immediately. At the top of the stairs, the photo showed them engaged in a tug of war. She appeared to be pulling him up the stairs and he appeared to be resisting, pulling away from her, trying to distance himself from her and go back down the stairs. In spite of the smiles on their faces, the message was clear: She wanted closeness and intimacy; he was distancing himself and pulling away from her. This pattern was to persist in their relationship and culminated in their divorce. They could only relate through and about the girl. The triangle briefly stabilized their relationship.

Their verbal interpretation was consistent with the visual communication. The physical distance in the pictures reflected the emotional distance in their relationship. She was the pursuer and he the distancer. Interestingly, in his memory of the wedding photographs, he was positive there was a picture of him pulling her up the stairs, with her resisting. That picture, if it existed at all, was not included in the "official wedding album." Which pictures are selected for inclusion in the documentation of events, which are left in the yellow Kodak envelopes, and which are discarded completely are often significant.

FAMILY THEORY, FAMILY ALBUMS, AND FAMILY ICONS

These investigations and explorations into the nature and functions of photographs provide a new way of looking at family pictures and family albums. The Bowen theory provides a framework to guide the formation of questions and hypotheses about individuals and relationships as expressed in photographs. They depict the social reality and constitute the visual diary of the family, documenting its changing and enduring concerns and relationships. Family albums reflect a continuation of generational rhythms in the family life cycle, presenting a recurring pattern of relationships linking people, the passage of time, and the organization of space far more systematically than is generally recognized.

ACKNOWLEDGMENTS

Some of the material in this chapter has previously appeared in different form in "Photo Therapy: Family Albums and Multigenerational Portraits," *Camera Lucida* 1 (2): 39–51 (1980), and Gurman, A. (Ed.), *Questions and Answers in the Practice of Family Therapy,* New York: Brunner/Mazel (1981). I wish to thank Robert Muffoletto, the editor of *Camera Lucida*, and Alan Gurman, Ph.D., for their permission to use the material here. I am indebted to Jules Arginteanu, Ph.D., for his critical reading of the manuscript, and I appreciate the assistance of Donald K. Bruce, Ph.D., and Phyllis C. Entin, M.A., for their insightful and critical reading of the chapter. And I thank the families with which I have worked, for their contributions of ideas about the ways photographs and albums function as icons.

REFERENCES

1. Anonymous. Personal communication (October 1979).
2. Akeret, R. V. *Photoanalysis.* New York: Peter H. Wyden (1973).
3. Anderson, C. M. and Malloy, E. S. Family photographs in treatment and training. *Family Process* 15 (2):259–264 (1976).
4. Bowen, M. Family and family group therapy. *In:* Kaplan, H. and Sadock, B. (Eds.). *Comprehensive Group Psychotherapy.* Baltimore: Williams and Wilkins (1971).
5. Bowen, M. Toward the differentiation of a self in one's own family. *In:* Framo, J. (Ed.). *Family Interaction – A Dialogue Between Family Researchers and Family Therapists.* New York: Springer (1972).
6. Bowen, M. Theory in the practice of psychotherapy. *In:* Guerin, P. (Ed.). *Family Therapy: Theory and Practice.* New York: Gardner (1976).
7. Bowen, M. *Family Therapy in Clinical Practice.* New York: Aronson (1978).
8. Bradt, J. and Moynihan, C. (Eds.). *Systems Therapy.* Washington, DC: Georgetown Family Center (1971).
9. Entin, A. D. Family systems theory: An introduction. Unpublished paper presented at the Southeastern Psychological Association (April 7, 1973).
10. Entin, A. D. Family, identity and the future of psychology. Unpublished paper presented at the 28th Annual Conference of the New York Society of Clinical Psychologists (February 22, 1976).
11. Entin, A. D. The genogram: A multigenerational family portrait. Unpublished paper presented at the American Psychological Association (August 29, 1978).
12. Entin, A. D. The use of photography in family psychotherapy. Unpublished paper presented at the American Psychological Association (September 2, 1979).
13. Entin, A. D. The differentiated eye: The use of photographs in family psychotherapy. Unpublished paper presented at the Georgetown University Symposium on Family Psychotherapy (November 1979).

14. Entin, A. D. Photo therapy: Family albums and multigenerational portraits. *Camera Lucida* 1 (2):39–51 (1980).
15. Entin, A. D. The use of photographs and family albums in family therapy. Gurman, A. (Ed.). *Questions and Answers in the Practice of Family Psychotherapy.* New York: Brunner/Mazel (1981).
16. Fredrick, A. Photographic announcement. Richmond, VA (February 3, 1980).
17. *Georgetown Family Symposia: A Collection of Selected Papers.* Andres, F. and Lorio, J. (Eds.), Vol. I (1974); Lorio, P. and McClenathan, L. (Eds.), Vol. II (1977); Sagar, R. (Ed.), Vol. III (1978). Washington, DC: Georgetown University.
18. Hattersley, R. *Discover Your Self Through Photography.* Dobbs Ferry, NY: Morgan & Morgan (1976).
19. Hattersley, R. Interview in the *Richmond Times Dispatch,* K-15 (May 7, 1979).
20. Kaslow, F. W. and Friedman, J. Utilization of family photos and movies in family therapy. *Journal of Marriage and Family Counseling* 3:19-25 (1977).
21. Kaslow, F. The use of photographs, scrapbooks and diaries in marital and family therapy. Paper presented at the American Psychological Association (August 25, 1978).
22. Kaslow, F. What personal photos reveal about marital sex conflicts. *Journal of Marital and Sex Therapy* 5 (2) (1979).
23. Kotkin, A. The family album as a form of folklore. *Exposure* 16 (1):4–8 (1978).
24. Krauss, D. A summary of characteristics of photographs which make them useful in counseling and therapy. *Camera Lucida* 1 (2):7–12 (1980).
25. Lennon, Yoko Ono. In gratitude. *The Washington Post*, A5 (January 18, 1981).
26. Loellbach, M. The uses of photographic materials in psychotherapy: A literature review. Unpublished master's thesis, George Williams College (1978).
27. Milgram, S. The image freezing machine. *Psychology Today* 10 (8):50 (January 1977).
28. Sontag, S. *On Photography.* New York: Farrar, Straus & Giroux (1977).
29. Stewart, D. Photo therapy: Theory and practice. *Art Psychotherapy* 6 (1):41–46 (1979).
30. Stewart, D. Photo therapy comes of age. *Kansas Quarterly* 11 (4):19–46 (1979).
31. Titus, S. L. Family photographs and the transition to parenthood. *Journal of Marriage and the Family* 38 (3):525–530 (1976).
32. Toman, W. *Family Constellation.* New York: Springer (1969).
33. Zakem, B. Photo therapy: A developing therapeutic approach. Unpublished paper (1977).

Poetry therapy is the application of poetry to the therapeutic process and is used on a one-to-one basis and/or as a group experience. It is an adjunctive modality employed in diverse settings with individuals of diverse ages who have wide-ranging problems.

Poetry therapy is an old-new field groping for its own identification and rationale as it emerges into a viable therapeutic tool. At this stage of its development, it appears that each school of psychotherapy can find a place in its armamentarium for poetry, as well as the other arts.

A poem may act as a catalyst through which feelings are filtered and brought into the realm of awareness. A poem may also act as though it were another person who is absent, except symbolically. In a very real sense, the poem acts as a projective device.

The examples presented in the following chapter are from the author's own experience in using poetry in therapy, both on an individual and group basis. However, the primary emphasis here is on the use of poetry in the group setting. This chapter does not purport to be all-inclusive, nor does it exhaust the possibilities inherent in a consideration of poetry therapy in the group experience.

14

Poetry Therapy in the Group Experience

Arthur Lerner, Ph.D.

Poetry therapy is the application of poetry to the therapeutic process. *It is a tool, not a school,* an adjunctive modality in the therapeutic experience, very much on the order of art therapy, music therapy, dance therapy, and the like. In this chapter, poetry therapy simply means *poetry in therapy.*

Poetry therapy is used in such diverse settings as hospitals, clinics, mental health institutions, jails, prisons, educational milieus, private practice, and the like. My discussion of poetry therapy is drawn from this tool in private practice, hospital settings, mental health and educational centers, and experiential workshop sessions given at the Poetry Therapy Institute and at seminars and meetings throughout the country. The primary emphasis here is on the group. My excerpts and examples illustrate some of the cogent and pertinent aspects of poetry therapy in the group experience.

One must bear in mind that while the material in this chapter is accurate in detail, it represents only selected aspects of a more complete experience. My main purpose is not to present a total picture but to illustrate the therapeutic potential inherent in poetry therapy as practiced by one therapist. My hope is that the reader will be thus exposed to both theoretical and practical aspects of the poetry therapy experience.

In general, a poem is a catalyst through which we filter verbal and non-verbal information bits. We may choose to hide behind our information bits, and a poem can help us to further locate, identify, and define our vague feelings by bringing them into the realm of awareness and cognition. As a result of integrating our newly acquired reality, we may develop new attitudes, reorient present ones, learn to make new responses, and develop skills in the art of self-management. It is amazing how under these circumstances a person acquires wholesome and acceptable views and at the same time a new sense of one's effectiveness.

A reader of poetry will often come up spontaneously with a "eureka" feeling, as if to validate the idea that a word or a line has touched an affect. How closely the poet and psychotherapist see eye to eye can be gleaned from a reading of the following lines from Wordsworth's "Intimations of Immortality."

> To me alone there came a thought of grief;
> A timely utterance gave that thought relief,
> And I again am strong.

One can easily see the parallel in a psychotherapeutic interpretation that is offered at the appropriate time.

A patient in poetry therapy wrote these lines:

> I feel something wanting to come out
> I can't scream I won't shout
> I know I feel something right
> Like I'm getting special sight
> To see and feel a certain way
> And make me fuller every day.

When pressed for an explanation, May, a 23-year-old single woman stated:

> I feel what I'm feeling is this. I have just caught on to the idea that you have to listen to people carefully and then match what they say with what they do. In that way, you'll learn how to protect yourself against too many false hopes. People don't always say what they mean or mean what they say. I've just flashed onto it after all these years because of some problem I've been having with my boyfriend. My problem is that I've made a new discovery for myself and I want to share it. But somehow or other, while I can't put together the right words, I think they'll come to me soon.

SELECTION OF CLIENTS

It has been my experience that selection of individuals for poetry therapy sessions depends to a large extent on the dynamics of the individual, the therapist, the setting, and the vast array of intangibles that every therapist encounters. From my vantage point, I have often found that individuals coming for individual or group therapy will give me some of their written material or favorite poems. Usually, a discussion will follow in which they will state their views, feelings, hopes, frustrations, etc. The poem, in other words, may be thought of as a projective device. Clients will often bring poems session after session and then stop. Or they may follow up their poems with the writing of some lines during the therapy session. Sometimes I will also write some lines of poetry. What is important is that the aim of the therapy session is not a poetry writing experience for the sake of writing poetry. Every therapist has had the experience of the patient or client trying to avoid getting at feelings by presenting examples of excellence in various fields and activities. Poetry is no exception. Hence, the dynamics of the individual must not be ignored during the time when poetry is the medium of interaction with the therapist.

In selecting individuals for the poetry therapy group experience, I have found that the same criteria prevail that apply to regular group therapy sessions. What I have found unique is my labeling of a group therapy session as a "poetry therapy group." It has also been my experience that individuals coming to poetry therapy groups do not need to read or write the language in use at the moment. I have had foreign-speaking clients in my groups who caught the flavor of the feeling at the moment and insisted on reciting a poem they had memorized in their early years or one they had recently learned. For this reason, I try to have available books of poetry that are bilingual — Russian, French, Italian, German, Spanish, and Oriental languages such as Chinese, Japanese, Korean, and Thai.

SETTING

The setting refers to the specific area or room in which the poetry therapy session is taking place. My experience has dictated that the room should be big enough to move around in without people getting lost or feeling cramped. There are usually from seven to twelve people in attendance. Seats are arranged in a circular fashion, with no obstruction, such as a table or the like, in the center. Poetry books, typed poems, and pencils with paper are in abundance. These conditions are particularly useful in a hospital setting.

In a hospital setting, such as the Woodview-Calabasas Hospital in Calabasas, California, and the Van Nuys Psychiatric Hospital in Van Nuys, California, our sessions are designated as poetry therapy. The primary therapist is, of course, the one who determines whether a patient shall attend whatever sessions may be helpful. As the poetry therapist, I also like to be in the vicinity of a duplicating machine, since patients will often ask for copies of poems that have been read.

It is important to have a variety of poems on hand. These include, but are not limited to, poems on love, hate, grief, joy, decision-making, and doubt. One doesn't know what affect may arise.

I conduct my poetry therapy sessions for one hour. In a hospital setting, one should remember that the time for holding a session is often determined by a host of other scheduled activities. Also, in a hospital setting, there may be interruptions, such as the patient being called out by his or her own individual therapist. As a rule, however, interruptions can be kept to a minimum.

When a session ends, my job is to chart each patient, noting what I thought his or her main reactions were during the meeting.

FACILITATORS

In my experience at the Woodview-Calabasas Hospital, I am helped by poetry therapy facilitators. These are individuals, not licensed or certified therapists, who have a feel and love for poetry and are preparing to become therapists. They often pick up clues and nuances of the group process and use poetry to facilitate interaction and communication. But the primary responsibility of what goes on in the session is mine. The facilitators work under my supervision while being a vital part of the group experience. They also chart patients' progress, and I read and sign their entries.

The point here is that facilitator and therapist work as a team. Before each group session, we usually discuss such matters as the composition of the group, types of difficulties that might be encountered, any special problems since the last session (medication, stressful events that may have occurred), progress reports, the patients' individual therapists' reactions, etc. After each session, we have feedback on what took place.

Obviously, in a discussion of this kind, one can't point out everything that is going on. It suffices to say that the general highlights at poetry therapy sessions contain common experiences that therapists can relate to as part of their experience in their own milieu.

It is important to note that not all psychotherapists are interested in poetry or have the skill to use it as a tool in their work. Until appropriate professional programs are developed, we may have to rely on facilitators working under professional supervision.

It is, of course, the therapist's responsibility to help create an accepting, non-judgmental atmosphere where people in the poetry therapy group can relate to one another and verbalize their feelings with a minimum of doubt, guilt, and hostility. The facilitator, working under supervision, aids in selecting poems for group members to read, enters the discussion from time to time, and becomes a part of the group experience. By his or her own actions and skill, the facilitator helps the therapist effect a wholesome therapeutic atmosphere. The following example illustrates this point.

Malcolm [a 17-year-old boy who was having "problems with girls," opening the third session]:   Kate [facilitator], last week you weren't here and I missed you. I know you're helping Dr. Lerner and are involved with his work. But I felt you had no right to be absent from the group. You kind of let me down.

Kate: Malcolm, I hear you saying you're angry at me. What happened?

Malcolm: You really pissed me off by not being here —

Jackie [a 15-year-old girl whose main problem, she said, was "just to get along with my parents"]:   Malcolm, Kate is asking why you were . . . well — I mean you're not answering her question. You always are like this. You avoid! Avoid! Avoid!

Malcolm: Screw you! You think you're smart! You're not the therapist here. Come to think of it, why don't *you* talk, Dr. Lerner?

Poetry Therapist: What do you want me to say? Can you answer Kate?

Malcolm: Well, I'm angry. The week before, when you were here, Kate, I told you I was going to write some poetry about myself. Then last week when you weren't here and I had the poetry, I felt cheated, that you didn't care. That's what I mean. You let me down!

Poetry Therapist: Malcolm, did you ever stop to think that Kate has as much right not to be here as you have. Maybe she got sick. Maybe she had an emergency. Isn't this what happens at home with your parents, sisters, and brothers when you don't get what you want?

Malcolm: I guess so. Well, let me read what I wrote. I mean the poem I wanted to read last week. Here it is:

> My parents don't read me
> My brothers and sisters too
> Only in here do I feel true
> Only in here do I feel free.

Kate: Are you saying that you're getting something from this group you're not getting at home?

Malcolm: Right. I feel you are all like my brothers and sisters and Dr. Lerner is big daddy.

Joan [a 19-year-old who was "having difficulty making up my mind about what college I should enroll in in the fall"]:   It's really strange This is the way I feel and have felt ever since I entered the group.

Kate: Have you a poem too?

Joan: I don't have a poem but I must say I was angry too last week when you weren't here. I too felt cheated.

Poetry Therapist: Do you often feel cheated, Joan?

Joan: Only when I can't get the things I want when I want them. I suppose you call it being immature.

Kate: Malcolm, doesn't the same hold for you? Why don't you talk about it? Maybe you would like to ask me why I wasn't here last week.

Malcolm: Well, I'm afraid maybe you'll tell me to mind my own . . . damn it — it is my business! Why weren't you here?

Kate: Do you feel better now that you've asked?

Malcolm: Yes, I do, but you still haven't answered me.

Kate: I can see why you're angry. One of the rules we made up at the beginning of our sessions was if we know we can't be here at a session we would let the group know if at all possible. I had a serious illness in my family and had to attend to personal matters.

At this point the Poetry Therapist suggested we all write a two-liner beginning with the words, "I feel." These were read individually as we went around the group. (I am only presenting the contributions of the four participants in this interaction segment.)

I feel sometimes things are good, sometimes they're bad
But whichever, you shouldn't feel like you've been had.

— Malcolm

I feel closer to the people here
Because they help me see things so clear.

— Joan

I feel stymied when at first I write
But soon feel out of sight.

— Kate

I feel like a seedling soaking up rain
As I listen to tales of joy and pain.

— Poetry Therapist

The lines presented here are certainly not great poetry. One can even question if they're poetry at all. But these are the basic materials from which poetry therapists gain much information about how to help people help themselves. It is well to remember that a poem presents an imaginative perception that illuminates or interprets an experience that has emotional appeal and possibly universal significance. Above all, a poem is not an editorial or an intellectualized comment.

INITIAL SESSION

This presentation of a portion of a poetry therapy group session illustrates what is commonly thought of as the orientation session. Incidentally, this was the first of twelve sessions. The group was composed of eight individuals, five females and three males, ranging in age from 23 to 56. The primary problems facing the group concerned employment and relating to friends, husbands, wives, children, and family. None of the group members were psychotic.

The poetry therapist has given a brief explanation of poetry therapy, re-emphasizing some of the points he had made to individual members at the time they were selected for the poetry therapy group session. The most significant of these ideas are: (1) poetry therapy groups are not poetry workshops; (2) poetry therapy groups consist primarily of the application of poetry to the group therapy process; (3) the poetry therapist and the group are interested primarily in feelings; and (4) in poetry therapy we bring our favorite poems, poetry books, or other materials, including poems that we have written before or during a session.

George [a 33-year-old father of three, a checker at a supermarket, whose main complaint was, "I can't get along with my wife at all"] : This is the first meeting. I still don't buy the idea that poetry can be of help. My problems are too deep for anything to help. Why am I here?

Alice [a 37-year-old divorced mother of two, a computer operator, whose main complaint was, "I find it hard to meet men"] : George, you remind me of my ex-husband. He was a real home-run slugger in his work, but when he came home he was ineffective. You just couldn't talk to him. He was always right about things. Even when I asked him to go for help he used to say that no one can help him and therapy was a lot of crap — and —

George: Remember, I'm not your ex-husband. I'm me. I don't know what your hangups are, but —

Alice: That's what I mean. Just like my ex-husband, even the interruptions.

Frank [a single, 28-year-old auditor, whose main complaint was, "I can't find a girlfriend who believes in me"] : You both act as though you were meant for each other. I mean you both have lots of problems

— and you both remind me of my parents — how they used to argue and bicker all the time.

Poetry Therapist: I have some lines, written by a young man in one of my previous sessions, which seem to have some meaning right now.

> Sometimes I blame my father
> At other times my mother
> For things I cannot achieve
> And when I start the blaming
> I am suddenly filled with grief.
> It's not my father, mother, or other
> With whom I have to bother
> When I deal with my inner life.
> It's my "me," not my wife.

George: Easy to write, hard to live.

Alice: True!

Frank: I agree. But what does one do when so much crap is piled on you. It's normal — or is it? To blame —

Gene [a 40-year-old grandfather, a salesman whose main interest was the outdoors, and whose complaint was, "My wife doesn't like to do the things I like to do, like hunting and fishing"]: I'm always blaming my wife.

George: My wife is a fine lady. She is a good wife and mother. Maybe I expect too much. You told us [turning to Poetry Therapist] to bring in some lines. Here's what I picked up on a bulletin board at a supermarket. It was part of a throwaway sheet.

> He or she who blames without looking into their own person will soon pay interest in the way they delay their best self from coming out.

Poetry Therapist: How do you others feel about this?

Toni [a 35-year-old executive secretary at a computer corporation, a mother of two, whose main complaint was, "I don't have enough time to do what I need to do. I'm always under stress"]: Before I received individual psychotherapeutic help I felt like a two-edged sword. One side was the sharp edge of guilt, the other was the sharp edge of feeling bad about not pleasing others. What would people think if I acted a certain way? I now see the guilt and pleasing trips as part of the same thing. It's all in the person. I mean me. Listen to what I've written:

> Guilt and pleasing others was me
> No more! I'm beginning to feel free.

Poetry Therapist: You are telling us then that you are capable at this time of assuming responsibility for your own behavior. Am I correct in what I'm hearing, Toni?

Toni: Yes. I wish I could assume more responsibility. But I've also learned patience. You've got to learn to take short and easy steps before you take the leaps and jump. Here's another poem I've written which points to this:

> Along with any ideas I share
> This is one that's really rare
> For me who've felt otherwise.
> I sense to grow and leap ahead
> I need to make my way
> And slowly learn each day
> To see the green and not the red.

The above example of an opening session pinpoints some of the interaction and feelings a group can engender, even at the first meeting. I think of the initial session as one where is a lot of emotional shadow boxing, getting acquainted with each other's style of reaction and problems, and getting the "feel" of poetry in the group experience. All of this is involved in the formulation of a sense of trust, which forms a powerful dynamic leading to honest self-disclosure.

AMBIVALENCE

If art is the response of our inner being to the outer world and *vice versa,* poetry by the very nature of its being also finds a rightful place in this experience. And if therapy is a process that involves healing, then poetry in therapy is a useful additive because it acts as a facilitating agent in the healing process and as an adjunctive aid in one's reality orientation. An individual may have a good deal of ambivalence, which the poem may reflect and ultimately help resolve in the course of the poetry therapy group experience. A case in point occurred during a poetry therapy group session, representing a short segment of a six-session poetry therapy group. (We are in the middle of the fourth session.)

John [a 36-year-old father of two, a salesman, whose main complaint was, "I can't make up my mind about anything"]: I don't know if I can say how I feel.

Poetry Therapist: John, for the past half-hour you have literally not said anything. Up to this session you complained a good deal about how
"weak" you are in making decisions. I see you were writing. Is
that a poem or a line you have?

John: Well . . . I don't —

Mary [a 42-year-old mother of three, divorced, and working as a computer
operator, whose main complaint was, "I seem to be drawing away
from my family"] : Come, John. This is your time to say what
you feel. Read it — if you've written anything.

John: O.K. — here it is. [reads]

> Sometimes I'm yes, sometimes I'm no
> Whichever I am it'll really show.
> But this I know to be the case
> I'm trying hard to find my place.

Facilitator: Right on! What does it say to you?

John: I'm like in a battle — trying to fight my way out. I suppose you
can say, "I'm half-slave and half-free."

Poetry Therapist: Can you tell us more?

John: As far back as I remember it's always been a struggle. Just when
I think I've made a decision that I think is O.K., I start feeling it's
not O.K. Even when I was a kid, I remember this happening. My
mother and father would often say something to make me change
my mind.

Facilitator: Is that why you've often challenged and rebelled against Dr. Lerner
and other members of the group? I remember you saying, when
you were questioned, "Can you do it better? What would you do
if you were in my place? Have you anything else to offer?" I
always felt you weren't seeking more information about what
happened. You wanted to be assured that what you did was the
so-called right way to act.

John: I think you're right.

Sarah [a 51-year-old widow, the mother of four adult children, a schoolteacher,
whose main complaint was, "I can't seem to feel right about the
things I do or say"] : I can relate to you, John. I remember when
my husband passed on. I used to say, "I just can't make it anymore.
What a nasty person he was to die when I needed him. I'll die too
just to get even with everyone." How silly I was! It has dawned
on me as you were talking, John, that I too have had many doubts
about actions. In all my life I can't remember a moment when I
felt right about any decision I've made. And that includes marriage,

children, and my job. But I suppose the thing that has helped me the most was — I kept on repeating that I was responsible for my behavior. It's only been in the last month that I've done more than repeat. I now believe and feel this to be true and that goes when I say I don't know what I want to do and act anyway.

John: I see your point. It's true.

George [a single, 27-year-old recent law school graduate preparing for the bar exam, whose main complaint was, "I work hard under pressure and make wrong decisions"] : John, let me tell you you've helped me see my own situation better. Here is what I wrote two weeks ago and never showed it or read it to anyone before:

> I work under steam with boilers breaking.
> My body pains, my mind is aching,
> And when I say "yes" I feel like saying "no."
> I really don't know which way to go.
> But I think I have found the clue to me
> Whether yes or no. I have to be
> The best I believe and the best I feel.
> Only then can I truly be real.
> I may not solve all my ills
> But it's better than paying doctor bills.

The ensuing discussion revolved about feeling doubtful and still having to live in a positive manner. At the end of this session, one of the members, Jane, a 25-year-old bank teller and recent bride, whose main complaint was, "I wish I could feel more positive about myself," read the following lines, which she had written during the previous session.

Jane: No matter how much doubt you have
There is no ready salve
To heal your wounds and frame of mind
If you're trying to be two of a kind.
Sometimes my body says no and my mind says yes
At best I feel it's only a guess.
What I've learned in recent days
Is not to be afraid of my performing ways.
You've got to be your own best scout
Acting fully though torn by doubt.

Poetry Therapist: Jane, it has taken some time for you to write and say what you've just said. Do you remember at the first session you asked, "How long will it take me to get well?" When the group asked what was wrong, you said, "Nothing really except that I never seem to be positive about anything I do." Here you are sharing your feelings with us in an open way using your own lines. Isn't this a positive step in itself?

Jane: I remember quite well what happened. I see now the problem I have is one where there are no easy answers. You just need to work things through and even then things aren't going to break the way you'd want them to. I know this too is a way of becoming positive. But it sure takes time.

The group closed at this point, with each person making a statement regarding the session. The underlying theme was that people waste time looking for assurances when life dictates that people need to take risks in many instances in the process of becoming mature individuals.

Nothing in this exposition should be construed as final or as indicating that the flow of interaction and conversation does not hide or arouse other affects. A segment of a session or the presentation of a session can present only what occurred at a specific time. Of course, clinicians can pick up nuances, defenses, dynamics, etc. from the process.

VALIDATION OF FEELINGS

Poetry may be of help in validating a person's feelings and outlook. For example, a 15-year-old girl who was having difficulty in her math classes wrote the following lines after the third session in a poetry therapy group.

I often feel that numbers
Cause the problems I have
I have feelings which are scary
When I think in the deep
I believe I can't make it
That my mind won't ever keep.
Now I know the truth
Of what is really the scare
It's me that is the problem
And not the math out there.

Another member of a poetry therapy group wrote about himself in a different vein. He was a 38-year-old father of three and a successful businessman. He felt he wanted to switch occupations and become a teacher, and he spoke of his problems as a "mid-life crisis." He told the group he had always wanted to teach and had gone into business to "earn a living for myself and my family. I really am stuck."

At the seventh meeting of the poetry therapy group, he began the session by reading the following lines.

Last night I thought hard
Of all the things I feel
And found myself to be
Afraid to be real.
One reason for my complaint
Is that I have no restraint
On what I want when I want.
If I really want to teach
I can easily reach
Into my business life
And without any strife
To me, my family or wife
Create another way
To share my time each day
And still reach my goal.
My reason for wanting to teach
Is to go beyond my father's reach,
Who wanted me to be
Like him and not just me.

Another young man, an 18-year-old who was having "trouble" with his girl-friend, who he claimed was "very demanding," came to his second poetry therapy session and read the following lines he had written.

I blame Sue for faults really mine
When I'm the one who is out of line.
I am most demanding
I need more understanding
Of myself and my friend Sue,
If I am to be honest —
I'm demanding, not Sue. How true!

By the time affects begin to impinge on our psyches, we have usually had many crossings and interweavings of other feelings, forgotten episodes, remnants of memory patterns and behavior, and the like. What comes out is often other than what we thought of originally. Poets have always written or sung about love, hate, greed, pathos, and all human emotions. The more honest the poem, the more honest the emotion or feeling. Some years ago, a 40-year-old woman put it this way in her initial poetry therapy session:

I declare and swear this is what I mean
And when I'm through it's either fat or lean.
I never know what will be
Until the moment lets me see.

LEARNING THROUGH SHARING

Patients are often reminded that the important thing about therapy is what they do with what they learn about their behavior. In this regard, the poetry therapy group session becomes a shared learning experience. Members encourage each other to act appropriately when outside the group. The following excerpt from a session pinpoints this idea further.

The session was the third in a series of an open-ended group. The group members had already been together for the first two sessions. Each session was an hour in length, and I was assisted by a facilitator. There were 10 individuals in the group, in addition to the facilitator and me. The group was divided into five men and five women. The facilitator working under my direction was female. (We are now fifteen minutes into the session.)

Poetry Therapist: Jan, I've heard you say on several occasions in previous sessions, and you've said it again just now, something to the effect of, "What's the use of all this poetry and therapy? We become wise and act stupid." What do you mean?

Jan [a 46-year-old mother of five, a schoolteacher at the elementary level, whose main complaint was, "I have a nice husband but can't talk to him at times"]. Well, I really don't . . . I guess I . . . well . . .

Facilitator: Would you like to tell us what happened when you left the group last week?

Jan: You mean everything? I really can't remember . . . oh — I see. Yes [pause]. I left the group and went to meet my husband Al for dinner. I had so much to tell him and seemed to forget everything I was planning to tell him — once I met him.

Poetry Therapist: On several occasions, when you brought his name up, you said he was a good father, a kind man, but topics like money and his family were off limits as far as he was concerned.

Thelma [a 41-year-old mother of two, a department store auditor, whose main complaint was, "Many times I'm nice to people when I'd like to tear them apart"]:   Jan, remember when you spoke about Al last week, I said he reminded me so much of Mike, my husband. I mean, the only thing I can't talk to Mike about is money. He says he is the boss and the provider, even though I make a good living myself and make as much as he does. It's like I hit him a low blow or something. Is it his male ego?

Jan: I don't know. But Al likes to show off to his family and it always seems like we're just barely cutting things financially. It's real hard for us, especially at the end of the month. You know, this year I took a personal leave from school, so I'm not getting paid. I already had had my sabbatical.

Poetry Therapist: Jan, was your husband always touchy about money matters?

Facilitator: Listen to what I wrote last week after the session. It's a two-liner.

> We've talked and now are put to the test
> In action. Can we lay our problems to rest?

What I'm saying is that we can have a shopping list of problems. But what can we do about them?

Jan: I know what you mean. We get good material here. Actually, I feel a little wiser and somewhat helpless when I leave here. I say things I'm learning are true. But what do I do when I have this knowledge? I'm talking about when we're away from here.

Frank [a 30-year-old newlywed, an auto mechanic, whose main complaint was, "I lack motivation to do anything else besides what I'm doing"] : I know what's being said. You know, I never wrote any lines of poetry before and read them. Maybe this can help:

> What I'm frightened of is me.
> My fears are there and make me weak.
> Can you guys just see
> I have a scared streak.

Martha [a 25-year-old divorced court reporter, whose main complaint was, "I'm tight about everything"] : Frank, it's all of the same cloth; your problem, Jan's problem, my problem — like someone was saying why are we afraid to do . . . that's the thing to do.

Thelma: It sure isn't easy. It's easy to talk. But to do —

Facilitator: Can you be more specific, Thelma?

Thelma: Well, I'll be . . . I mean I can give you a good example. Last week, after our meeting, I went home and tried to talk to Mike about needing to take care of a few bills. At first, he didn't say anything. After about five minutes, he told me if I was a better manager we wouldn't be in a bind from time to time. I resented his comment and didn't tell him. I didn't want to make him angrier than he was. So I changed the subject.

Poetry Therapist: Has this been going on for a long time?

Thelma: As far back as I can remember. It was this way ever since I was a
             kid in school with other kids and teachers. Also with my parents.
             I guess what I'm saying is that money is the tip of the iceberg. It's
             my total makeup. I'm afraid of being turned down or something.
             Even when I went for individual therapy, this was a problem.

Jan: You're right on. I can feel what you're saying, like we've hit the
             same experience. Anyway, here is what I wrote before coming to
             the group. It seems to say it all.

> Poetry therapy is like going to school
> At each session I learn another rule
> That's not a rule because it's more
> Like keeping a personal score.
> The best way to heal is just to act
> Your best self. This is a fact.

Poetry Therapist: Remember, we have discussed on several occasions in here
             the difficulty of making new adjustments and reactions.

Gary [a 40-year-old father of two, the manager of a supermarket, whose main
             complaint was, "I tighten up when I feel I'm doing a good job"] :
             Yes, I know what you mean. We have all agreed that when we
             leave here we may encounter shakiness and doubt, especially
             when we have to act. [pause] I'm a good example. Anyway, I
             want to say this. Getting better means taking chances. You
             spoke about risk, Dr. L., and risk it is. I guess when one gets
             older, one is not as flexible as when one was young, especially if
             you have family responsibility.

At this point, the members of the group decided to write a "group poem" or
group reaction. Each person wrote one or two lines. The following 12 lines are
the collective enterprise of the 10 participants, the facilitator, and the poetry
therapist. They are presented in the order they were collected. No person knew
what any other person was writing. The lines were also read to the group in the
order presented here. (Incidentally, this constituted our closure.)

1. The hardest thing is to be free inside.
2. You must follow your own conscience.
3. If you lie to yourself you'll pay with interest.
4. What I get in here is fine;
   What I do on the outside is finer.
5. Pain is part of growing
   It's the price you pay for knowing.

6. It's not what you say you do
   It's what you do about your saying.
7. I ve got a lot of growing up to do.
8. How easy to talk about your thing
   As long as you can talk and don't have to sing.
9. Jive talk is fine and keeps my peace
   But it doesn't stop showing my crease.
10. Good talk. Tough act.
11. At the end your talk
    May be out of line with your deeds.
12. Inside or out you're one human being
    Of many parts, striving and seeing.

The point is that, often, before a group becomes aware of individual responsibility on the part of its members, a poetry therapy session may find itself in the throes of the experience just described, a kind of soul-searching admission moment — when individual members suffer from a common inability to act in their own personality interests. Of course, this may involve other sessions too, but often one session can pinpoint the ordeal.

CONCLUDING COMMENTS

This chapter has emphasized the use of poetry in the therapeutic process, an experience known as poetry therapy. Nothing in this discussion is meant to suggest that a poet is automatically a therapist. A poet, like many sensitive artists, may have insight and understanding that see deeply into the psyche. This in no way means that the poet can treat neurotics or psychotics and the like, unless the poet also happens to be qualified as a therapist. Likewise, a qualified therapist may be able to come up with insights that have a poetic character. This does not mean that the therapist is necessarily a poet. Poetry and psychotherapy are two distinct entities which by their very nature often cross over into each other's territory.

This presentation has been just one practitioner's view of a growing field. This view is at best a limiting one, since other practitioners with other frames of reference will have their own ways of perceiving and practicing poetry therapy. The truth is that the field of poetry therapy is groping for a central rationale. There are as many ways of approaching poetry therapy as there are individuals practicing this modality. But one thing is clear: There is, at present, a need for refined research. Every school of psychotherapy can find a place in its rationale for poetry. This is especially so if poetry therapy means, as it does here, poetry *in* therapy.

BIBLIOGRAPHY

Barron, J. Poetry and therapeutic communication: Nature and meaning of poetry. *Psychotherapy, Theory, Research and Practice* 11 (1):87–92 (1974).

Blanton, S. *The Healing Power of Poetry.* New York: Crowell (1960).

Brower, D. Bibliotherapy. *In:* Brower, D. and Abt, L. E. (Eds.). *Progress in Clinical Psychology* 2: 212-215 New York: Grune and Stratton (1956).

Buck, L. A. and Kramer, A. Poetry as a means of group facilitation. *The Journal of Humanistic Psychology* 14 (1):57–71 (Winter 1974).

Edgar, K. A case of poetry therapy. *Psychotherapy: Theory Research and Practice* 16 (1): 104–106 (Spring 1979).

Forrest, D. V. Poiesis and the language of schizophrenia. *Psychiatry* 28:1-18 (February 1965).

Freud, S. The relation of the poet to day-dreaming. *Collected Papers* 4. Jones, Ernest (Ed.). New York: Basic Books (1959).

Gordon, D. *Therapeutic Metaphors.* Cupertino, CA: Meta Publications (1978).

Greifer, E. *Principles of Poetry Therapy.* New York: Poetry Therapy Center (1963).

Greifer, E. Poetry therapy. *The Brooklyn Psychologist,* 6-7 (September 1964).

Harrower, M. Poems emerging from the therapeutic experience. *Journal of Nervous and Mental Disease* 149:213-223 (August 1969).

Harrower, M. *The Therapy of Poetry.* Springfield, IL: Charles C. Thomas (1972).

Heninger, O. E. Poetry therapy: Exploration of a creative righting maneuver. *Art Psychotherapy: An International Journal* 4:39-40 (1977).

Jung, C. G. *Modern Man in Search of a Soul.* New York: Harcourt, Brace & World (1963).

Lawler, J. G. Poetry therapy? *Psychiatry* 35:227-237 (August 1972).

Leedy, J. J. (Ed.). *Poetry Therapy: The Use of Poetry in the Treatment of Emotional Disorders.* Philadelphia: Lippincott (1969).

Leedy, J. J. (Ed.). *Poetry the Healer.* Philadelphia: Lippincott (1973).

Lerner, A. Poetry therapy. *American Journal of Nursing* 73:1336-1338 (August 1973).

Lerner, A. Poetry as therapy. *American Psychological Association Monitor* 6 (9, 10):4 (September/October 1975).

Lerner, A. Entries from a journal on poetry and therapy. *Voices: Journal of the American Academy of Psychotherapists* 2 (4):69-71 (Winter 1975-76).

Lerner, A. Editorial: A look at poetry therapy. *Art Psychotherapy: An International Journal* 3 (1):i–ii (1976).

Lerner, A. Poetry therapy and semantics. *ETC: A Review of General Semantics,* 417-422 (December 1976).

Lerner, A. (Ed.). *Poetry in the Therapeutic Experience.* Elmsford, NY: Pergamon Press (1978).

Lerner, A. A note on poetry therapy. *Art Psychotherapy: An International Journal* 6: 197-198 (1979).

Lerner, A. Some observations on the poetic element in psychotherapy. *Voices: The Art and Science of Psychotherapy* 15 (4):29-31 (Winter 1980).

Lerner, A. Poetry therapy. *In:* Corsini, R. J. (Ed.) *Handbook of Innovative Psychotherapies.* New York: Wiley (1981). pp. 640-649.

Pietropinto, A. Poetry Therapy in groups. In: Masserman, J. H. (Ed.) *Current Psychiatric Therapies* Vol. 15. New York: Grune and Stratton (1975). pp. 221-232.

Prescott, F. C. *The Poetic Mind.* Ithaca: Cornell University Press (1959). [1st Ed., New York: Macmillan (1922).]

Rogers, C. R. *On Becoming a Person.* Boston: Houghton Mifflin (1961).

Rothenberg, A. Poetic process and psychotherapy. *Psychiatry* 35:238–254 (August 1972).

Rubin, R. J. (Ed.). *Bibliotherapy Sourcebook*. Phoenix: Oryx Press (1978).

Rubin, R. J. (Ed.). *Using Bibliotherapy: A Guide to Theory and Practice*. Phoenix: Oryx Press (1978).

Schloss, G. A. *Psychopoetry: A New Approach to Self-Awareness Through Poetry Therapy*. New York: Grosset & Dunlap (1976).

Shrodes, C. *Bibliotherapy: A Theoretical and Clinical Experimental Study*. Unpublished doctoral dissertation, University of California (1949).

Four strategic systems therapies are the core of an emerging paradigm: (1) the brief, problem-focused therapy of Watzlawick, Weakland, Fisch et al. (1974); (2) the strategic family therapy of Haley (1976) and Madanes (1981); (3) the structural family therapy of Minuchin and Fishman (1981); and (4) the systemic family therapy of Palazzoli-Selvini et al. (1977, 1980). Each view is rooted in a systemic epistemology of pattern that assumes that problems, regardless of their origin, are maintained in ongoing cycles of interaction and inextricably interwoven with their social context. The approaches are strategic because the therapist (or team) intervenes deliberately, on the basis of a specific plan, to resolve the presenting problem as quickly and efficiently as possible. This may involve interdicting problem-maintaining solutions (Watzlawick et al.), reorganizing relationship structures (Haley, Minuchin), or challenging dysfunctional family rules (Palazzoli-Selvini et al.). The therapist's strategy is not often shared openly with clients, nor is change assumed to depend on insight, catharsis, or acquiring personal skills.

Three modes of strategic intervention (prescribing, reframing, positioning) are described in the following chapter, and theoretical and technical issues within the orientation are highlighted. The strategic systems therapies are less a way of living than a way of working. Paradoxically, they represent a move away from therapy as a solution to human problems.

15

The Strategic Systems
Therapies*

Michael Rohrbaugh, Ph.D. and Joseph B. Eron, Psy.D.

These are several examples of strategic systems therapies.

Example 1. A client complaining of intense anxiety in public places is asked to have a panic attack deliberately as the first step in bringing the symptom under control [Weakland, Fisch, Watzlawick, and Bodin (1974)].

Example 2. After reviewing a voluminous history of unsuccessful medical and psychological therapies, a psychiatrist tells a headache patient that her condition is probably irreversible and that therapy should concentrate on helping her live with the problem. Despite persistent pessimism by the doctor, the headaches improve [Watzlawick, Beavin, and Jackson (1967)].

Example 3. A therapist asks a symptomatic husband to *pretend* to be irresponsible and inadequate three times before the next session and the wife to try to find out whether he is really feeling that way [Madanes (1980)].

Example 4. A depressed stroke victim, who would attend only an initial family interview, improves dramatically over six meetings in which a therapy

---

*The ideas in this chapter grew in part from the "Recent Developments in Strategic Family Therapy" conference organized by the authors at Skidmore College, Saratoga Springs, NY (August 21-22, 1980). We are indebted to Lynn Hoffman, Peggy Penn, Duncan Stanton, and James Coyne, who participated in that conference, and to Skidmore College, for making it possible.

team coaches his spouse and grown children to be helpless and ineffectual in his presence [Watzlawick and Coyne (1980)].

Example 5. A therapist asks that a disengaged father and his dog-phobic son buy a puppy together and teach it to be comfortable around people. The boy's overinvolved mother is asked to defer to her husband, who, as a mailman, is an expert on dogs [Minuchin (1974); Haley (1976)].

Example 6. As a condition for discharge, an in-patient therapist requires that the parents of a "schizophrenic" young adult establish firm rules and a specific plan for dealing with "irresponsible" behavior at home [Haley (1980)].

Example 7. A team of therapists gives a family a letter to read aloud at pre-scribed times before the next session. The letter praises the identified patient for acting crazy to protect his father, explaining that by occupying his mother's time with fights and tantrums, he allows his father more time for work and relaxation [Palazzoli-Selvini, Boscolo, Cecchin, and Prata (1978a)].

Example 8. A letter to another family prescribes that, on even days of the week, for a specified period of time, the father alone will decide what to do when the child behaves symptomatically, and mother will act as if she were not there. On even days, the procedure must be reversed, with each parent carefully recording infringements by the other throughout [Palazzoli-Selvini *et al.* (1978b)].

The foregoing examples of "strategic" intervention, each successful, typify a new orientation to therapy, which is the subject of this chapter. The technical aspects of this approach, while intrinsically fascinating, are not its essence. More important is a new way of thinking about clinical problems, which follows from adopting a systems vantage point [Sluzki (1978)]. Because strategic techniques can be so powerful, it is doubly important that they be based on coherent (systemic) assumptions about problem maintenance and clinical change.

THE TERRITORY

In our view, at least four therapy models define the core of the emerging paradigm:[1] (1) the brief, problem-focused therapy developed at Palo Alto's Mental Research Institute [Watzlawick, Weakland, and Fisch (1974); Weakland *et al.* (1974); Coyne and Segal (1981)]; (2) the structural family therapy of Minuchin and others at the Philadelphia Child Guidance Clinic [Minuchin (1974); Aponte and Van Deusen (1981); Minuchin and Fishman (1981)]; (3) the strategic/structural approach of Haley (1976, 1980) and Madanes (1981), associated with the Family Institute of Washington, D.C.; and (4) the systemic therapy pioneered at the Center for Family Studies in Milan, Italy [Palazzoli-Selvini *et al.* (1978, 1980)] and applied in this country at New York's Ackerman Institute [Hoffman (1980, 1981); Papp (1980)].

Besides having common roots in systems and communication theory,[2] these models have co-evolved in ways that reflect the interwoven careers of their authors. Weakland and Haley were colleagues in Bateson's seminal research project on communication [Sluzki and Ransom (1976)]; Haley was later with Minuchin in Philadelphia; Watzlawick was an important consultant to the Milan group; and so on. Yet, despite their similarities and common heritage, the models are unique in both concept and technique. We do not believe that they represent different stages in the evolution of a paradigm, or that one model is farther along than another in technical or theoretical sophistication. Although some practitioners have moved from one to another in what, for them, was a logical progression, the approaches themselves evolved in parallel, at roughly the same time.

For better or for worse, the common territory is not easily labeled. Words like "systems," "family," "brief," "strategic," "interactional," "communicational," "contextual," and "ecological" each capture some but not all of it. The approaches are family-oriented, but to identify them exclusively with "family therapy" would not be accurate. Family therapy comes in many varieties, only some based on a systems paradigm [Madanes and Haley (1977); Gurman and Kniskern (1981)]; furthermore, therapy based on systems principles need not be limited to families [Watzlawick et al. (1974)]. What the core models have most in common is a systemic (circular) view of problem maintenance and a strategic (planned) orientation to change. Even so, a strategic therapy need not be systemic [e.g., Rabkin (1977)], nor a systemic approach strategic [Keeney (1979)]. Still, the words "strategic" and "systemic," when combined, seem to mark the territory as well as any others.[3]

"Strategic" means that the therapist (or therapy team) acts on the basis of a specific plan, formulated in advance, for resolving the presenting problem as quickly and efficiently as possible [Haley (1963)]. The strategic orientation owes a large debt to the late Milton Erickson, whose clinical methods, particularly his use of indirection, have profoundly influenced the new systems therapies [Haley (1973)]. Unlike other newer therapies [Marmor (1980)], strategic approaches do not assume that change depends on achieving insight, awareness, or emotional release. Nor do they attempt explicitly to promote the growth and development of the person: The objective is to solve problems through minimal but sufficient intervention so that people can get on with life.

"Systemic" refers to the "epistemology of pattern" introduced to the social sciences by the late Gregory Bateson (1972, 1979). Doing therapy systemically means looking for pattern, difference, process, and relationship. The intrinsic characteristics of individuals – their personality traits, biological predispositions, unconscious conflicts, social skills, etc. – are secondary to the ongoing communicational patterns in which problems are embedded. Schizophrenia, for example, is understood less as a disordered mental state than as a patterned process, invariably involving several people, which usually arises as a solution to some dilemma of family life, and may incorporate conventional psychiatric services in its maintenance [Dell (1980b)]. The epistemology of pattern shifts therapists away from the familiar linear/etiological language of cause and effect to circular, recursive descriptions of mutual regulatory processes. Finding an antecedent cause in patterns of nagging and withdrawal, distancing and pursuit, depression and reassurance reduces to arbitrarily punctuating a circular sequence of interaction. Pattern and problem are inseparable. The binder is as bound as the victim.

Systems therapists also assume that reality is more "constructed" than "discovered" [Minuchin (1979)]. Watzlawick (1978) makes the point in discussing a particular therapy technique, "reframing," which offers clients more useful ways to look at their situations.

> . . . When talking about reality we are likely to confuse two very separate orders of reality: one that deals with the physical properties of the objects of our perception, and a second-order reality based on the attribution of *meaning* and *value* to these objects. [p. 119] . . . Reframing is a therapeutic technique that utilizes the fact that all "rules," all second-order realities, are relative, that life is what you say it is. [p. 126]

Constructed realities govern therapists also. While such esoteric matters as epistemology seem far removed from the consulting room, therapists are inevitably influenced by the assumptions they make, if only implicitly, about people, problems, and change. "In therapy, the theory determines what we do" [Watzlawick (1978)].

THEMES

We will characterize the strategic systems therapies by tracing some of the themes that run through them.

Circularity: Cycles, Structures, and Rules

A systems view assumes that how problems are maintained is more important than how they originate — that present causes are more relevant than past causes. Altering current, circular patterns of problem-maintaining behavior is assumed sufficient to resolve the problem, regardless of its origin or duration [Weakland *et al.* (1974)].

Haley (1980) has said that the chief value of systems theory is that it teaches therapists to recognize repeating sequences and so make predictions. Indeed, if there is a fundamental concept in the strategic systems therapies, it is the idea of *sequence*, or, as we would prefer, *problem cycle*. In the Palo Alto brief-therapy framework, problem cycles center quite simply around well-intentioned but inappropriate attempts to solve a problem. The assumption is that problems would be self-limiting were it not for the persistent but misguided problem-solving attempts of the people involved. Insomnia, for example, may be maintained by trying to go to sleep deliberately, or depression by well-intentioned reassurance and prodding. In this view, the problem *is* the solution, and interdicting the solution paves the way for change [Watzlawick *et al.* (1974)].

In the structural approaches, circular sequences usually involve at least three people and are the basis for inferring anomalies in organizational structure. According to Haley (1980):

An organization is merely a system of repeating sequences of communication. As people communicate with each other in systematic ways, that communication becomes the organization. When one person tells another what to do, and the other does it, a hierarchy is being defined by that process. [p. 25]

For Haley and Madanes, incongruities in such an organizational hierarchy are the basis of most clinical problems. Thus, with severely disturbed young people, a therapist might look for sequences in which "the parents tell the youth what to do but he does not do it or the parents do not tell the youth what to do but complain about what he does or the youth tells the parents what to do and the parents do it" [Madanes (1980), p. 190]. Many problem sequences indicate a confused hierarchy in which covert coalitions cross generation lines (e.g., a parent or grandparent nurtures a child after another parent attempts discipline). Minuchin's use of the sequence concept is similar but adds a horizontal dimension of structure — whether people are too involved with each other (enmeshed) or not involved enough (disengaged). In both approaches, therapy attempts to alter interaction sequences in ways that support a workable family structure. In practice, this may mean challenging patterns of overinvolvement and protection, helping parents join together to take charge of a child, or arranging that a grandparent back off to an appropriate supporting role.

In the Milan approach, forming a "systemic hypothesis" follows in part from a careful tracking of circular interaction sequences. For example, a therapist might ask:

When Lorenzo begins to loose [sic] control and pushes your mother, what does your father do? And how does your mother react to what he does (or doesn't) do? And what do you do? etc., etc. [Palazzoli-Selvini *et al.* (1980), p. 9].

Or each family member in turn may be asked to comment on the relationship of two others, a technique called "gossiping in presence." The patterns that emerge from such circular inquiry, considered in the broader context of family development, are the basis for a hypothesis about the "rules of the family game."

The hypothesis concerns the "homeostatic imperatives of a family system in danger of change" (1980, p. 7). Ideally, this formulation specifies both the nature of that danger (e.g., that someone may leave the family) and the ways in which the interlocking behavior of family members protects against it. The thrust of intervention is to change the family rules, which is never done by pointing them out directly. More often, the rules are challenged indirectly by positively connoting and prescribing the very sequences of interaction which define them [Palazzoli-Selvini *et al.* (1978a)].

Inside/Outside Position: Therapist as Ecological Part

A systems approach requires that a therapist be able to include him/herself in descriptions of interactional patterns. Such an "inside" position is explicit in Minuchin's (1974) emphasis on joining a family before attempting to restructure it. When a structural therapist joins or engages, he or she is *inside* the system, entering family conflicts, joining coalitions, and intensifying or blocking expressions of affect. When restructuring, he/she is more *outside*, marking boundaries, creating contexts, and (re)channeling pathways of communication.

The Milan team applies the inside/outside concept to control the "therapist-family suprasystem" [Palazzoli-Selvini (1980)]. Resistance is recast from an inside vantage point as an aspect of therapist-family interaction rather than as an intrinsic property of either a family or its individual members. The Milan team goes to great lengths to protect therapeutic messages from transactional disqualification (resistance). By delivering major interventions by letter, and at the end of the session with no opportunity for discussion, and further, by restricting contact during the long interval between sessions, the therapists maintain maximum outside leverage. The intervention becomes a constancy around which the (family) system must reorganize.

An inside vantage point is especially important when the therapist, by his or her actions, contributes directly to the problem. The Palo Alto group makes clear that problem-maintaining solutions can be applied by therapists as well as by clients and family members. It may be unhelpful, for example, to encourage a depressed person to cheer up, a romantic utopian to be realistic, or an ambivalent, indecisive client to take some definitive action — particularly if family members and other helpers have been dealing with the problem in these ways. In brief therapy, knowing what to do is less important than knowing what *not* to do: Any of many interventions may work as long as they avoid more of the same.

Recognizing the therapist as a potential part of the problem unit is also a theme in Haley's writings (1976, 1980). Here, one of the hazards is getting entangled in confused professional hierarchies, as easily happens when the primary therapist is not in charge of decisions to medicate, hospitalize, or discharge;

when a supervisor inadvertently aligns with the client against the therapist; or when several agencies or therapists work with a case simultaneously.

One of the difficulties in evaluating one's own role in a system (or contribution to a problem) is that doing so requires an outside vantage point. How can a therapist be outside and inside at the same time — objectively observing and intervening while acting and reacting as a member? The logical problem is in reconciling the idea of therapist as ecological part with the idea that a system has difficulty changing itself from within. The practical problem is keeping one's moorings. One solution is what Hoffman (1980b) has called the "bi-cameral" (two-room) form: With a consultation team and a one-way mirror, some team members can be more outside than others in relation to the immediate therapist-client interaction. The solution is only partial, however, because observers can never be totally separate from what they observe. It is simply grappling with the problem that distinguishes a systemic therapy from most others.

Context: Patterns of Transaction, Tasks of Transition

Problems do not occur in a vacuum but are inextricably interwoven with context. There are two general dimensions of context, one immediate or cross-sectional, the other developmental or longitudinal. The immediate context of symptomatic transaction — the cycles, rules, and structures mentioned above — can be understood in a broader context of family life transitions. The Palo Alto group shows how problems can arise from the utopian view that these transitions should go smoothly [Watzlawick et al. (1974)]. Haley's latest book, Leaving Home (1980), is about the most difficult of all transitions, where the task is for one generation to disengage from another. At this juncture, "mad" or "bad" behavior by an offspring may stabilize an immediate pattern of family transaction while preventing the leaving home transition from taking place. Similarly, Hoffman (1980a) describes the "missing leaps" which can be inferred when symptoms arise in families on the verge of transition (and transformation). Problem cycles are thus embedded in life cycles, and the strategic systems therapies address both.

Brevity: Minimum Contact, Maximum Impact

Another theme, brevity, distinguishes the strategic systems therapies from most other schools: The Milan and Palo Alto groups usually limit their contact with a case to 10 sessions, and Haley (1980) reports that 42 cases (most involving "schizophrenic" young people) were treated with a structural/strategic approach in an average of 10 to 11 sessions.

One reason for brief intervention is to prevent therapy from becoming part of the problem. Despite the importance of joining the system, there is general agreement that being inside too long is not a good idea.

. . . It seems to be in the nature of human relationships that the therapist has a rather limited period of grace in which to accomplish [his or her] goal. Relatively soon the new system itself consolidates to the point where the therapist is almost inextricably caught in it and from then on is much less able to produce change. [Watzlawick *et al.* (1967), p. 236]

In a broader context, the brevity theme is probably a reaction against the increasing reliance on therapists and experts generally in our "psychological society" [Gross (1978)]. With the burgeoning mental health and human potential industries, and the accelerating medicalization of human affairs, "therapy" is itself a growing social problem. As a habit, it can be enormously expensive and time-consuming; as a solution, it may only perpetuate the problem.

Strategy: Planned Change, Loving Manipulation

Strategic therapy is "strategic" because the therapist or team acts on the basis of a plan for resolving the presenting problem. A controversial aspect is that the therapist usually does not share this plan openly with the clients. The therapist's strategy and the client's or family's strategy are treated as distinct and of a different order: the former attempts to incorporate the latter, following Erickson's principle of accepting and using what the patient brings. Thus, in working with a withdrawn, paranoid patient, a strategic therapist probably would not challenge the client's self-defeating strategy directly by suggesting that he/she adopt a different, more reasonable approach to dealing with people. Rather, the therapist might agree that the client's suspicions about others' motives are probably well justified, and on that basis go on to suggest that the patient be even more cautious by approaching people directly to check out their intentions. If the client does this, of course, the habitual pattern of isolation and withdrawal will be altered. The point is that the therapist does not tell the client explicitly what he or she (the therapist) is doing. Instead, the client's strategy is extended to encourage a different course of action, one which will be likely to initiate change [Watzlawick *et al.* (1974)]. The strategic *modus operandi* is thus a kind of therapeutic judo. However, the stance it requires may be distasteful to some: The therapist becomes

. . . more a chameleon than a firm rock in a sea of trouble. And it is at this point that many therapists dig in behind the retort, "Anything except that," while for others the necessity of ever new adaptations to the world images of their clients is a fascinating task. [Watzlawick (1978), p. 141]

Another uncommon feature of strategic approaches is the lack of importance they attach to cherished assumptions about change — namely, that it depends on achieving insight and awareness, acquiring personal skills, or having a corrective emotional experience. The problem with insight, for example, is that attempts to impart it may provoke defensiveness and stiffen resistance to change. Haley (1980) suggests it is better to assume that people at some level "know" what they're doing; forcing them to acknowledge it is not only discourteous but unhelpful. Nor is it assumed that change with awareness is more efficient or enduring. "If a problem can be solved without the family knowing how or why, that is satisfactory" [Madanes (1980c), p. 75].

One of the distinctive features of strategic systems therapy as a method is the use of the consultation team. It might even be said that the consultation team is to systems therapy as free association is to psychoanalysis. But while in psychoanalysis the therapeutic relationship is inviolate, in systems therapy it is often scrutinized very carefully, as it is happening, by colleagues or a supervisor in another room. In practice, the consultation team participates in strategy planning and provides the external (outside) mooring that keeps inside therapists abreast of their roles in the system. In addition, the team supplies a powerful source of therapeutic leverage in the form of high-impact, hard-to-disqualify messages from unseen experts. These messages, which in the Milan approach are usually written, can be used to strengthen interventions or to co-opt resistance through subtler triangulation methods. Papp (1980), in an interesting paper likening the consultation team to a Greek chorus, shows how some (outside) team members may align with clients by warning against change, so that others, including inside therapists, can encourage it more directly. Similar strategies are used by the Palo Alto group [Weakland et al. (1974), p. 161].

The question arises: To have a "systems" orientation, is it necessary to be strategic and manipulative? Perhaps not. Yet systems, by definition, are controlled. To a large extent, the study of human communication in a cybernetic framework is the study of reciprocal influence and control. In therapy, therefore, one cannot not influence, just as one cannot not communicate [Watzlawick et al. (1967)]. The question is not whether to influence, but how to do it most constructively (or lovingly). Needless to say, the practices of strategic systems therapists raise important ethical questions, such as what is a reasonable degree of informed consent, and should it (or can it) be obtained from all whose lives may be touched by an intervention?

FINDING THE SYSTEM

In actual practice, a given clinical problem can always be understood in a number of alternative and equally systemic ways. The purpose of assessment is to identify and describe the "system(s)" that are most immediately relevant. The description specifies not just the people involved, but the patterns, rules, and relationships that govern their behavior. A clear formulation provides a map showing where to intervene. If assessment is on target and a problem-maintaining pattern can be identified and broken, change can be expected to follow. Hoffman (1976) has observed that when an expert systems therapist spots such a cycle, he or she will direct an intervention toward it "with the precision of a laser beam."

Depending on the therapy model, one might "find"[4] a system by investigating solutions (MRI), tracking interaction sequences in a confused organizational hierarchy (Haley), or teasing out unspoken analogical rules through circular interviewing (Milan). We will not review specific guidelines for doing this, but instead outline some interrelated dimensions along which systemic descriptions may vary. The importance of these conceptual dimensions is that they shape what is actually done in therapy. They also account for the major theoretical differences among the therapy models.

Problem versus Organization Focus

Some system descriptions center around the presenting problem, while in others the problem is secondary to the organizational structure surrounding it. In the latter, the problem or symptom is understood to serve a function in keeping the family organization stable or preventing a transition. The Palo Alto brief-therapy model is exclusively problem-focused (no function assumed). Minuchin's structural therapy and the Milan approach are organization-focused. Haley's strategic problem-solving therapy is both: While concerned with organizational structures (confused hierarchies), he gives more attention to the specific problem cycles on which those structures are based [Madanes and Haley (1977), p. 95].[5]

This dimension influences how (or whether) the therapist will set goals in therapy and what criteria will be used to evaluate change. For the problem-focused therapist, "problem resolution is a sufficient index of positive change, while for the structural therapist change in the identified problem without concurrent change in the structure of relationship patterns that underlie the problem is quite insufficient" [Gurman and Kniskern (1981), p. 328].

Narrow versus Broad Context

System descriptions also vary according to the breadth of context considered relevant to understanding how a problem is maintained. Earlier we said that context itself has two dimensions, one immediate and the other developmental or historical. Both are factors in whether context is defined narrowly or broadly.

One way of describing the immediate context is in terms of the therapist's conception of the problem unit — whether it is one person, two people, three people, or more.

The issue here is not how many people are actually involved in a problem or how many people are actually seen in the interviews, but how many people are involved in the therapist's way of thinking about the problem. A family of eight can be thought of as eight individuals or four dyads or as a variety of triangles. [Madanes and Haley (1977), p. 90]

By focusing almost exclusively on the presenting problem and how people try to solve it, the MRI brief-therapy approach reduces the system to an interactional nexus [Wilder (1979)]. Context is defined narrowly and precisely, since only those behaviors immediately contiguous to the problem are considered relevant. The emphasis throughout is on what people are doing in the present; history is seldom explored. The problem unit is sometimes monadic (e.g., trying to "be spontaneous"), but is most often dyadic. If more than two people are involved, they are usually seen as applying the same kind of problem-maintaining solution in parallel, in which case therapy focuses on getting them all to do less of the same. Sometimes it is possible to infer a triadic problem unit from a brief therapy intervention: For example, a covertly sabotaging parent may be asked to pay a misbehaving child a quarter, without explanation, when the other parent is provoked [Berenson (1976)]. In no case, however, is it assumed that the problem serves a function for the family.

The narrow contexts of brief therapy contrast with the broader structural formulations of Haley and Minuchin in which the problem unit is usually triadic (or larger), sometimes dyadic [Madanes (1980a)], but rarely monadic. Symptoms are functional in a broader (organizational) context, and symptom change depends on changing the context. History is important only if it sheds light on current organizational patterns. For example, if the history reveals broad cycles in which a troubled or troublesome young person has been repeatedly unable to leave home, it will be assumed that family stability in some way depends on his/her continuing failure [Haley (1980)].

Of all the systems therapists, the Milan group defines context most broadly. Here, the problem unit is usually triadic, symptoms are functional, and historical (cross-generational) data are essential to hypotheses about family rules. Palazzoli-Selvini et al. (1977) describe a case in which a severely anorectic 15-year-old, her nuclear family, and extended family all were enslaved by a myth of "one for all and all for one" created over 60 years and three generations of an Italian clan. The Milan team challenged the myth (and resolved the anorexia) by prescribing a family ritual which implicitly defined the nuclear family as a unit distinct from the clan. Another indication of the contextual breadth of this approach is that some of its practitioners at the Ackerman Institute use genograms and family event charts as assessment tools. They do this not to educate clients, but to generate systemic hypotheses on which to base strategic interventions.

The important point about breadth of context is that how one construes it profoundly influences what is done in therapy — who is seen, what is looked for, how much attention is paid to history and extended-family relationships, and ultimately, the locus and thrust of intervention.

Positive versus Negative Feedback[6]

The cybernetic notion of feedback loop is central to the strategic systems therapies. In a *positive* feedback loop, increases in one variable in a system are associated with increases in another (the more X, the more Y). *Negative* feedback, which is necessary for a system to maintain equilibrium or homeostasis, links increases in one variable to decreases in another (the more X, the less Y). Systemic clinical formulations tend to emphasize one of these mechanisms or the other.

A common formulation is of a self-regulating, error-activated process in which fluctuations in some homeostatic variable (e.g., the level of conflict between parents) are linked through a complex network of feedback loops to the state of some other variable (e.g., the symptomatic behavior of a child). For such a system to maintain equilibrium, it must include at least some negative feedback loops. Usually the symptom itself is assumed to play a role in keeping an homeostatic variable within tolerable limits. For example, in psychosomatic families, exacerbations of the illness may detour (lessen) conflict between the parents [Minuchin, Rosman, and Baker (1978)]. Such negative-feedback formulations lend themselves to the idea that symptoms are functional in the family system.

Whereas negative feedback is the backbone of structural and systemic approaches, simple *positive* feedback loops are emphasized in the MRI brief-therapy model. Whether the problem unit is monadic, dyadic, or otherwise, more of the same solution promotes more of the same problem Cybernetically, the picture is of a simple system in runaway. Problems arise from small causes through an escalating (snowballing) process of deviation amplification. The apparent stability of many problem configurations is explained, not by negative feedback or homeostasis, but by the dampening of deviation-amplifying positive-feedback processes which proceed to a certain ceiling magnitude and then level off [Wender (1968)]. Since virtuous as well as viscious circles can develop, seemingly minor changes in a problem cycle can be sufficient to initiate progressive (therapeutic) developments — hence the brief therapy emphasis on introducing only small changes [Weakland *et al.* (1974)].

Again, the theory determines what we do. Negative feedback models make change more formidable since a homeostasis will have to be altered or an organization restructured. A positive feedback model simplifies the task (though some would add too much so): The therapist need only introduce a small change and let it ripple.

Low versus High Inference (and Concrete versus Abstract Concepts)

All of the systems approaches emphasize careful observation and description of behavior, but they differ on how much inference or "construction" is helpful for effective therapy. For the Milan group, therapy is a deductive process of sequential hypothesis testing through which formulations about family rules are progressively confirmed, revised, or discarded. The structuralists also hypothesize about the symptom's function in the family organization, but structural concepts – boundary, enmeshment, hierarchy, etc. – are less abstract than the cybernetic rule-formulations of the Milan group [e.g., Palazzoli (1980)]. Most concrete are the problem cycle descriptions of the MRI group. In this inductive approach, functional hypotheses and higher-order structural concepts are avoided, lest they contaminate direct observation of behavior. To organization-centered therapists, this ruthless parsimony and apparent disregard for family dynamics are too simplistic: The baby is thrown out with the bathwater. On the other hand, Fisch (1978) has argued that to view problems as manifestations of underlying organizational dynamics is reminiscent of the psychodynamic "iceberg" formulations that systems approaches should move beyond.

INTERVENING

One way to describe what strategic therapists do is in terms of three interrelated modes of intervention – prescribing, reframing, and positioning.

Prescribing means telling people what to do, either directly or indirectly. Some prescriptions are compliance-based, in the sense that change follows from doing (or attempting to do) what the therapist suggests. Others are defiance-based: Change follows from rebellion [Rohrbaugh, Tennen, Press, and White (1981); Tennen, Rohrbaugh, Press, and White (1981)].

Reframing involves redefining the meaning of behavior in a way that makes change more possible. For example, a therapist might reframe a "mad" young person's behavior as "bad" so that the parents will be able to deal with it differently. If it is assumed that symptoms serve systemic functions, then redefining what behavior means may undermine those functions, rendering symptoms unnecessary [Sluzki (1978)]. Although reframing may appear to be interpretation, its goal is not insight. The accuracy of redefinition is less important than whether it provokes change [Watzlawick (1978)].

Whereas prescribing and reframing imply an outside vantage point, *positioning* is a term for interventions that address the therapist's role *inside* problem-maintaining systems. For example, when clients have sought help repeatedly but failed to benefit, or when therapeutic movement is stuck after straightforward approaches have failed, the therapist may reverse the cycle by adopting a restraining position and advising against change. If multiple helpers are involved with a case, the purpose of positioning is to establish a clear professional hierarchy [Haley (1976, 1980)]. Some positioning strategies are ways to avoid inside entanglements; others are ways to escape it. In either case, outside colleagues or supervisors — or, ideally, a consultation team — can be an invaluable resource.

In practice, the prescribing, reframing, and positioning modes are interwoven — each is at least implicit in any strategy or intervention. When a therapist prescribes having an anxiety attack deliberately, he/she implicitly reframes an uncontrollable symptom as voluntary. When, in the presence of a family, he or she redefines mad behavior as protective sacrifice, and warns against the dangers of improvement, there is an implicit (paradoxical) prescription for the family not to change. By advising against change, the therapist may also be reversing or neutralizing his/her own role in a problem cycle, and so on.

How prescribing, reframing, and positioning are used depends on the system level they address. Thus, prescribing and reframing might be applied with monadic, dyadic, or triadic problem units, and in each case their rationales would be different. The simple symptom prescription at the beginning of the chapter (Example 1) aims at a monadic cycle. In Examples 2, 3, and 4, the problem unit is dyadic; in Examples 5, 6, 7, and 8, it is triadic or larger. Since positioning (Example 2) addresses a therapist-client system, the problem unit, by definition, must be at least dyadic.

The particulars of intervention technique vary from model to model. The following is a brief summary of some dimensions of difference. Most parallel the broader issues in systemic assessment outlined earlier.

Small versus Large Changes

Therapy may target a small, even trivial, change in a problem pattern and allow it to amplify (Palo Alto), or force a broad reorganization of the entire system by inducing a crisis (Minuchin) or detonating an "underwater explosion"[7] through systemic paradox (Milan).

Direct versus Indirect Influence

Intervention may be direct and straightforward, with change following from compliance (Minuchin), or more indirect, paradoxical, or subtle, with change sometimes resulting from defiance (Milan).

Seeing All versus Parts of the Client System

Therapists may routinely see the entire family, addressing interventions to everyone (Milan) or meet with one or several members only, introducing change through them (Palo Alto).

Explicit versus Implicit Goal Setting

Therapists either set goals with clients explicitly (Haley, Palo Alto), or have implicit goals, corresponding to workable organizational structures (Minuchin), or the stages of broad-based, though unpredictable, systemic change (Milan).

Engaged versus Disengaged Therapist

Therapists may grapple actively with the "system" as members, entering coalitions and (un)balancing structures (Minuchin), or remain neutral and detached, avoiding coalitions, tracking circular patterns, and preserving outside leverage (Milan).

One-Up versus One-Down Position

The therapist takes charge of the therapy, assuming an expert position (Haley, Minuchin), or is deliberately one-down to minimize resistance (Palo Alto).

Change in Therapy Room versus at Home

Problem patterns are challenged directly, with new behavior enacted and rehearsed during the session (Minuchin), or change happens later, in response to interventions at the end of the session (Milan, Palo Alto).

COMMENTS

Why should the territory be called "systems therapy" rather than "family therapy?" One reason is that an exclusively family-level focus is limiting: As the brief-therapy model illustrates, a systems approach can be meaningfully applied to other levels in the systems hierarchy, including the level of the individual [Bloch (1980)]. Another reason is that "family therapy" is now so pluralistic that its many varieties (psychodynamic, experiential, behavioral, etc.) share less with one another than with their individual-therapy counterparts. The common denominator, then, is only a procedure (seeing families), not a new epistemology, or way of viewing problems. As Bateson (1971) warns, " . . . the important polarization of opinion is not simply between practitioners of individual and family therapy, but between those who think in terms of systems and those who think in terms of linear sequences of cause and effect" (p. 243).

While working on the edge of a new paradigm is exciting, the paradigm itself must soon move beyond the formative stage of conceptual clarification to verification through empirical research. There are two major tasks: One is to document further that interactional/contextual/organizational factors contribute significantly to the development and maintenance of clinical problems [Minuchin *et al.*

(1978); Wynne (1978); Coyne (1976); Madanes, Dukes, and Harbin (1980)]. The other is to demonstrate that the strategic systems therapies are effective and compare favorably to other treatments [see Stanton (1981); Gurman and Kniskern (1981)]. Dell (1980) and Abeles (1976) point to knotty methodological issues in studying clinical phenomena systemically, within an epistemology of pattern. While these make the first task more difficult, they should not delay the second. Research on clinical outcome requires the most rigidly linear of experimental contexts. Until the "effects" of the strategic systems therapies are thus documented, the scientific credibility of the new paradigm will remain in question.

In closing, we think that two features of strategic systems therapy as a method deserve special comment. Unlike many therapies, it is more a way of working than a way of living. While values are implicit in this approach as in any other, the emphasis is on solving problems rather than teaching skills or beliefs for a better life. In this sense, systems therapy is poorly suited for popular consumption in self-help programs or manuals for personal growth. Systemic thinking is for *therapists'* use in doing clinical work: It is not necessary that clients think systemically also.

The final point is a paradox: The thrust of this therapy is *away* from therapy as a solution to human problems. By following a principle of minimal intervention and assuming that living systems have within themselves the capacity for constructive change, the new approach may be sowing the seeds of its own demise. On the other hand, in a field of therapies plagued by excesses, "less is best" may be an idea whose time has come.

NOTES

[1]The boundaries of an orientation can never be drawn satisfactorily. We have included these four models because each is well-established (developed over at least a decade) and embodies both systemic *and* strategic principles. Other approaches [e.g., Andolfi's (1979)] might have been included also. Of all the models, Minuchin's structural therapy is probably least strategic because it is occasionally educational. Structural therapy, however, is very similar to Haley's strategic therapy and sufficiently pragmatic, we believe, to be grouped with the other models.

For a comprehensive review of "strategic approaches to family therapy," see Stanton (1980).

[2]For discussions of systems therapy as it relates to the broader frameworks of general systems theory, cybernetics, and communication theory, see Watzlawick, Beavin, and Jackson (1967); Sluzki and Ransom (1976); Haley (1980); Hoffman (1976, 1980a); Wilder (1979); and Dell (1980).

[3]The words "strategic" and "systemic" are in the title of a new periodical, the *Journal of Strategic and Systemic Therapies,* edited by Donald Efron, M. S. W., 779 Viscount Road, London, Ontario N6J 4A4, Canada.

Interestingly, some who work "this way" prefer not to name the approach at all, lest the label associate them with a particular camp or limit prematurely the evolution of a broader paradigm [Hoffman (1980b)].

[4]It would be more accurate to speak of "constructing" a system than "finding" it. A system, after all, is only a conceptual tool, which, as the Duhls point out, can never be kissed! Different system constructions are not more or less real or truthful, only more or less useful.

[5]Problem-focused system formulations tend to highlight *temporal* sequences of discrete communicational acts, whereas organizational systems are more likely to be represented *spatially*, with people close or far (enmeshed or disengaged) or arranged vertically in a hierarchy [Steinglass (1978)].

[6]The importance of this dimension was suggested by Harold Goolishian, Ph.D.

[7]Lynn Hoffman's metaphor.

REFERENCES

Abeles, G. Researching the unresearchable: Experimentation on the double bind. *In:* Sluzki, C. E. and Ranson, D. C. (Eds.). *Double Bind.* New York: Grune & Stratton (1976).

Andolfi, M. *Family Therapy: An interactional Approach.* New York: Plenum (1979).

Aponte, H. J. and Van Deusen, J. M. Structural family therapy. *In:* Gurman, A. S. and Kniskern, D. P. (Eds.). *Handbook of Family Therapy.* New York: Brunner/Mazel (1981).

Bateson, G. A systems approach. *International Journal of Psychiatry* 9:242–244 (1971).

Bateson, G. *Steps to an Ecology of Mind.* New York: Random House (1972).

Bateson, G. *Mind and Nature: A Necessary Unity.* New York: E. P. Dutton (1979).

Berenson, D. An interview with Richard Fisch. *The Family* 3:24–30 (1976).

Bloch, D. A. The future of family therapy. *In:* Andolfi, M. and Zwerling, I. (Eds.). *Dimensions of Family Therapy.* New York: Guilford (1980).

Coyne, J. C. Toward an international description of depression. *Psychiatry* 39:28–40 (1976).

Coyne, J. C. and Segal, L. A brief, strategic interactional approach to psychotherapy. *In:* Anchin, J. C. and Kiesler, D. J. (Eds.). *Handbook of Interpersonal Psychotherapy.* New York: Plenum Press (1981).

Dell, P. F. The Hopi family therapist and the Aristotelian parents. *Journal of Marital and Family Therapy* 6:123–130 (1980a).

Dell, P. F. Researching the family theories of schizophrenia: An exercise in epistemological confusion. *Family Process* 19:321–326 (1980b).

Fisch, R. Review of *Problem-Solving Therapy* (by J. Haley). *Family Process* 17:107–109 (1978).

Gross, M. L. *The Psychological Society.* New York: Random House (1978).

Gurman, A. S. and Kniskern, D. P. (Eds.). *Handbook of Family Therapy.* New York: Brunner/Mazel (1981).

Haley, J. *Strategies of Psychotherapy.* New York: Grune & Stratton (1963).

Haley, J. *Uncommon Therapy: The Psychiatric Techniques of Milton H. Erickson, M.D.* New York: W. W. Norton (1973).

Haley, J. *Problem-Solving Therapy.* San Francisco: Jossey-Bass (1976).

Haley, J. *Leaving Home: The Therapy of Disturbed Young People.* New York: McGraw-Hill (1980).

Hoffman, L. Breaking the homeostatic cycle. *In:* Guerin, P. J. (Ed.). *Family Therapy: Theory and Practice.* New York: Gardner (1976).

Hoffman, L. The family life cycle and discontinuous change. *In:* Carter, E. A. and McGoldrick, M. (Eds.). *The Family Life Cycle: A Framework for Family Therapy.* New York: Gardner Press (1980a).

Hoffman, L. *Foundations of Family Therapy.* New York: Basic Books (1981).

Hoffman, L. Behind the looking glass. Paper presented at Recent Developments in Strategic Family Therapy Conference, Skidmore College (August 1980b).

Keeney, B. P. Ecosystemic epistemology: An alternative paradigm for diagnosis. *Family Process* 18:117-129 (1979).

Madanes, C. Marital therapy when a symptom is presented by a spouse. *International Journal of Family Therapy* 2:120-136 (1980a).

Madanes, C. The prevention of rehospitalization of adolescents and young adults. *Family Process* 19:179-192 (1980b).

Madanes, C. Protection, paradox and pretending. *Family Process* 19:73-85 (1980c).

Madanes, C. *Strategic Family Therapy.* San Francisco: Jossey-Bass (1981).

Madanes, C. and Haley, J. Dimensions of family therapy. *Journal of Nervous and Mental Disease* 165:88-98 (1977).

Madanes, C., Dukes, J., and Harbin, H. Family ties of heroin addicts. *Archives of General Psychiatry* 37:889-894 (1980).

Marmor, J. Recent trends in psychotherapy. *American Journal of Psychiatry* 137:409-416 (1980).

Minuchin, S. *Families and Family Therapy.* Cambridge, MA: Harvard University Press (1974).

Minuchin, S. Constructing a therapeutic reality. *In:* Kaufmann, E. and Kaufman, P. (Eds.). *The Family Therapy of Drug and Alcohol Abuse.* New York: Gardner (1979).

Minuchin, S. and Fishman, H. C. *Pathways to Change: Techniques in Family Therapy.* Cambridge, MA: Harvard University Press (1981).

Minuchin, S., Rosman, B., and Baker, L. *Psychosomatic Families.* Cambridge, MA: Harvard University Press (1978).

Palazzoli-Selvini, M. Why a long interval between sessions? The therapeutic control of the family-therapist suprasystem. *In:* Andolfi, M. and Zwerling, I. (Eds.). *Dimensions of Family Therapy.* New York: Guilford (1980).

Palazzoli-Selvini, M., Boscolo, L., Cecchin, G., and Prata, G. Family rituals: A powerful tool in family therapy. *Family Process* 16:445-453 (1977).

Palazzoli-Selvini, M., Boscolo, L., Cecchin, G. F., and Prata, G. *Paradox and Counterparadox.* New York: Jason Aronson (1978a).

Palazzoli-Selvini, M., Boscolo, L., Cecchin, G. F., and Prata, G. A ritualized prescription in family therapy: Odd days and even days. *Journal of Marriage and Family Counseling* 4:3-9 (1978b).

Palazzoli-Selvini, M., Boscolo, L., Cecchin, G., and Prata, G. Hypothesizing, circularity, neutrality: Three guidelines for the conductor of the session. *Family Process* 19:3-12 (1980).

Papp, P. The Greek Chorus and other techniques of family therapy. *Family Process* 19:45-58 (1980).

Rabkin, R. *Strategic Psychotherapy.* New York: Basic Books (1977).

Rohrbaugh, M., Tennen, H., Press, S., White, L., Raskin, P., and Pickering, M. R. Paradoxical strategies in psychotherapy. Symposium presented at the American Psychological Association meetings, San Francisco (August 1977).

Rohrbaugh, M., Tennen, H., Press, S., and White, L. Compliance, defiance, and therapeutic paradox: Guidelines for strategic use of paradoxical interventions. *American Journal of Orthopsychiatry* (April 1981).

Sluzki, C. E. Marital therapy from a systems theory perspective. *In:* Paolino, T. J. and Mc-Grady, B. S. (Eds.). *Marriage and Marital Therapy: Psychoanalytic, Behavioral and Systems Theory Perspectives.* New York: Brunner/Mazel (1978).

Sluzki, C. E. and Ransom, D. C. (Eds.). *Double Bind: The Foundation of the Communicational Approach to the Family.* New York: Grune & Stratton (1976).

Stanton, M. D. Strategic approaches to family therapy. *In:* Gurman, A. S. and Kniskern, D. P. (Eds.). *Handbook of Family Therapy.* New York: Brunner/Mazel (1981).

Tennen, H., Rohrbaugh, M., Press, S., and White, L. Reactants theory and therapeutic paradox: A compliance-defiance model. *Psychotherapy: Theory, Research, and Practice* (in press).

Watzlawick, P. *The Language of Change.* New York: Basic Books (1978).

Watzlawick, P., Beavin, J. H., and Jackson, D. D. *Pragmatics of Human Communication.* New York: W. W. Norton (1967).

Watzlawick, P. and Coyne, J. C. Depression following stroke: Brief, problem-focused treatment. *Family Process* 19:13–18 (1980).

Watzlawick, P., Weakland, J., and Fisch, R. *Change: Principles of Problem Formation and Problem Resolution.* New York: W. W. Norton (1974).

Weakland, J. H., Fisch, R., Watzlawick, P., and Bodin, A. Brief therapy: Focused problem resolution. *Family Process* 13:141–168 (1974).

Wender, P. Viscious and virtuous circles: The role of deviation amplifying positive feedback in the origin and perpetuation of behavior. *Psychiatry* 31:309–324 (1968).

Wilder, C. The Palo Alto group: Difficulties and directions of the interactional view for human communication research. *Human Communication Research* 5:171–186 (1979).

Wynne, L. C. Knotted relationships, communication deviances, and metabinding. *In:* Berger, M.E. (Ed.). *Beyond the Double Bind.* New York: Brunner/Mazel (1978).

Network therapy is defined in the following chapter as an approach that aims to provide a family in crisis an opportunity to mobilize the supportive resources available within the family and the larger social system in a collaborative attempt to search for alternatives for resolving the crisis. It can serve as quite a powerful therapeutic intervention, particularly during an intense crisis in the family.

The intervention modality described here is of the full-scale network therapy process. It is a process that can begin once an intervention team, consisting of experienced mental health professionals, meets with members of the ailing family (usually at their home) to decide on a course of action which may reduce the crisis in the family to manageable proportions. The network therapy process involves therapeutic intervention with an assembled network of family and friends, who meet together for one or more four- to five-hour sessions in an attempt to find alternative solutions, new options, and productive resolutions of a previously unmanageable family problem. The network therapy process also includes six distinct phases which occur in each successful network session. Members of the intervention team need to be familiar with each of these network phases, as well as able to work as an effective team.

The roles and strategies used by team members during the network therapy session are described. Emphasis is on mobilizing the entire family and social network to become involved with members of the ailing nuclear family, discussing their concerns, sharing and becoming engaged in the creation of support groups for each family member. The goal is to develop commitments and investments of additional efforts and energies for the constructive resolution of a difficult family crisis.

16

Network Therapies: Involving the Extended System in Healing Family Crisis

Uri Rueveni, Ph.D.

WHAT IS NETWORK THERAPY?

Network therapy is an intervention process that aims to help a family, community, or organization in a crisis mobilize the supportive resources available within its social system in a collaborative effort to search for alternatives, crisis resolution, and/or healing. Similar definitions of this process can be found in the literature [Speck and Rueveni (1969); Speck and Attneave (1973); Rueveni (1975, 1976, 1977, 1979); Trimble (1980)].

In most cases, network therapy is a short-term, goal-oriented intervention process. It is usually undertaken by a team of professionals when crisis in a system has developed to unmanageable proportions, or where it is perceived or experienced as difficult and emotionally draining to handle by either members of the family or the helping professions systems.

The literature on family and social networks, community networks, social support systems, and the utilization of network resources for healing is growing and includes both theoretical and conceptual formulations as well as clinical applications utilizing innovative frameworks and models. Familiarity with the following contributors will increase the reader's appreciation and scope of this growing field [Attneave (1969); Bott (1971); Cohen and Sokolovsky (1978); Collins and Pancoast (1976); Curtis (1973); Cutler and Madore (1980); Erickson (1975); Garrison (1974, 1976, 1978); Gatti (1976); Pattison (1973); Rueveni (1975, 1977); Sarason (1977); Speck and Speck (1979); Todd (1979); Tolsdorf (1976); Trimble (1980)].

This chapter is concerned mostly with the full-scale network intervention process undertaken to help a variety of difficult emotional concerns which occur in dysfunctional and crisis-oriented family systems. The view taken here is that most families need to be able to maintain on-going relationships with their extended families and social networks. The importance of maintaining an on-going relationship with one's extended kin and social network should not be underestimated.

Mental health professionals and particularly family therapists need to become increasingly familiar and skillful in utilizing the powerful healing forces available within one's own extended social and family network.

Network therapy (also called family networking and network intervention) is a therapeutic process that mobilizes the social network support systems of family, relatives, and friends in a collaborative effort to solve a difficult emotional crisis. Most families, if need be, can reactivate 40 to 50, or more, of their extended kin and social systems with relative ease. This large-scale intervention effort is generally undertaken when other therapeutic efforts have not been able to modify the existing crisis, and the mobilization of such a large-scale assembly is usually undertaken by a team of experienced professionals, who work in concert under the leadership of a designated team leader to achieve specific goals aimed at the resolution of the family crisis.

There are growing indications that our emotional and physical well-being as individuals is closely related to our ability to effectively maintain active, functional, and well-balanced relationships to our own family, family of origin, our friends and community. All of these can, and do, function as productive resources for healing, growing, and change — particularly when crisis occurs.

The inclusion of a chapter on network therapy in a book dealing with new therapies is important, since the professional who works with dysfunctional family and crisis-oriented systems should be able to become familiar with the process, criteria for use, and techniques for utilizing network therapy. The remainder of the chapter concerns itself with these and other related issues.

THE PROCESS OF NETWORK THERAPY

Criteria for Use

The networking process often can begin when the team of professionals (hereafter called the Intervention Team) can determine whether members of the nuclear family will benefit from calling on their extended family and social system for help. This process also needs to allow time for members of the family to decide whether they wish to become involved in such an activty.

It is quite important for the mental health professionals interested in the potential use of this approach to become familiar with some of the factors that might indicate the usefulness to a family of mobilizing their own network system. This intervention modality could be quite useful and effective when the following factors are indicated.

1. *The existence of an on-going emotional crisis within the family system, which affects family members to the point of their feeling desperate.* The crisis usually involves all family members and has been present for quite a while with little sign of change or improvement.

Feelings of desperation and helplessness expressed by members of the family concerning their on-going difficulties are a good indication for considering network therapy as the preferred intervention modality.

When family members feel quite desperate, experiencing little relief, and no alternative options can be perceived, mobilizing the extended network system can often provide the needed support for additional explorations of alternatives tending toward increased coping and crisis resolution.

2. *Dysfunctional relationships which may result from severe family disorganization associated with excessive enmeshments, especially between parents and children; frequent emotional breakdowns by one or another family member, requiring psychiatric hospitalizations; threatened suicide attempts on the part of a family member; parental conflicts resulting from chronic alcohol use; runaway situations or violence in the family, creating chaos and lack of trust; feelings of isolation by family members; and excessive secrecy within the family system.*

3. *In situations where a temporary separation between family members is needed.* When family members feel helpless and depend on other people within their own extended family or community, the network therapy approach should be considered.

4. *The ability of the family members to mobilize 40 or 50 of their extended family and social network to be available to participate in the network therapy sessions.* Although one can frequently utilize a network therapy approach by mobilizing the friendship systems, effective crisis resolution needs to include both family members and the friendship system, as well as others within the client's social support system.

The availability of the client's social support system is then of importance, as well as the commitments and motivation of members of the distressed family to initiate the process by calling on their network for help. Motivation and willingness to collaborate with the intervention team are quite important. Although consensus for becoming involved in this process may not be possible by all members of the nuclear family, the intervention team in looking for commitments on the part of some, if not all, of the family members to become involved in the networking process.

The following case represents an appropriate decision on the part of an intervention team to help a family in crisis to mobilize its extended system for support and help.

Mrs. J called on this author for help with her on-going family struggles. She was in her 60s, living with her 40-year-old, schizophrenic son, who had frequently been hospitalized and had been diagnosed as a paranoid schizophrenic. Mrs. J had two married sons and a daughter, all living away from home. She stated on the phone that since her husband died 10 years ago, her son had been difficult to manage, threatening to kill himself, threatening his brothers, and acting quite irresponsibly. Past hospitalization periods were difficult for the entire family, and presently since her son had been discharged from the hospital and was living in a halfway house he still would make it difficult for her, demanding money and a great deal of attention, which drained her emotionally and physically. Mrs. J and her three children had read one the recent books on family networks and felt that the mobilization of their extended network could provide their family system with alternative solutions for resolving the crisis.

Team members visited the family's home and discussed the existing family members' concerns. This exchange provided team members an opportunity to assess the appropriateness of mobilizing Mrs. J's extended family network. A mutual decision was made by both family members and the team to attempt network therapy. The team members felt that mobilizing the extended family and social system could provide support for all family members for a continued search for alternatives and coping relationships that would minimize the existing crisis.

The Home Visit

Past experience indicates that the home is usually a sound location for conducting network therapy sessions. To establish whether a family in crisis meets the criteria for becoming involved in a network therapy session, the therapist should stress the importance of making a home visit. A two-hour meeting at the home usually provides ample opportunities for team members to become familiar with most of the family's concerns, assessing the appropriateness of the network approach.

During the home visit, both team members and family members attempt to become familiar with one another. The professional team members need information about the nature, extent, and severity of the existing crisis. They must assess the important criteria mentioned earlier in order to determine whether or not mobilization of the family's extended system is warranted. Family members, on the other hand, need information on costs, time commitments, and their involvement in the attempt to mobilize their family network.

In many cases, dysfunctional family systems can benefit from the full-scale mobilization of their extended family system. However, delaying and blocking tactics on the part of one or more members of the family are to be expected. Intervention team members need not necessarily seek family consensus regarding the implementation of the network therapy process. When some family members can demonstrate their commitment and motivation for becoming involved with network therapy, it is often sufficient to make a decision to try family network therapy despite the protestations of others in the family who may threaten to boycott or undermine the network meetings.

In a recent case, a 17-year-old family member had twice threatened suicide, and when serious consideration was given by his parents to mobilize their extended system, the young man threatened not to show up for the sessions. When the team leader confronted him with a counter-demand, which stipulated that he need not show up since the network therapy was assembled not necessarily for him but rather for his parents and family, he showed up promptly the next day in spite of his on-going threats to undermine the process.

When network therapy is planned as the appropriate intervention modality, each family member is usually instructed to prepare lists of people he or she wishes to invite. The invited family and friends are told that their participation and help are needed in order to discuss the family crisis. They are asked to attend the session, which usually lasts from four to five hours. All members of the family, including children age 10 or older, can and should be able to attend the session. The list of invited people need not be restricted to only family and friends. Neighbors, peers, work mates, school mates, and others within one's own social system may need to be considered, especially if a family has for one reason or another an unusually small number of members available for this purpose. Experience indicates that it is best to set a time for one network intervention session, and at the conclusion of this session to determine which family members would be needed for additional sessions.

There may be circumstances that require the network therapy sessions to be held at a location different than the home. If need be, the sessions can be conducted in a hospital, a residential facility, or a friend's or relative's home. During the last 15 years, this author has led family network sessions in various settings in addition to the home. The location for the network session is not the most critical factor for its success; it is rather the adequate mobilization of each of the network phases that determines an effective outcome.

THE PHASES OF NETWORK THERAPY

A fully mobilized network therapy session unfolds into six distinct phases. The first phase is *retribalization*, an initial period where network members begin to reconnect with one another. During this phase, team members encourage participants to mill around and meet as many people as possible. Some group activities can also be suggested, such as singing a song, swaying and humming, and similar activities which will allow for network participants to mobilize energies involving themselves as a more cohesive group.

The next phase is that of *polarization*. During this phase, participants exchange differing points of view regarding the problems in the family. The polarization phase is quite critical for the unfolding of the networking process. It allows for an exchange of information in the form of feelings and ideas as they are perceived by different persons concerning the factors that have contributed to the existing crisis. During this phase, team members continue to encourage participants to verbalize and share their perceptions of what factors, issues, and problems contribute to the existence of the crisis in the family.

Mobilization is the next phase. During this period, some people in the network begin to mobilize themselves, take leadership positions, and offer ideas that may lead to the reduction of the crisis. The team continues to encourage further exploration of all aspects of the family's concerns.

The phase of *depression* usually follows. During this phase, many people begin to express frustration at their inability to help. Others feel that the problems are too difficult and that they cannot be solved. The task of the intervention team is to acknowledge the difficulties but also to insist on the collective ability of the network to solve the crisis. The team leader can usually activate the network into action by choreographing some strategic moves, usually psychodramatic experiences that will allow for both family members and others in the network to become further involved in experiencing the difficult issues at hand.

The final two phases are *breakthrough* and *exhaustion elation*. During these two phases, some solutions and alternatives can begin to be formulated. The team strategy is to encourage the development and formation of temporary support groups. The feeling on the part of many in the network is not only that of exhaustion, but also of elation. There is a feeling of some accomplishment and the realization that positive changes in the family may be forthcoming as a result of their efforts and of the formation of the task-oriented support groups.

FORMATION OF SUPPORT GROUPS

The intervention team members need to allocate time, toward the end of the network therapy session, to allow network participants to join support groups of their own choice. It is quite important that each member of the ailing nuclear family be involved with a support group of his or her own choosing whose members can discuss specific alternatives for resolution of the immediate crisis.

The support group members need to activate their resources and organize themselves in a manner that will allow for on-going and continuous weekly meetings with members of the nuclear family, for at least a number of weeks until the immediate crisis can be reduced and solutions that were formulated during the network therapy session can be translated into the daily lives of the family in crisis.

It should be emphasized that the motivations and continued efforts on the part of active members of each support group can and do often ensure the search for constructive alternatives for productive coping by members of the nuclear family. Although such groups are usually temporary in nature, it is not uncommon to find support groups whose members have decided to continue meeting once a month sometimes over a period of years.

STRATEGIC INTERVENTION IN NETWORK THERAPY

The intervention strategy in any network session is best developed and carried out by a team of network therapists (interventionists) familiar with the family's concerns. the goals of intervention, and the network phases.

The general goals for network therapy sessions correspond to the major network phases. These are:

1. The facilitation of rapid connections among network members and an increase in the level of involvements (retribalization phase).
2. Stimulation of increased sharing and exchange of different viewpoints (polarization phase).
3. Increased communication among members of the nuclear family and their extended system, stressing the need for active leaders (mobilization phase).
4. Providing for direct intervention for deeper exploration of the crisis during impass periods (depression phase).
5. Assistance in the formation and development of temporary support groups which serve as resources for crisis resolution (breakthrough and exhaustion-elation phases).

The task of the intervention team is to mobilize all network members to work toward these goals. The strategic intervention by members of the team needs to be aimed at both the nuclear family level and the extended family level. The task of the network intervention team is to work in concert with the team leader, who directs and guides the networking process in a manner such that it will maximize the attainment of the five specific goals mentioned above.

To be effective in mobilizing the network for solving the crisis, the team leader needs to use a variety of effective strategies. Such strategies vary from the use of psychodramatic techniques to taking sides and the giving of directives, to direct confrontation and the use of choreographic strategies.

ROLES OF THE NETWORK THERAPIST

Each network session can be identified by the specific roles undertaken by members of the intervention team — family convenor, family mobilizer, family choreographer, and family resource consultant.

The Therapist as a Family Convenor

Members of the intervention team function often as family convenors specifically during the home visit and during the initial retribalization phase during the network session.

During a home visit to one family about to call on its extended family members for help with their suicidal daughter, team members helped in preparing family lists and in charting a family tree.

During another home visit, team members arranged to convene the network session on the same day a 20-year-old son was released from hospitalization necessitated by a previous depressive episode and his attempted suicide.

In still another case, Mrs. K needed desperately to utilize resources available within the family and social network to gain additional strengths in coping with her two daughters, one of whom was diagnosed as schizophrenic, the other as cerebral palsied. Team members realized during the home visit that Mrs. K's family network was quite small and most members were unavailable. A family network was convened, consisting of a few family members and professional therapists and mental health workers, who came for a day's workshop with this author.

It is not uncommon that team members will urge members of the nuclear family to call on their friends and neighbors. On a number of occasions the author and other team members were able to function as family convenors by involving nearby neighbors, and members of the church to which the client belonged, to join and participate in a family network session.

During the retribalization phase, team members function as family convenors by facilitation of the members' active involvement in the network process. Team members lead the assembled network of family and friends in a sequence of activities designed to increase participants' expenditure of some physical energy. These are activities such as milling around, shaking hands, singing in unison, humming a favorite family melody, and Indian whooping.

In another network, during a Friday night meeting with a Jewish family, designed to help family members deal with their son's on-going depressions, the role of convening the network became easier when one cousin, a Rabbinical student, agreed to lead the participants in the traditional Jewish ceremony of lighting the candles and offering the blessing welcoming the Sabbath.

The retribalization phase offers the network team a chance to function in the role of convenors of the family network assembly and allows for the proper unfolding of the remaining network phases.

The Network Therapist as a Family Mobilizer

The network therapy process requires active involvement both on the part of family network members and members of the intervention team. During the mobilization phase, the therapist's role can be described as that of family mobilizer. During the mobilization phase of any network, the team members need to encourage the formation of the network "activists." "Activists" are persons within the family or social network system who are willing to become increasingly active and lead others in a search for information helpful to the family, and to encourage others in the network to participate more fully and actively. Members of the intervention team function as family mobilizers by identifying such activists, and encouraging them to continue their productive leadership efforts. A few examples will demonstrate this role.

During a network assembled to help a young man find alternatives to his use of drugs, his uncle indicated that there were many other problems in the family. His wife and other family members ignored his comments. However, the team leader insisted that he clarify his statement, which revealed that an important and active family member (the young man's aunt) was not invited to attend since she used drugs and was believed to be a bad influence on the family. The insistence of the team on dealing with this issue helped the network become mobilized around the issues of drug use and abuse, scapegoating, and the relationships that existed between the young man and his parents.

In another network assembled to provide support and crisis resolution for a woman, her five children, and her 14-year-old psychotic daughter, the 14-year-old refused to attend the meeting, hid in the garage, and tied herself to the door with a rope. During the network meeting, one team member found a note in the girl's bedroom demanding that she be considered a sane person, and requesting a change in her shcool and privileges (which, if granted, would stop her "bizarre" behavior). The efforts of the team were directed toward mobilizing the network to consider the letter. Some network activists were able to encourage the young girl to leave the garage and stay in the basement, where communication developed between her and her family and also with her activist support group.

The Network Therapist as a Family Choreographer

Papp (1976) described this role as "a method of actively intervening in the nuclear and extended family by realigning family relationships through physical and movement positions."

To facilitate the network process from one phase to the next, the intervention team members often function as choreographers. This role frequently requires team members to use sequenced psychodramatic activities which can activate or reactivate additional energies for further involvement by members of the nuclear family and their extended network. It requires familiarity with such skills as family sculpting and a host of psychodramatic approaches that can be used, particularly during the depression phase, when there is a lull in activity.

A network meeting was assembled to help members of a family develop new strengths in dealing with an on-going crisis — the death of their father. The mother, a woman in her 50s, had had increasing difficulty in relating to her 15-year-old daughter, who had begun intensely acting out following her father's death. She began using drugs, attempted to set fire to her home, and attempted to overdose frequently. Although this child was under psychiatric care on an outpatient basis, her behavior seemed to be rapidly deteriorating. Her two older brothers and one sister were married and living away from home. They were working in the same business, however, and frequently rotated in having their younger sister visit them in their homes, but they were finding the experience difficult to cope with. The relationships between the mother and all of her children remained stressful at best. During the network meeting, the team strategy included an experience that would allow the young girl, as well as her family, to express feelings of loss and mourning. A choreographed move was designed by the intervention team, whereby members of the nuclear family stood in a circle sending verbal "postcards" to their dead father, expressing their feelings toward him when he was alive, how much they missed him, and what commitment they could make to ensure that their lives without him could continue and get the family free from pain and strife. This experience provided an excellent opportunity for further network mobilization and involvement by the family members and their support network.

Another example of this role occurred during the second network therapy session with the same family. The mother was sitting at the center while most of the immediate family members were seated around her, exchanging feelings and thoughts concerning their own contribution to the existing problem. They were also attempting to search for ways to develop more appropriate relationships with her. When family members completed this part of their discussion, the leader, following a brief consultation with his team members, suggested another choreographic experience, which required all members of the nuclear family and their spouses to stand around and hug the mother, forming a tight inner circle, while the remainder of the network participants formed a second, outer circle around them. This experience provided additional opportunities for many in the network to express feelings and contribute to the network process of sharing and supporting members of the nuclear family.

In another network meeting, assembled to stop a suicidal attempt by a 25-year-old divorced woman, whose relationship with her mother was very stressful, the therapist and team choreographed a psychodramatic event, in which the daughter was asked to step up on a chair, looking down toward her mother, who was seated. The daughter, who had previously felt helpless and controlled by her mother, was encouraged to communicate her feelings towards her. This initial confrontation provided the daughter with a new opportunity to express her feelings openly, with the support of her sister, and to begin the healing process.

Another example of this role occurred during a network meeting to help a mother begin the process of minimizing her enmeshment with her psychotic son. A mock funeral ceremony was conducted; the son was considered to be "dead," was covered up, and the mother proceeded to eulogize him. This choreographed experience provided a new opportunity for both the mother and her family network to express their feelings toward the son and begin a healing process whereby the network support system could provide new alternative arrangements for a temporary separation between mother and son.

The Network Therapist as a Family Resource Consultant

The role of a resource consultant is undertaken by the network team primarily during the formation of the support groups. At this stage, team members usually provide initial leadership for the formation and composition of the support group. This role is also maintained as network meetings are completed and is followed by support group meetings with members of the nuclear family.

Toward the end of a series of sessions with one family, the network intervention team remained active in helping to form a support group for the young daughter and for her mother. They provided consultations and offered ideas of additional resources to be explored by members of the support group. The daughter considered the team's suggestion to make arrangements for her to go back to school, for taking a part-time job, and for providing ongoing social contact during the week. The mother's support group helped her in forming new social contacts, and reopened new and old friendships resulting from the two network sessions.

In the network that met to help the enmeshed mother and her psychotic son, the therapist and the team were instrumental as resource consultants to the support groups. Following the second network meeting, the son was helped by his support group to take an apartment at the YMCA. He attempted to return home the following evening, only to find the locks changed. Mother's support group had provided her with the strength not to allow her son to return that evening. The son's support group was instrumental in encouraging him to visit his mother only on a weekly basis, to find a new job, and to stop his self-destructive behavior patterns.

TEAM DEVELOPMENT

Preparing for each of the network therapy sessions is a must even for the most experienced intervention teams. An intervention team should consist of two to four members. Prior to each intervention, team members need to address themselves to a number of important issues. The following is a brief list of the most important of these issues: Leadership functions and roles during the sessions; the goals to be accomplished; strategies to be used; and timing and sequencing of intervention strategies to be used during the network session.

Prior to a network therapy session, team members need to agree on the "division of labor." There is much to be accomplished during each session. New or inexperienced therapists may feel a need to intervene either too prematurely or to delay their responses inappropriately. There is a great deal of skill needed by network therapists in dealing with large groups, family dysfunctions, and psychodramatic strategies. It is best that one leader be designated in each intervention team, a therapist who is sufficiently skillful in coordinating intervention strategies and providing leadership for effective teamwork. The decision to have a team leader tends to facilitate team communication and appropriate timing of the intervention sequences.

During network sessions, team members frequently consult with one another, providing additional feedback to the team leader on various issues at hand. Frequent team consultations are a must prior to, during, and following any network therapy session.

One of the most important goals of the intervention team is to provide the opportunity for members of the nuclear family and their extended network of family and friends to formulate alternative solutions leading toward the reduction and/or resolution of the crisis at hand.

The successful unfolding of each of the network phases usually leads to a breakthrough in the crisis through effective formation of family and social network support groups. These support groups, which can, and do, consult with the team members, eventually need to come up with effective and practical alternatives for the resolution or the alleviation of the family crisis. The energies and skillful talents of members of the intervention team should be directed to achieve the above-stated goals.

REFERENCES

Attneave, C. L. Therapy in tribal settings and urban network intervention. *Family Process* 8:192–210 (1969).

Attneave, C. L. Social networks and clinical practice: A logical extension of family therapy. *In*: Freeman, D. S. (Ed.). *Perspectives on Family Therapy*. Vancouver, B. C.: Butterworth & Co. (1980).

Bott, E. *Family and Social Network* (2nd Ed.). London: Tavistock (1971).

Cohen, C. I. and Sokolovsky, J. Schizophrenia and social networks: Ex-patients in the inner city. *Schizophrenia Bulletin* 4:546–560 (1978).

Collins, A. H. and Pancoast, D. L. *Natural Helping Networks: A Strategy for Prevention*. Washington, DC: National Association of Social Workers Publications (1976).

Curtis, W. R. The future use of social networks in mental health. *In*: Pattison, E. M. (Chair). *Clinical Group Methods for Larger Social Systems.* Symposium presented at the 33rd Annual Conference of the American Group Psychotherapy Association, Boston (February 1976).

Cutler, D. and Madore, E. Community-family network therapy in rural settings. *Community Mental Health Journal* 6(2):144–155 (1980).

Erickson, C. E. The concept of personal network in clinical practice. *Family Process* 14: 487–498 (1975).

Garrison, J. E. Network techniques: Case studies in the screening-linking-planning conference method. *Family Process* 13:337–353 (1974).

Garrison, J. E. Network methods for clinical problems. *In*: Pattison, E. M. (Chair). *Clinical Group Methods for Larger Social Systems.* Symposium presented at the 33rd Annual Conference of the American Group Psychotherapy Association, Boston (February 1976).

Gatti, F. and Colman, C. Community network therapy: An approach to aiding families with troubled children. *American Journal of Orthopsychiatry* 40:608–617 (1976).

Papp, P. Family choreography. *In*: Guerin, P. J. Jr. (Ed.). *Family Therapy: Theory and Practice.* New York: Gardner Press (1976).

Pattison, E. M. Social system psychotherapy. *American Journal of Psychotherapy* 18:396–409 (1973).

Pattison, E. M., DeFrancisco, E., Wood, W., Frazier, H., and Crowder, J. A psychosocial kinship model for family therapy. *American Journal of Psychiatry* 132:1246-1251 (1975).

Rueveni, U. Network intervention with a family crisis. *Family Process* 14:193-204 (1975).

Rueveni, U. Family network intervention: Healing families in crisis. *Intellect,* 580-582 (May–June 1976).

Rueveni, U. Family network intervention: Mobilizing support for families in crisis. *International Journal of Family Counseling* 5:77-83 (1977).

Rueveni, U. *Networking Families in Crisis.* New York: Human Sciences Press (1979).

Rueveni, U. and Speck, R. V. Using encounter group techniques in the treatment of the social network of the schizophrenic. *International Journal of Group Psychotherapy* 19:495-500 (1969).

Rueveni, U., Speck, R. V., and Speck, J. *Interventions: Healing Human Systems.* New York: Human Sciences Press (in press).

Rueveni, U. and Wiener, M. Network intervention of disturbed families: The key role of network activists. *Psychotherapy: Theory, Research and Practice* 13:173-176 (December 1976).

Sarason, S. B., Carroll, C. F., Maton, K., Cohen, S., and Lorentz, E. *Human Services and Resource Networks.* San Francisco: Jossey-Bass (1977).

Speck, R. V. Psychotherapy of the social network of a schizophrenic family. *Family Process* 7:208-214 (1967).

Speck, R. V. and Attneave, C. L. *Family Networks.* New York: Pantheon Books (1973).

Speck, R. V. and Rueveni, U. Network therapy: A developing concept. *Family Process* 8:182-191 (1969).

Speck, R. V. and Speck, J. L. On networks: Network therapy, network intervention and networking. *International Journal of Family Therapy,* 333-337 (Winter 1979).

Todd, D. M. Social networks and psychology. *Connections* 2(2):87-88 (Spring 1979).

Tolsdorf, C. C. Social networks, support, and coping: An exploratory study. *Family Process* 15:407-417 (1976).

Trimble, D. A guide to the network therapies (1980). Unpublished paper.

Part IV
Adjuvant Therapies

The five chapters making up Part IV cover a large territory. Some are clearly therapies in their own right, while others can perhaps be more properly considered as aids to, or means of, implementing other approaches. However the reader may consider them, all represent sources of fruitful ideas and practice.

Chapter 17, on comprehensive vocationally-oriented psychotherapy, should be especially interesting to those who have responsibilities for working with adolescents, since it indicates quite precisely how important it is to meet the adolescent on his or her own terms — that is, in relation to the adolescent's emerging needs, principal social setting, and the problems he/she faces in preparing for a vocation. Based on years of experience, the authors believe that this approach should find useful — and successful — application in the hands of many other workers in this area.

As presented here, dance-movement therapy is a source for experiencing feelings, conflicts, and the fantasies associated with them. Some of its theoretical views, as well as certain of its practices, are certainly applicable to other therapeutic approaches. Moreover, it is a practice that merits application on its own in a variety of situations, and with many kinds of clients.

Art therapy, discussed in Chapter 19, stresses the prior nature of images, particularly visual images, to words. Reminiscent of early 20th century controversy concerning "imageless thought," some readers may not find this view entirely acceptable — in spite of evidence from many sources that lends support. Art therapy is clearly a primary therapy as well as an adjuvant one.

Primal therapy is one of the newer therapyies and one that has enjoyed a certain vogue by provoking considerable interest in the community of therapists. Perhaps its claim to being an especially effective depth therapy cannot be accepted everywhere, but there is little doubt that in focusing again on the significance of early trauma in fashioning personality and developing conflicts, this view of the nature of therapeutic theory and practice has won a significant number of adherents.

The final chapter is the only one in the book in which therapeutic attention is directed chiefly to hospitalized patients — and in this instance it is the elderly. This kind of supportive humanistic psychotherapy, as reported here from Cushing Hospital, where it has been pioneered, will surely find application, in both theory and practice, in other institutions serving elderly people who are too ill to care for themselves and thus to live in any environment except that provided by a hospital dedicated to meeting their manifold needs.

Comprehensive vocationally-oriented psychotherapy was developed to help individuals who have multiple areas of dysfunction — social, educational, emotional, vocational, behavioral, etc. — and who have not been able to be helped by traditional mental health intervention techniques. Such individuals are frequently a significant drain on community resources. Comprehensive vocationally-oriented psychotherapy requires that the therapist assume a number of different roles, undertaking a flexible, concrete, multidimensional involvement, with stress on outreach as a technique and on meeting individual needs.

Using jobs as the entree for other services, the aim is to incorporate educational and mental health components into activities in a real-life employment situation. A significant element is the constructive use of crisis situations (such as dropping out of school.) The approach differs significantly from many other approaches to the hard-to-reach, multi-problem individual, but is similar in many respects to recent Job Corps and CETA programs. Research has shown this program to be successful for a group of chronic adolescent delinquents, who were found to change profoundly in personality and behavioral dimensions, changes that continued at least to the last follow-up some 15 years later.

17

Comprehensive Vocationally-oriented Psychotherapy: Empirical and Practice Issues

Milton F. Shore, Ph.D. and Joseph L. Massimo, Ph.D.

Comprehensive vocationally-oriented psychotherapy arose because of the minimal success mental health personnel had in attempting to assist young people with antisocial problems through the traditional methods of mental health service delivery. For many years, a highly skilled multi-disciplinary mental health team operated within a suburban public school system to help youths who had long histories of disruptive behavior, chronic academic failure, serious problems with authority, and a juvenile police record. Unfortunately, efforts to reach these youths in school through a traditional multi-disciplinary approach met with little success. Often the young people would come for one scheduled appointment and never again. Indeed, the youths literally went through all the school-helping resources of guidance counselor, pupil personnel worker, resource teacher, and school social workers, as well as a number of administrative personnel, all of whom could not assist them. School personnel were all frustrated and annoyed by their feelings of impotence.

A number of assumptions underlay the development of comprehensive vocationally-oriented psychotherapy for adolescents. First, there must be a focus on the unique developmental tasks of adolescence. It was our belief that the values underlying many of our intervention techniques too often ignored the emerging developmental needs of adolescents, such as vocational planning and the role of a job. As a result, many of our programs have been aimed at getting youths back to school where, when they return, they often continue to fail, never obtaining the skills necessary to compete for positions in the employment marketplace.[1]

Second, any program must be based on a theory of psychopathology with clearly delineated diagnostic dimensions determining the nature of the intervention. For our theoretical framework, we chose psychoanalytic ego psychology and built a program around the theoretical and clinical articles written by August Aichorn (1935) and Fritz Redl (1951, 1952). What is appropriate for one group is inappropriate for another: The program elements and techniques need to be geared to theoretical understanding of the nature of the specific pathology. Youths with long histories of antisocial behavior — often labeled "character disordered youths" — have typically been described as concrete, action-oriented, impulsive, present-time-oriented, non-verbal, lacking compassion, manipulative, lacking in guilt, uncooperative, resistive, and untrusting. Yet unlike the psychotic, all of these characteristics are within the context of good reality testing.

Third, such youths have profound problems encompassing many areas of adjustment — social, educational, vocational, emotional, etc. Thus, any program geared to help them would have to be multidimensional.

Fourth, the clinical perspective needs to be broad. One could not limit oneself to only certain isolated behaviors or certain discrete activities. There needs to be total investment in all aspects of the youth's life along many clinical levels.

Fifth, the program needs to be evaluated. Unfortunately, there are very few evaluations of treatment programs. The evaluation of this program was an integral part of the development of the program, and served to provide an understanding of the changes that occurred. Although this chapter does not deal with the evaluation (see *Bibliography*), the results of evaluation give us an insight into how personality change was related to intervention (what aspects of personality one hoped to change) as well as the long-term effects of psychotherapy.

Certain principles underlie comprehensive vocationally-oriented psychotherapy:

1. *Contacts are initiated at a crisis point.* Unfortunately, the unique opportunities for intervention offered by a crisis are often lost in many of our psychotherapeutic programs, for initial contact is frequently made after the crisis is over. It was our belief that a crisis is an extraordinarily opportune moment for intervention in a group such as chronic adolescent delinquents, where it is important that any opportunity where distress or anxiety is produced be utilized therapeutically. Leaving school was seen as a crisis, for it required readjustment on the part of the youth. Therefore, it was a major principle for undertaking comprehensive vocationally-oriented psychotherapy that we select youths that had dropped out of school. The names, addresses, and telephone numbers of

the youths who had dropped out or had been suspended from school were obtained from the Supervisor of Attendance, who knew all the youths who had left school and whether or not this had been for antisocial reasons, academic failure, or other reasons.   In suburban neighborhoods, leaving school is particularly stressful, since gang structures tend to be loose, and a boy has no social group that he can enter and in which he can find some security after leaving school. He, therefore, often sleeps during the day until he meets his friends for the evening. (The Supervisor of Attendance was notified about the boy's status in the program, since the school was legally responsible for the boy until he turned 16 unless the parents, in writing, assumed such responsibility.) Requirements for admission into the program were that the youths had to be 15–17 years of age (so they could be employed legally) and not be psychotic, retarded, or brain damaged (such groups would require a different program).   In addition, youths had to have been on probation at least once and not have had therapy that lasted more than a month.

CASE.   Mark, age 15, was thrown out of high school in his sophomore year because of his overt, hostile, destructive behavior. He was not only preoccupied with violence but participated in any physical fights he heard about. Although considered above average in intelligence, he did not work in school and was failing in all subjects. His provocative behavior in school included placing firecrackers in the ventilating system. Mark was reading at a fifth grade level. He was in trouble with the police, having been put on informal probation for drinking, and later on formal probation for car theft. The initial interview revealed that Mark's destructive impulses were so overwhelming that he could talk only about his desires to destroy everything and anything. Clearly understanding that Mark's primitive orientation was based on a fear of attack and that it was not possible initially to deal with Mark's psychological conflicts, the therapist attempted to redirect Mark's hostile behavior into more constructive channels.

---

2. *Initial contact was made by offering youths an opportunity for looking for a job.* Each youth was offered the possiblity of looking for a job. No jobs were pre-selected. The jobs were related to the youth's needs, problems, and interests. The purpose of the job was to establish an arena around which therapeutic intervention and remedial education could occur.[2] All job opportunities were worked out with the youths, who went along with the therapist to explore job possiblities. At no point was the employer to act as therapist. If the youth was not performing adequately on the job, he could be fired. The only arrangement with employers was that the therapist be notified if the boy's performance was poor or if termination was imminent, so that the experience could be used therapeutically.

CASE. As occurred in each initial interview, the focus was on jobs that not only were available if the boys wanted them, but that also were in some way related to the youths' dynamics. For example, only after much discussion did the therapist realize that Mark might be interested in working with a construction company that did house-wrecking. Since this job was not one of the jobs known to the therapist, he and Mark combed through newspaper advertisements and visisted a firm where Mark was immediately employed as a helper in demolishing houses – in this way, we hoped, directing his destructive impulses into somewhat more constructive channels.

CASE. Much work went into preparing Jerry, age 17, for his first job. He finally was hired at a gasoline station. At work, many problems arose that nearly cost Jerry his job. Finally, when he was accused of stealing desk pads from the office, he became angry, fought with the boss, and was fired. Together Jerry and his therapist explored the possible reasons for this occurrence in an effort to gain some insight from his performance at work.

3. *Outreach.* Youths were seen in the community either at their homes, on street corners, in restaurants, in automobiles, or at their place of employment. Rarely were they seen in an office setting. If an office setting was used, it was emphasized that the therapist was not affiliated with any known social institutional settings, such as courts, clinics, or schools. The youths, all of whom were on probation, voluntarily agreed to the program: Participation was not one of the conditions of their probation.

CASE. George, age 15, had been hired for a job but he needed a number of state and county documents to get his Social Security card and work permit. Transportation was not good, and George had no automobile license or money to purchase a car. He also had no friends. It would have taken many hours to get to the various governmental offices by public transportation and wait in line. This would have further discouraged him and probably would have led to his giving up any attempt to follow through. The therapist drove George to these various places, and within a half-day the documents were obtained and George was ready to start on the job. Meanwhile, while driving the youth, the therapist noticed the boy's discomfort. Discussion led to concerns about being taken advantage of, which then led to talking about homosexual fears that had been aroused when the boy was in jail overnight.

CASE. Jerry's academic deficiencies emerged clearly one day at a restaurant. Jerry always ordered the same thing when he and the therapist went out to eat. When the therapist asked about this and confronted him with a menu to read, Jerry's eyes filled with tears as he admitted that it was not possible for him to do so. The next day's tutorial work contained a period of time devoted to the reading of menus, thereafter a regularly pursued activity.

4. *Flexibility of hours and contact.* The therapist was available to the youths any time of the day or night and for extended periods of time if necessary. Each youth had the therapist's home telephone number. Unlike extremely dependent youths who might misuse such an opportunity, when these resistant youths chose to contact the therapist, it was clearly a sign of reaching out and of increasing trust.[3] As might be expected, the youths began by testing the limits. The first call to the therapist usually came between midnight and 4:00 AM. The therapist showed the boy that he had meant what he'd said and was willing to talk over the telephone, but made it clear that there must be a legitimate reason for such a call and that he would not always respond favorably to the specific demands ("come and save me") made upon him. Once this testing took place, the boy rarely called at such an hour except in an actual emergency. There were few time limits: Sometimes contacts extended for many hours; at other times for a very short period of time.

CASE. Jim, age 16, called at 3:00 AM from a pay telephone to say he was in difficulty with the police and wondered if the therapist could help. The therapist called him back and discussed the situation for over an hour and the available alternatives for handling it. He told him he would see him in the morning. When they met in the morning, the situation had worked out satisfactorily.

---

5. *Stress on mobility, action, and real-life issues.* Field trips to explore job opportunites constituted an initial phase. There was practice at filling out application forms, role play, practice on first interviews with employers, and visits to various clinics or agencies. The therapist accompanied the youth to the first job interview or to court. While the therapist was involved in these activities, there was constant discussion with the youths about the meaning of what was going on. The therapist entered all aspects of the youths' lives and was able to see what the youths were talking about, what was occurring, and how he could be of help in real-life situations.

CASE. Jerry said he was interested in becoming an auto mechanic. The therapist inquired into his notion of this job — what the nature of the work was, the training necessary, the pay, and future opportunities. Jerry did not know the answers to the questions so he and the therapist found them together. They took several trips to automotive and auto body shops and then discussed thier first-hand observations of this occupation. Much work had gone into preparing Jerry for the day he would have his first job appointment. Practice at filling out forms and meeting a potential boss had been extensive, with the therapist playing various employer roles. Two months were spent practicing driving the therapist's car and studying the driver's manual so that Jerry could get the needed driver's license.

---

6. *Intensive individualized learning.* As an integral part of the program, a detailed plan for improving academic skills was evolved for each of the youths, often tied in with their current employment. (As a requirement for being in the program, the young people had to have had severe learning difficulties. The average reading grade level was third grade, despite the youths being in high school.) No attempt was made to have a boy return to high school unless he chose to. Instead, such alternatives as night school, on-the-job training, and/or correspondence courses were arranged specifically as they related to performance on the job. The skill programs were oriented to each youth's specific interests. For example, a reading program was developed from the driver's manual when one youth was highly motivated to get a driver's license. A second reading plan arose from a need to read menus in restaurants.

CASE. Jerry's performance on his first job had exposed his academic deficiencies, a source of great embarrassment to him. Around the sixth month of treatment, a tailored remedial program was developed. At first it was solely job-oriented — reading mechanics manuals, using fraction concepts in considering the use of wrenches, and trouble-shooting on the therapist's car. Soon the activities became more general, although always concrete in nature.

---

7. *All the parts of the program (job placement, remedial education, and psychotherapy) were administered by one person.* It was our belief that working with the youths demanded total commitment and that dividing the areas of difficulty by departments with specialized personnel having different roles would be artificial and counter-productive. The youths had a long history of playing one person against another and could easily precipitate intense rivalries between staff members. Coordination of various elements of a program such as this one is extremely difficult if the parts are administered separately. There were also theoretical reasons for the choice of one person. Most of the youths were hypothesized to have had disturbances in an early "predifferentiated" level of personality development. They truly did not understand the different roles and specialties that so many mental health professionals take for granted. They need the early experience of working on many levels with one individual in which one is able to work out a variety of feelings aimed at one person, rather than splitting the world into the "good" and the "bad" in the ways they have done in the past.

There was no specific order to the elements of the program. All the parts of the program depended on what was needed at a given time as the therapist was able to change roles from therapist, to teacher, to job counselor, to parent, or to advocate.

CASE. The therapist had spent many weeks preparing Jack, age 17, for his written driver's test. Jack took the test and failed by one question. He was very upset and felt that one of the questions he had missed was unfair. Eager to give up completely, he started to leave the room. But the presence of the therapist, who had accompanied him to the test, led to a discussion of what could be done. The therapist also had some doubts about the question. They agreed to discuss it with those in charge of the agency and appeal the decision. The authorities accepted the explanation, and Jack was permitted to take the road test, which he passed easily. Having a driver's license permitted him to get a job as a driver, a major step in helping him.

8. *Stress was placed on coping, not pathology.* Although the therapist recognized the way early needs were affecting current performance, the focus was on dealing with specific reality situations and the development of particular skills to deal with such situations. Such a stress, however, was not necessarily on a conscious, congitive level but was frequently one that took account of both cognitive and affective elements in mastering situations.

CASE. John, age 17, was working in an auto body shop. He was very fearful of learning how to use a blow torch, yet tried to deny these fears lest he be considered weak. The therapist explored John's fears of the gases mixing and blowing him up. He and John talked about the different safety measures used and how one is able to regulate and master a potentially dangerous tool.

9. *All aspects of the program were organized and carried out according to therapeutic principles.* Each activity was evaluated in terms of the effect it had on the relationship and its therapeutic significance. Parents were not seen.[4] Since the youths were well aware of reality and the risks of antisocial activities, the therapist made no effort to intervene with courts or police, or reduce or change the legal consequences of actions. However, he was available to discuss what had happened, to be supportive, and to think about alternatives. (If the youths were psychotic or did not understand reality, one might consider being more protective in regard to correctional agencies.) There were indeed times when the therapist was aware that the youths had to experience failure in order to be able to be motivated to change.

CASE. The therapist first reached Jerry by telephone and told him that individual help in finding work was available to boys who left school early. Jerry's distortions and denials, such as his insistence that he left school because "the work wasn't hard enough," were directly examined. The therapist was constantly on the side of reality, and Jerry began to realize that contradictions in his statements would be noted and pointed out. Finally a job possiblity was selected and Jerry went for an interview. This was not for a job as a mechanic — a grossly unrealistic expectation for Jerry at this time — but for a job as a general helper at pay far below his earlier expectation of $2.50 an hour. Jerry was fired from his first job. He was able to express his rage and concomitant shame over what had happened on the job. His attempts to project the blame on everyone but himself were not allowed to pass unchallenged. Soon it became apparent that the core of the problem lay in Jerry's intense hatred of the boss and his attraction to the boss's secretary, a recapitulation of his feelings toward his father and his mother. This was a pattern observed in many of Jerry's other relationships. The therapist worked with him in considering his home life and the problems he had with both parents and in relating to people. Parallels were gradually drawn between some aspects of his past experience and behavior and his present mode of response. Only after two more job attempts had the boy achieved enough stablility to maintain his position and gained some valuable insights into the meaning behind some of his actions.

10. *The focus of the intervention was on developing initiative and independence.* Dependence was not encouraged. A major focus was on the adolescent's taking responsibility for actions and stressing the youth's capability in dealing with situations.

CASE. In an auto salvage job, Mark did very well. He enjoyed going to scenes of death and destruction in order to obtain the wrecked cars. As his performance improved on the job, Mark was given more responsibility. This required taking phone calls, reading auto sections of books, and writing orders. It was at this point that remedial education became important, and the therapist and Mark worked on spelling and reading. Because of Mark's high intelligence, he was able to learn rapidly. Following his job in salvage work, at the eighth month of treatment, Mark became interested in auto body mechanic work. This meant further involvement in terminology, catalogs of body parts, and other academic-like pursuits. The therapist and Mark visited auto body shops to find out the necessary requirements for a body mechanic job.

STAGES OF TREATMENT

As with any psychotherapeutic intervention, one can identify certain states in the process of comprehensive vocationally-oriented psychotherapy. The therapy in the initial program lasted ten months. (The youths were aware of termination after that period of time.) A period of ten months, however, was chosen arbitrarily (although it was found to be adequate for change to take place in this particular group). There is no need to stick to the ten-month time frame. For example, youths from training schools or from urban settings, where there is more severe personal and social pathology, or where possible incarceration is considered, may need more extensive time.

The Initial Phase

In dealing with antisocial, character-disordered youths, the contact is often called "the biggest hurdle," for such patients are intensely resistant to any relationship that implies needing help. One of the important initial goals is to deal with this distress so that the youth may at least be willing to take a risk of making contact to discuss the possibilities of getting assistance in any area. The use of jobs as an entree to such a discussion was found to be extremely useful. Such youths are eager (as are many adolescents) to make money which can be spent to purchase things they greatly value ("money is power," as someone has said). The jobs were not jobs designed for the program or artificial situations such as being paid to talk into tape recorders. They were meaningful, real-life jobs in the community. With minimal skills and severe personality difficulties, the youths' chances of finding meaningful jobs without help, however, were slight, thus narrowing options and often leading to a life of daytime sleeping and antisocial activity at night. In addition, the first interview often took place on a street corner, in a car, or in a coffee shop.

It is very characteristic of these youths, who use primitive defenses, to spend the initial interview hour literally spewing forth a great deal of vivid sado-masochistic material, partially to impress the therapist and partially to hide their own intense fears and anxieties. We found that permitting such uncontrolled detailed "spilling" was not helpful, and that the youths, after having done so, would not return for a second session. The first interview, therefore, was spent getting acquainted with some of the realities of job-finding and job interest, with personal issues being tied specifically to job activities. This task orientation and psychological distance were found to be extremely helpful as plans were made to continue exploring the youths' vocational interests, planning for field trips, etc. The anxiety the youths had in their first interview was obvious when they appeared for the initial session with friends or brought along knives or other weapons.

During the initial interview, the therapist made clear that he was available to discuss any issues at any time. The significance of this type of initial interview was highlighted by the fact that the youths, within the first few months, commented very favorably about the way they had been approached and the meaning and significance of the job as a way of getting them involved.

CASE. Ray, a 15-year-old boy, was expelled from school in his sophomore year. He was described as looking like a "huge bull," and was belligerent, defiant, and physically aggressive to peers and teachers. Known at school and in the community as a "terror and brute," he had had many contacts with the police and was on probation. After obtaining Ray's name, the therapist called twice but met with no success. He finally reached Ray around 5:15 PM, when the boy was eating supper and didn't seem to appreciate being interrupted. The therapist apologized to him and indicated that he had attempted to reach him before, but that when he had had no luck, he had "sat down and figured out that supper time would probably be best." Ray grunted a glib "Yeh." The therapist introduced himself and said that he had gotten his name from Mr. ____ (Supervisor of Attendance – name intentionally mispronounced) as a young man who had recently left school (actually, Ray had been expelled that very morning). The silence from Ray's end was pronounced. Continuing, the therapist indicated that he had worked with young people who had left school early, helping them find jobs or with "anything else they felt they wanted – no strings attached." Ray responded to this by saying that he was anxious to find work and had been looking. (At this point the coin dropped, and the operator asked for another dime.)

The therapist wondered if Ray would be willing to get together to discuss this a little further, and at that time he might decide if it sounded as though his help was something he could use. Ray agreed to do this with slight hesitation, asking where and when. He was told that the therapist had no real office anywhere that could be called his own but that they could probably find room in the old brick building on ____ Street, which he guessed "used to be a school." If not, his car would have to suffice. As for when, this was to be at Ray's convenience, although some possibilities could be suggested. They agreed on a date and time. Ray arrived at the scheduled time with three friends but was seen alone. The therapist opened the initial interview by reiterating part of the phone conversation for clarification, saying that he realized that this was short notice, but maybe Ray could use help (purposely kept vague). Ray responded by saying that all he was interested in was getting a job; the therapist said he could assist in this but that certain information might make him better able to help Ray find a job. Continuing, the therapist made clear that anything he and Ray discussed was strictly between them. Ray just nodded. He was asked to talk about his present situation. There was a short pause, and then Ray began by indicating that he had been thrown out of school for "f____g around," and that his "old lady and ____" (Supervisor of Attendance) had felt that this was best. The therapist wondered what he thought of it. Ray said that he was glad to be out, and he would have continued getting in trouble until it happened anyway.

The therapist wondered if he could tell more about the kind of trouble he had been in. (Ray lit a cigarette, throwing the match on the floor, although an ashtray was right in front of him on the table.) At this point Ray asked, "Who the hell do you work for?" The answer was given immediately: "I was hired by the city to help young people who leave school early." There was a pause. Ray made no comment. The therapist spoke again and repeated his earlier question. Ray responded and discussed his school life. He was an academic failure and kept busy with acts of truancy and disobedience. He woul "jig" (leave) school on the average of twice a week — go with the boys and "dip our dobbers" (solicit a prostitute) or "raise a little hell" or just "sit down at the park and f____ around." He had a reputation for giving the teachers a difficult time — swearing in class, throwing erasers, and so forth. Ray sneered at authority, and relentlessly attacked established school rules. Ray went on to say that he and his friends didn't take anything from anyone — for example, "If you gave me any s____ or took a swing at me, I'd get you no matter how many guys you had around." The therapist told Ray he realized this was a difficult thing to face and could understand his anger. He indicated that he had no intention of taking a swing at Ray and hoped Ray wouldn't find it necessary to come after him. Ray grunted.

Continuing, the therapist suggested that there seemed to be some mix-up in what had been said. Since the therapist could be gotten, even if surrounded by a group of people, wasn't Ray afraid the same thing could happen to him regardless of gang membership? Ray seemed flustered. He did not respond but reached into his pocket and withdrew a small switchblade knife, which he opened, asking if the therapist had even seen one. The therapist indicated that he had seen several and wondered if Ray had ever used his knife. Ray showed a small scar on the back of his hand and told a long tale. After listening awhile, the therapist changed the subject, bringing the focus back to the main purpose. "Now, Ray, about getting a job — what kinds of things are you interested in?" Still somewhat taken aback, Ray lit another cigarette. He seemed considerably more at ease. He indicated that he was fond of auto mechanics or auto body repair. The therapist wondered how he had gotten interested in this. He said that his father owned a gas station and he occasionally worked there. At this time Ray gave some sketchy information about his family. The therapist suggested that since Ray liked to learn by seeing, maybe it would help him decide about a job if they made a few field trips to body shops and then went for a position. Once Ray was on the job, the therapist would continue to help him any way he felt he wanted such help. Ray was asked if he felt that this would be something he would be willing to give a try. Ray thought for a few moments and said, "Sure, what can I lose?" They agreed that the therapist would call for him in his car (a 1955 Chevrolet) at the prearranged time. Ray was given the therapist's home phone number, indicating that he could call any time to change an appointment or for any other reason Ray felt important. Ray put his last cigarette out in the ashtray instead of stepping on it as he had the others. Both left the office together. Ray said he would see the therapist and silently shuffled off with his companions.

The Middle Phase

The middle phase of comprehensive vocationally-oriented psychotherapy focused more on job performance and the need for remedial education and therapeutic insights to improve performance on the job. One of the important early therapeutic tasks was to gain the youths' confidence in establishing realistic vocational expectations. Youths frequently wanted high-level jobs without having had the training or background. Although advancement was never seen as impossible, efforts were made to work with the youths toward developing a plan that would permit movement from low-level to high-level jobs. (One boy began by pumping gas. At the end of ten years he owned a body shop employing 15 people.) Presence at the first job interview permitted the therapist to see how the youth presented himself and to deal with any problems that arose if the youth was not hired (or the fears that sometimes arose when he *was* hired). The youth's experience on the first job was crucial. It was made clear that the relationship with the therapist was not contingent on success or failure at work.

Once the youth was working full-time, focus was able to shift to performance in and around the job. It was at this point that remedial education became important. Each remedial program was individualized, since the work experience served to confront the boy with his academic inadequacies. Sometimes jobs were lost as youths were unable to handle academic demands. At other times a boy was fired because he could not deal with the experiences of frustration or humiliation that sometimes occurred on the job. However, by using various requirements from the job, one could develop special reading programs (for example, using labels of oil cans, menus from local restaurants, the driver's manual, or magazines about cars).

As mentioned, once on the job, the personal problems would often contribute to impaired performance. The therapeutic focus was then on attitudes toward work, toward the boss, and/or toward fellow employees. This would generalize to relationships with peers and others. The therapist went shopping with the boy, helped open a bank account, visited the youth in jail, or accompanied him to a dentist. The therapist particularly helped the youth handle intense feelings, such as anger, which arose on the job. The two would discuss how the youth would provoke anger from others.

In this particular diagnostic group, one could directly make interpretations and correct distortions without fear of ego collapse. In fact, directness, frankness, and openness often served to gain the respect of the young people, who often tried to shcok others with their "openness." As the boy continued to be successful on the job and as his skills improved, he turned almost exclusively to personal problems. Boys would frequently begin discussing their fantasies and intimate feelings about themselves and others (particularly homosexual and dependency fears, as well as strong depressive feelings). These would be handled within the context of the current work reality, which continued to be satisfying, and from which the boys derived concrete rewards, both financial and personal. In this way, it was possible to dose the feelings so as to give the youths better control over what they were revealing and how psychologically close they wanted to come.

CASE. Arthur, age 16, was permanently suspended from high school in his junior year. After much preparation, Arthur was placed in a job as a grease monkey in a gasoline station. However, he was not able to read adequately, a deficiency the therapist knew about but which Arthur tried to deny. When other workers discovered the deficiency, they demanded that Arthur read the labels of oil cans in the garage. Suddenly exposed, Arthur was enraged and started a fight that led to his being fired. The therapist used this opportunity to start Arthur on a remedial reading program. Beginning with oil can labels, the therapist went on to books on automobile work of all kinds. Later they branched out to other kinds of reading. Arthur was now motivated and eagerly learned to read. It took some three months before Arthur's skills and his emotional state, following the devastating experience, could be brought up to a level where he could be placed in another gasoline station. The second placement, accompanied by a great deal of support by the therapist, was highly successful. Three years following treatment Arthur was still working with automobiles, but, having continued in remedial education on his own, was a car salesman.

Termination

A major principle of comprehensive vocationally-oriented psychotherapy was not to encourage regression but rather to stress the emergent aspects of personality development. Although earlier developmental problems were not ignored but were dealt with within the context of realistic everyday experience, the emphasis was on the opportunity to develop skills and to master situations that left the youths with feelings of accomplishment and independence. In the ten-month treatment period of our program, we hoped to initiate autonomous decision-making that would bring about changes and be helpful to the youths in the future. Throughout the ten months, the youths could evolve new ways of handling situations with opportunities for these new approaches to be tested concretely, often in the job situation. Follow-up studies have indicated that indeed these youths did continue to improve even after therapeutic contact ceased. Our evaluation showed highly significant changes in legal areas, job performance, and personal adjustment. The youths were able to increase their social activity. For example, many successfully treated youths married within a few years. (Some of the marriages had difficulties, but the youths were better able to use available resources in the community, such as family agencies, to help with their marital problems.) Nevertheless, despite all efforts to minimize, reduce, or eliminate feelings of loss at the end of treatment, such anxieties inevitably occurred.

CASE. Three of the treated boys with long antisocial histories had come to see the therapist together. Each knew that the relationship was to be discontinued on a formal basis within a week. The therapist had left his hat, coat, and briefcase, familiar objects to the boys, in the third floor waiting area of the building where the meeting took place. As they were about to leave, the three youngsters looked at each other and suggested that they examine the "doc's bag of tricks." (This referred to the briefcase, which they realized contained job leads, personal records, a *Hot Rod* magazine, and other materials of significance to these youths.) The therapist indicated that they should look in the bag and discover for themselves once and for all that it contained no magic or secret potion and that the changes that had come about in their behavior were the result of their individual hard work. After the boys had examined and carefully returned the contents of the briefcase, one put on the therapist's hat, another his coat, and the remaining boy carried the case, as all three began to depart. The therapist did not interfere with their leaving but suggested they were in actuality taking something important of the relationship with them but that it was not merely a concrete object such as a hat or coat. He went on to indicate that they now had identities of their own that they could be proud of. Later, as the therapist left for home, he found the three items neatly placed where expected, one on each landing of the building's three floors.

HOW COMPREHENSIVE VOCATIONALLY-ORIENTED PSYCHOTHERAPY DIFFERS FROM OTHER THERAPEUTIC APPROACHES

Critical comments have been made about comprehensive vocationally-oriented psychotherapy. Some have stated that the program could not be called psychotherapy (the terms "sociotherapy" or "educational therapy" have been suggested). The term psychotherapy, they say, should be used only for office-based 50-minute interviews focused around specific psychological issues with limited involvement of the therapist. Unfortunately, such classic techniques do not work with chronic antisocial youths.[5] It is our belief that psychotherapy, to be successful with hard-reach groups, needs to be broadened rather than narrowed. The success of our program suggests the possible directions for such broadening.

Comprehensive vocationally-oriented psychotherapy has been compared to vocational counseling. Although the job focus is common to both, the two differ greatly. In comprehensive vocationally-oriented psychotherapy, jobs are used as an entree and arena for other intervention techniques, not as an end in themselves. The job is used as a way of enabling youths to accept help and serve as a meaningful opportunity to bring in needed remedial education and psychological understanding. All too often vocational counseling merely consists of narrow, job-focused discussions, culminating in a list of employers whom the client is to contact for job opportunities. With youths such as ours, approaches of this kind certainly would not have been successful. They needed not only preparation for the job but the presence of the therapist at the initial job interview.

They needed not only the job itself, but the skills to perform on the job. In addition, they needed continued contact and psychotherapeutic involvement.

More recently, there have been reports of a number of behavioral management programs aimed at assisting people to find employment. These programs tend to be narrow in scope. Although jobs may be found, long-term follow-ups of such programs are needed. It was our assumption that personality changes had to be brought about in our youths in therapy so that they could continue to improve after the program ended. Thus, in addition to job placement, they needed to learn academic as well as interpersonal skills. We believe that the youths also must must not feel that they can only have "dead end" jobs, something that inevitably leads to frustration and anger. The therapist worked with them toward moving on in the job market as their skills increased. Advancement is important, for it offers, among other things, increased hope and increased status, as well as greater financial rewards. (Indeed, although the youths had intellectual ability measured in the average range, the score was not an indication of their true ability. Many were extremely creative and talented and able to use their abilities effectively once some of their problems had been resolved.)

There have been a number of suggestions that the jobs themselves without the other services (remedial education and therapy) might have been the sole reason for the success. Indeed, a number of people have asked the question, "What was *the* therapeutic element?" We cannot say what specific individual elements were therapeutic since all the elements were woven together into one fabric. We cannot determine what elements can be eliminated until we know what is needed and how to do it. Some attempts have recently been made to eliminate the job element of the program but continue remedial education and psychotherapy. Other attempts have focused on jobs but have not included remedial education or psychotherapy. Neither of these approaches has been found to work as effectively as the total, comprehensive program. One has to recognize that with no job and with constant failure, certain adaptive personality changes occur (such as pervasive opposition to socialization) that need to be altered in order to produce better social and personal adaptation. By eliminating jobs, one may compromise the concrete focus and reality base which is most meaningful to the youths. By focusing only on jobs, one may miss opportunities to effect significant long-term change.

Comparisons have been made between comprehensive vocationally-oriented psychotherapy and "Big Brother" programs, especially with regard to how the therapist in vocationally-oriented psychotherapy is involved in the youth's daily life. The program outlined here required an understanding of psychotherapy (psychological interviewing skills are prerequisite) very different from the purposes of "Big Brother," which is a caring but an essentially social relationship. Although Big Brothers can offer a great deal as friendly adults, their major purpose is not basic personality change. Techniques such as catharsis, reflection, confrontation, and interpretation can only serve to impair the special relationships that Big Brothers develop and that often lead to their unique success.

The only programs that had been developed that seem similar to comprehensive vocationally-oriented psychotherapy are those of the Job Corps, Neighborhood Youth Corps, and some CETA programs (comprehensive vocationally-oriented psychotherapy antedated all these programs by many years). In the evaluation of Neighborhood Youth Corps and CETA programs that incorporate the three elements of remedial education, job training, and psychotherapy, positive changes have been reported.

PRACTICE AND TRAINING ISSUES

Training in comprehensive vocationally-oriented psychotherapy requires an understanding of both normal psychological development and psychopathology. But academic training or even basic training in psychotherapy doesn't ensure that one can do comprehensive vocationally-oriented psychotherapy with groups of youths that can profit from the technique. Although one may understand the principles of psychotherapy, working with character-disordered, antisocial youths requires special personal talents. In vocationally-oriented psychotherapy, it is necessary to avoid identification either with authority figures or with the acting out of young people. One has to be flexible and comfortable enough to assume various helping roles and to involve oneself deeply in a number of different ways. One needs to be willing to try out new techniques and take risks. One needs to be confident in undertaking activities such as outreach. Training in one discipline is not so essential as the opportunity and willingness to evolve creative ideas and feel comfortable in carrying them out. It is impossible to understand all aspects of the fields of remedial education, vocational job finding, and psychotherapy. Many of the specific details are learned concurrently by the therapist and the youth. (Consultation is sought from experts in specialized fields, when needed.) The authors have found a number of talented people in the poverty programs of the 1960s and in some of the alternative youth programs (hotlines, runaway houses, free clinics, drop-in centers) who have been functioning in ways similar to comprehensive vocationally-oriented psychotherapists and who with special training could easily become expert in the area. Indeed, practice in these community and alternative settings may serve as a proving ground for undertaking such therapy.

Most important is the ability to invest deeply in a few people. One cannot, for example, work with more than 10 youths at a time. Because of the intense involvement of time, varying the contacts with the youths is important. At the beginning, one may spend a great amount of time, then gradually less, as the youth is able to take more responsibility and begins to do well. Despite the limited number of youths that can be helped by one therapist, the program has been found to be cost-effective. The prognosis for these youths is very poor without help, with many of them becoming criminals in later life. Incarceration at the present time costs over $25,000 per year per person. Such incarcerated youths are an enormous expense to the community, contributing both to destruction of property and personal injury. Over 15 years, it is estimated that community savings are in the hundreds of thousands of dollars for each 10 youths seen.

EVALUATION

Although an important feature of the development of comprehensive vocationally-oriented psychotherapy was its evaluation, space prohibits detailing the results (which may be considered by going to the *Bibliography*). When compared with an untreated group of youths, those seen therapeutically showed significant changes in overt behavior, academic functioning, and personality structure, changes which have remained over a 15-year period. Detailed study of the changes show that many structural internal changes had taken place, consistent with many theories of psychotherapeutic change. Such areas as future time dimension, guilt, object relations, verbalization, and perception of people all showed marked improvements.

OTHER APPLICATIONS

As stated initially, comprehensive vocationally-oriented psychotherapy is not a specifically outlined set of techniques but a way of combining and adapting various techniques already known. It is one possible approach to getting psychotherapeutic services to groups that are in desperate need but that have rarely been helped in the past. Although comprehensive vocationally-oriented psychotherapy has been used with delinquent youths, it appears also to be relevant to helping non-delinquent, disadvantaged groups that present adjustment problems. It seems to also be relevant (with adaptations) to work with psychotics. A recent attempt to adopt many of the principles of comprehensive vocationally-oriented psychotherapy to help psychotic individuals who have returned to the community from a mental hopital has been found to be successful [Fisher, Nackman, and Vyas (1973)]. The program, using outreach, contacted patients in a state hospital on admission to the hospital to be able to assist them continuously through their hospital stay and upon discharge. The therapist followed the patient and family through the discharge process into the community and offered multiple services along many dimensions. The services were offered in a concrete manner with flexible time involvement. The stress of resocialization was set forth as a crisis for the whole family, a time that offered a unique opportunity for help. Therapists were available on a 24-hour basis to the family. Jobs were used as one area through which the family could mobilize a number of other services.

The use of comprehensive vocationally-oriented psychotherapy for still other groups also appears to be feasible. High costs of institutional care require that we think of a less expensive community-based program of mental health intervention. But what directions can such programs take? Comprehensive vocationally-oriented psychotherapy differs philosophically from some of the recent trends toward unidimensional, mechanistic, managerial, and simplistic approaches to behavioral change. It aims to integrate in a broadly creative, flexible fashion all aspects of services related to the personal and social functioning of the individual, using jobs as the focus for intervention. It offers directions for meeting the multi-service needs of populations that have been consuming vast resources in our society, helping the individuals become happy, constructive, and productive citizens.

NOTES

[1] Indeed, it appears that the contemporary school system perpetuates a group of failures. If one accepts the "normal curve" concept, those who succeed in the competitive struggle in school do so at the expense of those who fail. If there is failure and the youth is not a behavior problem, then he is able to remain in the school setting, often without learning a great deal or preparing himself for the future. On the other hand, if the yough acts up and becomes disruptive, he is referred for help and if such help is not successful, he is encouraged openly to leave school, by suspension, or subtly, by the school pursuing him when and if he drops out.

[2] A similarity has been noted between this approach at the vulnerable time of leaving school and that of drug pushers who frequently utilize the sensitive period to get youths involved in the use of drugs. The youths in the program were from suburbia, with a majority lower class. Most of the families were intact.

[3] We believe that the essence of diagnosis is to know to whom one gives one's home telephone number. Diagnostic skill is required to make sure to give the number to individuals who would least likely call. When they do call, often in the early morning, as in the case of youths, it is clearly a sign of the development of a meaningful relationship, though this relationship may still be based on magical expectations, such as trying to get the therapist to bail the young person out of jail or to help in a different situation. If one were to give one's telephone number to individuals who are borderline, alcoholic, or seriously dependent, contact could be constant and not therapeutic. In one adaptation of this approach, a recent program gave each youth the agency telephone number with an answering service being available 24 hours a day, 7 days a week. With adequate coverage, the youth is promised that an individual in the project will return the call within two hours.

[4] The advantage of being adolescent is that the youth can be seen alone. There are times, however, when there is intense family conflict in which the youth is an integral part and where one needs to work with the family. In the families of our youths, such conflict was not present. Parents cooperated, and in fact were eager that someone was interested in their children and could relieve them of some of the responsiblity. Most of the families were lower class families struggling economically to survive. The parents were grateful that they no longer had to take time off from their jobs to be called to school or to court since someone was active in outreach. They therefore felt less helpless with regard to social institutions whose work they frequently could not understand. The independence of the youths from their families can be seen by the fact that many of them left home shortly after they had gained some financial independence.

[5]Even a classic psychoanalyst such as August Aichorn was aware of the need to become involved differently with antisocial youth, even suggesting the importance of work when he described in a case (1935), "If a change could be brought about in his relationship to his mother and sisters and if he could find suitable work, it seemed that a greater improvement would result. Mother was easily dissuaded from her plan to force the boy out of the house to seek work as a laborer. I was able to arrange to give him credit for his first year of apprenticeship and go on with learning carpentry. He began work two weeks after our first meeting and did well. He gave no indication of laziness."

REFERENCES

Aichorn, A. *Wayward Youth.* New York: Viking (1953).

Fisher, T., Nackman, N. S., and Vyas, A. Aftercare services in a family agency. *Social Casework* 54:131-146 (March 1973).

Redl, F. and Wineman, D. *Children Who Hate: The Disorganization and Breakdown of Behavioral Controls.* Glencoe, IL: The Free Press (1951).

Redl, F. and Wineman, D. *Controls from Within: Techniques for the Treatment of the Aggressive Child.* Glencoe, IL: The Free Press (1952).

BIBLIOGRAPHY

Massimo, J. L. Alienated youth and socialization: New opportunities for schools. *In:* Landy, E. and Kroll, L. (Eds.). *Guidance in American Education — II: Current Issues and Suggested Action.* Cambridge, MA: Harvard University Press (1965), pp. 199-212.

Massimo, J. L. and Shore, M. F. The effectiveness of a vocationally oriented psychotherapy program for adolescent delinquent boys. *American Journal of Orthopsychiatry* 33:634-643 (1963). Reprinted in Riessman, Cohen, and Pearl (Eds.). *Mental Health of the Poor.* Glencoe, IL: The Free Press (1965).

Massimo, J. L. and Shore, M. F. Job focused treatment for anti-social youth. *Children* 11:143-147 (1964).

Massimo, J. L. and Shore, M. F. Comprehensive vocationally oriented psychotherapy: A new treatment technique for lower class adolescent delinquent youth. *Psychiatry* 30:229-236 (August 1967).

Ricks, D., Umbarger, C., and Mack, R. A measure of increased temporal perspective in successfully treated adolescent delinquent boys. *Journal of Abnormal and Social Psychology* 69:685-689 (1964).

Shore, M. F. Jobs and youth: Educational, vocational, and mental health aspects. *Journal of Youth and Adolescence* 1(4):315-323 (1972). Reprinted in G. Williams and S. Gordon (Eds.). *Clinical Child Psychology.* New York: Behavioral Publications (1972).

Shore, M. F. A model of services for youth: Making community mental health programs marketable. *In:* Claiborne, W. and Evans, D. (Eds.). *Mental Health Issues and the Urban Poor.* New York: Pergamon (1974), pp. 129-136.

Shore, M. F. Evaluation of a community-based clinical program for antisocial youth. *Evaluation* 4:104-108 (1977).

Shore, M. F. What adolescent delinquents taught me about psychotherapy research. *In:* McMillan, M. F. and Henao, S. (Eds.). *Child Psychiatry: Treatment and Research.* New York: Brunner/Mazel (1977), pp. 116-129.

Shore, M. F. Some psychoanalytic perspectives on adolescent delinquency: Implications for practice. *In:* Greenspan, S. and Pollock, G. (Eds.). *Psychoanalytic Contributions to the*

Understanding of Human Development. Washington, DC: U.S. Government Printing Office (in press).

Shore, M. F., Massimo, J. L., and Mack, R. The relationship between levels of guilt in thematic stories and unsocialized behavior. *Journal of Projective Techniques and Personality Assessment* 28:346-349 (1964).

Shore, M. F., Massimo, J. L., and Ricks, D. F. A factor analytic study of psychotherapeutic change in delinquent boys. *Journal of Clinical Psychology* 21:208-212 (1965).

Shore, M. F., Massimo, J. L., and Mack, R. Changes in the perception of interpersonal relations in successfully treated adolescent delinquent boys. *Journal of Consulting Psychology* 29:213-217 (June 1965).

Shore, M. F. and Massimo, J. L. Employment as a therapeutic tool with adolescent delinquent boys. *Rehabilitation Counseling Bulletin* 9:1-5 (1965).

Shore, M. F. and Mannino, F. V. The school dropout situation: An opportunity for constructive intervention. *Federal Probation* 29:41-44 (1965).

Shore, M. F., Massimo, J. L., Kisielewski, J., and Moran, J. K. Object relations changes resulting from successful psychotherapy with adolescent delinquents and their relationship to academic performance. *Journal of the American Academy of Child Psychiatry* 5:93-104 (January 1966).

Shore, M. F. and Massimo, J. L. The mobilization of community resources in the outpatient treatment of delinquent adolescent boys. *Community Mental Health Journal* 2:329-332 (Winter 1966).

Shore, M. F. and Massimo, J. L. Comprehensive vocationally oriented psychotherapy for adolescent delinquent boys: A follow-up study. *American Journal of Orthopsychiatry* 36:609-616 (July 1966). Reprinted as a Monograph of the Harvard Research and Development Center on Educational Differences (Reprint #11).

Shore, M. F. and Massimo, J. L. Verbalization, stimulus relevance, and personality change. *Journal of Consulting Psychology* 31:423-424 (July 1967).

Shore, M. F., Massimo, J. L., and Moran, J. K. Some cognitive dimensions of interpersonal behavior in adolescent delinquent boys. *Journal of Research in Crime and Delinquency* 4:243-248 (July 1967).

Shore, M. F. and Massimo, J. L. The chronic delinquent during adolescence: A new opportunity for intervention. *In:* Caplan, G. and Lebovici, S. (Eds.). *Adolescents: A Psychosocial Approach.* New York: Basic Books (1968), pp. 335-343.

Shore, M. F., Massimo, J. L., Moran, J. K., and Malasky, C. Object relations changes and psychotherapeutic intervention: A follow-up study. *Journal of the American Academy of Child Psychiatry* 7:59-68 (January 1968).

Shore, M. F., Massimo, J. L., Mack, R., and Malasky, C. Studies of psychotherapeutic change in adolescent delinquent boys: The role of guilt. *Psychotherapy* 5:85-89 (June 1968).

Shore, M. F. and Massimo, J. L. An innovative program for the treatment of adolescent delinquent boys within a suburban community. *In:* Shore, M. F. and Mannino, F. V. (Eds.). *Mental Health and the Community: Problems, Programs and Strategies.* New York: Behavioral Publications (1968) pp. 163-179.

Shore, M. F. and Massimo, J. L. The alienated adolescent: A challenge to the mental health professional. *Adolescence* 4(13):19-34 (1969).

Shore, M. F. and Massimo, J. L. Five years later: A follow-up study of comprehensive vocationally oriented psychotherapy. *American Journal of Orthopsychiatry* 39(5):769-774.

Shore, M. F. and Massimo, J. L. An innovative apporach to the treatment of adolescent delinquent boys. *In:* Golann, S. and Eisdorfer, C. (Eds.). *Handbook of Community Psychology and Mental Health.* New York: Appleton Century-Crofts (1972) pp. 659-668.

Shore, M. F. and Massimo, J. L. After ten years: A follow-up study of comprehensive voca-
tionally oriented psychotherapy. *American Journal of Orthopsychiatry* **43**(1):128–132
(January 1973).   Reprinted in H. Strupp *et al.* (Eds.). *Psychotherapy and Behavior
Change, 1973.* Chicago: Aldine (1974), pp. 174–181.

Shore, M. F. and Massimo, J. L. Fifteen years after treatment: A follow-up study of comprehensive vocationally oriented psychotherapy. *American Journal of Orthopsychiatry*
49(2):240–246 (April 1979).

Dance-movement therapy is a form of psychotherapy that uses the body and its movement patterns to achieve therapeutic goals. The roots of dance-movement therapy extend to ancient times, when dance was used by primitive societies as communication. Through the dance, societal values and norms were passed down from generation to generation, thus reinforcing survival mechanisms of the culture. Moving together to a common rhythm during ritual dance fostered the development of unity and harmony. For the individual, dance can stimulate and give form to feelings, conflicts, and fantasies. It allows for a symbolic expression of one's inner life and a growing consciousness of self. It was the recognition of these psychological and sociological elements natrually inherent in dance that led to the eventual use of them in dance-movement therapy.

Based on the assumption that the body and mind are interrelated, dance-movement therapy attempts to effect changes in feelings, cognition, and behavior. Clients are helped to develop self-awareness, work through emotional blocks, gain a clearer perception of themselves and others, and effect behavioral changes.

The therapeutic process involves developing one's emotional content into fuller expression on a body level and facilitating an integration of feelings, thoughts, and behaviors.

Other mental health professionals can utilize some of the tools of the profession in their work. These include developing themes and issues into body action, transforming the movement into expressive action, and the use of exaggeration and kinesthetic empathy. Movement activities can help stimulate social interaction, maintain the physical level of activity or range of movement, and provide relaxation. All require that the mental health professional develop a sensitivity to nonverbal communication, as a vehicle of personal expression, and a willingness to go beyond the safely and security of just using words in the therapeutic work.

18

Dance-movement Therapy

Arlynne Stark, M. A.

In dance-movement therapy, by working with muscular patterns and focusing on the interrelationship between psychological and physiological processes, clients are helped to experience, identify, and express feelings and conflicts. From this kinesthetic level, individuals and groups are led to further discovery of emotional material through symbolic representations, images, memories, and personal meanings of their life experiences. Through movement interaction, the dance-movement therapist helps clients to develop their self-awareness, work through emotional blocks, explore alternative modes of behavior, gain a clearer perception of themselves and others, and effect behavioral changes that will lead to healthier functioning.

Dance-movement therapists are employed in clinical work, research, and education. Dance-movement therapy clinicians work with emotionally disturbed children, adolescents, and adults in hospitals, clinics, and special schools. Other clients may include retarded individuals, geriatric patients, and persons with learning disabilities. Employment opportunities for the trained professional also include the teaching and training of dance-movement therapists and consulting work in educational institutions.

HISTORICAL DEVELOPMENT OF THE PROFESSION

The roots of dance-movement therapy go back to ancient civilizations, where dance was an important part of life. People probably began to dance and use bodily movement as communication long before language was developed. Dance was used to express and reinforce the most important aspects of the culture. In their cross-cultural observations of dance in societies, Bartenieff, Pauley, and Lomax[4] found that everday movements utilized by the members of a society as they do their daily work are incorporated into the dance style and dance forms of that culture. For example, the wide and firm stance of the Eskimo, with quick darting arm movements, necessary for ice-fishing and spearing, are incorporated into their dance. Societal values and norms are passed down from generation to generation through the dance, thus reinforcing a survival mechanism of the culture Rites of passage; preparations for, and celebrations of, wars; and hopes for a bountiful harvest are other examples of the use of dance in cultures. In many societies, dance continues to serve these important functions. It is the expressive and communicative aspect of dance, the direct sharing of emotions on a pre-verbal and physical level, while moving together to a common rhythm, prevalent in primitive societies, that have been influences towards the development of dance-movement therapy. The feelings of unity and harmony that emerge in group dance rituals provide for empathetic understanding between people.

For the individual, dance may safely allow all that can and cannot be put into words; it can both stimulate and give form to the expression of deeply buried fantasies, thus allowing symbolic expression of one's potentials and conflicts. Because dance makes use of the natural joy, energy, and rhythm that are available to all, it fosters a consciousness of self. Movement itself changes sensations. These ever-changing physical sensations are often sharpened in dance. They provide the basis from which feelings emerge and are expressed. That which has been at a pre-verbal and unconscious level often becomes crystalized into a direct feeling and personal experience. It was the recognition of such elements naturally inherent in dance that led to their eventual use in dance-movement therapy.

The revolutionary changes in dance during the first half of the 20th century have been instrumental in the developmental of dance-movement therapy. Pioneers such as Isadora Duncan and Mary Wigman believed that emotional and individual expression was of paramount importance for the dancer. Casting aside the strict and structured technique of ballet, they encouraged direct communication of the individual through dance. It was their experience and conviction that through the body we directly experience and respond to life. It is through dance that this communication with ourselves and the environment is formed. These innovative dancers believed that dance makes use of the totality of the person — body, mind, and spriit — as a vehicle for expression and communication.

The development of dance into a therapeutic modality is most often credited to Marian Chace, a former teacher and performer. From her teaching of dance to normal students she began to discover the psychological benefits that dance offered. Gradually she changed her focus from dance technique to expression of individual needs through movement.[9] She began to work with children and adolescents in special schools and clinics as well as in her own studio. Psychologists, psychiatrists, and other members of the health professions, impressed with her work, began sending her referrals. This aspect of her work was instrumental to her understanding the importance of the body's relationship to emotional difficulties. During this period she began to formulate many of her ideas, which were then carried over into her work with the emotionally disturbed. Dr. W. Overhosler, then superintendent of St. Elizabeth's Hospital in Washington, D.C., had heard about Ms. Chace's work and invited her to try out her methods with hospitalized psychiatric patients. Over the years, the success of her work with extremely regressed, nonverbal, and psychotic clients at St. Elizabeth's gained national recognition. Patients who had been considered hopeless were able to engage in group interaction and expression of feelings in the dance therapy sessions. Establishing a movement dialogue and supporting it with verbalizations that related to feelings, images, thoughts, and memories in the dance therapy sessions often provided the first step for the client toward his or her ability to make use of the more traditional verbal psychotherapies.

It is important to note that in the 1940s and 1950s there were similar developments in other parts of the country. Other modern dancers were beginning to explore the use of dance as a therapeutic agent in the treatment of emotional disturbances. Trudi Schoop and Mary Whitehouse on the West Coast, and Franziska Boas on the East Coast, are also given credit for stimulating the development of dance as therapy. Although each of these pioneers developed a different approach, all believed that the roots of their work were in dance. Through the work of each ran common threads. Each understood that psychological and physical processes are interrelated. Each shared a deep commitment to the use of dance in developing body-mind awareness: To foster integration in the body, thus leading to a feeling of wholeness and aliveness for the individual; to utilize movement and dance as a means of experiencing and expressing the full range of feelings; to share group and individual expressions of feelings through rhythmic body action; and to externalize and express emotional material (e.g., dreams, fantasies, memories) through symbolic action.[9]

THEORETICAL BASIS

Dance-movement therapy is therefore based on the assumption that the soma and the psyche are interrelated; changes in emotional feeling, cognition, and behavior effect changes in each of the other areas. The body and mind are seen as having equally important influences in integrative functioning. Dance-movement therapist Berger divides the body-mind relationship into four categories for study — muscular tension and relaxation, kinesthetics, body-image, and expressive movement.[6]

Awareness of feelings and the corresponding emotional expression involve muscular tonus in the individual. When a high degree of bodily tension exists, individuals are usually unaware of their feelings. In the process of trying to deal with stress, a person may defend against the fear of losing control by suppressing the recognition of feelings in the body. Allowing the tension to be built up and held in the body serves to protect the individual from directly experiencing and thus confronting the conflict. For example, the degree of tension in the shoulder and arms may be unconsciously increased just enough so that this part of the body is cut off from feeling; it becomes dissociated. With such a person, the dance-movement therapist may choose to have the client slowly begin to move the arms in a swinging motion to relax the muscles associated with the particular emotional state the patient is denying. By first working with the muscular patterns related to emotions, one can experience feelings through the musculature, sharpened, made conscious in movement, and then recognized or clarified cognitively. The connection that develops between physical action and inner feeling state results from muscular memory associated with the feeling. With another client the therapist may want to take the bodily experience into an action so that the emotion and the movement reinforce each other. Movement can then become a direct expression of inner feelings. For someone functioning at a more integrated level, the therapist may help the client focus on the specific part of the body to identify what is being done on a body level, perhaps unconsciously, that is creating a particular emotional experience. In such a situation, the therapist may assist the client in verbally exploring the associations, images, fantasies, or memories that come into consciousness in the process of connecting the movement response in the body and its emotional components.

Every thought, action, memory, fantasy, or image involves some innovative muscular tension. Individuals can be helped to discover how they change, alter, redirect, destroy, or control these subtle muscular sensations which affect the experience or expression of feelings. This process is similar to, and corresponds with, the ego defense mechanisms. Reich's work with character formation illustrates how the identical process is evidenced in both the physiological and psychological areas. He writes:

In the melancolic or depressed patients, speech and facial expression are stiff, as if every motion required the overcoming of a resistance. In a manic condition, on the other hand, the impulses seem to suddenly flood the whole personality. In the catatonic stupor, psychic and muscular rigidity are completely identical, just as a dissolution of the condition brings back psychic as well as muscular motility.[32] [p. 352]

In order to be aware of one's feelings, there must be some degree of body awareness. The kinesthetic process enables us to have a direct experience of our muscular activity. Changes in position and balance of the body, coordination of motor activities, and the planning of movement involve both the perception of external objects or events and our motor reaction. This kinesthetic sense, critical to carrying out everyday tasks, is also paramount in the formation of our own emotional awareness and responses. There seem to be two ways in which emotional awareness develops. One is by learning the correct label or word that corresponds to the emotional state. This learning has its beginnings in infancy and early childhood. One only needs to remember picking up a crying baby and asking, "Why are you so sad?" or saying, "You're hungry, aren't you?" to be aware of how this learning comes about. Our nonverbal behavior communicates. Others recognize our experience and provide us with the correct words to identify and later talk about our feelings.

The second way in which emotional awareness develops is based on our recognition and interpretation of the motor actions of others. Clynes' research[12] on how emotions are communicated indicates that each emotion has a distinct physiologic code and a characteristic brain pattern governed by the central nervous system and biologically coordinated, a process that is similar in all people. In addition, experiencing the same emotions and similar corresponding muscular reactions is also universal. Because of this, we are able to perceive and recognize emotional states in others. Our emotional responses to other people usually arise from our interpretations of the bodily actions and reactions of others experienced through our kinesthetic recognition. This kinesthetic empathy, which occurs mostly on an unnconscious level, contributes to the verbal and nonverbal communication between people.

Another concept that addresses the body-mind relationship is body image. In one of the earliest comprehensive studies of body-image research, Schilder[36] states that "The image of the body means the picture of our own body which we form in our mind, that is to say the way in which the body appears to ourselves" [p. 11]. He views the body image as being in a state of continual development or change. Movement evokes changes in body image. Articulation of body parts, recognition of bodily sensations such as breathing, or awareness of muscular activity, are just a few examples of how kinesthetic sensations can contribute to the recognition and development of body image. Mahler's work on emotional development or "psychological birth" lends support to the premise that there must be a recognition of the self as a separate physical entity before the individuation process can successfully occur.

The image we have of ourselves affects and is affected by all our perceptions, experiences, and actions. A man who perceives himself as weak and fragile will move differently from one who perceives himself to be strong. Likewise, if a child is treated as though he were stupid, his body image would incorporate his reactions to other people's impressions and to his own. Schilder writes:

The postural model of our own body is connected with the postural model of the bodies of others. There are connections between the postural models of fellow human beings. We experience the body images of others. Experience of our body image and experience of the bodies of others are closely inter- woven with each other. Just as our emotions and actions are inseparable from the body image, the emotions and actions of others are inseparable from their bodies.[36] [p. 16]

Specifically focusing on the connection between movement change and psy- chological change in dance therapy, Chace states, "Since motion influences body image, and a change in the psychic attitude, then if you can work a feeling of distortion of body image out in motion, then this will change your psychic attitude about yourself" [p. 228].[9]

With regard to the body-mind interrelationship, it is the fourth area, expres- sive movement, which most dance-movement therapists seem to stress in their work. Through the body, emotional expression is manifested. The position of the body, gesturing movements, and breathing patterns are a few examples of movement behavior that can be examined within the framework of expressive movement. It is the qualitative aspect of movement — how it occurs, rather than the static positioning — that reflects individual expression.

Allport and Vernon write:

. . . no single act can be designated exclusively as expressive. Every act seems to have its nonexpressive as well as its expressive aspects. It has its adaptive . . . character, and also its undividual character. In unlocking a door, for example, the task prescribes definite coordinated movements suited to the goal, but it allows a certain play for individual style in executing the prescribed movements. There are peculiarities in the steadiness, pressure, precision, or patience with which the task is executed. It is only these individual peculiari- ties that are properly called expressive.[1] [p. 21]

Expressive behavior is the motor manifestation of emotions, both interrelated and in a functional system. Clynes[12] sees expressive movement as an emotional state being expressed. His research on how emotions are exprienced and com- municated helps explain how dance-movement therapy affects feelings and their actions. If we produce an action or a gesture that corresponds to an emotion (e.g., angrily kicking away a stone), we begin to experience the corresponding visceral response generated. If this action is repeated a number of times, there is an increase in the intensity of the emotional experience. In order to encourage the experience and expression of emotions, the dance-movement therapist works with the movement patterns associated with the emotion. For example, to work with anger, the therapist may suggest curling the hands into a fist, clenching them tightly, and shaking them toward another person. Other instructions may include standing firmly in place and tensing the whole body. By encouraging the shaking of the fist, the movement is generating a more specific bodily experience of the emotional state. This provides a feedback and interactive loop between the expressive act and the emotional experience.

Emotions can be generated by a real situation (e.g., sadness when one loses a friend); by perceiving another's emotional state (e.g., contagiously experiencing another's fear); in an imagined fantasy situation (e.g., remembering or imagining being trapped in an elevator); or by perceiving a fantasy state in another (e.g., contagiously experiencing hurt or guilt as demonstrated by an actor).

The therapist's use of imagery, action, and emotion thus helps to crystallize and integrate the physiological and psychological.

GOALS

It is necessary for the dance-movement therapist to formulate therapeutic goals based on the developmental level of the individual or group. Some patients are unable to tolerate identification and direct expression of feelings. Still others are unable to make the cognitive connection of their movement behavior as a reflection of themselves.

It is important to keep in mind that what is a reasonable and appropriate goal for one person may be too complciated for another. A developmental model which uses a continuum of dysfunctional behavior to functional behavior seems to allow for a more holistic framework. The goals of dance-movement therapy can be divided into three areas — the body and its action, interpersonal relationships, and self-awareness.

The Body and its Action

The dance therapist works with the client in order to help foster a healthier body, one that is not constricted from holding onto tension, conflicts, and feelings. Goals include helping the client activate the body, cathartic release of tension and feelings, experiencing a sense of bodily integration and coordination, and constructing a realistic body image. These goals are accomplished by using already existing movement patterns of the individual, and encouraging an awareness of body sensations, developing a broader range of movement, exploring choices in movement, and encouraging communication and expression through body action. Movement associated with feared events or feelings is often used in sessions to enable the client to practice, or become more familiar with, and thus overcome what is feared. This process allows for a lessening of the fear when the actual feeling or event arises, since the body has already experienced it in symbolic form.

Interpersonal Relationships

Research indicates that dance-movement therapy helps to establish or reestablish interpersonal communication on a body level.

Condon's research[13] in synchrony of movement is based on the premise that there is a neurophysiologic organization of speech and body movement in human communication. Self-synchrony refers to movement in relation to one's own speech — a rhythmic unity of speech and body movement. Interactional synchrony is defined as the synchronous movement of the listener with the speech and movement of the speaker. Condon describes interactional synchrony as ". . . a basic, dance-like sharing of movement on the part of the interactants during communication" [p. 33] .[13] The heightened synchrony that occurs duing communication is enhanced when moving together.

Self-synchrony and intreactional synchrony can be seen in all persons except those with neurological impairments (e.g., Parkinson's disease, aphasia) and schizophrenia.

Dance-movement therapy can assist the development of this basic level of communication as it directly uses rhythm and kinesthetic patterns. A reaffirmation of self and self in relation to others naturally evolves.

Kendon[21] views the coordination of bodily movement with others as a necessary ingredient for achieving satisfactory social interactions. He suggests that in dance-movement therapy, individuals who have disturbances in social interactions or communications can relearn the necessary behavior (rhythmic coordination with others), which can then be carried over to other social settings. As a result of the dance-movement therapy, most clients experience a richer level of intimacy as they share feelings through body actions while moving to a common rhythm.

The dance-movement therapist may use speficic types of movement to encourage interaction. Reaching arms forward, toward another person, stretching sideways to touch the person next to you, or having the group members hold hands for balance as they lean back are just a few examples of how movement can facilitate and encourage the development of interaction.

The group dance therapy experience allows for an increased awareness of self through visual feedback that occurs while observing others move. Noticing feelings being expressed in the bodies of others may elicit a new recognition and awareness of one's own feelings. The dance therapy group is a microcosm of other social situations. As a result, clients can receive direct and visible feedback about themselves and learn to develop a broader range of behavioral options.

Self-Awareness

Intrinsic to dance-movement therapy practice is the belief that one must be aware of bodily experiences and their meanings (sensory and kinesthetic experiences and emotional states) for self-understanding. Gendlin[17] proposes two levels of experiencing that must be present if personal growth is to occur. The felt level of experiencing is a bodily experience or body-sense or the experience of experiencing one's experience. Gendlin states: "A body sense of a problem or situation is pre-verbal and pre-conceptive . . . it is not equivalent to any one verbal or conceptual pattern" [p. 88].[2] The next level of experiencing is the *symbolic level*. It is here that one is able to conceptualize and verbalize the felt experience and attach specific meaning to it. The *felt level* must be present before one can make adequate use of the *symbolic level*.

The most direct experience one can have with one's self is through one's body. The physical experience of one's muscular actions and kinesthetic sense provides an immediate way of knowing and experiencing one's self. Thus, self-awareness begins on a body level. Dance-movement therapist Kleinman feels that the first stage in therapy, the *exploration stage,* must address itself to awakening inner sensations and feelings. The patient must be assisted in learning to be receptive to the messages of the body and their expression in outward movement.

Kleinman writes:

He begins to recognize his body as an important aspect of himself. His experiences of inner motions and experimentation with outer motion stimulate and promote the identification with his body. The separation between body and mind becomes weaker as links of awareness integrate the whole of the person. His words become an expression of his body as he explores himself in motion. As his senses awaken and he begins to directly experience himself, he begins to form a bond with his body.[24] [p. 10]

When the importance of words is lessened, there is often a more direct observation of one's nonverbal behavior. In particular, for individuals with strong verbal defenses, movement allows for a more reliable expression of feelings than words; direct information and knowledge of the inner self can become realized as a result of the integrated connection between physical and mental processes. Movement naturally evokes memories, images, fantasies, and associations. Because bodily experience tends to draw out the psychological context, the body can be used to further explore and crystalize this material, thus enhancing self-awareness.

THE THERAPEUTIC PROCESS

Dance-movement therapy works at various levels within a movement framework, each dependent on treatment goals and the developmental level at which clients are functioning. Stark and Lohn[41] feel that there are two major ways in which dance-movement therapy affects change: (1) as a stimulus for body action, for differentiation and individuation of self and for the recognition and expression of feelings; and (2) to aid in clarifying and providing insight into the emotional symbolic content of the movement.

In order to achieve therapeutic change, a process similar to verbal psychotherapy is used. Using an interactive approach to the treatment of psychotic individuals, Chace describes her dance therapy sessions as follows.

The movement used in establishing initial contact with a patient may be qualitatively similar to those of the patient (not an exact mimicking, since this is often construed by the patient as mocking) or they may be expressive of an entirely different emotion with which the therapist has responded to the patient's gestures.[9] [p. 221]

The following example may serve as clarification.

On this particular day, patients in the dance therapy group appeared depressed and resistive. Most of them sat slumped down in their chairs with arms crossed over their chests, and either looking down at the floor or staring off into space. Noticing that most of the patients had their bodies set in a position of defiance, with jaws tense and arms rigidly folded, the therapist put her body in a similar position. She suggested to the group that they tighten their bodies and pull themselves closer, as if to shut out the world and not budge from that position. Directing them to curl up even further, she asked if anyone had an image or an association to what he or she might be closing off from. One woman replied, "My psychiatrist." Another person offered, "My problems." Suggesting that they close off and turn away from whatever was bothering them, the therapist directed the movement in their chairs so that group members began to turn away from one another. Noticing that one patient was twisting his body in a strong thrashing movement, she encouraged the others to try it. She then expanded upon the thrashing movement by suggesting that the shoulders and arms move in a similar manner. As the movement crystallized into a pushing of the body, she asked, "What do people want to push?" No one responded verbally. However, the movement became more forceful. Patients were directed to push with other parts of their bodies. Within a few moments, all were pushing and slashing the air. She requested that they make a forceful sound to accompany the movement. Grunts and groans emerged at first, followed by words ("Get away, stop, leave me alone"). Group members were asked to try out the different phrases and see if they could find one that seemed to fit their mood the most. As anger began to emerge more in the body, the quality of movement changed; it became limp. In order to assist them in direct experience and expression of anger, the therapist encouraged the group to press their hands against the hands of people on each side. More strength emerged as the patients tried to press as hard as they could. When they began to tire, the therapist structured the movement so that push changed into a gentle lean and support of one another. The group swayed from side to side, holding hands and leaning on one another.

Within a short period of time, the therapist had picked up the emotional content of the group, developed it into fuller expression on a body level, facilitated an integration of feelings, thoughts, and actions, and developed the material in a way that allowed for group interaction and activation of self. Once these angry and resistive feelings were given form through movement, the group was able to relate in a more meaningful way.

While differences in approaches do exist, the core of dance-movement therapy remains the same. Emotional material (feeling, themes, symbolizations, etc.) is developed by using the body representation to elicit and explore material. The flow of the session develops as the therapist facilitates one spontaneous expression and connects it to another. This linking of material is based on the on-going process that unfolds.

In the group described above, the members were rubbing their hands to get the circulation going when one of the members began to clap. Picking up on the movement, the group was encouraged to clap. This developed into an acknowledgment of one another as each spontaneously moved into the middle of the circle and took a bow. Shortly thereafter, one patient changed the claping into a slapping of her hands. The therapist commented on this and encouraged the others to try "Jenny's movement." As they tried out the new movement, the therapist asked, "Did you ever have your hand slapped?" One woman offered, "No, my hands were never slapped, but my father used to whip me with a belt." Other members began to relate incidents in which they had been punished or physically abused. As these tales of punishment unfolded, the movement died. Some people stayed extremely still. A woman began to cry and got up, asking if she could leave the group. The therapist said, "See if you can tell what you just did with your body to cut off the painful feelings and memories you began to experience."

With this approach, the therapist structures the movements in response to the patient's movements. Through kinesthetic empathy, an attempt is made to capture the feeling observed in the patient. By mirroring the expressive behavior, ther therapist encourages the paitent's awareness of self through visual feedback. The patient's movement behavior is then expanded upon and developed into a symbolic dance, reflective of conflicts, wishes, and dreams.

The therapist may initiate movement, introduce imagery or content. How the movement is transformed and structured is based on the evolving therapuetic process and the patient's needs.

Dance therapist Mary Whitehouse describes a different approach.[7] Instead of focusing on group interaction, she pursued the meaning of the movement for the individual through a process called Active Imagination. She used a Jungian frame of reference in which the client was led to discover the content of the unconscious, notice how it was manifested in physical form, and integrate this material for greater self-knowledge. Because her clients were normal and neurotic individuals and not hospitalized, there was no need for her to be an active participant and role model in the movement itself (as in the model Chace developed). However, she too functioned as a catalyst, guiding the therapeutic process through suggestions of movement possibilities, asking questions, making interpretations — all of this based on the observable and often subtle movement behavior. Whitehouse writes:

> In one particular session, a dancer wanted to work with an object in the studio — a box that was square, rigid and unyielding. No mater how she tried she got nowhere; no life would start. She spent the whole session trying to find a working relationship to that box. Complete frustration was followed by giving up. In discussing it afterwards, she said without thinking, "It's just as damn unyielding and rigid and ungiving as my relationship to R . . ." This was a revelation to her. She had been dancing out the relationship without knowing it. Those same feelings in movement perfectly mirrored the agonies she constantly struggled with at that time.[7] [p. 64]

For those functioning at an early developmental level, such as the autistic child, the movement goals take a different form. The therapist's aim is to reach the child at the primitive sensory-motor level at which he/she functions.* By initially imitating the child's movement, rhythm, and vocalizations, the therapist seeks to build psychic structure, form a body image (the autistic child has not formed a mental representation of his/her body or of others), and develop a therapeutic relationship. Initially the therapist mirrors the child's movements as a way to speak the child's langauge and gain entry into his or her world. As the child allows the therapist to enter his/her world, imitation begins to drop away. The therapist transforms movement so that instead of its being used as a mechanism to keep others away, it is used as a way to establish a relationship and to communicate. Thus, the repetitive movement patterns that served as sensory stimulation for the child are used as the basis for developing reciprocal interaction. The way in which the therapist mirrors, shares, and develops the child's movement is crucial. Too much imitation or spatial closeness and the child pulls away. Not enough results in the therapist's failing to make contact. Once the relationship has been established in movement, the therapist is able to introduce particular movement sequences to accomplish higher level goals. Kalish writes:

> After several months of "meeting her level" and slowly striving to build a relationship with her, [Laura] began to show signs of trusting me and her movement began to change. She would run to me, holding on around my waist, while I moved her body "fused" to mine. She would sit in my lap in front of the mirror and watch intently as I slowly moved my arms and

*EDITORS' NOTE: See appropriate chapters in Part II of this book.

then gently moved hers in the same movement phrase. At this point she did not seem able to imitate any movements on her own. As discussed earlier, Laura had no body image. The process of learning to imitate was just beginning, it seemed. After much repetition, Laura was able to finish a movement sequence that we would begin together. She could be observed at other times during the day, experimenting with a movement that had been introduced to her in the therapy session.[20] [p. 57]

With the developmentally disabled, the therapeutic process involves the acquisition of perceptual-motor skills along with the development of expressive behavior and social interaction. Movements that encourage an interaction of correct motor development are utilized within the context of the unfolding psychotherapeutic process. Special emphasis is given to help the child or adult to move reciprocally with others, to express feelings and anxieties symbolically through movement, and to provide alternatives for dysfunctional behavior. Here, too, the therapist works in a process-oriented manner, developing the expressive and affective components of the movement while encouraging higher levels of cognitive, social, and motor development. Populations and individuals may require different types of goals; however, the process-orientation of dance therapy remains consistent despite differences.

DANCE-MOVEMENT THERAPY TRAINING

The clinical and academic training of dance-movement therapists occurs on the graduate level. Included in the core courses are studies in human behavior (both individual and group); movement observation and movement behavior; and dance therapy theiry and skills. Clinical field placements and an internship are vital parts of the curriculum. Conducting a dance-movement therapy session requires astute sensitivity to the unfolding therapeutic process manifested in movement, the skills to draw upon a full range of movement experiences to facilitate communication and expression, and the ability to adjust and transcend one's own movement style in order to work with clients of various cultural and socioeconomic groups. Using a variety of movement activities does not make the experience psychotherapeutic. Rather it is how the on-going movement process is guided and directed by the dance-movement therapist to achieve therapeutic goals that transforms creative movement and dance into psychotherapy.

While most mental health professionals lack the specialized training and skill of the dance-movement therapist, there are some ways in which some of the tools of the approach can be utilized. These include providing movement activities and developing a sensitivity to the uses of nonverbal behavior. Paying attention to the nonverbal aspects of behavior can shed some light on the relationships among group members, couples, or therapist and client. Movement reflects social, cultural, and personality traits, thus providing additional information which can be used in therapy.

TECHNIQUES IN DANCE-MOVEMENT THERAPY

Kinesthetic Empathy

As mentioned previously, placing yourself in kinesthetic empathy with another serves two important functions: it can give pertinent information about how someone else is feeling, and it can foster the development of rapport. In using kinesthetic empathy to get a sense of what another is feeling, it is important to incorporate into your own body the same posture, muscular tension, breathing pattern, and body movement. However, it is crucial to remain in empathy for only a short period of time. Otherwise the intensity of the emotional experience will be hard to shake off as it becomes incorporated into your body. Another area of difficulty may occur by projecting your impressions, values, and judgments on the other person rather than recognizing that the material that emerges may be your own.

Kinesthetic empathy is useful as a way to make contact with extremely regressed nonverbal clients. Sharing the same movement pattern while walking with them helps to establish the beginnings of a relationship. In a way similar to working with the autistic child, the therapist needs to pay attention to the client's need for spatial and emotional distance.

An awareness of the client's movement behavior makes it possible to use this information as part of more traditional verbal psychotherapies. In mirroring back the movement, the therapist may ask the client what he/she feels or thinks if either saw someone else move in this way, or inquire if there is an image that the movement evokes.

Exaggeration

Usually there is a particular aspect of someone's movement behavior that catches our attention (e.g., a deliberate or controlled quality, quick and sudden movements of the hand, or a sunken and heavy feeling). After getting the client to notice this pattern first, the therapist may suggest exaggerating the movement so that the characteristic quality stands out more. The client can be asked to explore expressive or communicative aspects. On a movement level, the therapist can suggest that the client allow more feelings to emerge and to allow movement to go where it feels like going. It is also possible to take movement quality into a different part of the body to notice if there is a similar or different emotional response. The client can be directed to verbalize what that particular part of the body may be saying or what it wants to do.

Transforming Movement into Communication

Another technique utilized is to take movements that are dysfunctional in nature (e.g., self-stimulating, repetitive, or used to keep others away) and use them as a basis in which to engage the client in a movement interaction. Finger wiggling near the eyes, a characteristic of some autistic children, can be transformed into wiggling the fingers toward each other as in a wave of hello.

In attempting to use this technique, it is important not to mimic the other person. What seems to work best are movements similar to the client's or ones that are in direct response to what the client is doing.

Developing the Themes into Action

Despite the client's best intentions, words sometimes cover over or get in the way of experiencing the full impact of a particular feeling or situation. Developing this material into a body expression often crystallizes and deepens awareness. In addition, there is sometimes a discrepancy between what one says and what one does. Nonverbal behavior is hard to conceal or change. As a result, it often pinpoints precisely what is occurring.

For exmaple, a client was working on separating emotionally from her father. Despite saying all the correct words to indicate that she now felt free of this entaglement, her movement behavior indicated otherwise. Using a stretch band as the connecting link to illustrate the discrepancy, the therapist (taking on the role of the father) asked the client to hold the other end. The client was instructed to imagine that the band represented the strong emotional ties that existed between her and her father and to see how she could disengage herself from the situation. She was unwilling to let go the of the band. For her the movement task clarified and demonstrated her true feelings.

Another useful theme to take into movement is trust. Allowing one's self to fully lean on another or physically support someone else can pinpoint individual styles or patterns. Totally giving up one's grounding and balance to another's support is a different bodily emotion from not giving in completely. Clients can become cognizant of which people they do trust, if they do trust at all, or only partially trust, and of how this represents their life patterns.

Some other issues that can be developed on a movement level include resistance, passivity, cooperation, and being a leader or a follower.

Attention to the Interactional Aspect

All of the techniques suggested require astute sensitivity to nonverbal communication. Subtle changes in body posture can often indicate changes or adjustments in relationships. Particularly in a verbal therapy session, take note of which people share similar positions or move in synchrony (rhythm) with one another. People can use themselves physically to unconsciously block another person, cut off or interrupt nonverbal sequences, or change position to avoid being in a movement interaction with others. The nonverbal level can provide information regarding status, power, relationships, cohesiveness, rapport, conflict, defenses, and emotional expression.

Another important area for professionals to use is movement activities (e.g., exercise, games, creative dance). Benefits include increasing or maintaining physical activity level, development of self-esteem, increasing socialization, tension release, and relaxation.

Use of Rhythm

Movement activities that make use of rhythmic body action, such as folk dances or exercise, foster a sense of togetherness for group members. The rhythmic action also helps sustain involvement in the activity and encourage an integrated use of the body.

Tension Discharge

For people who are stiff or tense, working with movement helps to loosen up the uncomfortable or stiff body parts. This usually results in increased blood flow, deeper breathing, and release of tension. Sometimes vigorous shaking of body parts (such as pretending to shake off water or dust) will allow for a carthartic release.

Use of Props

For some people, relating directly to others can be a painful or frightening experience. At these times, the use of inanimate objects can serve to connect group members. Moreover, props can allow for the direct expression of feelings when real feelings are too frightening. Foam balls can be thrown, smacked, and squashed; pillows thrown or punched; and sheets pulled or shaken hard. Holding onto a stretch band can help people feel part of the group even when they experience a lack of social relatedness. Using props encourages a natural bodily response; one will usually try to catch a ball or at least duck so as not to get hit. Likewise, their use can elicit memories of other times when play, competition, and group participation occurred.

SUMMARY

Dance-movement therapy is a unique profession. It engages the total person in a process toward healthier functioning. The nonverbal aspect allows for it be to used with all ages and all populations. It is particularly valuable for those with cultural, language, or socioeconomic differences. It works with the already existing strengths of people — bodily movement — and uses this as the basis out of which personal growth and exploration occur.

REFERENCES

1. Allport, G. and Vernon, P. *Studies in Expressive Movement.* New York: Macmillan (1933).
2. Alperson, E. Movement therapy — a theoretical framework. *Writings on Body Movement and Communication* 3:87–99 (1973–1974).
3. Bartenieff, I. and Lewis, D. *Body Movement: Coping with the Environment.* New York: Gordon and Breach (1980).
4. Bartenieff, I., Pauley, F., and Lomax, A. Cross-cultural study of dance: Description and implications. *In*: Bartenieff, I., Davis, M., and Pauley, F. (Eds.). *Four Adaptations of Effort Theory in Research and Teaching.* New York: Dance Notation Bureau (1973).
5. Bauer, R. and Modaressi, T. Strategies of therapeutic contact: Working with children with severe object relationship disturbances. *American Journal of Psychotherapy* 3(4):605–617 (1977).
6. Berger, M. Bodily experience and expression of emotion. *Writings on Body Movement and Communication* 2:191–230 (1972).
7. Bernstein, P. *Theory and Methods in Dance-Movement Therapy.* Dubuque, IA: Kendall/Hunt (1972).
8. Burton, C. and Ancelin-Schutzenberger, A. Nonverbal communication in the verbal and nonverbal interaction: A research approach. *American Journal of Dance Therapy* 1(1):20–23 (1977).
9. Chaiklin, H. (Ed.). *Marian Chace: Her Papers.* Maryland: The American Dance Therapy Association (1975).
10. Chaiklin, S. Dance therapy. *In*: Arieti, S. (Ed.). *American Handbook of Psychiatry* (Vol. 5). New York: Basic Books (1975).
11. Chaiklin, S. Defining therapeutic goals. *American Journal of Dance Therapy* 1(1): 25–29 (1977).
12. Clynes, M. *Sentics.* New York: Anchor (1978).
13. Condon, W. Linguistic-kinesic research and dance therapy. *Proceedings of the Third Annual Conference of the American Dance Therapy Association* (1968), pp. 21–42.
14. Davis, M. Movement characteristics of hospitalized psychiatric patients. *Proceedings of the Fifth Annual Conference of the American Dance Therapy Association* (1970), pp. 25–46.
15. Davis, M., Dulicai, D., and Climenko, J. Movement researcher and movement therapist. *American Journal of Dance Therapy* 1(2):28–32 (1977).
16. Dratman, M. Reorganization of psychic structures in autism: A study using body movement therapy. *Proceedings of the Second Annual Conference of the American Dance Therapy Association* (1967), pp. 39–45.
17. Gendlin, E.T. Focusing. *Psychotherapy: Theory, Research, and Practice* 6:4–15 (1969).
18. Hanna, J. L. African dance: Some implications for dance therapy. *American Journal of Dance Therapy* 2(1):3–15 (1977).
19. Hunt, V. Neuromuscular organization in emotional states. *Proceedings of the Seventh Annual Conference of the American Dance Therapy Association* (1972) pp. 16–41.

20. Kalish, B. Body movement therapy for autistic children. *Proceedings of the Third Annual Conference of the American Dance Therapy Association* (1968) pp. 49-60.
21. Kendon, A. Movement coordination in dance therapy. *In: Committee on Research in Dance, Workshop in Dance Therapy: Its Research Potentials. Proceedings of a Joint Conference by the Research Department of the Postgraduate Center, Committee on Research in Dance, American Dance Therapy Association* (1970).
22. Kestenberg, J. *Children and Parents: Psychoanalytic Studies in Development.* New York: Jason Aaronson (1975).
23. Kestenberg, J. Suggestions for diagnostic and therapeutic procedures in movement therapy. *Proceedings of the Second Annual Conference of the American Dance Therapy Association* (1967), pp. 5-16.
24. Kleinman, S. A circle of motion. Unpublished master's thesis, Lone Mountain College, California (1977).
25. Lavender, J. Moving toward meaning. *Psychotherapy: Theory, Research, and Practice* 14(2)123-133 (1977).
26. Lefeo, H. *Dance Therapy.* Chicago: Nelson Hall (1974).
27. Leventhal, M. (Ed.). *Movement and Growth.* New York: New York University Press (1980).
28. Levick, M., Dulicai, D., Briggs, C., and Billock, L. The creative arts therapies. *In*: Adamson, C. and Adamson, E. (Eds.). *A Handbook for Specific Learning Disabilities.* New York: Gardner Press (1979).
29. Lowen, A. *Betrayal of the Body.* New York: Macmillan (1974).
30. Mahler, M., Pine, F., and Bergman, A. *The Psychological Birth of the Human Infant.* New York: Basic Books (1975).
31. North, M. *Personality Assessment Through Movement.* London: MacDonald and Evans (1972).
32. Reich, W. *Character Analysis.* New York: Farrar, Strauss, and Giroux (1949).
33. Rosen, E. *Dance in Psychotherapy.* New York: Columbia University Press (1957).
34. Sandel, S. Dance therapy in the psychiatric hospital. *Journal of the National Association of Private Psychiatric Hospitals* 11(2):20-26 (1980).
35. Sandel, S., Orleans, F., and Stark, A. Mothering in the dance therapy experience. Paper presented at the Fourteenth Annual Conference of the American Dance Therapy Association (October 1979).
36. Schilder, P. *The Image and Appearance of the Human Body.* New York: International University Press (1950).
37. Schmais, C. Dance therapy in perspective. *In*: Mason, K. (Ed.). *Focus on Dance VII.* Washington, DC: American Association for Health, Physical Education and Recreation (1974).
38. Schmais, C. and Orleans, F. Dance/movement therapy with the minimally brain-damaged child. *In*: Ochroch, Ruth (Ed.). *The Diagnosis of M.B.D. Children.* New York: Human Sciences Press (1981).
39. Schoop, T. and Mitchell, P. *Won't You Join the Dance? A Dancer's Essay into the Treatment of Psychosis.* California: National Press Books (1974).
40. Stark, A. Symbiosis. *In*: Feder, E. and Feder, B. (Eds.). *The Expressive Arts Therapies.* Englewood Cliffs, NJ: Prentice-Hall (1981).
41. Stark, A. and Lohn, A. Verbalization and dance therapy: What, where, when, how and why. Paper presented at the Fifteenth Annual Conference of the American Dance Therapy Association (October 1980).
42. Zwerling, I. The creative arts therapies as "real therapies." *Hospital and Community Psychiatry* 30(12): 841-844 (December 1979).

Art therapy seeks to promote self-expression and self-exploration toward both healing and growth. Its basic premise is that images are prior to words, and a secondary view is that dreams are primarily visual in nature. Art therapists generally feel that artistic expression is natural, as may be seen in the spontaneous productions of young children.

A mental health professional may look forward to using art therapy if he or she has had considerable experience personally with catharsis and integration through some form of art expression, is comfortable with the use of art materials, and is sufficiently self-aware not to project into the patients' art expressions his or her own needs and views.

Art therapy finds present application in a wide variety of situations – in private practice, in- and out-patient psychiatric clinics, with addicts, children and the elderly, in schools and prisons. It may be especially useful in working with physically handicapped persons. The chapter that follows explores, through examples, some of the many uses of art therapy with different populations and in different settings.

19

Art Therapy

Harriet Wadeson, Ph.D.

Art therapy may actually be one of the "older therapies." Its roots extend back in time to the misty realms of pre-history, when our ancestors expressed themselves and explored meaning in their lives through cave paintings and crudely formed sculpture. Our ability to trace human history rests on this dependence upon imagistic symbolization [Greek *syn* ("together") and *ballien* ("to throw")]. For primitive people, meaning became established by the "throwing together" of the known and the unknown. For example, in 2500 B.C., a crude Greek stone carving with protuberances to indicate breasts served as a fertility goddess. The imagistic symbol represented the powerful, mysterious force that created life.

As removed as present day psychotherapy may appear from such a primitive process, in actuality there are some significant traces of our ancestral antecedents in the current practice of art therapy. Today people use images to express and explore their feelings, to make sense out of their lives and their perceptions of the world. Reciprocally, as a profession, art therapy seeks to promote self-expression and self-exploration through the use of art media toward the goals of healing and human growth.

But before moving toward amplification of how this is done, let's fill in the history a bit between ourselves and our remote ancestors. Over the ages, expression in art as a vehicle (if not as the main means) of understanding an individual's or a culture's view of its life and world are well documented. In the modern era of psychotherapy, art therapy is rooted directly in the work of Freud and Jung. Finding dreams the "royal road" to the unconscious, Freud predicted art therapy when he wrote:

> We experience it [a dream] predominantly in visual images; feelings may be present too, and thoughts interwoven in it as well; the other senses may also experience something, but nonetheless it is predominantly a question of images. Part of the difficulty of giving an account of dreams is due to our having to translate these images into words. "I could draw it," a dreamer often says to us, "but I don't know how to say it." [Freud, in Strachey (1963)]

Jung went further, encouraging his patients to draw or paint their dreams. In fact, the graphic rendering of dreams is often the major component of a Jungian analysis.

Art therapy has some heretofore undiscovered roots in a totally different area I have been happily surprised to unearth recently. Having a degree in social work myself and as director of an art therapy master's degree program which offers basic clinical courses in a school of social work, I was delighted to discover the emphasis on art expression starting almost 100 years ago in early social work. At Hull House, a museum at the University of Illinois, where I teach, and previously a settlement house founded in Chicago by Jane Addams, a pioneer of the settlement house movement, I found old photographs and program descriptions emphasizing the expressive value this activity had for the immigrants the settlement house served.* Thus art therapy can be seen to have grown out of both the sister fields of psychiatry and social service.

Art therapy *per se* began in the 1930s, 1940s, and 1950s, when a few independent practitioners began experimenting in using patient artwork for therapeutic purposes. During the 1960s, the idea began to spread; independent art therapists started to communicate; a professional journal was established; and, by the end of the decade, a professional association was formed, the American Art Therapy Association. During the 1970s, the profession exploded into a recognized and sought-after therapeutic modality, and numerous training programs were developed. As of this writing, the master's degree is the terminal degree in the profession, although increasing numbers of art therapists are obtaining doctorates in related fields.

WHAT IS ART THERAPY AND WHY AND HOW DOES IT WORK?

Art therapy is based on the premise that we think in images — that we probably thought in images before we had words. For example, an infant no doubt

---

*I am indebted to Mary Ann Johnson, Administrator of Jane Addams Hull House, for bringing this information to my attention.

recognizes "mother" long before the child has a name for her. Dreams, our primary access to those recesses in ourselves we know least, are mainly visual experiences. It is unfortunate that our Western Civilization, with its emphasis on linear thinking and rational processes, heeds so little the important imagistic component of our inner experience.

Art therapy is also based on the premise that artistic expression is natural. This is inferred from the spontaneous production of young children, and from history, which tells us that throughout all cultures and ages of civilization, people have reflected upon themselves and their cultures through art expression. In art therapy, these natural processes are encouraged and utilized for the purpose of therapeutic gain.

There is an important difference here between an enlightened art class and an art therapy session. In the latter, the importance is placed on the process rather than on the product. The goal is the utilization of creativity in the broader aspect of creating one's own life rather than in the narrower sense of artistic creativity. Thus, an art therapy client might produce a picture of no artistic merit but which is extremely productive in terms of enhanced self-awareness, insight, and growth. Conversely, one might create a painting of high artistic excellence that leads to little personal growth. (Naturally, personal integration and artistic creativity may also enhance each other, as they so often do.)

Why is art therapy beneficial? To try to cull its various advantages exemplifies one of the difficulties art therapy was developed to counter. We experience its many aspects all at once, but I can write or talk about them only one at a time. Pictorial or sculptural expression, on the other hand, obviates this problem, because when you look at a work of art, you see it all at once, just as you experience concurrently the many processes that we can describe only in components. Furthermore, a description is limited. If you attended an art therapy workshop, you could experience the process yourself and know through its impact on your personal awareness what art therapy can be. With those caveats in mind, I will attempt a description and explanation.

Imagery

As stated previously, we think in images. In art therapy, the image of a dream, fantasy, or other experience is depicted in image form rather than having to be translated into words, as in purely verbal therapy. (Words, nevertheless, are useful in amplification and exploration of the image.) In addition to the *reflection* of images, the art process often stimulates the *production* of images, tapping into primary process material, enhancing the creative experience, both narrowly (in the artistic sense) and broadly (in the creation of solutions in living).

Spatial Matrix

Verbalization is linear communication. First we say one thing, then another. Art expression need not obey the rules of language — grammar, syntax, or logic. It is spatial in nature. In art, relationships occur in space. Sometimes this form of expression more nearly duplicates experience. If I were to tell you about my family, I would tell you about my mother, *then* about my father, *then* about their relationship to each other, *then* about each one's relationship to me, etc. Obviously, I experience all of this at once. And in a picture I can portray it all at once, I can show closeness and distance, bonds and divisions, similarities and differences, feelings, particular attributes, context of family life, *ad infinitum.*

Creative and Physical Energy

For years I taught an evening art therapy course attended mostly by professionals. They had worked all day and were tired when they came to class. It was primarily an experiential course, but often there was discussion at the beginning. I was struck time and again by how sleepy we all were until we began the artwork. Then everyone seemed to wake up, and the discussion following the picture-making was much livelier than the initial interchange.

There seems to be an enlivening quality to be found in engaging in art expression. I have noticed a comparable phenomenon in on-going art therapy groups. In the discussion following the drawing period, group members are often more open, revealing, and receptive than in the initial discussion, even though it, too, may have been quite intense and probing. I have experienced the change in energy level in myself as well, over and over again, as I have become "activated" in art activity. I believe that this is due to a release of creative energy and a more direct participation in experience than in talking, especially "talking about." At times the creative activity even takes on the character of play, and art therapy becomes more like fun than like work.

Decreased Defenses

Because verbalization is our primary mode of communication, we are more adept at manipulating it and more facile in saying what we want to say and refraining from saying what we don't want to say, than through other communication modes. Art is a less customary communicative vehicle for most people and therefore less amenable to control. Unexpected things may burst forth in a picture or sculpture, sometimes totally contrary to the intentions of its creator. This is one of the most exciting potentialities in art therapy. Unexpected recognitions often form the leading edge of insight, learning, and growth.

A common misconception about art therapy is that artistic ability is necessary for self-exploration through art expression. On the contrary, an artist may be less prone to accidental "slips of the brush" due to a high degree of ability in manipulating the materials. In this sense, non-artists may more readily respond productively to the art activity.

Objectification

In additon to working in images, another unique attribute of art therapy is the production of a tangible product. A particular advantage here is that it is often easier for a resistant patient to relate to the picture than to the self. For example, a hospitalized depressed man initially spoke of the angry expression on the face in his picture. He hadn't intended it to look that way and didn't understand why it had come out that way, since he did not feel angry himself, he said. Eventually he came to identify with the figure in his picture and recognized his own anger. In this way, the art expression can form a bridge. I call this process "objectification" because feelings or ideas are at first externalized in an object (picture or sculpture). The art object allows the individual, while separating from his or her feelings, to recognize their existence. If all goes well, the feelings become owned and integrated as a part of the self.

Permanence

Unique to art therapy is the permanence of the object produced. The advantage here is that the picture or sculpture is not subject to the distortions of memory. It remains the same and can be recalled intact months or years after its creation. Reviewing art productions with clients is extremely beneficial. Sometimes new insights develop. Particularly helpful is noticing emerging patterns which may not be apparent when the work is viewed singly. There have been times when clients have forgotten a piece of work and seeing it recalls the feelings that were present at its creation, sometimes producing new insights. In this way, it is possible for both therapist and client to derive a sense of the on-going development that occurs in the therapeutic process. Such awareness can be very encouraging to a client who thereby comes to recognize his or her own progress. A series of pictures can provide ample documentation of the significant issues and their affectual components.

WHO IS QUALIFIED TO PRACTICE ART THERAPY?

Art therapy training usually requires two years of graduate work with an ample background in psychology and studio art as prerequisites. In graduate art therapy training, specific art therapy theory and methods are combined with a basic clinical preparation and extensively supervised art therapy field work. Some programs require art therapy research as well. Obviously, graduates of art therapy master's degree programs are qualified to practice art therapy. But what about others? There is disagreement within the profession on this issue. Although experience in studio art is a necessity, few would agree that any artist without clinical training, and specifically art therapy training, is qualified. The disagreement occurs regarding other mental health professionals with sound clinical training but without extensive art therapy training. Some art therapists hold that one must be an artist, not necessarily successful, but with the sort of commitment to a life of making art to develop the identity of "artist." I do not agree. I have worked with non-art therapist colleagues who were sufficiently interested to learn quite a bit about art therapy through working with me and other art therapists to enable them to introduce some art therapy into their own work. Nevertheless, their work was limited to occasional use of art materials at appropriate times, rather than the more thorough-going imagistic therapeutic journeys art therapists are trained to take.

For a practitioner to utilize art therapy, I believe there are some important requirements. First, the therapist must have experienced the releasing and integrative aspects of creating art. It is unlikely that one who has not had rather extensive experience of this sort will be able to encourage another in this mode of expression. Second, the therapist must be comfortable with art materials. Third, the therapist must be open to whatever expression comes forth from the client, in images, artistic style, and verbal elaboration. Fourth, the therapist must be willing and able to improvise as the client's needs demand, rather than to attempt art therapy "techniques" for their own sake. Fifth, the therapist must be particularly alert lest there be self-projection onto the client's art. Art products can be especially evocative and therefore seductive in this regard.

In sum then, a mental health professional with sound clinical training might make use of the advantages of art in conjunction with his or her usual therapeutic approach *if* he or she has had extensive personal experience of catharsis in, and integration through, art expression; is comfortable with art materials; is sufficiently self-aware not to project onto the patient's art expression; can be open to the patient's needs; and is sensitive to the place of artwork in the therapist/client relationship, as will be discussed below.

THERAPEUTIC RELATIONSHIP *VIS-A-VIS* THE ART PRODUCT

Added to the usual therapeutic relationship is each one's relationship to the art product itself. As an expression of self it becomes an extension of the client and must be respected as such. Therefore, the way the therapist regards it, handles it, puts it away, and recalls it, becomes extremely important. Obviously, in recognizing the art creation as an extension of the client, the art therapist does not work on it. One may demonstrate technical assistance on another piece of paper, but the integrity of the client's expression must be respected but not interfering with it.

Even the most minimal drawing is an expression that has something to say. Many people with whom I have worked, particularly hospitalized depressed patients, have been convinced on entering art therapy that their artwork was meaningless and inadequate (which is how they saw themselves). As a result of my interest in the meaning to them of their art expressions, however, they soon became interested themselves.

To whom does the artwork speak — to the therapist, to the client? Both, but differently: For the client it is self-revelation. Therefore, the responsibility for interpretation should be the client's. What the art therapist reads in it is an echo of his or her own personal life experience. Many times that experience may connect with the client's and augment understanding. This is the stuff of which intuition is made. Too often, however, art therapists act as if they *know* what a picture is saying without any confirmation from the client.

And yet an art therapist *does* come to know clients through their art. One comes to understand their language of imagery, their style, their individual themes, and their specific symbols, so that explanations don't need to be redundant. Art expression is a language, but not a common one. It is unique and not immediately understood. The client is encouraged to tutor the art therapist in its meaning. Once this language of the individual's symbolic imagery is understood, it need not be explained over and over again: There can be immediate communication from client to art therapist through the image. For many people, the language of symbolic imagery is undeveloped. As a result, it is not a ready-made language that becomes communicated, but a language in process, as the client explores and builds his or her own visual mode of expression.

Just as the therapist responds to a client's facial expression, or voice tone, without a description of the feeling being necessary to convey it, so does the art therapist respond to the mood of a picture. One can tell if it's empty, lively, disorganized, rigidly organized, chaotic, tranquil, etc. But what it means to the client is for the client to say.

The Mamas and the Papas sang:

Words of love, so soft and tender,
Won't win a girl's heart anymore.
If you love her, you must send her
Somewhere where she's never been before.*

Psychotherapy is like that. It's not what people already know that grabs them. It's the new places that challenge them. One of the joys of art therapy is its

*Lyrics from "Words of Love," by John Phillips (published by Trousdale Music, Inc.).

potential for sending the client "somewhere where she's never been before." Although the art therapist doesn't offer cut-and-dried interpretations, he or she does encourage the client to explore the potentialities of the art. For example, if a client of mine is engrossed in the old and familiar meaning of the pictorial objects, I may direct attention to the mood of the picture. I try to make my queries open-ended, rather than suggestive of an answer. I'll ask, "What sort of mood does the picture have?" rather than, "It looks bleak, doesn't it?" I won't make assumptions about objects, either. I'll ask, "What does that green shape represent?" rather than, "Is that a snake?"

To help clients explore further, I'll suggest that they fantasize about their pictures. I might ask them to tell me a story about it, or, if a person has been drawn, I might ask what the person in the picture is doing, thinking, feeling.

I don't begin this way, however. After the picture (or sculpture) has been completed, I wait for the client to tell me about it. I may ask questions for clarification. I will start out questioning any unexplained objects in the picture so that I can be sure I understand what has been intended, rather than making assumptions. I'll follow the client's lead in what seems important to him or her to pursue in the associations to the picture. Sometimes I might respond to a particular issue because of some indication that this is an important area for the client. This may be based on material that has come up previously, or on something in the client's manner when it comes up, or just on a hunch whose basis I can't identify.

In the initial phase of art therapy, some people with whom I have worked have felt they were making pictures for *me*. This was particularly true in the hospital, where patients weren't seeking art therapy, but where it was part of the program. For some patients, in addition to viewing the picture as a gift for me, they felt that the quality had to meet with my approval. If an art therapist truly wants his or her clients to orient their lives to satisfying themselves, rather than constantly seeking the approval of others, the therapist must be consistent in reactions to the pictures. That is, one must not dole out praise or criticism on the basis of artistic merit, but rather reinforce the client's self-exploration through art. When a relatively minimal picture leads a client to startling new insights, for example, the art therapist might remark on the importance of the picture to the client.

The therapist must be accepting and non-judgmental of the art product as well as of the client. Although I would recommend such an approach to many aspects of the therapy, it is especially necessary in relating to the artwork. Most people who are inexperienced in art are reminded of their early picture-making experiences in school. They feel like children in relation to a teacher who is expecting an adequate performance. If a therapeutic alliance is to be established, it is important that the art therapist decline the clients' overtures to relate in this manner and remain interested in the clients' experiences and help them to reflect on their expectations and feelings about the therapist's responses.

The mantle of confidentiality extends to artwork as a visual form of privileged communication. Therefore, art exhibits of the work are not appropriate. In addition to being a possible violation of confidentiality, they give the message that the goal is creation of a product, rather than a process. If the artwork is to be shown to other staff members, the art therapist should make explicit to the client who is to see it and under what circumstances. It is helpful for the art therapist to reassure the client that the pictures and related information are shared only with the treatment staff and are not randomly displayed.

Since the artwork is viewed as an extension of self, if a client wishes to destroy it, that is his or her prerogative. It is my habit to request that the action be considered so that it be done with awareness, rather than on "automatic pilot." In this way, the destruction of a personal expression, as well as its production, may lead to insight and understanding.

The question of whether the art therapist should participate in the artwork must be addressed. Usually I don't, for several reasons. First, the field of exploration is the client's life, not mine. It's a matter of role. Second, for those clients who feel inadequate in art, my more experienced drawing might prove intimidating. Third, the processing of my picture or sculpture would take up valuable therapy time. Nevertheless, there are times when I *do* do artwork with clients. This occurs more often in group art therapy, when it is important for me to join the others in a group expression, especially when the subject has to do with the experience of being part of the group. Sometimes there is a particular reason for my participating in individual therapy as well. For example, a severely depressed man with whom I had worked became mute after a serious suicide attempt. I found that although a verbal interchange with him was impossible, we were able to communicate nonverbally by making several pictures together. In them I followed his lead, responding with color, form, or symbol to his graphic ideas as we took turns adding to the picture.

Of course, one of the problems faced by art therapists is the frustration they may experience in watching others dig into the art media when they would love to do so themselves. This problem highlights another personal reason why I refrain from artwork in the sessions. I tend to become so absorbed in my own expression that I neglect the client. Since observing the manner in which a piece of art develops is often revealing, and since clients may want to verbalize as they are working, it is important to be available to them rather than lost in one's own world, as I tend to be when I'm personally immersed in art materials.

APPLICATION OF ART THERAPY

The term "art therapy" is a huge umbrella covering the use of art expression for many purposes, with diverse populations, in a wide variety of settings. Art therapists in private practice work with clients on an insight-oriented basis for a relatively long-term course of treatment. In short-term settings, such as crisis-intervention units and many hospital programs, patients are seen in short-term art therapy. Art therapy is probably utilized on in-patient psychiatric wards more than any place else, where patients may be seen individually or in groups. It is utilized in out-patient services as well, and it is increasingly becoming a part of programs for drug addicts, the elderly, and the imprisoned. In addition to treatment facilities, art therapy is employed in school systems for the emotionally disturbed, retarded, learning disabled, or socially disadvantaged child, and, increasingly, for so-called "normal" children. In recent times, art therapy has found a place in working with physically handicapped people. For many of these populations, family art therapy may also be useful.

Obviously, the goals and design of art therapy sessions are based upon the needs of the particular individuals being treated and the setting in which the treatment occurs. Therefore, art therapy sessions in a home for the elderly would be very different from those in a out-patient drug addiction program, for example. Session structure, therefore, should be tailored toward enhancing the goals of treatment. Structure, in this sense, includes frequency and length of meetings, manner of referral, decisions about ending treatment, missed sessions, particular activities (i.e., structured exercises), art media, discussion periods, etc. In most instances, an hour is sufficient time for an individual session and an hour and a half or two hours for a group or family session (since there needs to be time for both the production and the discussion of the artwork). Some people like to do artwork outside the sessions as well, and bring it in to discuss. Session time may be influenced by the art media used and *vice versa* (see below).

Another factor in the structure of the art therapy sessions is the approach, or style, of the art therapist. Since there is something of a polarity in the profession, with some art therapists placing an emphasis on the "art" and some on the "therapy," this difference in emphasis naturally affects several aspects of session structure. Those who emphasize the "art" consider artistic creativity a synthesizing, integrating force, often at an unconscious level. Art therapists of this persuasion are likely to devote more session time to the actual production of art and to use more elaborate materials. Those who emphasize the "therapy" consider the artwork more of a vehicle to enhance insight. They are likely to devote less session time to the production of art, structuring the session so that the process of creating is quick and spontaneous, and to devote more time to the processing of the art expressions. They usually use simple, fast art media. (Naturally, many art therapists fall between the two extremes. Also, some populations and settings lend themselves better to one approach and some to the other.)

The baseline activity is the "free" picture or sculpture. This is the activity most frequently used. Patients work spontaneously, depicting whatever occurs to them. These productions are likely to express current significant issues in their lives or defenses against them. In selected instances, the therapist may suggest an art exercise. Sometimes the suggestion is based on the client's concerns.

For example, if a client initiates a discussion of complaints about his wife, the art therapist might suggest that he draw a picture of their relationship.

There are many standard art therapy exercises [see Nadeson (1980), Appendix]. It is important to utilize them only when appropriate, not simply because some of them seem interesting. For example, a picture of one's family of origin is helpful in gaining a history; joint picture-making in dyads or by whole families is useful in exploring relationship among people. The timing of such an exercise is most advantageous when relationships are at issue. Drawing a self-image might be requested to highlight the patient's view and experience of self. Sometimes a picture of the person one would like to be is an illuminating contrast (and so forth).

Most art therapy sessions are structured so that there is time for the discussion and dynamic processing of the artwork. Although the manner of inquiry was discussed above in regard to the therapeutic relationship, it is worth adding that no piece of artwork need be plumbed to its ultimate depths. And, in fact, such is probably never possible. There is likely to be some meaning that always escapes both client and therapist. Either may be limited by time, resourcefulness, or imagination, as well as the usual blocks (in the sense, understanding artwork is very much like investigating dreams). The important thing to remember is that if significant material is not fully explored in any one art expression, it is bound to surface again and again in one form or another.

Physical Environment

Some aspects of structure should apply to all art therapy, regardless of type. These highlight the importance of the physical setting and material necessities, which are of less consequence in most other forms of therapy. For artwork there should be ample space, adequate lighting, suitable art materials, clean-up equipment, and a room that does not have to be protected from stains. Quiet and privacy, requisite for other forms of therapy, of course, are needed for art therapy, too. Sometimes art therapy programs in hospitals have been relegated to activity or social areas which are also open to other patients and staff during the sessions. It is not likely that any information the patients wish to be kept confidential will be shared in such an environment.

There are times when a patient cannot come to the art therapy room. If there is a physical disability, the art therapist may have to visit the patient's room and bring the art supplies. I have held sessions in the seclusion room when a patient was confined there.

Certain specific aspects of the physical environment have an impact on the nature of the art therapy experience. In a group setting, the physical distance among members, both while engaged in the artwork and in the discussion of it, can influence the experience. Furniture makes a difference too, such as sitting and drawing on the floor or using easels and chairs. The former usually creates a less formal environment.

An important consideration in art therapy is the physical relationship between the art producer and the art product. Many art therapists have the productions hung on the wall for discussion purposes. Sometimes patients may be asked to describe their pictures from across the room. I usually like to encourage a close proximity between creator and creation. Most often, participants hold their pictures or display them in front of them so that others can look at the producer and the product at the same time. Holding the picture emphasizes the connection between the two so that the art product is more readily experienced as an extension of the self. There may be occasions, however, when the art therapist wishes to encourage distance between patient and picture for the purpose of greater objectivity. At such times, the patient may be asked to step back from the picture.

The storing of the art products may pose a logistical problem. Ideally, it is best to have all the previously artwork handy in case a present picture or sculpture relates to a previous one. It may then be brought out and the two viewed together. Sometimes, however, space considerations make storing all the material impractical.

Art Media

The art therapist may use a variety of art materials. As is the case with other elements of session structure, media should be selected purposefully. In a relatively loose studio setup, art supplies might be arranged for the patients' choosing, particularly in art therapy where the emphasis is on the art activity. If the artwork is more a vehicle for free association, for family or group communication, relatively fast media such as pastels, crayons, or felt-tip pens would be most suitable. Material preparation and clean-up certainly are factors to be considered. Unless there is time for the patient to participate in these responsibilities, the art therapist might prefer media that require little preparation or cleaning up. Handicapped individuals, very young children, and some elderly people might need materials that are easily manipulated.

Two important considerations in the selection of media are the dimensions of facilitation and control. A sufficient variety of colors, adequate size of paper or canvas, and enough clay, should be provided, along with an adequate working space to facilitate spontaneity in the client. An overabundance of materials may overwhelm and confuse some clients. Since clients differ in this regard, the art therapist must be sensitive to the individual's needs. Obviously, frustrating materials should be avoided (such as newsprint which tears easily if pressure is applied to it, or chalks that have worn down so much they can hardly be grasped).

Some media are more easy to control than others. Pencils lend themselves to tight control. Watercolors and clay are more difficult to control because there are technical problems in manipulating them. Again, the art therapist must be sensitive to the client's needs. The opportunity to smear might be enlivening for a severely inhibited individual or it might be extremely frightening. Sometimes, changing the medium can be facilitating for an individual who is in a rut. The point is that it is necessary for the art therapist to be familiar with what may be evoked by the different media, what advantages each offers, and what limitations each has, so that media can be selected appropriately.

In much of my work, the art product is a vehicle for psychological insight. Since I want to devote as much time as possible to processing the image and the experience of creating it, I prefer a quick and simple medium. Also, I usually like to combine the possibility to control and to smear. For these purposes, I have found wide, soft pastels in a variety of vivid colors to be my "happy medium" — neither too tight not too loose. They are easy to wash off hands and clothes as well.

DIAGNOSIS

Some art therapists use the art productions for diagnosis. Here we are on shaky ground indeed. There are no convincing empirical studies to indicate that certain pictorial characteristics correlate with specific diagnostic variables. The present state of the art does not allow us to determine a "schizophrenic picture" or a picture augering a poor prognosis. Nevertheless, there is much that the artwork can tell us, particularly when combined with other information. If we listen to what patients tell us about their art expressions, there is much we can understand of their dynamics. If we also observe the patient's behavior in relation to the art, there is more we can learn. Especially fruitful is the examination of a series of art expressions over time. We can note changes in the patient's course. As mentioned earlier, the art expressions come to evolve into personal language from which the art therapist may discern the dimensions of the patient's world.

CONTRAINDICATIONS

Art therapy is facilitating for diverse populations and is rarely contraindicated. In almost two decades of treating hundreds of clients of many kinds under varying conditions, I can remember only two instances in my own work in which the therapy was contraindicated. One was a hospitalized young man whom the staff was trying to "patch together" to prepare him for discharge. My opinion was that the patient was in need of long-term hospitalization; as this was not feasible, the plan was for him to continue in out-patient treatment. In our first art therapy session, he drew extremely bizarre pictures full of blood, themes of vengeance, sex, and many disjointed images. He became more upset as the session progressed, in contrast to his usual pleasant behavior. I communicated my concern about him to the rest of the staff and cancelled further art therapy sessions. Although it appeared that art therapy was an excellent modality for the release of his very disturbing feelings, the timing was all wrong. The art activity opened up powerful inner forces for which he needed a protected environment to face. Shortly before discharge was not the time to begin. These issues had not emerged in his verbal therapy. Unfortunately, he was not able to have the continued hospitalization he needed to enable him to deal with his difficulties. He managed out-patient life successsfully for a while, holding a job and seeing his psychiatrist regularly. It is likely, however, that he did not deal successfully with the material that had emerged in the art therapy session. His psychiatrist had not anticipated the severity of his disturbance (despite my communication with him about the art therapy material) and failed to rehospitalize him. The patient committed suicide. One can only speculate that he was finally overwhelmed by the sort of feelings revealed in the pictures.

The point here is that there are moments when the art experience can provoke an activation of unconscious onslaught, requiring a protective environment and understanding and supportive additional therapists on an on-going basis to help patients face their overwhelming fears. If such is not available, art therapy is often better avoided. This caution is particularly important for beginning art therapists, who are more likely to believe that the work is worthwhile if the patient is uncovering repressed conflicts.

The other instance in which art therapy turned out to be contraindicated also involved a suicidal individual, but in this case the reasons were quite different. The patient was a young woman I saw in private practice for several years. She had previously been hospitalized briefly following a suicide attempt and began therapy with me because she was once again experiencing suicidal feelings. This client had very low self-esteem and lived an impoverished interpersonal existence; she had no friends and had difficult family relationships. She was afraid to explore her inner life. Repeated suggestions toward fantasy were met with resistance and increased feelings of worthlessness as she experienced difficulty in giving herself over to fantasy. Although many patients feel inadequate in drawing, most get over it quickly and become involved in their own expressiveness. Such was not the case for this young woman, however, probably partially due to her conviction of worthlessness and her extensive history of feeling coerced by her parents. At the same time, she was quite responsive to a more cognitive approach. Since the goal was the client's improvement, rather than the use of one modality or another, cognitive work was continued over the course of treatment with a most successful outcome. Although a situation such as this is rare, the art therapist should be sensitive to the possibility that, for a few individuals, pushing the artwork may only strengthen resistance and ultimately sabotage the therapy.

For most clients and patients, however, art therapy proves to be an illuminating and integrative process. The examples below are presented in order to provide a view of the kinds of phenomena art therapy taps in various settings with diverse populations.* Exigencies of space allow for only brief vignettes, with many kinds of clients and settings left unrepresented, but it is hoped that these illustrations give a glimpse of art therapy's potentialities.

DEPRESSION AND SUICIDE

The depressed patients with whom I worked for nine years on wards for affective psychoses at the National Institutes of Health Clinical Center taught me much about feelings of hopelessness, worthlessness, guilt, and suppressed anger. Many of them suffered psychomotor retardation for some portion of their hospital stay. In such a condition, they found almost any activity overwhelmingly difficult, having little available energy for anything other than internal preoccupations.

As a result, the request for self-expression through picture-making was often resisted. Many patients associated drawing with a childhood activity and felt embarrassed. The patients' feelings of self-worth were challenged by their expectations that whatever they would draw would show their childish inadequacies. I stressed that the purpose was to provide another mode of expression in addition to words (rather than artistic accomplishment) and that I had no expectation that patients have artistic talent or experience. Nevertheless, patients often protested that they didn't know how to draw. Such statements seemed both an expression of inadequacy feelings and a warning that I shouldn't expect anything. I often suggested experimenting with the colors and not worrying about "making a picture."

In the initial difficulties in working with severely depressed patients, usually the objection to art production embodies a projective expectation — that my judgment of the patient will be as harsh as the patient's judgment of him/herself. As experience accrues and the patients see that I am genuinely interested in whatever they do for its meaning to themselves, they begin to internalize my approach and stop judging themselves.

Although many depressed individuals draw empty, rather meaningless pictures [Wadeson (1971)], with concerted work they are able to push past their lethargy to the more tumultuous feelings within. Such was the case for Mary, a young mother of three children. She was hospitalized following a serious suicide attempt. At her first art therapy session, I suggested she make a picture of that experience (Figure 19-1). Although colorless and rather empty, "Spiral" was meaningful to her.** She said that each circle represented an argument with her husband and that the circles became smaller as her "tolerance" decreased. She

---

*Some of these examples have appeared in Wadeson (1980).

**For a discussion of the spiral symbol as expressive of suicidal feeling, see Wadeson (1975).

Figure 19-1. "Spiral," a depiction of feelings leading up to a suicide attempt by Mary, a young woman hospitalized for depression. Reprinted, with permission, from Wadeson, H. *Art Psychotherapy*. New York: Wiley 1980.

felt that what they said to each other no longer had meaning and that they had both lost control. At the center she came to a "dead stop," could "no longer face another day," and made a suicide attempt.

After several weeks of twice-weekly art therapy, Mary's artwork became more expressive as she began to delve into long-unresolved feelings. Figure 19-2 is an abstract piece of sculpture that she worked on very intently. She immediately saw it as herself. The portions that would be the face, guts, and a breast are gouged out. Her association was that she has "chopped away" at herself, that the figure is leaning back because she is still resistant to exploring her painful feelings. As she probed further, however, she connected it with her identification with her mother, whom she, at age 11, had nursed through terminal cancer. She related that experience to her own kidney removal four years ago, saying that she had never expected to survive what was labeled an "exploratory operation" (which she connected with her mother's exploratory operation shortly before her death). Mary felt that things were "rotting" inside her, and that if her kidney had been "dead" for a long time without her knowing it, other things inside her could have gone wrong, too. Apparently the kidney suffered

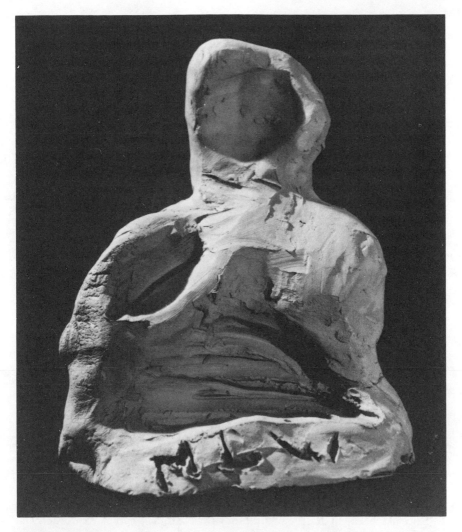

Figure 19-2. Sculpture by Mary, a young woman hospitalized for depression, depicting fear of death. Reprinted, with permission, from Wadeson (1980).

damage during her first two pregnancies. It was removed before her third pregnancy, but she felt that she would not live through the delivery of her third child and that the child would be deformed (further evidence of things being wrong inside her). In this work, she was beginning to deal with her experiences of loss and her fears of death.

Although Mary's treatment course was anything but smooth, eventually she returned to a less conflictual relationship with her husband and to the care of her children. She was especially pleased to be able to hold a demanding job, finding work pressure preferable to the constant demands of her family.

When Mary first entered HIH, her artwork was typical of the impoverished style characteristic of depression [Wadeson (1971)]. Although she never developed much skill in artistic expression, she was able to make good use of the process, both as a means of self-expression and release and as a tool for self-exploration. She dealt with the problems she encountered regarding loss, death, suppressed anger, and feelings of harmfulness to others with resultant guilt. Many of these feelings are typical of depression. Art therapy was a useful process for her in examining these problems and overcoming them sufficiently to live more satisfactorily.

MANIC-DEPRESSIVE PSYCHOSIS

Full-blown mania has become a relative rarity on psychiatric wards, as the excessive characteristics of this condition have succumbed to the control of lithium carbonate. Nevertheless, occasionally an art therapist will see such a patient who has not been medicated, has not responded to the medication, or, as is sometimes the case, has managed to avoid the medication in order to experience the "high" of mania.

Rachel, a woman in her 40s, is an example of a hospitalized patient receiving no medication. Hers was a very rapid cycle between mania and depression, often with depression one day and mania the next. This 48-hour cycle continued with unrelenting regularity for two years.

Her behavior in our sessions varied according to her mood. A few times, when manic, she deliberately spilled the materials, ran out of the room, or talked so much that she never got around to doing artwork. Sometimes, when depressed, she dozed off in the middle of making a picture and had to be awakened. Most of the time, however, she enjoyed the sessions and tried to cooperate, in contrast with her behavior on the ward, which was withdrawn when she was depressed, and often combative or, at best, unreasonable when she was manic.

Since Rachel's explicit communication was minimal, her art expression was particularly important in conveying her experience. Like other manics, her insight was also minimal, but the art sessions provided her a significant avenue of catharsis and relationship. Although I called her attention to recurrent themes and variations in her pictures, she did not sustain continuity in integrating them meaningfully. These themes, however, provided a useful comprehension to me and the rest of the staff.

Rachel's most frequent manic symbol was a spiral (Figure 19-3).* It was usually bounded by straight horizontal lines. These coils often filled the paper and

---

*Rachel's spirals coiled outward, as opposed to the suicidal spirals, which were involuted.

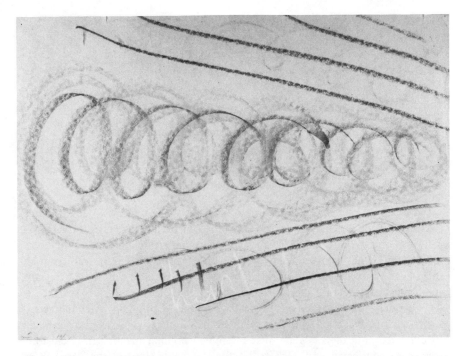

Figure 19-3. Spiral symbol by Rachel, a hospitalized manic-depressive patient. Reprinted, with permission, from Wadeson (1980).

gave the appearance of much motion. She did not draw spirals when depressed, with one exception.

Usually when she drew spirals there was so much flight of ideas and distract-ability that it was impossible to determine what this image meant to her. The rapid manner in which she made them suggested in part that they reflected her manic energy. Frequently, she expressed a great deal of anger as she produced them, and in this connection it is interesting to note that the spiral symbol is associated with anger in a previous study by Naumburg and Caldwell (1959) as well. One of their obese patients, who often felt depressed, entitled her picture of spirals, "Rage."

The one time Rachel drew a spiral when depressed, the symbol appeared in her final picture of the session and was accompanied by a marked change in mood — from sobbing to a forced optimism, which seemed at least in part pro-duced by denial of her realistic difficulties. This particular spiral was small and tight compared to the larger, expansive ones produced in mania.

In this instance, the art therapy provided catharsis and a meaningful relation-ship for the patient that was more easily formed around a creative activity than the more sedentary, purely verbal therapy sessions. The patient developed little insight from her art expressions. Rachel's repeated themes were helpful, however, in providing the staff some measure of understanding of the issues confronting her.

SCHIZOPHRENIA

As is the case with mania, some of the more bizarre attributes of schizophrenia, such as hallucinations and delusions, are presently controlled by medication. Where they do surface, however, they provide important indices of conflictual issues. Hallucinations, which are often visual in nature, and delusions are especially expressible in art.

The example of Craig, a young man diagnosed as a paranoid schizophrenic, demonstrates the accessibility to art expression of the idiosyncratic, private, and often isolating experience of delusions. Although afraid to trust anyone with his "secrets," Craig's love of drawing and the gratification he derived from another's interest in the private world pictured in his drawings caused him to transcend his fears and reveal his inner world.

Craig's delusional system was intricate, complex, and highly systematized. I gleaned various facets of it as he explained his pictures to me. I never gained a full understanding of it. Much of it resembled popular mysticism. Delusional ideas were manifested in Craig's belief that he could control the weather, especially in regard to punishing his enemies ("I make nervous cuts with brain waves through the weather to people"). He believed that he was the guardian of Mother Nature's secrets. Threading through the pictures are symbols of sexuality, destruction, and women. They also exhibit Craig's fine sense of design, imagination, humor, and technical skills. The interest his pictures aroused was extremely gratifying to him.

Craig believed he was in a "life and death struggle too important to talk about," because people were trying to steal his secrets. These secrets dealt with the forces of nature, which were usually represented by images of conception or the figure of a woman. In an early picture (Figure 19-4), Craig drew himself traveling in an astral body on an astral plane. He explained that this was an actual experience, not imaginary. At lower left are sperms emanating from testicles. At upper right is a sun-ovum, which has already been fertilized. The astral body in which he is traveling (the form with an eye) protects him from being drawn into the sun-ovum. Later he labeled this picture "psychotic," and said that it would make someone who looked at it psychotic.

NEUROSIS

Out-patient private practice art therapy is most likely to involve people with problems in living who are capable of a great deal of insight and ability in re-

Figure 19-4. Delusion depicted by Craig, a young man diagnosed as a paranoid schizophrenic. Reprinted, with permission, from Wadeson (1980).

fashioning their lives. For them, the graphic images often produce dramatic revelations and a springboard to deeper reflection. Art expression for this group of people often speeds up the therapeutic process markedly.

Laura was a young woman who made good use of the images she produced in private practice group art therapy sessions. Several months after drawing her first picture, in which she introduced herself to the group (Figure 19-5), she wrote the following about it.

Lion Picture — Self-Introduction

This is me, cloaked in my shield of long hair and in my favorite, gentle colors. I am aware that as I smile timidly, there lurks behind me, within me, a fierce, aggressive, hating lion. I am afraid of him in me but want his energy and confidence. Above me flies a beautiful butterfly, delicate and full of life. I

Figure 19-5. Self-introduction picture by Laura, a patient in private practice. Reprinted, with permission, from Wadeson (1980).

want to accept my beauty, inner and outer, and not be ashamed of it. These parts of me were not integrated when I drew this picture but now I am more whole. These parts were in conflict with each other and unacknowledged, although I was well aware of them.

Through the art therapy medium, Laura was able to confront and share her self-destructive fantasies that made her feel "crazy" and became a more assertive and confident person.

ADDICTION

As is the case with individuals in the other diagnostic categories, addicts display a variety of concerns and problems. Many deny their condition. Others feel helpless to change it. Art therapy can be useful in helping addicts to review and assess their lives and come to terms with their present condition, often necessary for the difficult decision and follow-through of the abstinence needed for change. A prominent feature of such a review is often the realization of loss. Figure 19-6 was drawn by a middle aged man diagnosed as an alcoholic. The broken clock and hour glass represent missed time and opportunities, he said. When he was jailed for drunkenness, he feared he had lost everything.

Figure 19-6. Missed time and opportunities depicted by a middle-aged alcoholic man. Reprinted, with permission, from Wadeson (1980).

CHILDREN

Art therapy is used extensively in both treatment settings and in schools for work with children. In fact, there are those who hold the misconception that art therapy is a form of play therapy used for children only. The goals of art therapy with children are very similar to those of play therapy. The arena of expression and communication is often the realm of fantasy; naturally, insight-oriented work occurs much more often with older children and adolescents than with young children.

Clark was a six-year-old referred to therapy because of disruptive behavior in school and at home. He was diagnosed as minimally brain-damaged with presenting symptoms of hyperactivity and learning disability. In individual art therapy sessions, however, he was cooperative and well-behaved, not having to cope with the stimulation and competition of school and family life. In pictorial form, Clark was able to express the conflicts between his attempts to please and his aggressive urges. For example, the third picture of sessions one, two, and five was of a bear hiding in a cave. At the first session, he didn't draw the bear (because it was "hiding") and explained that he hadn't drawn a cat, since it was hiding in the trees, being attacked by birds. He spoke of wishing to hide from his mother and fantasized her looking for him. He was identifying with the bear. At the second session, he drew the bear in the cave (Figure 19-7), saying it growled at the birds and would eat him up, as well as his mother, me, and a number of friends he named, but not his father (because Daddy would shoot the bear with a gun). He then said that he didn't want to be that bear – he would like to be a friendly bear. There seemed to be ambivalence about identifying with the aggressor or the victim. In his third picture of this theme, the bright colors of the previous bear pictures became murky, and the bear larger. Clark said the bear was "smiling because it's going to eat me." He then retracted and said that it was smiling because it liked him and wouldn't eat him – but then he changed his mind again and said when he got in the cave the bear would eat him. Here he was a victim.

Many of the changes in his mood and pictures were correlated with changes in dosage of medication. Eventually a moderated dose was stabilized, and Clark reported that he was "happy at school and home most of the time now." He drew a self-portrait depicting himself that way. It was much more complete than his previous self-images. It also looked like a little boy rather than the "monsters" he had drawn previously to represent himself.

Figure 19-7. Bear hiding in a cave, by six-year-old Clark, showing his ambivalence of identification with aggressor and victim. Reprinted, with permission, from Wadeson (1980).

GROUP ART THERAPY

The most important contribution of group art therapy, I believe, is the sharing of images. We think in images to a greater or lesser extent, but seldom share this important aspect of our experience with others. In an art therapy group, members come to know one another and be known by the images they keep. Recurrent symbols, themes, and motifs do not have to be re-explained. There is a feeling of knowing and being known at a very deep and personal level. For example, whenever Lenore used an olive drab sort of color, group members would say, "Lenore is using her 'ick' color." They knew it expressed her feelings of disgust. Many aspects of feeling states are noted by group members in this way — change in pictorial style, such as more formed pictures or amorphousness, sensuousness, bleakness, etc. At the same time that participants sometimes surprise themselves with the nature of their art expression, they communicate it to others. The reactions of the others are often illuminating for one's own self-exploration.

Role of the Art Therapist in the Group

The possible roles the art therapist may assume in a group range from being a strong leader, to a facilitator, to a group member. If there are co-therapists, they may assume similar or different roles. Sometimes the co-therapist is not an art person but another member of the mental health team, such as a psychiatrist, psychologist, social worker, or nurse. The sort of group leader one chooses to be depends on such factors as type of population, size of group, treatment goals, length of treatment, setting, structure of sessions, and personal style.

Structure

There are many different kinds of art therapy groups. Some may be very informal and loosely structured, while others are highly structured. An example of the former might be a hospital art studio, where patients may wander in at will, work as long as they like, and discuss their work with the art therapist and/or others in the room or not. Such a group is unlikely to form much cohesiveness, and some therapists would more likely designate it a gathering rather than a group at all. Meetings such as this, and even some that are more structured and that meet for the purpose of art production, might more accurately be called art groups that are therapeutic. A more structured group would have specific membership, meeting time, place, and procedure, including group discussion.

Certain aspects of structure unique to art therapy differentiate it from conventional group therapy. Space, lighting, and art supplies are obviously important considerations. The art therapist may supply the art materials, or the group participants may furnish them. The sessions will be structured very differently according to the type of media used (i.e., material that may be quickly used and requires no elaborate preparation or clean-up, such as magic markers, pastels, ink, or crayons, or more time-consuming projects, such as clay, stone carving, or oil paints). The media used and the length of the sessions should be determined according to the treatment goals.

Another aspect of the structure is the use of various techniques. Participants may work spontaneously; they may respond to projects suggested by the art therapist or other group members; and they may work together on shared projects in dyads or small groups, or as a total group.

Obviously, the nature of the population will influence the nature of the group structure. For example, some groups, such as insight-oriented, out-patient ones, may be eager to share their art expressions with one another; others, such as a group of retarded individuals, may find sharing very difficult.

In considering the structuring of the sessions, the art therapist must make some decisions about time. As already mentioned, the sort of art materials selected will influence the time spent on artwork. Naturally, the therapist will not want to interrupt the artwork, yet if there is to be sharing and discussion, time must be allowed for it. If the priority in the group is art production, then discussion time may have to be sacrificed, and *vice versa*. The art therapist must be very clear about goals for the group in this sense. On the other hand, if an important goal is that the group take responsibility for its own functioning, the art therapist may leave it up to the members to determine the structure around the division of time for artwork and discussion.

Although in conventional group therapy sessions, there may be material that gets postponed due to lack of time, these issues aren't usually recognized in such a way as to incur the frustration that an unexplained, provocative picture does. In conventional group therapy, at any particular session, some members may be relatively passive or simply reactive to others rather than introducing issues of their own. When each member creates an art expression, however, each introduces material, so there is much out on the table, so to speak. In another respect, this phenomenon is advantageous in groups with members who otherwise are withdrawn. Through their art productions they capture attention, which helps to integrate them into the group.

Although needs of various populations differ, generally speaking, an art therapy group session requires more time than a verbal group because executing the artwork is time-consuming. Usually at least one and a half or two hours are required for a session. Discussion time depends upon the population and the number of group members. Usually a half-hour discussion is the minimum, with an hour or more desirable for most groups.

Related to the sharing of images is the question of whether the art therapist creates art productions in the group or not. At times, when I wish to share images with the group, I do so, but more often I refrain, as stated previously. My sharing with the group, though quite extensive, is limited to what I think will advance the therapeutic process. Often this includes my feelings about the group and individual members and some of my own experience, both past and present.

Examples of instances where I have participated in picture-making have been when a member wanted to know how others perceived her and requested of the group that each one make a picture of her, and when a group was terminating and I too wanted to express my feelings about its ending, along with the others.

There are some general characteristics of hospital groups that distinguish them from out-patient art therapy groups. An obvious one is that often patients are not in the hospital by choice and therefore may be resistant to the activities scheduled for them. On the other hand, in the hospital setting, the tone during art production is often more relaxed than in other hospital therapy situations. Concentration is centered on the activity. In verbal therapy, patients often feel pressured to bring up specific problems. In the art group, problems frequently come to light naturally and spontaneously as a result of their appearance in the artwork.

Paradoxically, art activity in the hospital, which draws some people close to the group, may also help to isolate certain members. Sometimes patients become so absorbed in their work, they are almost oblivious of others. This is beneficial when they are fully engrossed in creative pictorial expression. On the other hand, solitary absorption in the work may serve as a defense against closeness and exchange with others.

Because each patient produces a tangible object, the experience for the more withdrawn and less verbal patients may take a more favorable course than in conventional group therapy. As stated previously, patients who remain isolated in verbal therapy groups and on the hospital ward become participants in group art therapy through their art productions. Even when they do not contribute to the discussion, their artwork may provide a means of contact with others. A picture by a withdrawn patient sometimes displays an unexpected aspect of his or her personality which may stimulate interest and eventually serve to draw him or her closer to the group.

As in other group therapies, a common pitfall for the therapist is that of being monopolized by some patients so that effectiveness with the group as a whole is lessened. In some respects, the introduction of art heightens this possibility when the art therapist must make materials available and is occasionally called upon for technical assistance. This problem occurs more often in the hospital with the dependency institutionalization fosters; these demands may also be used to manipulate the therapist.

Art production in groups introduces a new element of pride or shame in performance. Added to verbal performance is the production of pictures and sculpture. Some may feel initially inadequate in this activity compared to other group members. Others may derive great satisfaction from it from the start. For some mental patients, artwork may be the only area in their lives where they feel some degree of competence. At any rate, it is possible in the art therapy room for people to recognize in themselves and each other expressive abilities they had not seen before.

I have found results from art therapy groups in private practice to be more substantial than those in the hospital. There are several obvious reasons, including higher motivation, longer duration, greater consistency of membership (not influenced by hospital admissions and discharges), and greater intrapsychic and interpersonal resourcefulness of the members.

Examples

Figure 19-8 was drawn by Marty, a member of a private practice group. The group met for two-hour sessions in which there was some initial discussion, picture-making, then discussion of the pictures. Sometimes the opening discussion produced a common theme that touched all group members. At such times, the group often decided to make pictures of it. In this case, the theme was the feeling of being judged.

Figure 19-8. Marty's picture of feeling judged, made in group art therapy. Reprinted, with permission, from Wadeson (1980).

After Marty made a picture related to judgment, she spoke of the "dark, angry, dead" face of her mother she had depicted. Her voice became very quiet and controlled. When I commented on this, she said her mother's voice was like that. She wrote the following comments about her picture.

The Good and the Bad Mother in Me

I tried to draw that part of me that sits in judgment of myself. I had just become aware of how I criticize myself. How nothing I do is right for myself that sits inside. And that to others I am a good mother — caring about, forgiving, accepting — and I tried to do this each moment for myself. It shows the me now, in the center — the inside hating, yelling at me — and on the left that care-worn, hurting part of me, and above, that good mother, hands holding and caring about all these parts of me. Judgment — I judge myself and begin to want to forgive myself.

Feedback in pictorial form is another especially important advantage of group art therapy. Often it is clearer and more complete than in verbal messages. Group members have drawn their perceptions of the group as a whole, specific relationships within it, as well as representations of one another. Figure 19-9 is an example of pictorial feedback that differed markedly from verbal exchanges. It was drawn in a hospitalized adolescent group by Alan to depict another member, Stanley. There was a great deal of tension between the two, as they feuded constantly. Stanley drank a great many Cokes and in fact had brought one with him to this particular session. Alan found that he could tease Stanley pictorially in a way his withdrawn nature did not permit otherwise. Stanley reacted to the picture good-naturedly, obviously pleased that Alan had chosen to portray him and using it as an opportunity to revel in his "addiction" to Coke. On this occasion, the usual tension between them was relieved through the comical pictorial communication.

FAMILY ART THERAPY

As in group art therapy, family art therapy provides its participants the unique experience of sharing images. In this case, however, the family enters art therapy with fixed assumptions about one another and the relationships within the family. Depicting these perceptions and actually seeing those of the other members is often a dramatically eye-opening experience. Members may be amazed at how they are viewed by their family and how the other family members view the various dynamics of the intra-family relationships. Building on sharing perceptions within the family is the art activity's possibility to serve as a vehicle for the exposition of fantasy material as well. Members' expectations, wishes, and

Figure 19-9. Alan's portrayal of another member of his art therapy group. Reprinted, with permission, from Wadeson (1980).

fears are extremely important aspects of family dynamics that are seldom shared and may be done so most effectively through art expression.

Another special contribution of art therapy to family therapy is the generational leveling aspect of art expression. Although parents are often more articulate verbally than their young children, in art activity the children are usually on an equal footing with the adults. Frequently they feel quite comfortable with the media and find a way of making themselves "heard" within the family that may not be possible for them in their regular family interactions.

Besides having a generational leveling effect, differences among members in art expressiveness may provide benefits in reshuffling the usual family hierarchy. The same sort of influence can apply to family members who may be more withdrawn, intimidated or submissive. Although role relationships are often inflexible or assumed initially, the introduction of this new mode of expression can supply leverage so that a family may provide more space within itself for the movement of its members, both in family roles and position. Through art expression, a family member can cause the entire family to shift its shared perception of him or her dramatically.

Generally, family art therapy sessions are structured so that art activity is quick and spontaneous, with maximum time for discussion. Planned exercises, such as pictures of the family, the home, ancestral families, important family events, and joint pictures, often provide illuminating material. All family members may be present or the family may be seen in functional units around particular relationships, such as the marital couple only, or a parent and child. In most instances, the focus is on interrelational aspects of each person's experience.

Example

Figure 19-10, 12-year-old Jonathan's drawing of his family, displays activity and turmoil that contrasted sharply with his subdued and unexpressive manner. Although he had expressed a wish to move in with his father, rather than live with his mother and stepfather as he was now doing, he had revealed nothing of his experience of his family life. In his picture, however, may be seen some of his perceptions of home life. He explained that on the right is his mother yelling at the dog. His stepfather is yelling at his crying children, and Jonathan and his sister, on the left, look forlornly at each other. Jonathan had previously wished to attend an art therapy workshop I had conducted, perhaps realizing that he could say in pictures what he could not put into words. He had refused to participate in verbal family therapy or in individual therapy. Eventually, he did move in with his father, experienced some difficulties there, and continued in individual art therapy.

Although art therapy is a "newer therapy" and a still relatively small profession, it is a field more vast than can be summarized in a single chapter. I have tried to present the highlights with the hope that interested readers will investigate the field further. Exploring images is an exciting way to work.

Figure 19-10. Family portrait by 12-year-old Jonathan, drawn in family art therapy. Reprinted, with permission, from Wadeson (1980).

REFERENCES

Freud, S. *In*: Strachey, James (Ed.). *New Introductory Lectures on Psychoanalysis. Part II: Dreams, Vol. XV.* London: The Hogarth Press (1963).

Naumburg, M. and Caldwell, J. The use of spontaneous art in analytically-oriented group therapy of obese women. *International Journal of Group Psychotherapy and Psychosomatics, Special Education.* (1959).

Wadeson, H. and Bunney, W., Jr. Manic-depressive art: A systematic study of differences in a 48-hour cyclic patient. *Journal of Nervous and Mental Disorders* 150:215–231 (1970).

Wadeson, H. Characteristics of art expression in depression. *Journal of Nervous and Mental Disorders* 153:197–204 (1971).

Wadeson, H. Suicide: Expression in images. *American Journal of Art Therapy* 14:75–82 (1975).

Wadeson, H. *Art Psychotherapy.* New York: Wiley (1980).

RECOMMENDED READINGS

American Journal of Art Therapy
The Arts in Psychotherapy.
Betensky, M. *Self-Discovery through Self-Expression.* Springfield, IL: Charles C. Thomas (1973).
Kramer, E. *Art as Therapy with Children.* New York: Schoken (1971).
Kwiatkowska, H. *Family Therapy and Evaluation through Art.* Springfield, IL: Charles C. Thomas (1978).
Naumburg, M. *Dynamically Oriented Art Therapy: Its Principles and Practice.* New York: Grune and Stratton (1966).
Rhyne, J. *The Gestalt Art Experience.* Monterey, CA: Brooks/Cole (1973).
Robbins, A. and Sibley, L. B. *Creative Art Therapy.* New York: Brunner/Mazel (1976).
Rubin, J. *Child Art Therapy.* New York: Van Nostrand Reinhold (1978).

Primal therapy, since its development about a dozen years ago, has focused on the reexperiencing of early traumatic events considered critical in the development of personality and leading to later symptoms. This therapeutic view has recently been broadened in scope and has enjoyed additional adherents not only in the United States but also abroad.

As the author of the chapter that follows suggests, primal therapy is considered a depth therapy that has certain qualities that enable a person to delve perhaps more deeply into his or her past, to reexperience it, and to resolve emotional difficulties associated with it than other depth-oriented approaches.

20

Primal Therapy:
Theory and Practice

Daniel Waldstein, Ed.D.

This chapter briefly reviews the developmental history of primal therapy, discusses its theoretical framework, and explains levels of consciousness and their relation to brain structure as well as to psychopathology. Pain and defense are examined, and it can be seen that an organism needs defense only when it is overloaded with the memory of pain and with anxiety.

The techniques of primal therapy are described and samples of portions of sessions are given. Patients usually start reexperiencing pain starting from very recent traumas and slowly descend to earlier and earlier events. Later, patients typically reexperience pain that they underwent at birth.

It is important to reexperience the point of origin of every major repression.

Reexperiencing of various phases and pains of the birth process and their relationship to later psychopathology and psychosomatic problems is discussed in detail.

It should be noted that psychopathology represents mainly disturbances in the R complex and the limbic system. These, however, tend to overwhelm the neocortex, which then cannot function properly.

Some of the main types of defenses are explored here, as well as primal insight and techniques and their value for the traditional therapist, the effect of pain and neurotic defense on interpersonal relationships, the danger to society from neurotic defense, adapting the educational system to tackle neurotic problems more adequately, genetic manipulation as a mode of altering proneness to psychopathology, and the need to enhance the ability of the individual to feel altruism and compassion and to diminish blocking and destructiveness to oneself and to society.

BACKGROUND HISTORY

In the late 1960s, Arthur Janov started developing the concepts and techniques of a method of psychotherapy that he termed "primal therapy." The term "primal" was used since this therapy involved the reexperiencing of early traumatic events. The theoretical framework and, to some extent, the techniques he used were first described in his book *The Primal Scream.*[2] Since then, Janov and numerous other professionals (for example, William Holden, Joseph Hart,[1] and Richard Corrier) further explored primal therapy, its theory, and its techniques. By now there are hundreds of therapists in the United States and in many other countries who either practice primal therapy or who involve many of the concepts of primal therapy in their psychotherapeutic approach. Many therapists using traditional therapy, who have been influenced by primal therapy, have been emphasizing the use of feeling rather than only intellectual understanding.

Professionals using primal therapy consider it a depth therapy which surpasses the ability of other therapies, even psychoanalysis, to help the individual delve into past pains, reexperience them, and resolve emotional problems.

PRIMAL THEORY

Primal theory asserts that in the course of an individual's development, starting from the prenatal period, during birth, and thereafter until adulthood, much pain will be experienced. The mind uses its defense system to repress the memory of the pain experienced so that the individual may function more efficiently. As birth is one of the most (perhaps *the* most) traumatic experiences in the life of most human beings, many serious repressions occur then. Much pain and repression occurs after birth. These repressions keep mounting as the individual grows up, distorting physical, emotional, and intellectual reactions in life. The inhibitions that the mind uses to cut off the memory of pain tend to shut off the ability of the individual to act naturally.

In general, repression occurs when the system gets overloaded with pain. This overwhelming pain cannot be integrated and thus becomes repressed. During primal reexperiencing, the pain is brought into consciousness in small enough doses to be integrated and dissipated.

LEVELS OF CONSCIOUSNESS

Primal theory recognizes three levels of consciousness, an understanding of which is essential if the therapist is to be of help to the person undergoing primal re-experiencing. These levels of consciousness roughly correspond to the functions of the three distinct parts of the human brain.[9] The human brain underwent steps of development during the course of evolution. First there developed the old brain segment, which is often referred to as the R complex. It is located at the very bottom center of the brain. This section seems to be the portion of the brain we possessed one to two hundred million years ago, when our ancestors were still fish and dinosaurs. It looks like a fish brain and hasn't changed much in its function in all these years. It is active when the child is born and mediates body sensations and reactions and helps repress body pain. It stores memories of body pain experienced at birth and shortly after birth. This is the most primitive part of the human brain. It reacts like a computer. Its initial modes of reaction to stimuli become the prototypical ways in which it later reacts to all similar stimuli. It is as though it becomes set to react in a certain way and thereafter cannot deviate from that mode of reaction. Since this portion of the brain mediates functions such as heartbeat and respiration, and since it has to do with responses of the bowel, the skin, and the stomach, and relates to hormonal regulation and the circulatory system, etc., it is obvious that disturbances of over-agitation and over-repression in it may affect any of the above body functions. In primal theory, the activity of this part of the brain is termed the first level of consciousness.

During the course of evolution, the brain developed one step further and new portions of brain matter were built around and on top of the initial segment. The second segment involves the limbic system. It contains, among other things, segments of brain governing emotions. This portion of the brain also cannot reason and evaluate logically. It works along primitive principles, many of which are described in books of abnormal psychology (e.g., identification, projection, introjection). This portion of the brain becomes active in the young child between the ages of one and four. Its activity corresponds to the second level of consciousness of primal theory. The third level of consciousness of primal theory corresponds to the activity of the "human" part of the brain (i.e., the bulk of the neocortex, which developed during the past few million years). This portion of the brain can reason, analyze, and discriminate well if not overwhelmed by aroused emotions or by distortion emanating from the lower levels of the brain. The activity of the third level of consciousness starts mainly after the second or third year of life. Disturbances in this area appear mainly due to repressive activity and to distortions emanating from the first and second levels of consciousness or due to faulty education.

Although the inner portions of the brain (levels one and two) are very primitive in their functioning, nature seems to have preferred animals and (later) humans, whose third level of consciousness can be easily overwhelmed by first- and second-level activity. It would seem that the animals that survived in the jungle and in the prairie were those in which unanalytic, impulsive action took place in times of danger. The thinking, analytic animals that stayed around to evaluate matters undoubtedly got eaten up first. Animals that reacted to danger with immediate, impulsive flight or fight activity survived more readily.

The tendency of levels one and two to overwhelm the third level exists also for internal reasons, namely to enable the third level to avoid remembering pain so that it may function more efficiently.

DO WE NEED DEFENSES?

The advent of primal therapy has enabled therapists to take a deeper look at the nature of pain and the organization of defense mechanisms. This enables us to clarify some notions that have confused some therapists all along. Some of the confusion centers around whether the individual needs to maintain defenses or not. Primal theory maintains that we do not need defenses to function well. When the defenses covering the memory of pain dissipate, the individual simply becomes him/herself and can act naturally. He or she stops being unreal and becomes real. When pain dissipates, defenses such as anger, anxiety, counter-phobic repression, and distortions of natural behavior such as overeating and drug use become unnecessary and the mind spontaneously tends to abandon them.

Natural modes of behavior are not defensive. The individual is not defending when socializing, functioning well at work, reading, or eating, provided he/she is free of pain and anxiety. If the individual still stores pain, activities such as the above may be used to defend against this pain.

Most systems of psychotherapy do not eradicate pain; they merely help the individual repress it (in other words, defend against it). Thus, professionals using these methods find it hard to conceive of individuals not needing defenses. Many systems of psychotherapy encourage the individual to shift from one defense to another. An eclectic therapist may, for example, help the individual eliminate overeating and help him/her to socialize instead. This socialization will, however, be as defensive as the overeating. When one eliminates the pain, socialization tends to lose its defensive nature and becomes a natural, fun activity. It must be noted that when the individual becomes him/herself (real), the tendency to develop new defenses is not lost when he or she is overwhelmed by new pains. If the individual "primals," though for a period of time about new pains, they will not become repressed.

POINT OF ORIGIN

In order for a neurotic defense to become truly eliminated, the pain at the point of its origin must be reexperienced. Thus, if a person has a neurotic defense, such as a tendency to overcome every obstacle in life through angry reactions, this person may reexperience memories of pain leading to anger on every age level in life. This tendency to become angry will not change thoroughly until it is reexperienced at the point of its origin, such as (perhaps) age nine months or at birth. Once this feeling is reexperienced at the point of origin, it will tend to disappear altogether and the individual will become less aggressive.

TRAINING OF THE THERAPIST

The theoretical framework, methods, and techniques of primal therapy are so different from those of traditional therapies that without specialized training and experience, the psychotherapist cannot hope to be successful in primal therapy. The therapist should be a professional in the field of psychotherapy and have training and supervision by an experienced primal therapist. In addition, he or she should undergo personal primal therapy prior to practicing in this area.

PREPARING FOR THE FIRST SESSION

When the patient is first seen, a history of symptoms and relationships with family members is taken. Details of birth are obtained, if available, and questions are asked about early development and physical health. Virtually all patients who come for primal therapy are at least somewhat familiar with this therapy through reading some of the material published in the field. If they are not familiar with this material, they are asked to do some reading.

Prior to the first session, the primalee (patient undergoing primal therapy) is instructed to avoid doing anything that is comforting, such as watching TV or eating sweets, and he/she may be encouraged to do things that are upsetting so that at the first session the patient will be as upset as possible. This helps the primalee get into his or her pain more readily. However, if the patient is already very upset prior to the first session, he/she is not encouraged to do anything to increase anxiety.

In general, primaling occurs most successfully when the primalee is not overanxious and not overwhelmed with pain. When overwhelmed with pain, the patient is said to be overloaded, and then feelings tend to shut down as they cannot be handled. On the other hand, if feelings are too controlled and repressed, primaling cannot take place at all.

The primalee should be off all drugs and should not smoke or drink liquor, nor should he/she drink caffeine-containing liquids prior to the primal sessions (caffeine may tend to block pain).

The primalee may be asked to spend 24 hours alone in a motel room prior to the first session, if this would make him or her feel lonely, anxious, and upset. Or, if staying home brings up more anxiety and unhappiness than being alone in a motel, the primalee may be asked to do that.

The primaling room should have no furniture and the walls should be padded so that the primalee may roll against them without being hurt and so that walls may be punched when anger is reexperienced. Noise from the outside should be at a minimum. The primalee should not wear makeup and should be dressed in clothing that he or she does not fear messing up. All of this helps the primalee focus on feelings rather than on external concerns and stimuli.

The initial part of the therapy usually involves a three-week period called the "intensive," during which time the individual will be seen every day, five to six days a week, for as long as the individual can reexperience. Most people tire after one or two hours and need a rest until later in the day or until the next day. After the intensive, the individual will join group sessions lasting a few hours each, two to three times weekly. Primaling in a group setting may last many months until the primalee feels satisfied with his or her progress.

THE INTENSIVE

During the first session, the individual will typically be asked to lie on his/her back on a mat and focus on a relatively recent experience that had been painful. The primalee may say: "I'm thinking about my girlfriend,"* Therapist: "What do you feel?" Primalee: "I feel very hurt." Therapist: "Tell me about it." Primalee: "My girlfriend left me." Therapist: "Try to feel it as though it is happening again here and now. What do you feel?" Primalee: "Very sad." Therapist: "Talk to her." Primalee: "Don't leave, don't leave, please stay with me, be good to me, be nice to me." Here the primalee may begin crying. Therapist: "Keep talking to her." A flow of crying may follow, suggesting that the primalee is getting to feel the pain of rejection by his girlfriend.

Here and throughout the therapy, we aim at genuine reexperiencing; i.e., to have the individual feel again now what happened then. The defenses tend to truly dissipate only when the individual emotionally reexperiences fully the painful events of the past. Merely remembering these events does not eliminate the defenses. Remembering and awareness as used in traditional psychotherapy tend to be intellectual activities that do not involve emotion.

The term "abreacting" as used in psychoanalysis also denotes mainly intellectual remembering and discussing. When merely remembering or abreacting, the individual may become aware of the source of his/her neurotic behavior and proceed to use this awareness to repress some of the symptoms. The neurotic structure, however, remains intact. When pains are actually deeply felt through

---

*Included are portions of an actual session.

reexperiencing, past pains reach consciousness and thus the inhibitions or defenses covering them tend to slowly, spontaneously dissipate.

Returning to our sample session: The primalee may cry briefly at first, getting to some of his pain, then begin defending by telling the therapist about his girlfriend's behavior or try to analyze why she left him. He will then be directed away from his narrative and from intellectual analysis back into his feelings. Therapist: "Go back to feelings. Tell me more about your sadness and hurt." The primalee may then begin crying again, indicating that he feels pain again. Primalee: "I loved you so much. Why did you leave? You are just like my mother. She would never stay with me." Therapist: "Talk to your mother." Primalee: "Don't leave, don't leave, Mommy." His voice reached a high pitch, with deepening pain. "Don't leave me all alone. Sue [sister] hates me. She will hit me and say nasty things . . . Oh! Don't yell at me, Mommy. You always yell. I love you. I'll be so good." And thus painful memory after memory kept flowing until the session's end.

The defense system consistently tends to try to shift the individual away from pain into defensive maneuvering. Anything that interferes with feeling pain is termed the defense. In fact, at times, the individual may stay with lesser pain in order to avoid feeling more intense pain. For example, primalees may focus on the pain felt in relation to their fathers too long in order to avoid feeling the greater pain experienced with their mothers.

Many individuals can get to their painful memories readily. Others are, at times, quite slow in getting to them. As the primalee reexperiences painful past events, personality changes tend to occur spontaneously. Symptoms sometimes tend to disappear dramatically.

Bess was in the process of reexperiencing early events when suddenly her crying became exceedingly intense. She screamed, "No, Grandma. No! It's not my fault. Don't die, please don't die. Help! Help! Don't . . . Grandma, don't be mad at me. Oh! Blood!" She cried intensely for 15 minutes, and later recounted as follows: "All my life I was terrified of blood. If anyone mentioned the word 'cut' or 'bleeding' or if I read it somewhere I went crazy, feeling terrified. While primaling, I suddenly remembered that when I was three my grandmother cut her hand and it was bleeding. She blamed me for getting her upset and making her cut herself. I felt she might die." After primaling once about this event, Bess reported that her fear had disappeared altogether and that the words "blood" and "cut" didn't bother her anymore. (Usually, however, the primalee must reexperience past traumas many times before a significant reduction occurs in the neurotic defense.)

TRANSFERENCE

In the course of feeling pain, the individual may transfer his or her primal feelings to the therapist. It is preferable to discuss this matter with the primalee, pointing out the difficulty that his/her mind is having in distinguishing between parents and therapist and encouraging the primalee to feel feelings toward the parents more deeply. Typically, as the individual gets deeper into pain, the transferred feelings spontaneously shift away from the therapist to the parents, about whom they were felt in the first place. Transference is thus treated as a defense. It is easier to transfer feelings than it is to feel the impact of one's own real pain — that it was really one's own mother or father who didn't care.

USE OF DEVICES

I do not condone the use of mechanical aids, drugs, coffee, deep breathing, body gestures, etc., in the therapy session. Typically, when the primalee talks to his or her parents during the sessions, feelings spontaneously begin and eventually proceed with less and less prodding by the therapist. Drugs often tend to throw the process of therapy out of sequence and may tend to bring up certain feelings before the primalee is ready to face them. Deep breathing often may induce the primalee to focus on earlier body feelings when perhaps he or she is really chronologically involved in feeling painful emotions about his/her parents. Techniques used by some people to get a whole group into the same type of feeling, or do the same kind of thing at the same time, or merely run about screaming, are not primal in nature and induce the individual to avoid personal feelings and to go along with other people's feelings. It is best to let the primalee work on what is foremost on his or her mind at the moment. The therapist may simulate the attitude of the parents, or may talk like the parents did or apply some body pressure. But this should be done only when the primalee is feeling those particular feelings at the time. Thus, the therapist merely enhances what the primalee is already spontaneously feeling.

The therapist's effort is directed toward aiding the primalee to stay with his or her pain, and thus saying or doing things that may comfort the primalee is avoided. Comforting may sometimes reduce symptoms rapidly, but it would mask deeper feelings and prevent the primalee from truly eliminating defenses. In general, when the primalee is reexperiencing pain on the emotional level, he/she is working on the second level of consciousness. When repressed second-level pain is felt, it reaches third-level consciousness and tends to dissipate.

The primalee may spend many weeks reexperiencing events, usually relating to significant people in his or her life — lovers, father, mother, sister, teacher, grandparents, relatives, etc.

Reexperiencing tends to spontaneously descend to earlier and earlier periods of life. The primalee's voice may begin sounding younger. It is at times hard to tell the difference between the primalee's voice and that of a real baby when he/she is reexperiencing events from crib time. Body motions during primaling also tend to become babyish. Primaling on the infant level seems so genuinely babyish that the unsophisticated observer may mistake it for psychotic behavior. Numerous patients who have spent time in mental hospitals have observed that if they did primaling in the hospital they would probably have been dragged to the isolation room and sedated. Hospitals typically do not allow much expression of feeling. The difference between true psychosis and primaling is that the primalee knows that he or she has just reexperienced baby feelings and goes away from the session behaving relatively maturely again. The psychotic, however, remains regressed and disorganized after the session.

PRIMALING ON THE FIRST LEVEL

The aim in primaling on the first level is to bring memories of traumatic events from that period of time into consciousness through reexperiencing them. As the individual goes into earlier and earlier periods of life, he or she eventually spontaneously begins reexperiencing body feelings. For example, the patient may begin gagging, feeling pains like a ring around the head, feeling muscle pain, feeling restless, or needing to move about constantly.

Body memory tends to be of a very primitive nature. The body often remembers by feeling the pain now as it was felt in the past. When it comes to visual and auditory memory, the individual has more of a sense of distance from the event. In other words, the individual tends to be able to recognize that the visual and auditory events happened in the past even though the pain associated with those memories is felt now. The individual thus does not actually see the room and the parents while reexperiencing, nor does he/she actually hear them speaking. A primalee may, however, actually feel a father's slap on the face or actually feel the birth pressure on his/her chest as though it were happening right now. If this fact is not recognized by a physician, the physician may be tempted to do exploratory surgery, looking for a cause of unexplained stomach pain or chest pain, only to find nothing there. One cannot locate, see, and surgically remove a body memory. I have come across a number of patients who have had such fruitless surgery. Many of the aches and pains that patients complain about are merely body memories of past events. Their appearance merely indicates that the forces keeping these memories repressed have weakened and the pains have thus surfaced into consciousness.

As the individual begins feeling body feelings, the therapist may assist by placing a hand on the patient's chest and pressing it somewhat, or by putting the patient under a mat to simulate being enclosed in the womb. The current, or present, pressure exerted on the primalee's body by the therapist is helpful only if it triggers off the reexperiencing of old pains. If the individual feels only the current pressure, it would be of no help therapeutically.

Examples of First-Level Material and its Correlation with
Later Feelings and Behavior

Inasmuch as professionals are not familiar with material on this level, this section will be presented in somewhat greater detail.

Some of the typical first level of consciousness body experiences that primalees undergo are as follows, not necessarily in their order of appearance.

The primalee may be curled up in the initial prebirth position as though in the womb. Numerous people who curl up frequently during the therapy report that they did not wish to be born. They may sleep curled up, they may sit in a curled position when upset, or they may curl up in their lovers' laps, etc.

In general, initial reactions by the individual in response to stress, especially if they occur during the very impressionable period of birth, tend to become the prototypical modes of reaction of the individual in literally hundreds of somewhat similar situations later in life.

The individual reexperiencing events on the first level may straighten his/her body out, head thrust backwards just as the infant does in the womb on the way out. The primalee may push his/her legs backward, head thrust forward, as if an attempt is being made to move ahead. At this point, the primalee may suddenly feel a desire to withdraw backward. Primalees who were premature babies or who experienced much pain will typically feel like withdrawing and often will seem unwilling to come out. An infant at birth who feels this urge to retreat when urged to move ahead by the mother's birth contractions may always seek to hold back in life. Then it seems that every new situation the person has to face after birth reinforces the same tendency to hold back. An infant that holds back at birth may hold back in walking, talking, and social responsiveness. Such a person may be reluctant to undertake tasks. He or she may tend to become dependent, wishing others to do things, may feel unwanted and believe that people wish to get rid of him or her, may feel very angry when crossed, or may feel that other people must be resisted. After the primalee reexperiences birth feelings intensely, he or she often will express recognition of where such typical life feelings originated.

As mentioned above, a feeling must be experienced at its point of origin if it is to be thoroughly eliminated. Thus, for example, John reported: "All my life I became furious with women and hurt them physically when they did not do as I wished. I couldn't control myself and became violent with them. When primaling, I felt angry with my mother and felt like killing her because she left me alone and went to work. After much primaling about my mother, I still felt like hurting women. Later I felt like I could not get out of the womb [John was a 13-pound baby at birth] and felt like destroying everything in my way so that I could come out. I felt that if I didn't come out it would be a disaster for me. As I reexperienced this feeling again and again, I mellowed more and more.

By now I can't hurt women anymore. Women friends now tell me I am very gentle."

It is my impression that many criminals who have the uncontrollable urge to kill or hurt would not benefit from psychotherapy unless they reexperienced the point of origin of such a feeling, which may be rooted at birth. The intensity of the desire to kill could only develop in response to what the baby may sense as a life-and-death situation. The baby may feel: "Either I destroy everything in my way and come out, or I am doomed." Then the tendency to feel this way remains engraved in the mind forever. In general, responses emanating from the R complex (first level) often tend to be of a violent, destructive nature.

The primalee may feel a very high degree of anxiety when reexperiencing trying to come out and finding it impossible. This imprint of anxiety may stay with the individual for life. This anxiety may be triggered off any time the individual feels trapped in a room (claustrophobia), in a car, in heavy traffic, or in an uncomfortable marriage, or when trapped with kids, with tasks to do, when wrapped tightly in clothing, or even when wearing a turtle neck sweater (etc.).

When reexperiencing pressure around the head, the primalee will often recognize the pain as the same as that which he or she has felt throughout life when stricken by a headache. The patient may recognize the feeling of being intolerant of being touched on the head or of wearing hats or of having his or face covered by a sheet as the same feeling that was reexperienced during the course of birth.

The primalee may reexperience clenching teeth while making an effort to push ahead, tightening muscles to resist the immense pressure within the birth canal. While doing so, the primalee may realize for the first time that his/her muscles have been tense and tight throughout life and that all the chiropractor's efforts to loosen them came to naught as, soon after treatment, the muscles tightened again, causing further stress on the skeleton and spine.

The primalee may reexperience choking feelings with a sense of lack of oxygen and a need to cough and vomit. The throat may fill with mucus. This may be the result of the infant's umbilical cord not supplying enough blood and oxygen to the baby. Or perhaps it is due to intake by the baby of fluid from the birth canal into the lungs and the stomach. This person may have problems with nausea or with chronic coughing throughout life. The primalee may recognize asthmatic attacks as similar to the choking feeling experienced at birth, or recognize chronic stomach pains as exactly like those felt at birth when his/her stomach contracted in an attempt to throw up liquid. A choking sensation may be felt, or a lump in the throat, similar to that which the primalee almost always feels when tense.

A singer who trained for many years could not pursue a professional career because, when singing to an audience, her throat tightened and the voice did not come from the correct part of her throat. When she reexperienced the choking feeling at birth, her voice "straightened out" and she was able to sing success-fully. Incidentally, her reexperiencing many crucial traumas relating to her parents after birth had no effect on opening up her throat.

The primalee may experience an immense amount of anxiety at birth and feel an overall constriction of the circulatory system. The anxiety is a defense against the pain and the parasympathetic constriction is a defense against the anxiety. The defense of constriction may cause shallow and weak heartbeat, feelings of coldness, especially in the extremities, and, perhaps, an accompanying sense of doom. The primalee may say, "This is how I felt so often throughout my life."

The body may defend against pain due to pressure around the chest area by contracting (the breasts will then not develop in the female) or developing heavy layers of fat to protect against the memory of body pressure and pain (in such a case, a woman may develop very large breasts or large hips). Body parts, such as fingers, hands, torso, and feet, may not grow fully as determined by the genes. During the course of primaling, body parts may begin growing. In a few women, breasts grew after the age of 20 or 30, hips became smaller, chests wider, feet long-er, and fingers longer. Body growth, however, does not occur in all primalees.

One woman was unable to conceive until she was 36. Her examining physician told her he could not find semen in her womb after intercourse. This woman be-came pregnant easily after primaling for a number of months. It is assumed that the constricting muscles around the entrance to the uterus loosened up and al-lowed sperm to enter.

There are numerous studies presented in the literature indicating the lowering of body core temperature, the lowering of basal metabolism, and a decrease in heartbeat after primaling for a period of time.[6]

Thirty-year-old Janice writes about her birth reexperiencing: "All of these sensations in my lips have made my lips noticeably smoother and fuller and a better color. It is as if the blood had come to the surface. My vagina is lubri-cating more, and when I made love, the man I was with said he could feel my muscle tone better. Entry used to be very difficult, but now it is not so at all. My skin, in general, is softer and better feeling all over my body, as if the blood had come to the surface there, too. My acne seems to have gone away and, more important, my face used to look red and inflamed much of the time and now has calmed down considerably. My breasts have both grown, becoming fuller, and the nipple area is getting to look more mature and less unformed and adolescent. I am finally entering adulthood."

Numerous primalees become very restless and hyperactive as they reexperience being born. They report that unless they keep on moving and pushing constantly, they feel a sense of doom. Perhaps the baby feels that the only way to stay alive is to continually push. The imprint of this feeling may become permanent in the individual's mind. Thus, we may have a hyperactive child and later a rest-less, overactive adult, perhaps with the well-publicized Type A personality. On the other hand, some primalees may realize that their lifelong tendency to give up easily, and to want others to bail them out, originated at birth, when they felt that they could not move by themselves and that if they just lay there passively long enough things would be done for them. It becomes easy for such a child to assume a dependency role throughout life, especially if the parents tend to be somewhat protective or domineering. If the child is overactive, he or she may become a rebel and grow up to feel that success will come only by being independent and doing everything by him/herself — and if the parents are domineering, the child may become even more rebellious.

THE SENSE OF DOOM

Underlying the defensive feelings of anger and anxiety is usually a sense of doom, which is later on in life perceived as the fear of death. This sense of doom should be reexperienced by the primalee. A tremendous amount of body defensiveness is focused on trying to ward off the sense of doom. Primalees report sharp changes for the better in their adjustment when they reexperience a sense of doom. They report improvements such as the disappearance of mental confusion, the immediate reduction of a total level of anxiety, and the easing of psychotic thinking and behavior. Oddly enough, the sense of doom is often converted into a suicidal feeling, such as, "I wish I would die," to avoid the pain of doom. Thus, most suicidal primalees who did their therapy with me traced the origin of their suicidal thinking to birth, at which time they felt they would rather die than continue to feel the unbearable pain they were undergoing.

THE VALUE OF PRIMAL INSIGHT FOR THERAPISTS

To psychotherapists, who devote most of their efforts to a surface understanding of human behavior, and to surface techniques of symptomatic change, primal understanding would be of immense value. Understanding of the forces operating beneath the surface would help the traditional therapist to understand motivation and predict behavior considerably better. Furthermore, the therapist who experienced his or her own primal feelings would have a much better grasp of where the patient is "coming from" and what the patient is looking for in life.

THE NATURE OF THE DEFENSE SYSTEM

During the course of working with primalees, I have found that, among the many defenses the mind utilizes against feeling pain, one extensively used is self-deception. Human beings get themselves to believe in, and to argue for, almost any foolish notion if maintaining this notion eases their anxiety. Segmental thinking is another frequently used defense. Here the mind will avoid seeing the whole picture, as it may be threatening. Thus, the political thinker will see only his/her side of the argument. The husband will point out only where his wife was wrong and not see his share in creating the problem, or the therapist will see only the contribution of one party to the problem. (Or the mainstream of psychology will develop a theory recognizing only one approach to therapy and will not be able to acknowledge or act on another theory.)

It is amazing how tenacious defenses can be, especially when the individual feels a threat to security. The defense system appears to be organized around just one purpose — to prevent the individual from feeling pain at almost any cost. Thus, the defense system may lure the individual to commit suicide in order to avoid pain, to shift into a psychotic dreamworld, or to commit murder; to rob, overeat, indulge in the use of drugs, fall in love, fall out of love, or devote one's life to single-mindedly helping others or to destroying others; to remain in a state of constant or alternating anxiety so as to be alert against the repetition of pain, to chose a profession designed to make one appear desirable, to make believe all is well when in truth one is very worried, to fanatically believe in a cause (as perhaps without this belief one would feel helpless and vulunerable), or to be convinced, while undergoing therapy, that one is already fully well for fear of facing further pain.

The defense system is very convincing and misleads the individual, both psychotic and neurotic, to act, think, or feel whichever way is best to avoid pain. The defense system easily overwhelms the intellect and tends to make the individual become fully convinced that what he/she wants or intends to do is right. An impression is gained that, when emotion is involved, the individual really doesn't have too much freedom of choice. Choices in life are made along the lines that the defense system deems safe. Nature did not devise the defense system to lead us to truth. It devised it to help us survive in a hostile environment. It was developed in the jungle and in the prairie millions of years ago. Those who could defend themselves best against the memories of their pain, and thus free the rest of their energy to doing their best, survived.

When we look at the typical human being, we can see a whole array of surface, good, adaptive behavior that the neocortex has learned. Under this layer we typically find two levels of consciousness, the first and the second, which are in a tragic state of disarray, filled with inhibitions, distortions, and hang-ups. These levels constantly encroach into the activity of the third level, often distorting it.

So far as I can see, for the time being, and until a better system is developed, primal therapy offers us the greatest hope of eliminating from our minds a large array of defenses and neurotic distortions that afflict and tyrannize humanity.

Primalees eventually feel and act more freely, are more open, are more able to function, and are more able to avoid neurotic thinking.

RECOGNIZING THE MIND

The mind that nature developed in us is equipped to do a variety of things when it feels threatened — to become angry in order to defend itself against attacks; to become jealous in order to protect its belongings; to destroy, cheat, or lie to others or to ourselves so that we may survive longer; to wish to destroy when we fear being destroyed; and to become convinced that only what we believe in and like to do is right. This kind of mind, which tends to struggle and try to survive at everyone else's expense when it feels threatened, is not suitable to maintain a higher type of civilization, which may exist 4,000 or 40,000 years from now. It can maintain a primitive civilization such as ours, based on only 400 years of technological development and 1,000 to 3,000 years of changing social organization. The type of brain we have, although it is endowed with the ability to feel altruism, love, and compassion, tends to go out of order. So long as technological development is not really advanced, anger and hatred have a relatively limited destructive capacity. However, in years to come, when technological development goes far beyond atomic bombs, it may reach a point where even a very small group of disgruntled individuals, or perhaps even one disgruntled genius, can acquire or develop enough technological destructive power to blow up portions of the planet — or even the whole planet.

In order to increase immensely the chances of survival of our civilization, we must bring about alterations in the way our mind operates. Ways have to be found to make a transition between the kind of mind we possess to a truly peaceful, cooperative, compassionate mind that can be depended on not to fail and self-destruct.

ACHIEVING CHANGE

The means for achieving the transition discussed above can come from a few quarters: 1) from genetic engineering, through which scientists will eventually be able to achieve structural changes in portions of the brain, reducing the individual's tendency toward anger and hatred, desire to kill, and tendency to block compassion (it will be, however, many years before this can be accomplished); or 2) by introducing drastic changes in the methods of child delivery and in the programs of educational institutions.

Methods of child delivery today are virtually barbaric. The baby is treated like an unfeeling piece of meat, creating tremendous anxiety and anger during the delivery and later severe defensiveness within the realm of the child's personality.

LeBoyer[8] has devised new methods of child delivery, which eliminate much of the pain at birth and reduce the chances of the child's developing severe inhibitions and severe personality distortions, including the tendency to harbor violently destructive feelings emanating from the R complex.

Virtually all personality disturbances emanate from the R complex and the limbic system. Yet our educational institutions devote their time to the training of the third level intellect and deal very little with the training of the lower centers of the brain. It is as though educational institutions prefer to make believe that nothing exists below the level of the intellect. This absurd approach can only compound the difficulty.

At home, the family can do very little to bring about personality changes, as the parents do not have the training or the insight needed to achieve this. It appears imperative that elementary schools and high schools should devote much time to personality adjustment, with intensive programs devoted to the problems of relationships between people, between parent and child, between husband and wife, and between nations. What is the use in further training in history, geography, geometry, algebra, etc., if the individual can't get along with a spouse, can't work efficiently (or can't work at all), can't use his or her abilities to their fullest extent, can't use knowledge to good effect, hates other people, has constant accidents and endangers his or her life or the lives of others, has visions of grandeur, is blocked and can't love, can't comprehend well, can't stop working in order to relax and have some pleasures in life, can't talk with people in authority, can't enjoy but one kind of music, can't enjoy art at all, can't appreciate nature, is insensitive to the needs of others, or can't appreciate anyone but him/herself?

Almost every individual in the culture is partly or largely disabled and malfunctioning as compared with their full potential. But he and she don't realize how disabled they are. The defense system tends to keep them in the dark about it or gives them excuses as to why they are not doing better at the moment, so that they can avoid feeling pain.

Life can be a lot of fun, but it is not so for most people. Most people are not in radiantly good physical health, as they are too blocked intellectually and emotionally to be able to take care of their nutritional needs properly. They are too blocked to know that their neurosis prevents them from being physically healthy. And I would estimate that 70 to 80 percent of school programs are useless. But what can the educational system offer, then, that would be helpful, in addition to a good program designed to develop the intellect? It would be desirable to devise programs designed to improve the students' ability to relate to one another, to recognize a large array of hang-ups in themselves and in others, to help them avoid merely following the dictates of destructive impulses, to help them recognize what makes a relationship work, and to help them recognize problem areas within themselves, as well as to direct many into group psychotherapy programs involving the expression of feelings within the framework of the school program.

These programs should aim at loosening up undesirable inhibitions, enabling the individual to function better, help the individual find him/herself again, help the individual to become compassionate and loving, and help in reducing anger, jealousy, and hatred.

The details of such a vast educational reorganization would not be easy to develop and implement, but it would certainly be worth the effort.

Individuals who are less anxious, less inhibited, more open, and more insightful, and who can feel more empathy, can utilize what they learn in school much more effectively and can become acceptable citizens of an advanced world.

REFERENCES

1. Hart, J., Corrier, R., and Binder, J. *Going Sane.* New York: Jason Aronson (1975).
2. Janov, A. *The Primal Scream.* New York: Dell (1970).
3. Janov, A. *The Anatomy of Mental Illness.* New York: Putnam (1971).
4. Janov. A. *The Primal Revolution.* New York: Simon and Schuster (1973).
5. Janov, A. *The Feeling Child.* New York: Simon and Schuster (1973).
6. Janov, A. and Holden, M. *Primal Man.* New York: Thomas Y. Crowell (1975).
7. Janov, A. *Prisoners of Pain.* New York: Doubleday (1980).
8. LeBoyer, F. *Birth Without Violence.* New York: Knopf (1975).
9. MacLean, P. D. *A Triune Concept of the Brain and Behavior.* Toronto: University of Toronto Press (1973).

Old age has been characterized as "the final segragation," and the following chapter, on supportive therapy practiced within a state hospital setting for the aged, provides an insightful and encouraging picture of how such segregation can be minimized through effective, warm, caring intervention by hospital personnel especially selected for their ability to interact with elderly hospitalized patients.

The need for such therapy is widespread, and it is clear that it is a new approach utilizing a variety of more familiar types of therapeutic intervention. The authors, all of whom practice this new method, have been both carefully selected and trained. The reader is afforded an understanding of the criteria for such selection, the elements of training, and practice essential to effective therapeutic outcomes.

At a time when a "greying America" includes such a very large number of post-65-year-old people, the more elderly of whom are hospitalized, there is an ever-increasing need for different kinds of effective psychotherapy for this group, many of whom also have complicating physical illnesses.

21

Humanistic Supportive Therapy

**Sheryl C. Wilson, Ph.D., Beverly L. Ryder, B.A.,
Judith M. Doran, B.A., and Linda M. Enos, B.A.**

A model program of supportive therapy for patients in a geriatric hospital is described in this chapter. The aim of the program is to utilize supportive therapists with a B.A. or M.A. in psychology to minimize the loneliness, despair, and hopelessness of institutionalized elderly patients who lack meaningful human contacts. The chapter covers the following: 1) why a new service, supportive therapy, is needed in all extended care facilities, 2) the goals of supportive therapy, and how this therapy differs from traditional therapies, 3) the characteristics of individuals who make good supportive therapists, and 4) the variety of therapeutic approaches used in supportive therapy (e.g., unconditional positive regard, suggestive therapy, guided imagining, "re-living" the past, touch therapy, and thanatotherapy).

The model program described is one that we initiated at Cushing Hospital,[3] a 500-bed geriatric hospital. We have named this program "supportive therapy," and we believe it is needed in all geriatric centers, nursing homes, and chronic disease hospitals.

THE NEED FOR SUPPORTIVE THERAPY
IN EXTENDED CARE FACILITIES

In addition to their medical illnesses, patients in chronic disease hospitals, geriatric hospitals, nursing homes, and homes for the aged also suffer from a "malaise of the spirit." These ill, elderly individuals are found in increasing numbers in extended care facilities, where they will live for the remainder of their lives. Their lack of contact with old friends, spouses, children, and relatives is associated with feeling lonely, worthless, and unloved. The life of many of these patients is characterized by a lack of meaningful social contacts, a loss of useful social roles, and a posture of despair while waiting for death. Often they feel that nothing good is ever going to happen again in their lives – just more despair and misery and then a lonely death.

We believe that this malaise of the spirit and this loss of a feeling for life can be ameliorated by a new type of therapist, whom we call a supportive therapist. These therapists are needed for the following reasons.

Extended care facilities typically provide the services of many kinds of professionals (physicians, nurses, physical therapists, psychologists, social workers, dietitians, etc.) to care for their residents. Many facilities, such as Cushing Hospital, also provide for the recreational, social, and religious needs of their residents by offering a great variety of activities, such as counseling, religious services, occupational therapy, recreational therapy, movies, and outings for those who are able to participate. However, many of the residents do not participate in these activities either because they are too ill or because they are suffering from a malaise of the spirit (hopelessness, helplessness, and despair). These residents who have given up on living are emotionally unable to participate in activities or to socialize with other residents. A few even refuse to eat or drink anything, in a desperate attempt to end their despair.

These despairing elderly individuals are not seen in therapy by counselors, psychologists, or psychiatrists. They typically are not good candidates for traditional psychotherapeutic or counseling techniques. First, they rarely (if ever) view their problems as emotional or psychological. They typically feel that they have to live in the facility because they are old and sick, not because they are "crazy" or in need of psychological help. They often are upset even by routine psychological evaluations, and they definitely do not feel comfortable in the role of a psychotherapy client (e.g., being asked personal questions and disclosing themselves without reciprocal disclosures). Furthermore, owing to cerebral arteriosclerosis, strokes, aphasia, confusion, failing eyesight and hearing, etc., most of such residents are not suitable candidates for traditional psychoanalytic, behavioral, or cognitive therapies. When they are deemed unsuitable for traditionally available therapies, the choice generally becomes one of either medicating them or doing nothing special for them. Supportive therapy enters here as an alternative to medicating or doing nothing. Supportive therapists do not attempt to bring about fundamental changes in the patient's personality. Rather, supportive therapists spend their active work time on the wards with the patients, working within the patient's long-established lifestyle to improve the quality of the remaining days of their lives. In brief, the goal of the supportive therapist is not to produce a basic change in the patient but to reduce as much as possible the loneliness and despair of the patient and to help make his or her remaining life as good as possible.

CHARACTERISTICS OF GOOD SUPPORTIVE THERAPISTS

From our experience with this program at Cushing Hospital, we believe supportive therapists should be recruited from those with a bachelor's degree in the helping professions, psychology, counseling, nursing, social work, etc. More important, they should have obtained their degree out of a sincere desire to help people. They need to be highly empathic individuals who care deeply about others and are willing to give unselfishly of themselves to help others. They should also enjoy life and be as close as possible to Maslow's "self-actualized" person and to Carl Rogers[1] ideal therapist, who gives unconditional positive regard, is warm and genuine, and views each person as a unique individual unlike any other [Rogers (1961)]. Furthermore, they should be capable of forming close, caring, trusting relationships even with those who are unable otherwise to relate, such as severely depressed, withdrawn persons previously diagnosed as schizophrenic. Although we realize no one exactly fits this ideal, we have been surprised at how closely the supportive therapists who are now working at Cushing Hospital do fit this portrait.[4]

THE METHODS OF SUPPORTIVE THERAPY

Supportive therapists use a wide variety of therapeutic approaches, some of which are unusual or original. Underlying all of the approaches are two goals that differentiate supportive therapy from most other therapies: The general goal of supportive therapy is to relate to all individuals with absolute respect and unconditional positive regard, recognizing each individual as a unique human being — unlike any other person who ever was or ever will be, and the specific goal of supportive therapy is to work within the patient's long-established lifestyle toward improving the quality of the remaining days of his or her life. The general principle of supportive therapy is to focus on the positive attributes of the patients in order to help them feel good about themselves and to feel valuable and worthwhile; in other words, to build up self-esteem.

Although we can delineate the various therapeutic approaches used in supportive therapy, the therapists themselves utilize these approaches in a totally natural way. That is, each therapist is completely natural and genuine and feels free to be him/herself and to spontaneously engage in any activity the therapist believes to be immediately helpful to a patient as well as most appropriate to his or her long-term needs. Therapeutic approaches overlap considerably; however, unconditional love pervades all therapeutic relationships. By unconditional love, we mean that the therapist truly loves and respects the patient, has no behavioral criteria upon which the love and respect are contingent, and does not hesitate to convey this to the patient. Although we recognize that unconditional love is similar in many respects to what Carl Rogers has termed unconditional positive regard, we choose to refer to what supportive therapists give patients as love because of the intense closeness in the relationship, as well as the caring touches, hugs, and kisses that also are integral, natural aspects of these relationships.

Since the patients seen by supportive therapists are not "suitable" for traditional psychotherapy or counseling, supportive therapists use several therapeutic approaches that are taboo in traditional therapy. For instance, although touching the patient is inappropriate in traditional psychotherapy, it is a major therapeutic approach used by supportive therapists. In fact, they not only touch their patients, but they also feel free to hold, hug, or kiss their patients whenever hugs and kisses are a spontaneous, natural part of their therapeutic relationship.

Although the basic need for loving touch pervades all age groups [Montagu (1971)], the need is more intense for elderly, ill residents of extended care facilities. With few exceptions, their spouses, friends, and relatives have died and their children have moved away, either physically, emotionally, or both, and there is no one left whom they can touch or who can touch them in a caring, loving way. Elderly patients have a special need for loving touch, for hugging, and for physical closeness. We can also speculate that the meaningfulness of such physical contact may be magnified in elderly, ill patients, whose eyesight and hearing are fading but who can still feel a kind touch or a loving embrace.

Traditional approaches avoid touching or embracing patients because such actions are expected to intensify a counter-therapeutic transference relationship in which the patient unconsciously equates the therapist with an important person in his or her past. In traditional psychotherapy, transference is to be either avoided or dealt with ("worked through") when it occurs. Paradoxically, supportive therapists strive to establish transference relationships with their patients as often as they can and to the maximum strength possible. In fact, success in meeting the goals of supportive therapy at times seems to be correlated with the degree to which the patient sees the therapist either as a replacement for someone in his or her past with whom the patient was very close or as a friend or close family member, such as a daughter or granddaughter.

Some approaches used by supportive therapists overlap in many ways and are difficult to separate. Two such overlapping approaches are guided imagining and positive suggestive therapy. In both of these approaches, the therapist uses words with the aim of accomplishing such things as helping the person to relax, to re-live (in imagination) enjoyable times in the past, and to continue to experience these good feelings in the present. For instance, in one technique commonly used by supportive therapists, an anxious or agitated resident might be guided by the therapist's words to feel him/herself in a relaxing place, such as lying in the sun on a summer day, or sitting in the winter in front of a cozy livingroom fire-place. Prior to beginning the verbal guidance, the therapist asks the patient what he or she finds most relaxing and then tailors the suggestion to fit the pa-tient. The therapist may also ask the patient to close his or her eyes and to think, imagine, and feel along with the words or suggestions. This procedure could be labeled, with equal justification, as suggestive therapy or guided imagining. Other examples of the same technique include guiding a patient who is anxious, and thus unable to eat, to imagine herself as a young girl eating at a picnic, and guiding a patient with insomnia to imagine himself at a summer resort because he always had slept soundly there. A variation of guided imagining is used by one sup-portive therapist, Linda, during her sessions with Jenny, who at 74 years felt sad and upset because she no longer had her own home in which she could entertain friends. Linda helped her cope with this. Some of their therapy sessions now in-clude closing their eyes and imagining Jenny is having Linda over for tea, e.g., Linda asks Jenny to describe her home, tea service, what she is serving, etc.

Supportive therapists utilize sincere positive statements or suggestions as much as possible. For instance, since the therapist looks for the positive aspects of the patient, it is natural to tell the patient "You have been such a good mother," "You have done so many things in your life," "You've endured many things — you're such a strong person," "You could write a book about all the things that have happened to you," and "You are beautiful."

Supportive therapists deliberately use recall of the past as a therapeutic tech-nique. This may seem an odd procedure to employ with the elderly, since a typical complaint about the aged is that they live too much in the past. However, it can be therapeutic to guide a resident who is lonely and depressed to recall and "re-live" pleasant times in the past with friends and loved ones, and to fol-low this with the suggestion, "You will always have your happy memories to go back to whenever you wish. No one can ever take them from you." Along simi-lar lines, supportive therapists also encourage residents to make cassette tapes of events, people, and places in their lives as a historical record which the residents can keep to listen to themselves or, more commonly, give to grandchildren or other relatives. When a resident is having an anxiety attack, is very ill, or is dying, supportive therapists can use their previously acquired knowledge of the resident's life to formulate suggestions to guide the resident to reexperience memorable events from his or her past; e.g., living on a farm or in an Italian village as a child, taking an enjoyable trip to Ireland. This is also useful if a resident is undergoing a painful medical procedure, such as insertion of a catheter or re-insertion of a nasal feeding tube.

Supportive therapists also give suggestions to residents to help them heal or recover from illness. Such suggestions, which have a long history in hypnother-apy [Barber (1970)], may aim to indirectly hasten recovery and healing by reducing helplessness, hopelessness, and despair or by helping the patient to relax and to attain peace of mind [Barber (1980)]. At times, suggestions are more directly aimed to hasten healing. For instance, a supportive therapist might explain to a resident with an ulcerated leg how more blood flowing to the area can help to heal the sores; and then the therapist might suggest to the resident that he or she can bring more healing blood to the sores by thinking and imagining that the sun is shining on that leg, making it feel very warm, or that the leg is packed in warm towels or in a warm tub of water, etc. These kinds of suggestions for healing are difficult to separate from another therapeutic approach that is at times used by supportive therapists and that has a long history; namely, healing by laying on of hands.

Laying on of hands involves healthy individuals (healers) reaching out to ill individuals by touching in a concerned, loving way with the intention of "giving of themselves" to help the sick recover from disease or pain. The "giving of self" that is involved in laying on of hands is typically experienced by healers as a transmission of "energy" flowing through them to the sick while they serve as conduits. Supportive therapists are selected for "willingness to give of themselves" to the sick; if they also can feel "energy" flowing from them or through them to the patient, this can be a highly effective therapeutic procedure, especially when the patient believes in healing and in the therapist's ability to heal him or her.

Laying on of hands, as used by the supportive therapists at Cushing Hospital, is often combined with another useful therapeutic procedure — prayer. Supportive therapists who can sincerely pray with patients and also use laying on of hands are especially effective with patients who have compatible deep religious beliefs. Whether or not the therapist is actually transmitting a "physical healing energy" may be unimportant; by praying with the patients and also using "healing touch," therapists are clearly communicating their concern and love for the patient, are relieving the patient's feelings of loneliness and despair, and are thus assisting the patient's self-healing processes [Barber (1980)].

Another important aspect of supportive therapy is thanatotherapy, therapy at the time of death. In all extended care facilities, deaths and critical life-threatening situations, such as congestive heart failure and strokes, are not uncommon among patients. However, as we mentioned earlier, patients in such facilities are typically isolated, and it is unlikely that anyone will be present at the time of their deaths. In fact, anticipation of a lonely death is at times a part of their despair. The nursing staff, which usually is in short supply in such facilities, rarely has sufficient extra time to devote to critically ill patients. Consequently, there is a need for supportive therapists at this time. The goal of thanatotherapy is for the therapist to offer support to the patient, to help him or her relax, and to reduce fear and anxiety. In brief, the aim is to be supportive no matter what the outcome, not to encourage the patient either to live or to die. Supportive therapists at Cushing Hospital are also typically "on call" at night and on weekends if thanatotherapy is needed at those times.

Supportive therapists often serve what could be termed an intermediary function between patients and other hospital staff. In other words, they frequently find themselves in the role of "patient advocate." Why is this necessary? Even though all the hospital staff is working in the best interest of each patient, shortages among nurses and nurses' aides make it difficult for them to spend extended periods of time with any one patient. Nevertheless, the establishment of a close relationship, which requires time to develop, is precisely what is needed to determine individual needs and "best interests" of some patients. In addition, the nursing staff, faced with many patients to care for, often doesn't have the time or energy to work intensively with a patient who refuses to eat, or to be washed up, etc., or to provide extensive orientation programs for new patients. Furthermore, some of the patients who are without family or friends are filled with a terrifying feeling of anonymity, and no matter how kindly the hospital staff treats them, they truly need someone special (at least for a while) who they feel is "on their side" and whom they can rely on like family. The following are brief examples of some of the intermediary functions of supportive therapists.

When one of the wards was being moved on another ward area, the nursing staff was necessarily very busy trying to attend to all the details of the move. In all the commotion, Joan, a 75-year-old woman with Parkinson's disease, was terrified. Linda, who had been working with Joan and had a well-established relationship with her, was able to calm and reassure her. Joan told Linda, in reference to the staff, that "they are a gang that is going to hurt me." Linda replied that no one would hurt her and, utilizing Joan's term "gang," explained that they constituted a gang to *help her get well*. Accepting Linda's interpretation, Joan relaxed.

Another supportive therapist was called to one of the wards in the evening because a woman patient who was diabetic had refused to eat for the entire day. The therapist gently put one hand on her shoulder in a comforting way, thus conveying the non-verbal message, "Be calm, relax, I'm not fighting you." The therapist remained quietly like that for at least 10 minutes. Then, when she felt the patient had calmed down, she kneeled down by her (so she would not be above her) and softly suggested that she drink some milk. The patient drank the whole glass and also a second glass that the nurse asked the therapist to give her.

Often, when patients are first admitted to Cushing Hospital, they have difficulty finding their bed among all the beds on the ward — or, if they have a private room, finding which door is theirs. As one 81-year-old pleasant and sociable, but forgetful, woman said, "I'm afraid of walking into the wrong room. They all look alike from the outside." Supportive therapists make drawings for many patients, special for them, to help them locate their bed or room. However, sometimes a new admission, such as Leo, can find his room without difficulty but doesn't feel that it is really *his*. Judy greeted Leo and took him a picture to put up on the wall to make his room more home-like. He was pleased and wanted to put up more pictures. So Judy suggested they do drawings together, which they began working on, as well as rearrange his furniture. Leo soon felt "at home" in his room; however, he still was not content about being in Cushing Hospital. He was a man who had worked hard as a carpenter since eight years of age and now he felt too inactive. Judy is now introducing Leo to occupational therapy and the wood-working and carpentry available there. She is also helping his self-image by encouraging him to record cassette tapes of his life as a child in Italy to give his great grandson, who is now three years old.

Sometimes supportive therapists serve an intermediary function between a patient and his or her family. The hospital setting and/or impairments in the patient's functioning can put a severe strain on and interfere with a patient's previous family relationship. Supportive therapists can help the patient and the family feel more at ease and learn to interact in a new setting or possibly in a new way which can be rewarding to them.

Supportive therapists have been able to help family members communicate with a patient who is unable to speak (aphasia), by helping the family understand that the patient still can be aware of their presence and is still appreciative of their touch, hugs, and kisses, and also can understand more of what they say than they might have supposed.

Supportive therapists also are available to provide both immediate and long-term orientation for patients following strokes (CVA's) that leave them confused and disoriented. Therapists often spend many hours helping to calm and reassure stroke victims, and telling them what has happened and where they are now. Typically, when someone has sustained brain damage, people, including those once known as friends, treat him or her differently. Usually, no one explains to the patient what has happened, thereby adding to the victim's confusion and sometimes resulting in anger. Also, no one really talks to patients. Supportive therapists offer reassuring explanations and treat them with the same consideration and respect as they did before the stroke.

Since supportive therapists are free to engage spontaneously in any activity they believe to be immediately helpful to the patient, as well as most appropriate for the patient's long-term needs, the therapeutic approach selected is sometimes so highly individualized to fit the patient's needs that it becomes quite a unique form of therapy. For instance, a supportive therapist enrolled Mary, a 76-year-old patient, in an undergraduate biology course with a biweekly lab in a nearby college. The therapist arranged for Mary to audit the course because Mary had always wanted to go to college and, in fact, she had wanted to become a medical doctor, but back in her early days her father had said, "You're a girl. Of course you can't go to college," and that was the end of that. Mary, nevertheless, had pursued her interest by reading on her own and for a while had lived in a rooming house where there was a medical student who let her borrow and read the textbooks. Since Mary had maintained an intense interest in biology over the years, the supportive therapist felt it would be very beneficial to Mary's self-image and to her whole lifetime accomplishments to attend a college biology course. Mary loved the course and completed it with much satisfaction.

Mary is not the only patient that has been educationally helped. Whenever possible, therapists find out what patients can read and enjoy reading, and bring them as many books and magazines as they can possibly provide. Also, for patients who are blind, have impaired vision, or have difficulty reading and could benefit from the availability of talking books, there are some now available in the hospital library, and therapists are looking for more at this time.

There are many more aspects of supportive therapy — far too many to cover completely in a chapter of this length. One of the therapies that is extremely popular with residents of Cushing Hospital, and with the staff, is "pet therapy," which has been provided by supportive therapists, who have brought kittens in to visit patients. This met with tremendous popularity. Often, patients who previously seemed relatively non-responsive were very happy to pet, cuddle, and hold a kitten.

Another aspect of supportive therapy is that supportive therapists encourage patients who are capable of participation to attend various hospital activities, especially recreational therapy and occupational therapy, in order to increase their activities and social contacts. They also encourage socialization among residents. Sometimes this is done by enlisting the aid of one patient to help with another patient, thus developing a friendship between the two patients.

Supportive therapists at Cushing Hospital are free to be spontaneous and not adhere to a rigid "job description." In other words, they feel free to be themselves and to engage in any action they believe will be immediately helpful to a resident. This can be illustrated by the following examples: If a resident is distraught over a torn dress, the supportive therapist is apt to mend it; if a resident is upset because her hair is hanging over her eyes, the supportive therapist might ask the resident if she would like her hair trimmed; if the supportive therapist can sing and play the guitar, she might present a concert of World War I songs on a ward of ill, elderly men.

Additional goals and therapeutic procedures used by supportive therapists at Cushing Hospital are listed in the supportive therapy reporting inventory presented at the end of this chapter.

Finally, the following brief excerpts from illustrative cases exemplify the importance and prevalence of unconditional love and the use of suggestions by our therapists as well as the flavor of some of the various therapeutic approaches used in Supportive Therapy.

Alice

Alice is now 87 years old. She never married. When she was 32, she is reported to have had hallucinations and delusions for the first time. She reportedly "saw rats and terrible looking men getting after me," had temper tantrums and crying spells and was admitted to a state mental hospital with a diagnosis of "chronic schizophrenia, undifferentiated." Since then, she has been institutionalized and now she is a resident of Cushing Hospital. At present, she has persistent tardive dyskinesia (probably due to many years of anti-psychotic medications), which gives her a strange appearance.

Prior to Beverly's — the supportive therapist's — working with her, Alice chose to remain confined to her bed and chair. More important, she was periodically catatonic and became combative if anyone tried to move here. Beverly had received a request to work not with Alice, but with a patient in the bed next to Alice's. In her visits with Alice's neighbor, Beverly typically discussed philosophical topics and, unknown to Beverly, Alice was listening even though she was in an apparently catatonic state. These philosophical discussions seem to have stimulated this woman, who for 55 years had been basically withdrawn into "her own world." To Beverly's amazement, Alice suddenly "came to life" and asked, "Who are you?" Beverly responded by telling her her name and that she was a supportive therapist, which "has something to do with people loving and caring for other people." Alice then asked Beverly a surprising question. She asked why we come into this world, live a few years, and then die, when most of the time we are suffering. Not knowing at the time who Alice was, Beverly responded spontaneously that she had suffered too, although she was sure it was different from Alice's suffering and that she was trying to learn from her suffering and maybe she could help Alice learn from hers. Beverly continued with, "But I don't think it is meant that you suffer anymore. It seems to me that you have done your share of suffering." Alice responded by telling about herself: "I was born, went to school, lived my life the best I could and I was working as a bookkeeper when I had a nervous breakdown . . . and I was put into an institution and I've been there for 46 years [actually it had been 55 years] sitting like this, 46 years in an institution suffering and the only way I could think about it was that maybe it was meant to be." Although Beverly reported that at that point she just wanted to hug Alice and "cry my heart out for her" (which Beverly did later that night when she went home), Beverly responded by stating she didn't know why Alice had suffered so but she felt she did not need to suffer anymore and that she had gained much wisdom in her suffering. She said she'd like to come to visit her and learn from her and that perhaps together they could find the answers she was seeking. Alice said she'd like that and in all those years she had never had visitors and that she has no family. Beverly then suggested that she could be family to Alice and then she followed this with a philosophical discussion of "the universe, how we are connected and how I feel it was meant to be that we met today." Then in a natural, sincere way, Beverly left Alice with the positive suggestion that "something new and wonderful is going to open up for you and you will experience happiness, and your happiness will mean so much more because of all your suffering."

Beverly has continued supportive therapy with Alice. They have engaged in additional philosophical discussion about such things as suffering — why we suffer and how we need not suffer, freedom as a state of mind, etc. Beverly is always supportive to Alice and always emphasizes positive aspects in Alice's life and new possibilities for her to enjoy life and be happy. For Alice's birthday, Beverly gave her a statue of an elephant. But, more important, Beverly gave her the following suggestion written on the box: "Dear Alice, this is your good luck charm — this will protect you from all evil and bad dreams. It will watch over you and keep you safe." Alice was very excited about the gift, and keeps it by her side night and day. She hasn't had a nightmare since then, and she says it is all due to the elephant.

It is now five months since Beverly's first interaction with Alice. The head nurse on the ward reports that Alice has made a remarkable improvement; her behavior is better, she becomes more involved, and is less catatonic. Alice says repeatedly that Beverly is her loyal, faithful friend. She talks more to other people, has established another close relationship with a recreational therapist, and she has willingly left her bedside, which she never did before. Previously she was combative if anyone tried to get her to leave her bed and chair. Now, not only has Alice been out on the porch, but she has been around the hospital and even out for a drive for the first time in over 50 years! Also, Alice no longer has her previously frequent nightmares about devils coming to get her. The important factors in obtaining these results appear to have included philosophical discussions, positive suggestions, and an intense loving, caring friendship. Alice feels Beverly is someone she can trust completely and rely on as she explores the world beyond her bed and chair.

Maria

Maria, who is 80 years old, had been at Cushing Hospital for about a month before the supportive therapist, Judy, started seeing her. She had refused all food and drink, and she never spoke. In fact, Maria was born in Italy and never had spoken much English. Judy first made contact and established a relationship with Maria by holding her hand, speaking gently (e.g., telling her that she wanted to help and would be coming to see her daily), and staying with her, sitting by her bedside holding her hand. Thus, Judy effectively conveyed, both verbally and nonverbally, her concern for Maria's well being.

In order to help Maria, Judy empathized with her; that is, Judy imagined how she would feel if she were in Maria's position. This technique of empathizing is necessary when patients are unable to verbalize why they are bothered. Supportive therapists are tuned into and watchful for nonverbal communications from patients. By careful observation of Maria's nonverbal communications, Judy noticed Maria's increased terror when she heard certain unidentifiable sounds, such as the toilet flushing and the squeaking wheels on an unseen attendant's chart passing by in the hall. Although Judy wasn't sure how much Maria would be able to comprehend, Judy went ahead and explained the source of these "frightening" sounds. Following Judy's explanation, Maria seemed greatly relieved and even a bit amused that she had been so frightened for so long by such harmless sounds. Obviously, Maria did understand at least the intent of Judy's explanation; that is, that the sounds were harmless. Supportive therapists talk as Judy did to patients who themselves are unable to talk much or at all, and they talk to them on the assumption that they understand more than they can verbalize. Typically, this is true of those whose native language is not English, such as Maria, and it also tends to be true for patients who have primarily an expressive aphasia.

Susan

When Susan was admitted to Cushing Hospital in October of 1979, it was questionable whether she would remain at Cushing. The state hospital in which she had resided for nine years previously reported that she was unpredictably belligerent and assaultive to both staff and other patients, especially those less able than she. Susan, who was 69 years old, had been born prematurely and showed learning problems, and her family had accepted that she was retarded. They were always protective of her, and aside from an ill-fated marriage to an alcoholic, resulting in eight children (half of whom were placed in foster homes and half in homes of relatives), she had lived in the care of her mother until 1970.

Beverly met Susan soon after her admission to Cushing Hospital, and accepted a referral to work with Susan on her hostility, assaultive behavior, and depression, and to help her adjust to Cushing. Susan was given a private room and Beverly talked to her about helping her fix it up so it would be more homelike. She found Susan to be agitated and anxious, and it was difficult to understand her speech. Beverly came to see her every day and often twice a day. She always showed Susan unconditional love, even when Susan was assaultive. For instance, whenever Susan attempted to hit Beverly, she held her arms, preventing her from hitting, and at the same time she hugged Susan and told her, "I can't allow you to hit me." While she dealt with Susan's assaultive behavior in this way, Beverly strove to make Susan's room into "a little home for her." She took Susan many little things, such as a cup, a wastebasket, a special pillow, paper, and crayons. To help Susan feel at home and loved, Beverly took her a doll that kissed and a wardrobe of doll's clothes. Susan was delighted and washed the doll's pajamas, placing them on a radiator to dry. By the end of three weeks, Beverly had established a trusting relationship with Susan.

Susan still did occasionally act out her frustrations by hitting or pinching the doll. Once, when Susan was about to hit the doll, Beverly said, "That's OK. You can hit her. She'll always love you no matter what you do." Susan stopped and looked up at Beverly, who told her, "I'll always love you too." Susan hugged the doll instead of hitting it.

Now that Susan was not so assaultive and felt more "at home," Beverly's next goal was to involve Susan in hospital activities. She began taking her to the coffee shop and telling her about the beauty shop, the activities of the recreation department, etc. Two months after her admission, nursing reported that Susan was less nervous and more responsive to, and no longer afraid of, new people. The head nurse told Beverly how pleased she was at the dramatic change in Susan.

To increase Susan's relationships, Beverly introduced her to a new supportive therapist, Judy, who began working with Susan. Judy also has established a trusting relationship with Susan now, and Susan now participates in an art group Judy is conducting. Judy always lets Susan know she loves her no matter what. Susan now is more at ease and feels free to express herself verbally rather than by physical violence. Judy encourages her to express her feelings, tells her she's her friend, and always gives her a good-bye hug.

Unconditional love and caring, together with providing her with "a little home," helped make it possible for Susan to remain at Cushing Hospital. Susan feels more at ease, enjoys Judy's art group and other hospital activities, and knows she has at least two genuine friends (Beverly and Judy).

Margarette

Margarette is an 87-year-old woman who, although capable of verbal communication, had withdrawn and was not communicating – only counting to herself, apparently in an effort to control anxiety. Also, Margarette was not feeding herself, was in bed all the time, was lonely, and had impaired vision following lense removal in cataract surgery. Beverly was the first supportive therapist to work with Margarette. She made contact by placing her head next to Margarette's until their eyes met, putting her arm around her shoulder, telling her her name ("Beverly"), and asking her if she could come to visit. In other words, Beverly approached Margarette with gestures of genuine friendship.

As a result of Beverly's "visits," Margarette became more responsive and more lucid in conversation, and she began to initiate conversations. She began talking to others (nurses, attendants, physical therapists, etc.) and began to demonstrate a surprising degree of wit. Beverly also began working toward the goal of Margarette's feeding herself. She did this by very gently encouraging her and with empathy, being sensitive not to push her too fast. As a result, Margarette began to enjoy meals and, amazingly, began to eat with her former table manners, (e.g., taking her napkin and dabbing her mouth when she had finished her meal).

This case illustrates the successful transfer of a patient from one supportive therapist to another. Once Beverly had broken through Margarette's withdrawal and had established a relationship with her, it became possible for Margarette to relate to others. Beverly introduced Margarette to another supportive therapist, Judy, who also established a trusting relationship with her. This enabled Beverly to stop seeing Margarette without disrupting the therapeutic process.

Margarette tends to lack confidence in her ability to do things, so Judy gives her a lot of positive suggestions, encouragement, and praise. Furthermore, she is helping Margarette to experience success and recognize her achievements. As a result of Judy's working with her, Margarette has become less dependent and more motivated to do things herself. Sometimes she eats an entire meal without assistance, and although she was having a difficult time once with her jello, she even refused Judy's help. Margarette is also now more assertive. She feels it is safe to express anger to Judy. Judy lets her know that these are very natural feelings to have and that she will be there to help her cope with them and alleviate them.

NOTES

1. A portion of this chapter was presented by Sheryl C. Wilson at the American Psychological Association Annual meeting in Montreal, P.Q., Canada, September 1980 [Wilson, Barber, Kastenbaum, Ryder, and Hathaway (1980)].

2. We are deeply grateful to Robert Kastenbaum, Superintendent, and Theodore X. Barber, Director of Supportive Services, for initiating and maintaining the Supportive Therapy program at Cushing Hospital. Our thanks also to Michael S. Berdell, Andrea George, Lisa B. Hathaway, Patti Isis, Bob Johnson, Rosemary Kaupp, Susan M, King, Marge Rhodes, and Susan Solad, who participated in various facets of the program (discussed elsewhere) [Kastenbaum, Barber, Wilson, Ryder, and Hathaway (in press)].

3. Cushing Hospital is a geriatric hospital operated by the Department of Mental Health, Commonwealth of Massachusetts. Therefore, a large proportion of the patients were previously institutionalized in state hospitals and state schools for the retarded.

4. The supportive therapists whom we have hired for the program at Cushing Hospital are all women who have recently graduated from college with a bachelor's degree in psychology. (Men have not as yet applied.) The supportive therapists are supervised by doctoral-level psychologists. In-service training includes lectures, experiential workshops, and discussions on physiology, pathology, and therapeutic procedures.

REFERENCES

Barber, T. X. *LSD, Marihuana, Yoga, and Hypnosis.* Chicago: Aldine (1970).

Barber, T. X. *Medicine, Suggestive Therapy, and Healing: Historical and Psychophysiological Considerations.* Framingham, MA: Cushing Hospital (1980).

Kastenbaum, R. J., Barber, T. X., Wilson, S. C., Ryder, B. L., and Hathaway, L. B. *Old, Sick, and Helpless: Where Therapy Begins.* Cambridge, MA: Ballinger (in press).

Montagu, A. *Touching: The Human Significance of the Skin.* New York: Columbia University Press (1971).

Rogers, C. R. *On Becoming a Person.* Boston: Houghton Mifflin (1961).

Wilson, S. C., Barber, T. X., Kastenbaum, R. J., Ryder, B. L., and Hathaway, L. B. *Humanistic (Supportive) Therapy: A New Application to Hospitalized Geriatric Patients.* Paper presented at the 88th Annual Convention, American Psychological Association, Montreal (September 3, 1980).

Supportive Therapy Reporting Inventory (STRI)*

Reporting Therapist: _____

Patient: _____

Reporting Date: _____ Sex: ____ Ward: ____

I have been seeing _____ for Supportive Therapy
                          name

_____ since _____ .
daily? or times per week?   date (optional)

What Were Your Reasons for Working with Patient?

The reason(s) I have been working with him or her are:
____ to evaluate his or her potential for
____ benefitting from one-to-one relationship
____ self-feeding
____ communicating
____ _____
     other

____ to help reduce
____ depression   ____ sadness   ____ tearfulness   ____ crying
____ feelings of worthlessness   ____ feelings of helplessness
____ feelings of loneliness   ____ feelings of hopelessness
____ feelings of being unloved   ____ _____
                                       other

____ to help cope with feelings
____ of loss   ____ of grief   ____ about impending medical procedures
____ about physical disabilities   ____ _____
                                         other

____ to help minimize
____ anxiety   ____ fearfulness   ____ guilt feelings   ____ confusion
____ manic behavior   ____ bizarre behavior   ____ withdrawal
____ negativism/negative behavior   ____ agitation   ____ antisocial behavior
____ calling out/crying out   ____ _____
                                    other

____ to help reduce
____ anger   ____ assaultiveness   ____ verbal abusiveness
____ distrust of others   ____ striking out   ____ combativeness
____ _____
     other

____ to help him or her accept being at Cushing Hospital
____ to help him or her accept new ward
____ to help him or her accept other patient(s)
____ to help provide increased social stimulation

_____

*By Sheryl C. Wilson.

_____ to encourage
   _____ self-feeding   _____ increased intake of food and/or fluids
   _____ verbal communication   _____ nonverbal communication   _____ socialization
   _____ involvement in hospital activities   _____ development of trust relationships
   _____ decision-making   _____ _____
                                          other

_____ to attempt to increase his or her
   _____ self-esteem   _____ sense of well being   _____ feeling of competency
   _____ orientation to present surroundings   _____ ability to cope with pain
   _____ orientation, memory, and understanding of what has occurred following the
recent CVA(s)   _____ _____
                                  other

_____ to be a comfort and to help calm and reassure him or her
   _____ during his or her illness   _____ while he or she is in critical condition
   _____ while he or she is dying   _____ during this emotionally trying time
   _____ during recovery from his or her: _____ injury   _____ illness
   _____ CVA   _____ heart attack   _____ congestive heart failure
   _____ _____   _____ to maintain emotional well being
      other

   _____ _____
      other

_____ to help strengthen his or her body's natural healing and defense mechanisms by
   _____ increasing his or her feelings of being loved and cared for   _____ alleviating his
or her sense of loneliness   _____ comforting touch with implicit or explicit suggestions for healing or pain reduction   _____ positive suggestive techniques
   _____ guided imagery techniques   _____ relaxation techniques

_____ to provide increased intellectual stimulation
   _____ by reading inspirational material such as inspirational messages, poetry, etc.
   _____ by reading philosophical excerpts, e.g., passages from _Illusions_ by Richard Bach,
The Prophet by Kahlil Gibran   _____ by discussing intellectual or philosophical
topics such as favorite authors and their works or the meaning of life
   _____ by encouraging attendance at Dr. Barber's or Dr. Kastenbaum's lectures or other
hospital lectures   _____ by providing educational material; that is, books/magazines/
tapes/talking books/newspapers/_____   _____ by encour-
                                          other
aging him or her to go to the library   _____ _____
                                                              other

_____ to help transfer my relationship to others
_____ to maintain the progress that has been made
_____ to maintain our relationship

_____
other goals or reasons for working with the patient

What Did You Do To Meet Goals?

In order to accomplish these goals, I
_____ demonstrated unconditional love and caring
_____ reassured him or her that I really care and will be available to help with problems,
difficulties, etc.

_____ told him or her that we are good friends and discussed what friendship means
_____ emphasized his or her positive qualities by sincere compliments, etc.
_____ engaged in meaningful conversations with him or her
_____ discussed his or her problems
_____ shared parallel experiences
_____ talked to him or her about _____

_____

_____ gave him or her an opportunity to
_____ ventilate anger   _____ express feelings   _____ express fears

_____ _____
        other
_____ prayed with him or her
_____ told him or her I will be thinking of or praying for him or her
_____ gently touched him or her in order to
_____ bring comfort   _____ bring warmth   _____ express love
_____ convey that I really care and want to help him or her feel better
_____ convey reassurance   _____ _____
                                              other
_____ utilized positive suggestive techniques
_____ utilized guided imagery techniques to guide him or her to recall and re-live in imagination significant and pleasant times in the past
_____ utilized relaxation techniques
_____ deep breathing   _____ guided imagery   _____ Jacobson's Progressive
Relaxation   _____ _____
                              other
_____ utilized touch to reduce pain and encourage healing
_____ asked about and discussed events, people, and places in his or her life
_____ encouraged and helped him or her to make a cassette tape of events, people, and places
in his or her life as a historical record for family members (grandchildren, etc.)
_____ encouraged a conversation between him or her and another patient _____
_____ asked him or her to
        teach me his or her native language   _____ teach me how to knit or crochet
_____ give me advice   _____ _____
                              other
_____ brought him or her
_____ flowers   _____ a card   _____ a personalized gift of _____

_____ _____
        other
_____ helped him or her
_____ write a letter to _____   _____ find out about funds
_____ locate (glasses, false teeth, etc.)   _____ _____
                                                              other
_____ took him or her
_____ outside to the garden or for a walk   _____ to the coffee shop
_____ to the Captain's Chair (hospital pub)   _____ to recreational activities _____
_____   _____ to Occupational Therapy   _____ for a
ride on the hospital van to _____
_____ to visit _____   _____ _____
                name of other patient, ward, or area   other

_____ played music for him or her

_____ _____
      other

Do You Want to Note Any Progress or Decline You Have Noticed? (optional)

During _____ I noticed he or she has
                    time period

_____ fluctuated considerably: _____ in responsiveness _____ in mood, e.g. _____

_____ _____ _____ _____
                                    other

_____ not changed significantly
_____ improved noticeably as follows: he or she seems less
_____ decline noticeably as follows: he or she seems more
    _____ angry _____ assaultive _____ abusive _____ anxious
    _____ fearful _____ confused _____ agitated _____ negative
    _____ depressed _____ sad _____ tearful _____ lonely _____ tired
    _____ bothered by pain _____ fearful and anxious about dying

    _____ _____
          other

_____ improved noticeably as follows: he or she seems more
_____ declined noticeably as follows: he or she seems less
    _____ calm _____ comfortable _____ happy _____ content
    _____ relaxed _____ accepting of _____
    _____ trusting of me or others _____ sociable _____ friendly
    _____ able to speak better _____ communicative _____ involved in hospital
activities _____ able to feed self _____ able to perform ADLs
    _____ able to or willing to eat or drink fluids _____ _____
                                       other

_____ _____
      other

Do You Plan to Continue Seeing Patient, and How Often?

_____ I will continue seeing him or her _____
                              how often?

_____ I will discontinue formal sessions with him or her but will continue informal sessions
(by stopping by to talk awhile) in order to maintain or reinforce the progress that has
been made

_____ I will stop seeing him or her because
    _____ I feel he or she has progressed maximumly
    _____ I feel he or she is not benefitting from one-to-one
    _____ he or she is now involved in hospital activities

_____ _____
    other

_____ I will resume therapy should the need arise
_____ I will be on call in a crisis or emergency situation _____
_____ additional comments _____
_____
_____

Index